Edited by
STEVEN W. HAYS
University of South Carolina, Columbia

RICHARD C. KEARNEY
University of South Carolina, Columbia

PUBLIC PERSONNEL ADMINISTRATION
Problems and prospects

PRENTICE-HALL, INC., Englewood Cliffs, New Jersey 07632

Library of Congress Cataloging in Publication Data
Main entry under title:

Public personnel administration.

   Includes bibliographies and index.
   1. Civil service—United States—Personnel
management—Addresses, essays, lectures. I. Hays,
Steven W. II. Kearney, Richard C.
JK765.P797   353.001   82–7611
ISBN 0-13-737973-0   AACR2

Editorial production supervision: *Edith Riker*
Cover design: *Miriam Recio*
Manufacturing buyer: *Edmund W. Leone*

Printed in the United States of America

10 9 8 7 6 5 4 3 2 1

ISBN 0-13-737973-0

Prentice-Hall International, Inc., *London*
Prentice-Hall of Australia Pty. Limited, *Sydney*
Prentice-Hall Canada, Inc., *Toronto*
Prentice-Hall of India Private Limited, *New Delhi*
Prentice-Hall of Japan, Inc., *Tokyo*
Prentice-Hall of Southeast Asia Pte. Ltd., *Singapore*
Whitehall Books Limited, *Wellington, New Zealand*

TO
THE NEW SCHOLARSHIP
IN
PUBLIC PERSONNEL ADMINISTRATION

CONTENTS

PREFACE

Within the past three decades, the image of public personnel administration has undergone a rapid metamorphosis. Whereas public personnel administration was once perceived as a mundane and tedious facet of public management, it is now viewed in a much different light. Past criticisms of the field's static and unimaginative organizational role have given way to assertions that the personnel office is the nerve center of bureaucracy and the linchpin for public managers, politicians, and existent social values.

The causes of the transformed image of public personnel administration are apparent to anyone who is even remotely familiar with contemporary public administration. A number of important social and economic developments have converged to catapult public personnel administration into the forefront of the discipline. The drive for social justice, which was perhaps the most significant legacy of the 1960s, found new expression in the 1970s. Affirmative action and equal employment opportunity became spearheads of the social movement and forced personnel administrators to accommodate a whole new range of pressures, operating philosophies, and management practices. Likewise, the 1960s and 1970s were the heyday of the unionization and collective bargaining movement in the public sector, which complicated the personnel policymaking process by granting formal access to a powerful group whose interests and values often conflicted with those of public managers and politicians. The 1970s also witnessed the leading edge of a profound economic movement that threatens to alter permanently the criteria that have traditionally guided evaluation, compensation, and creation of public jobs. The so-called "taxpayer revolt" has thrust new demands upon the public administrator and is beginning to spawn dramatic changes in the ways in which personnel managers perform their functions. To this list of influences on the personnel function must be added such related factors as the changing nature of the public work force, the "constitutionalization" of public personnel administration through increased judicial intervention in the management process, and the altered relationships between federal and nonfederal personnel systems.

In part as a result of these social and economic developments, the merit system itself has been subjected increasingly to renewed scrutiny, evaluation, and attack. Because the traditional "way of doing things" is often incompatible with demands for social justice, employee access, and reduced government expenditures, the first major civil service reform movement in one hundred years also appeared during the last decade. This reform movement is indicative of the importance that the public personnel function has recently acquired and is stark testimony to the fact that public personnel administration is currently in a critical stage of its evolution.

One prominent consequence of the changing nature and image of public personnel administration is that the literature of the field has experienced a similar transformation. This phenomenon can be seen best in what we refer to as the "new scholarship" of public personnel administration. In brief, this new scholarship is composed of theoretical and empirical research that is intended to provide personnel practitioners with understanding and guidance in meeting the challenges imposed by the field's altered state. Thus, it attempts to apply contemporary theoretical and empirical constructs to old and new problems in the search for better methods of performing personnel functions. Implicit within this approach is a preference for analytical assessments of personnel issues, in contrast to the field's traditional preoccupation with prescription. The most important impact of the new scholarship is that it has added a vitality and relevance to personnel literature that was lacking during the first fifty years of this century.

The chief purpose of this anthology is to assemble a representative sample of research arising from the new scholarship. As such, the book contains a mix of "thought pieces," theoretical essays, descriptive treatises, and empirical research. As is evident in the title we have chosen, the theme around which the chapters are based is "problems and prospects." The selections summarize the major problems confronting personnel practitioners and offer substantive suggestions for improving the practice of personnel management. Thus, they focus more on the future of public personnel administration than on its past. They are intended to provide the reader with a clear sense of where the discipline is going rather than where it has been.

An important characteristic of the selections is that they are original articles that were prepared specifically for inclusion in this volume. The authors are all established contributors to the new scholarship of public personnel administration. They were selected on the basis of their recognized competence in, and past contritions to, the topical areas addressed in their essays.

The contributions are organized in four broad sections: The Environment of Public Personnel Administration; Techniques of Public Personnel Administration; Personnel Policies and Issues; and Merit System Reform and the Future. Part I (Environment) focuses primarily on the social, legal, political, and economic trends that have served as catalysts in the transformation of public personnel administration. Part II is composed of selections that summarize developments in the practice of public personnel administration, with particular emphasis on emerging personnel techniques that have arisen in response to certain nagging managerial dilemmas. Part III (Personnel Policies and Issues) discusses and suggests remedies for four of the most troublesome problem areas in modern personnel administration—financial retrenchment, equal employment opportunity and affirmative action, sexual harassment, and ethics. The final part (Reform and the Future) assesses the efficacy of recent reform measures and examines the prospects for further reforms of state, local, and federal merit systems.

A prime consideration in the design, preparation, and organization of the book was that it be sufficiently "readable" to make it appropriate for both graduate and undergraduate students. For this reason, the authors were asked to provide enough background information so that both beginning and more advanced students could understand and relate to the content. Additionally, the authors were requested to provide sufficient concrete examples and practical information to enhance the volume's applicability to practitioners who wish to broaden their perspectives on the field. We are satisfied that these objectives have been met in every respect.

As anyone who has ever undertaken a project of this nature will readily admit, a thorough recounting of all the debts incurred in assembling an anthology would consume more pages than the text itself. The authors whose works you are about to read richly deserve our most sincere thanks, for their efforts are the heart and soul of what follows. The names, affiliations, and accomplishments of each of these individuals appear in the "About the Authors" section, which precedes the index. Without exception, the authors produced quality manuscripts on very short notice and responded quickly to numerous requests for revisions, clarifications, and elaborations. If, after enduring so many "reminders" and proddings from the editors, they are still speaking to us, we hope that they are aware of the depth of our appreciation.

Also richly deserving of our gratitude are the scholars whose insightful reviews contributed enormously to the substantive and stylistic qualities of the manuscript: Walter F. Baber, Illinois State University; Barbara S. Romzek, University of Kansas; Allen K. Settle, Calfornia Polytechnic State University; and Russell L. Smith, Northern Illinois University.

A special thanks is owed to Professor Charlie B. Tyer, director of the Bureau of Governmental Research and Service at the University of South Carolina. The Bureau published an earlier, abbreviated version of this volume and thereby initiated the effort that culminated in the book you now hold in your hands. Given Professor Tyer's instrumental role in bringing the project to fruition, we would like very much to blame any errors, omissions, or inaccuracies on him. Obviously, however, any such mistakes are our own responsibility.

S.W.H. and R.C.K.

PART ONE
ENVIRONMENT OF PUBLIC PERSONNEL ADMINISTRATION

To a great extent, public personnel administration is a mirror of the society that it serves. Because of the critical role that public servants play in conducting the people's business, and because government jobs are government resources, society has a direct and appropriate stake in ensuring that the personnel function operates according to its wishes. Thus, a proper understanding of the problems and prospects of contemporary personnel administration must begin with an appreciation for the environmental factors that influence the practice of personnel management.

Since its inception, the merit system has been enmeshed in the fiber of the American political and social fabric. To say that "politics" exerts a profound influence on the public personnel function is hardly revealing or surprising. Yet, as is examined in the first four chapters here, the content and purposes of political intrusions into the personnel process have recently undergone important changes. In distinguishing between two broad types of politics—elective and generic—Thompson notes that much of the "real" political activity now occurs within the personnel arena itself, as opposed to being imposed by patronage-oriented elected officials. The differing perceptions of public managers and personnelists have become a catalyst for internal political battles over the means and ends of personnel policies and procedures. Klingner adds a theoretical focus to Thompson's theme by identifying and analyzing the environmental variables that can influence the policy debates occurring within personnel offices. He asserts that the organizational configuration of personnel agencies should reflect the goals of the organization and that these goals are often imposed by external forces that generate internal controversy.

The Rosenbloom and Reeves articles also envision dramatic alterations in the political environment, although from a very different perspective. Through an examination of the impact of judicial decisions on personnel administration, Rosenbloom describes the courts' attempts to derive a viable alternative for the anachronistic privilege doctrine. Despite nearly two decades of progressively increasing judicial involvement in employee-employer affairs, Rosenbloom suggests that, since the mid-1970s, the courts have engaged in a gradual withdrawal that will ultimately "deconstitutionalize" the personnel function. A similar theme is apparent in Reeves' analysis of the effects of President Reagan's economic and political policies on state and local personnel management. By trimming various federal aid programs, the federal role in dictating personnel policies to local governments will decline.

The final chapter in this grouping examines a different yet equally important form of environmental influence: the changing nature of the labor force. Focusing on increased professionalism among public workers, Neuse discovers that the presence of many professions within government agencies creates a diversity in job attitudes and personal characteristics that complicates the practice of personnel administration. He concludes with an observation that is appropriate to all the articles in the section—that the increasing complexity and dynamism of personnel's environment necessitates a "commitment to flexibility."

Frank J. Thompson
University of Georgia

CHAPTER ONE
THE POLITICS
OF PUBLIC PERSONNEL
ADMINISTRATION

The movement that galvanized approval of the Pendleton Act and other aspects of civil service reform in the late nineteenth and early twentieth centuries sought to exorcise politics from public personnel administration. The "neutral" application of sound merit techniques became the ideal. This perspective retained a remarkably tenacious grip on the personnel field even after World War II, when the politics-administration dichotomy fell rapidly from grace in the general field of public administration. Only in the late 1960s did momentum develop to lay the dichotomy to rest with respect to personnel administration. In 1968, Mosher observed that efforts to segregate administration and politics in the personnel field could hardly satisfy any but the "blind" (1968: 209). A steady stream of studies soon emphasized the political character of much of public personnel management (Heclo, 1977; Horton, 1973; Miewald, 1969; Nalbandian and Klingner, 1981; Rosenbloom, 1977; Shafritz, 1973; Thompson, 1975).

In a broad sense, virtually all public personnel administration possesses political ramifications. This is because it affects who gets what from government. Consider, for instance, the Professional and Administrative Career Examination (PACE) that the federal government used to fill many positions during the 1970s. Fifty-one percent of the whites taking this exam passed, whereas only 4 percent of the blacks did (GAO, 1979: 12). Although the staff of the Civil Service Commission used technically sophisticated validation strategies in developing PACE, the fact remained that the test placed certain groups in a better position to obtain a scarce public resource (a government job) than others. The same rationale could be applied to almost any aspect of personnel administration.

Failure to hire the most adroit may impair government's ability to deliver important services to some segment of society. Or it may push up the costs of public services, thus taking a toll on certain taxpayers. Any notion, then, that specialists in public personnel administration pursue a value-free, neutral, or apolitical art is chimerical.

Rejection of a simple politics-administration distinction in the personnel field does not, however, take us very far. When one turns to studying decision making in various personnel arenas, it is probably not very useful to view choice processes as equally politicized. If politics is everything, it may well be nothing. This leads to the central assumption that undergirds this chapter: *whereas public personnel administration invariably possesses political implications in the sense that it affects the outputs and outcomes of government, politics does not invariably permeate personnel decision processes.*

"Politics" here refers to the way in which choices concerning personnel administration get made as opposed to their implications for who gets what from government. Beyond this general distinction, it is useful to consider two major connotations of politics as it pertains to personnel management. First, observers have traditionally employed the term to indicate the involvement of elected officials and their allies in personnel decision making within an agency. For present purposes, this form of involvement can be thought of as *elective personnel politics.* Applying this definition, one can assert that public personnel management becomes less politicized to the extent that elected officials and their partisan associates play a smaller role in its conduct. Second, one can conceive of *generic personnel politics*. This refers to activities within the personnel arena aimed at acquiring and using resources to exert power (obtain some desired outcome) in a situation where disagreement about appropriate action exists (Pfeffer, 1981: 7). In other words, politics involves actors with different preferences about some personnel matter, attempting to ensure that their particular views prevail. Participants in the fray need not necessarily include elected officials; different congeries of administrators may comprise the major groups involved. The conscious plotting of strategies, the mobilization of coalitions, bargaining, and compromise are often key ingredients of generic personnel politics. Viewed from the perspective offered by this definition, personnel administration becomes less politicized to the extent that it does not feature the clash of different clusters of participants espousing different objectives.

This chapter suggests some major developments and prospects with respect to the two types of personnel politics. To this end, the first section addresses elective politics, both that involving spoils and that aimed at assuring bureaucratic responsiveness to top elected officials. The second focuses on generic personnel politics. A final section considers some implications of our current understanding of personnel politics for research into as well as the practice of public personnel management.

EFFECTIVE PERSONNEL POLITICS

Elective personnel politics assumes several guises. Spoils and leadership versions comprise two of the major ones. The former emphasizes the manipulation of personnel administration by partisan politicians who seek to provide followers with tangible material rewards such as jobs. Their machinations aim primarily at maintaining the electoral network that allowed these politicians to obtain office rather than at helping them to administer programs once in office. In this vein, they tend to emphasize patronage in the routine, lower-level jobs in government rather than top policy posts. By contrast, leadership politics stresses the importance of personnel administration as a vehicle for keeping the bureaucracy responsive and accountable to elected officials. Top policy jobs tend to be a central target of concern as elected officials strive to place people loyal to them in strategically sensitive positions. Elected executives view leverage over personnel administration more as a tool for allowing them to govern than as a means of building electoral machinery. The line between spoils and leadership versions of elective politics often becomes fuzzy. Still, the two remain sufficiently distinct to discuss them separately.

Spoils: Toward Depoliticization

An aversion to spoils politics spurred the early civil service reformers to introduce a host of institutional buffers aimed at sealing off personnel administration from the influence of elected officials. The "independent" civil service commission, with its formal authority over hiring, firing, and related personnel matters, serves as an obvious example, as do written employment tests. The spread of these merit institutions combined with other sociopolitical trends (e.g., greater education, the expansion of welfare programs) to reduce spoils politics. By 1960, the forces of depoliticization had progressed to a point that one observer viewed the "ethic of patronage, the naked political quid pro quo," as no longer "a natural and reasonable ingredient of politics" (Sorauf, 1960: 30). Some personnel specialists concluded that politics had attained a "maturity" whereby elected officials would no longer pose a threat to merit practices (Jones, 1964; Municipal Manpower Commission, 1962: 62).

But if spoils has declined in significance, it is pertinent to point out that pockets of patronage persist. Merit systems appear to cover no more than 60 percent of all state employees; more than 10 percent of the cities with populations of greater than 50,000 still lack formal merit systems (Shafritz, Hyde, and Rosenbloom, 1981: 53). The absence of a formal merit system need not imply the presence of spoils politics. However, more in-depth evidence from cities, such as Chicago and New Haven (Connecticut), as well as states, such as Pennsylvania, buttress the view that spoils politics lives on (Royko, 1971; Wolfinger, 1972; Lynn, 1980: 153).

Elected officials in many jurisdictions have kept a particularly vigilant eye out for patronage opportunities emanating from intergovernmental sources. The public jobs authorized under the Comprehensive Employment and Training Act (CETA) provide a case in point. This program allocated funds to state and local governments to hire the unemployed to perform new services in the community. The number of public jobs subsidized by CETA grew rapidly, rising from roughly 100,000 in 1974 to some 725,000 by the late 1970s. In Buffalo, New York, CETA employees amounted to roughly one-third of the city government's work force and in Hartford, Connecticut, about a quarter (Donnelly, 1978). The fact that CETA employees often obtained their jobs outside of regular civil service channels tempted some officials to use them for patronage purposes. In New Haven, Connecticut, for instance, party officials allocated some 675 positions primarily on the basis of ethnic political considerations rather than by calculating which parts of the city suffered most from unemployment. Wards that produced votes for Italian political candidates fared better in obtaining CETA positions (Johnston, 1979). By fiscal 1982, the Reagan administration had eliminated all funding for the public jobs component of CETA. But alternative manpower initiatives may ultimately rise and become a tempting source of spoils for local politicians.

Two Supreme Court decisions in the late 1970s, however, may well make the pursuit of patronage more difficult. One case involved the Cook County sheriff's office in Chicago. This office employed roughly 3,000 personnel, about half of whom enjoyed merit system protection. When a Democrat, Richard Elrod, took over as sheriff in 1970, he followed the long-standing practice of dismissing a number of incumbent employees who were not members of his party. But this time, certain employees brought suit on grounds that the action abridged their rights under the First and Fourteenth Amendments to the Constitution. By a vote of 5 to 3, the Supreme Court sided with the dismissed officeholders. The justices supporting the decision could not agree on a single majority position, but all objected to discharging an employee from a "nonpolicymaking" position solely on grounds of political belief and association (*Elrod* v. *Burns*).

The Supreme Court involved itself with patronage again in 1980, this time refusing to permit the partisan dismissal of certain assistant public defenders in Rockland County, New York. The majority opinion drew on the example of a football coach at a state university to argue that "the ultimate inquiry is not whether the label 'policymaker' or 'confidential' fits a particular position; rather the question is whether the hiring authority can demonstrate that party affiliation is an appropriate requirement for the effective performance of the public office involved" (*Branti* v. *Finkel*). Decisions such as these have fueled the fires of de-politicization already evident with respect to spoils.

Leadership: Persistent Interest in Politicization

The pattern with respect to leadership politics does not mirror precisely that in evidence with regard to spoils. Many elected officials who have little interest in party patronage remain firmly committed to influencing personnel decisions to keep the bureaucracy responsive and accountable to them. Within limits this motivation can be seen as quite healthy. Democracy requires that elected policymakers exert substantial control over the bureaucracy. One cannot assume that the bureaucracy will respond to an elected executive without the artful intervention of this official in certain personnel issues. For instance, one study of the federal bureaucracy during the early Nixon years found that many top civil servants lacked sympathy for his conservative social policies. While not excusing the excesses of the Nixon administration, the analysis concludes that the president's concern with the attitudes of these civil servants lends credence to the view that "even paranoids . . . have real enemies" (Aberbach and Rockman, 1976: 467). Others have pointed to the considerable insulation of local bureaucracies from elected political leadership. One study terms these urban agencies the "new machines" and argues that they are "relatively irresponsible structures of power . . . not readily subject to the controls of any higher authority" (Lowi, 1969: 200-201).

Gauging the presence of leadership politics is even more difficult than measuring the incidence of spoils. Some signs, however, point to renewed attempts by elected executives to garner more control over personnel processes. These executives have taken both informal and formal paths to this end.

Informal initiatives foreswear altering the rules of the game; instead, officials ignore or manipulate existing rules in the name of executive leadership. For example, Lyndon Johnson used the chairman of the Civil Service Commission not only to administer this "independent" agency but to provide advice concerning political appointments. This cooptative strategy won Johnson the support of the commission staff for a number of things he wanted done (Heclo, 1977: 35, 65). It was Richard Nixon, however, who manipulated personnel practices with particular vigor. Under Nixon, the White House staff prepared the "Malek Manual" (after Fred Malek who at one point headed the White House Personnel Office). This manual outlined the "realpolitik" of the federal personnel system, warned that the bureaucracy might sabotage the president's program, and offered advice on how to manipulate personnel processes. The manual strongly stressed that "There is no substitute in the beginning of any administration for a very active political personnel operation." It went on to underscore that officials could not "hope to achieve policy, program or management control" until they had "achieved political control." By influencing personnel practices, the staff hoped to permit Nixon to rule rather than reign ("Malek Manual," 1979: 187). Ultimately, Nixon's efforts to exert leverage over personnel decisions probably yielded some dividends. By the time of his Watergate demise, he appears to have reshaped the top levels of the civil service in a way that assured greater sympathy for his program priorities (Cole and Caputo, 1979).

Attempts by top elected officials to politicize the bureaucracy under the banners of greater responsiveness and accountability have not stopped with these informal efforts. Officials have also altered the formal rules of the game. The Civil Service Reform Act of 1978 serves as a good example. This law divided the old, semiautonomous Civil Service Commission into two agencies: the Merit Systems Protection Board and the Office of Personnel Management (OPM). OPM was to be the "personnel management staff arm" of the president (Campbell, 1979: 83). Furthermore, the reform act created a Senior Executive Service that within certain bounds also enhanced the leverage of the president by giving him greater discretion to place his appointees in sensitive policy jobs. The total number of noncareer, or "political," appointees may not surpass 10 percent of all positions in the Senior Executive Service. But the president's political appointees can equal 25 percent of the senior executive jobs in a given agency.[1] With the advent of the new senior service, the president also won greater authority to transfer, demote, and promote career civil servants.

Efforts to bolster the leverage of top executives over personnel administration have also found expression at the state and local levels. In some respects, changes in federal standards for merit systems symbolize the renewed interest in such leadership. These standards apply to state and local agencies involved in administering certain federal programs (e.g., Medicaid, Aid to Families with Dependent Children). When the Office of Personnel Management revised these rules in the late 1970s, it made them more sympathetic to an executive leadership model. The new rules specified that "to assure proper organizational responsiveness, appropriate numbers of top-level positions may be exempted from merit coverage if they determine and publicly advocate substantive program policy, provide legal counsel, or are required to maintain a direct confidential working relationship with a key exempt official" (*Fed. Reg.*, 1979: 10238, 10246). Other signs of leadership politics have also emerged. For instance, initiatives have surfaced sporadically to shift authority from local civil service commissions to the chief executives in these jurisdictions.

Whatever the virtues of providing elected executives with more leverage over personnel administration, a certain irony marks the attempt. As top officials gain more clout over this kind of administration, many important personnel decisions have slipped beyond the formal boundaries of government. Operations at the margins of government, or indirect administration, have become more common (Sharkansky, 1979). A host of organizations other than those designated formally as part of the civil service carry on the activities of the public sector. For instance, private insurance companies substantially administer the vast sums the government spends on Medicare. Relatively autonomous agencies, such as the Corporation for Public Broadcasting and the National Railroad Passenger Corporation (Amtrak), perform major public functions.

At least within the boundaries of public agencies, however, efforts by elected officials to foster bureaucratic responsiveness via the personnel arena seem likely to persist well into the 1980s. This is not to project the wholesale repoliticization of public personnel practices. Merit institutions continue to place checks on the authority of elected officials. For instance, a president bent on covertly increasing the number of political operatives employed by the Senior Executive Service would face significant barriers. Among other things, the law requires that 70 percent of the people in the service have at least five years' experience in the career bureaucracy prior to their appointment to these senior levels. Beyond the institutional barriers, many who work in the personnel field continue to mistrust elected officials. For instance, a survey of close to 1,000 public personnel administrators conducted in the mid-1970s found that only 25 percent of them agreed with the statement, "In this day and age, elected officials aren't much of a threat to merit hiring practices"; 68 percent disagreed (Thompson, 1979: 146). These views suggest that formal or informal attempts at politicization by elected officials will not be received uncritically.

GENERIC PERSONNEL POLITICS

Elective personnel politics has absorbed the lion's share of attention among personnel specialists. It is critical to recognize, however, that the personnel arena features another, far more basic brand of politics. Generic personnel politics usually requires the presence of five major conditions: heterogeneous preferences, interdependence, scarcity, issue importance, and the dispersal of power resources.[2] Each of these conditions receives attention in the paragraphs that follow.

Heterogeneous preferences comprise the first condition for generic personnel politics. Those involved must disagree about ends, means, or both. Such disagreements flourish in the personnel arena. Consider, for instance, the diverse objectives of many performance appraisal systems. Some within a public agency may see the appraisal system almost exclusively as a means of protecting themselves against grievances based on the equal employment opportunity laws (Schneier, 1978). Others may perceive the primary function as employee development, as a means of providing feedback to the employee about his or her performance along with strategies for improvement. Still another objective may be to rationalize the agency's allocation of rewards and punishments such as merit pay, promotions, dismissals, demotions, and reductions in force. The various goals to some extent (although not completely) imply different strategies. If officials wish to maximize the use of performance appraisal for employee development, creation of an organizational climate characterized by openness and trust looms as critical. Employees must be willing to admit their mistakes, learn from them, and request help if they cannot cope with some aspect of their work. But if the objective is also to rationalize the reward and punishment system, the cultivation of openness often becomes difficult. The employee being evaluated develops a stake in keeping his or her failures from view and not admitting errors. Valid information about performance tends to flow less freely (Brinkerhoff and Kanter, 1980).

Even where a consensus on objectives exists, preferences about means may differ sharply. The cost-effectiveness of many personnel technologies remains uncertain. This ambiguity permits a great diversity of opinion to exist as to how to accomplish some end. Officials might concur, for instance, on the need to identify middle managers with the most leadership potential. But they may differ sharply over the use of assessment centers or written promotional examinations as vehicles for singling out these potential leaders.

Interdependence is a second condition for the presence of generic personnel politics. Interdependence implies that organizational participants are tied together. The activities of one actor affect the operations or fortunes of another. Each participant, therefore, tends to be concerned with the behavior of the other. In many cities, for instance, the police chief's efforts to promote certain officers depends on the outcomes of written tests designed or selected by the city's central personnel staff. In cases where interdependence is absent, heterogeneous values matter less because each participant can operate independently. Different participants in the personnel arena may pursue conflicting objectives without ever fighting about them or bargaining with each other.

Scarcity constitutes a third and related condition for politics. If the pie is huge, participants will be less likely to fight with one another to get a portion. For instance, a city manager who can draw on a flush city treasury may be able to create a new agency by adding positions to the organization. Where fiscal scarcity reigns, the manager would probably have to strip slots from other departments to set up the new unit. The latter situation obviously holds out far greater potential for conflict. Consequently, the manager will probably have to plot available strategies carefully and take pains to muster a supporting coalition.

A fourth condition giving rise to personnel politics is issue importance. Participants in the personnel game hold many views but act on only a few of them. The gap between attitudes and action is often large. When participants perceive an issue as important, however, they tend to be much more inclined to follow up thoughts and words with deeds. If, for instance, minority leaders assign higher importance to fostering affirmative action at city hall than to fighting slum lords, politicization in the hiring arena is likely to increase.

Finally, politicization is likely to increase when power resources are dispersed among more participants in the personnel arena. If one set of participants monopolizes these resources, it becomes less likely that those who hold views contrary to this group will challenge it, even if they see the issue as important. The willingness to fight declines when those concerned see meager prospects for victory. The concept of power dispersion holds the key to understanding recent developments in the personnel arena. *The movement toward a dispersal of power, more than any other single factor, accounts for the greater generic politicization of public personnel issues in the last twenty years.*

Changes in the law along with other factors have fueled this dispersion. Representatives of racial minorities, women, the handicapped, the elderly and other special groups have acquired new leverage to press their respective causes in the personnel sphere. Unions through collective bargaining and in other ways have also gained strength. Then, too, the courts have intervened with some frequency to bestow legal rights (an important power resource) on individual employees or job hunters (Shafritz, Hyde, and Rosenbloom, 1981: 239-265). In *Board of Regents* v. *Roth* (1972), for instance, the Supreme Court established that an employee may have a constitutional right to a hearing for removal or nonrenewal of a contract under certain circumstances (although not generally).

In essence, then, the number of significant players in the personnel game has expanded. No one player can count on holding all the cards with respect to an issue. Instead, it has often been essential to plot strategies carefully, assemble a coalition, and engage in bargaining. In the words of the Office of Personnel Management, the point is often to distill "the best possible reconciliation of the various views put forward" (*Fed. Reg.*, 1979: 10238-10239).

The dispersal of power means that even highly technical subjects such as test validation provoke intense infighting. As one of the leading experts on testing has observed, "Personnel selection was once a quiet backroom specialty but those days are gone" (Cronbach, 1980: 37). Virtually no feasible validation strategy can eradicate all uncertainty about how well a given selection process singles out the most meritorious candidates for employment. Hence, a kind of "politics of proof" develops. Advocates for minorities and such federal agencies as the Equal Employment Opportunity Commission become research purists seeking to apply the strictest standards of selection validation. That way, employers who cannot meet these standards will more readily feel obligated to hire racial minorities to stay out of legal trouble. For their part, employers respond by saying "let's be practical" as they emphasize the enormous costs and other barriers to conducting such research. Conflict over appropriate research methodology and acceptable levels of evidence gets played out in the federal bureaucracy and in the courts. For instance, the promulgation of uniform guidelines on employee selection procedures took the better part of the 1970s because of intense bureaucratic infighting among the Equal Employment Opportunity Commission, the Civil Service Commission, the Department of Labor, and the Department of Justice (*Fed. Reg.*, 1978; Commission on Civil Rights, 1975).

The resolution or at least temporary mitigation of conflict in the personnel arena may be accomplished in a number of ways. Bargaining comprises a common means of achieving some kind of settlement. It deserves attention, however, that at times the rules of the personnel game do not permit explicit negotiations; instead they require that participants deal with each other at arms' length. For instance, by 1980 four federal agencies were involved with policy questions concerning performance appraisal in the federal bureaucracy: the Equal Employment Opportunity Commission, the Office of Personnel Management, the Federal Labor Relations Authority, and the Merit Systems Protection Board. When a Senate committee inquired as to whether these agencies had gotten together to coordinate policy decisions, officials at the Office of Personnel Management denied that getting together to reconcile differences would be appropriate. In the words of its staff, "These four agencies are independent of one another and operate in a 'checks and balances' way. For that reason, proactive coordination of policy is not appropriate" (U.S. Senate Committee on Appropriations, 1980: 321).

The generic politicization of personnel administration did not, of course, start with the rise of minority groups, employee unions, and activist courts. For instance, skirmishes between centralized personnel staffs and officials in line departments who want to sustain their control over certain personnel practices have long been present. But the sociopolitical developments of the 1960s and 1970s did much to increase the politicization of these processes.

What does the future hold in terms of generic personnel politics? Alternative scenarios present themselves. One scenario anticipates greater politicization because of growing scarcity. The cutbacks imposed by the Reagan administration, the approval of ballot propositions limiting government revenues or expenditures, and the more general sluggishness of the economy could well constrain government budgets. As a consequence, conflict over jobs, pay, and other personnel resources could intensify. An alternative scenario pointing to depoliticization also possesses some plausibility, however.

If the 1980 presidential election proves to be a conservative watershed, statutory changes, the appointment of conservatives to the judiciary, and other factors could reduce the clout of public employee unions and the proponents of equal employment opportunity. A growing sense of weakness might incline union leaders and advocates for affirmative action toward greater reluctance to press their causes. Power would therefore become less dispersed in the personnel arena. Top government officials could pursue certain employment practices with less fear of encountering any challenges. While serious arguments can be made for these and other scenarios, the safest bet may well be that the personnel arena will continue at a relatively high level of generic politicization. It is less than obvious, for instance, that the fiscal conservatism so much in vogue in the early 1980s will translate into a social conservatism that succeeds in gutting union bargaining rights and equal employment opportunity in the public sector. A dispersal of power resources could well persist and continue to spawn generic personnel politics.

Whatever the level of generic politicization present in public personnel administration, normative assessments of these developments require caution. No doubt organizational politics at times undermines an agency's cost-effectiveness and results in inappropriate adaptations to environmental contingencies. But as Pfeffer has pointed out, the available evidence with respect to work organizations "does not support the argument that politics leads to performance problems. Indeed, there is some evidence that the reverse may be true" (1981: 335). He goes on to argue that "organizational politicking" often facilitates useful change and the correction of an organization's errors (1981: 339).

The possible virtues of organizational politics deserve a particularly lengthy airing among personnel specialists because to a substantial degree the field rests on "the unfounded belief that conflict in the environment and practice of public personnel administration is absent, abnormal, and should be avoided" (Nalbandian and Klingner, 1981: 14). Instead specialists in public personnel administration have often labeled politics as irrational or pernicious or both. From a broader perspective, however, the interplay of political forces within the personnel arena may often lead to outcomes far more sensible, or "rational," than adherence to those "scientific techniques" that have been the hallmarks of the field. The propensity of personnel specialists to show slavish adherence to techniques at the expense of purpose has drawn attention in the past (Sayre, 1948). The clash of forces endemic to politicization can help to reduce unthinking commitment to procedures that have ceased to be useful; this clash can help personnel specialists to come to grips with the value assumptions that underpin their work.

SOME IMPLICATIONS

Public personnel administration cannot be "neutral" or value free; it is inescapably political in that it affects who gets what from government. By the same token, however, all governmental personnel systems are not politicized equally. Definitional ambiguities have to this point plagued discussions of the degree to which different governmental agencies feature personnel politics. Rather than attempt in some Procrustean fashion to define politics once and for all, we need to be more explicit about the diverse meanings of the concept.

This chapter has pointed to certain of these definitions. One broad type, elective politics, focuses on the degree to which elected officials and their partisan supporters intervene in personnel administration. Another variant, generic personnel politics, refers to whether different coalitions are in conflict with one another over personnel issues. Assessments of the current and future status of personnel politics vary depending on which kind of politics one is examining. Pockets of spoils persist, but on the whole this form of elective personnel politics appears to have ebbed and may well continue to do so in light of recent court decisions. The leadership version of elective personnel politics has persisted in many governments, and recent decades have produced initiatives to increase the leverage of top elected officials in the personnel arena. These initiatives seem likely to persist into the

1980s. Finally, the generic politicization of the personnel arena increased markedly during the 1960s and 1970s and may well continue at current levels during the 1980s.

If this analysis is correct, what are the implications for those interested in studying and practicing public personnel administration? A major research objective should be to explain the variations in the different types and levels of politicization and to trace their implications for the outputs and outcomes of government. Progress with respect to this objective depends on a number of developments. For one thing, we need to devise a better means of measuring the presence or absence of the different versions of personnel politics in public agencies. For another, evidence of both a qualitative and statistical nature needs to be gathered. Causal models must be constructed. Accomplishing these and related tasks will not prove easy. Even if a consensus develops on how to gauge the presence of different forms of personnel politics, a number of barriers may inhibit the acquisition of valid evidence. For example, those involved in personnel politics will often find it in their strategic interest not to be too open about what they do. Still, some progress in generating a theory of personnel politics seems possible.

Developments with respect to personnel politics also possess implications for those who practice and teach public personnel administration. Personnel administration in a milieu that features a high level of generic politicization requires more than an understanding of technical issues related to job analysis, test validation, performance appraisal, and the like. It commonly requires that officials be skilled organizational "politicians." This means that managers need to possess a tolerance for ambiguity plus the ability to confront and deal with conflict. Speaking and writing skills that serve them well in advocacy, bargaining, negotiations, and the general forging of coalitions become central. Managers must be able to map their strategic environments and develop a sense of timing. To do this, they must be adroit at establishing and using informal information networks that yield insight into the configuration of support, indifference, and opposition within the agency and its environment.

This politicized perspective on the personnel field will run against the grain of many practitioners. In some cases, it will violate their self-identities as professionals, as experts trained in scientifically grounded, objective techniques. In dealing with this concern, it needs to be stressed that a more politicized vision of personnel administration does not negate the importance of the field's technical aspects. To the contrary, an effective administrative "politician" generally has to possess a firm grounding in these techniques. Furthermore, it deserves to be reiterated that personnel politics need not be the enemy of rationality. Such politics can serve both noble and ignoble ends just as the traditional techniques of personnel administration can. Even these considerations may, of course, fail to soothe the discomfort that some personnel specialists experience in acknowledging the importance and legitimacy of political skills in their profession. But psychological comfort can hardly provide a raison d'être for personnel administration. In the words of one observer, it may well be "time to shake up the comfortable habits of thought in the personnel field" (Cronbach, 1980: 49).

NOTES

1. The figure can exceed 25 percent if the agency had a higher proportion of noncareer positions at the time of the act's passage.
2. This perspective draws heavily from the work of Pfeffer (1981).

REFERENCES

ABERBACH, J. D. and B. A. ROCKMAN. 1976. "Clashing Beliefs Within the Executive Branch: The Nixon Administration Bureaucracy." *American Political Science Review* 70 (June): 456-468.

Board of Regents v. *Roth.* 1972. 408 S.Ct. 564.

Branti v. *Finkel.* 1980. 100 S.Ct. 1287.

BRINKERHOFF, D. W. and R. M. KANTER. 1980. "Appraising the Performance of Performance Appraisal." *Sloan Management Review* 21 (Spring): 3-16.

CAMPBELL, A. K. 1979. "Testimony on Civil Service Reform and Organization." In F. J. Thompson, ed., *Classics of Public Personnel Policy.* Oak Park, Ill: Moore, pp. 77-102.

COLE, R. J. and D. A. CAPUTO. 1979. "Presidential Control of the Senior Civil Service: Assessing the Strategies of the Nixon Years." *American Political Science Review* 73 (June): 399-413.

COMMISSION ON CIVIL RIGHTS. 1975. *The Federal Civil Rights Enforcement Effort—1974.* Volume V. Washington, D.C.: G.P.O.

CRONBACH, L. J. 1980. "Selection Theory for a Political World." *Public Personnel Management* 9 (January-February): 37-50.

DONNELLY, H. H. 1978. "CETA: Successful Jobs Program or Subsidy for Local Governments?" *Congressional Quarterly Weekly Report* 36 (April 1): 799-806.

Elrod v. *Burns.* 1976. 96 S.Ct. 2673.

Federal Register. 1978. 43 (August 25): 38290-38315.

——. 1979. 44 (February 16): 10238-10264.

GENERAL ACCOUNTING OFFICE. 1979. *Federal Employment Examinations: Do They Achieve Equal Opportunity and Merit Principle Goals?* FPCD-70-46. Washington, D.C.: G.P.O.

HECLO, H. 1977. *A Government of Strangers.* Washington, D.C.: Brookings Institution.

HORTON, R. D. 1973. *Municipal Labor Relations in New York City: Lessons from the Lindsay-Wagner Years.* New York: Praeger.

JOHNSTON, M. 1979. "Patrons and Clients, Jobs and Machines: A Case Study of the Uses of Patronage." *American Political Science Review* 73 (June): 385-398.

JONES, R. W. 1964. "The Merit System, Politics and Political Maturity." *Public Personnel Review* 25 (January): 28-34.

LOWI, T. 1969. *The End of Liberalism.* New York: W. W. Norton.

LYNN, L. 1980. *The States and Human Services.* Cambridge, Mass.: M.I.T. Press.

"MALEK MANUAL." 1979. In F. J. Thompson, ed., *Classics of Public Personnel Policy.* Oak Park, Ill.: Moore, pp. 159-187.

MIEWALD, R. D. 1969. "Political Science and Public Personnel Administration." *Public Personnel Review* 30 (July): 178-180.

MOSHER, F. 1968. *Democracy and the Public Service.* New York: Oxford University Press.

MUNICIPAL MANPOWER COMMISSION. 1962. *Governmental Manpower for Tomorrow's Cities.* New York: McGraw-Hill.

NALBANDIAN, J. and D. KLINGNER. 1981. "The Politics of Public Personnel Administration: Towards Theoretical Understanding." *Public Administration Review*, 41 (September/October): 541-549.

PFEFFER, J. 1981. *Power in Organizations.* Marshfield, Mass.: Pitman.

ROSENBLOOM, D. H. 1977. *Federal Equal Employment Opportunity: Politics and Public Personnel Administration.* New York: Praeger.

ROYKO, M. 1971. *Boss.* New York: New American Library.

SAYRE, W. 1948. "The Triumph of Techniques over Purpose." *Public Administration Review* 8 (Spring): 134-137.

SCHNEIER, D. B. 1978. "The Impact of EEO Legislation on Performance Appraisals." *Personnel* 55 (July-August): 24-34.

SHAFRITZ, J. 1973. *Position Classification: A Behavioral Analysis for the Public Service.* New York: Praeger.

SHAFRITZ, J., A. C. HYDE, and D. H. ROSENBLOOM. 1981. *Personnel Management in Government.* New York: Marcel Dekker.

SHARKANSKY, I. 1979. *Wither the State?* Chatham, N.J.: Chatham House.

SORAUF, F. 1960. "The Silent Revolution in Patronage." *Public Administration Review* 20 (Winter): 28-34.

THOMPSON, F. J. 1975. *Personnel Policy in the City.* Berkeley: University of California Press.

——. 1979. "Professionalism, Mistrust of Politicians and the Receptivity of Civil Servants to Procedural Buffers: The Case of Personnel Officials." *Midwest Review of Public Administration* 13 (September): 143-156.

U.S. SENATE COMMITTEE ON APPROPRIATIONS. 1980. *Treasury, Postal Service and General Government Appropriations, Fiscal Year 1981.* Part 2. Washington, D.C.: G.P.O.

WOLFINGER, R. 1972. "Why Political Machines Have Not Withered Away and Other Revisionist Thoughts." *Journal of Politics* 34 (May): 365-398.

Donald E. Klingner

Florida International University

CHAPTER TWO
VARIABLES AFFECTING THE DESIGN OF STATE AND LOCAL PERSONNEL SYSTEMS

The United States is a technological society in that we believe that by developing new machines and processes we can overcome social problems or meet people's needs. We also accept the assumptions that different technologies will be suitable for various applications and that changes in objectives or conditions will require new technologies. As examples, we accept that different forms of transportation are required for different types of terrain (dunebuggies and snowmobiles) or that more economical cars are needed to combat increased gas prices.

However, our conception of public organizations is likely to be much more traditional. We are more likely to assume that there is "one best way" to design agencies with similar functions, regardless of cultural variations or changes in agency objectives. With respect to the design of state or local public personnel management agencies, this traditional conception is likely to be based on the beliefs that (1) the sole objective of these agencies is to make nonpolitical decisions that support agreed-upon managerial objectives and (2) personnel management activities are routine and noncontroversial.[1]

Yet the reality of contemporary public personnel management casts doubt upon both these beliefs. First, sweeping reforms in federal civil service structure in 1978 indicate that differences of opinion existed as to whether the primary objective of the Civil Service Commission was to coordinate federal personnel policy, to provide centralized personnel management assistance to federal agencies, or to protect the rights of federal employees. Clearly, these conflicts among the commission's roles led to drastic structural changes—the abolishment of the commission and the creation of two new organizations in its place.[2] Second, recent exploratory research suggests that, although some personnel activities are relatively routine and noncontroversial (e.g., orientation), many reflect widespread disagreement over goals and methods (e.g., affirmative action, labor-management relations, and motivation).

This chapter examines how variable environmental factors and alternative objectives influence the design of state and local public personnel agencies. First, three environmental influences are considered: laws, the relative power of subgroups, and the expected role of the personnel agency. Second, their effects on the objectives, structure, and function of these personnel agencies are evaluated. Third, some techniques of personnel agencies, according to their own perception of the agency's objectives and relevant environment, are suggested.

ENVIRONMENTAL INFLUENCES

Traditionally, public managers have assumed that they could use personnel management techniques to control employees so as to increase their productivity or the predictability of their behavior. However, contemporary theories emphasize the importance of environmental influences on organizations. Among these are the three subgroups (managers, employees, and outside groups) whose conflicting values and objectives create controversies during the decision-making process within each agency. For example, labor relations represent the influences of legislators, courts, regulatory agencies, and interest groups on a variety of employment practices—recruitment, selection, promotion, and training. Second, the fact that certain personnel activities exemplify the conflicting objectives of competing subgroups tends to discredit the traditional assumption that personnel activities are routine and noncontroversial. Recent commentary indicates that, whereas some personnel activities are characterized by agreement on goals and methods, others are highly politicized.[3] In fact, personnel managers select, from among several decision modes (computation, negotiation, and judgment), the one they consider appropriate to the decision context.[4] Third, problems with developing operational definitions of organizational effectiveness, and the resultant need to examine contextual and organizational variables, have tended to focus our interest on the relationship between perceived power and perceived subgroup effectiveness.

Predictably, additional research suggests that there is a high degree of correlation between the perceived powers of subgroups and their perceived effectiveness in influencing personnel decisions in controversial areas such as compensation, promotion, and labor relations. Not only do personnel managers find that subgroup objectives may conflict with managerial objectives, but also that these groups may exercise considerable influence over organizational policy in personnel activities.

Laws represent the second major environmental influence on public personnel management: the structure and functions of public personnel agencies are determined largely by enabling legislation, executive orders, court decisions, and administrative agency regulations. Recent federal civil service reforms illustrate this. In addition, state and local personnel systems are bound strongly by state collective bargaining laws, federal affirmative action requirements, and the "strings" attached to federal grants-in-aid.[5] In addition, the typical local budgetary process exerts a strong influence on the level and direction of agency activities. Law is among the most interesting variables because its impact has produced two contradictory trends: on the one hand, laws are seen as a means of protecting personnel agencies from political influence; on the other hand, laws reflect the conflicting values and objectives of competing subgroups.

The reasons why law has had this contradictory impact on personnel are worth examining. Since the reform era of municipal and state administration during the late 1890s, the growth of public personnel agencies has depended on the extension of "merit system" protections to an even greater proportion of public employees. By dichotomizing public decisions into two categories—political and administrative—and by insisting that personnel decisions be made solely toward uniform organizational objectives and based on the sole criterion of administrative efficiency, personnel theorists have supported the implicit assumption that "merit" is a value-free principle. Yet the law has also performed a second function: it has politicized personnel management by extending special protections to persons in certain groups and by requiring compliance agencies to enforce regulations that may contradict each other.

For example, personnel practitioners generally realize that legitimate conflicts exist among laws. There are at least nine federal affirmative action laws, each applicable to different employers, employees, and employment practices and each having different compliance agencies and procedures. As Sears, Roebuck argued in its 1979 class action suit against ten federal agencies involved in affirmative action compliance, an employer may find it difficult to hire more blacks and women and at the same time protect the rights of elderly white males (primarily veterans who are also protected by the Age Discrimination in Employment Act). Even the Supreme Court has had trouble deciding whether all persons are covered by affirmative action laws.[6]

The third environmental factor affecting the design of local personnel systems is the way in which various groups view the role of personnel agencies. The point here is that actors' conceptions of the purpose of the personnel agency and their perceptions of its environment will affect that agency. In general, central personnel agencies perform the following functions:[7]

1. *Legislative*—developing state or local personnel policy for enactment by state legislature, gubernatorial executive order, or city-county council.
2. *Administrative*
   a. providing other state or local agencies with qualified job applicants through centralized recruitment services.
   b. coordinating affirmative action compliance policies.
   c. providing reimbursable training.
   d. supporting client agency personnel procedures through the development of classification, pay, retirement, and information systems.
3. *Judicial*
   a. assuring agency compliance with state or local personnel management laws, rules, and regulations.
   b. hearing employee appeals concerning the adequacy of agency grievance procedures.

Given this general uniformity of functions, different personnel agencies will emphasize different functions or will perform them in different ways.

An agency's behavior will reflect managerial perceptions of the nature of the organization's task environment and the extent of influence exerted on managerial perceptions by outsiders. For example, personnel managers who perceive themselves as having the only significant influence on policy will tend to develop policies that reflect managerial objectives, make administrative decisions according to standardized decision rules, and enforce laws blindly. Personnel managers who perceive their organizations as operating in more open environments are more likely to develop policies based on mediation among conflicting subgroup objectives, make many nonroutine administrative decisions, and interpret laws by weighing their intent and effect on alternative subgroups. Table 1 shows this relationship between managerial perceptions and expected organizational behavior.

For example, a municipal personnel agency may be responsible for assuring merit system compliance (a judicial function), making personnel rules and regulations (a policymaking function), and making program decisions with respect to a range of personnel functions (a managerial function). If the personnel manager perceives the environment to be closed, personnel policies will reflect only the

TABLE 1 Managerial Perceptions versus Expected Organizational Behavior

PERSONNEL AGENCY FUNCTION	PERSONNEL MANAGER'S PERCEPTION OF THE ENVIRONMENT	
	CLOSED	OPEN
1. Policymaking	Clarify management objectives	Mediate among group's objectives
2. Managerial	Make routine decisions	Make contextual (political) decisions
3. Judicial	Enforce laws	Interpret laws
	Expected behavior	

objectives of the personnel agency or its line agency clients. If the personnel agency is perceived as being more open to pressure by employees and outside groups, it is more likely that the personnel agency will be viewed as having a mediating role among the diverse objectives of management, employees, and outside groups. This perception affects the second function—management. If policies are simply managerial objectives made explicit, then effective management is the making of cost-efficient decisions according to standardized rules. However, if policies are the result of mediation among competing groups, then decisions are likely to be contextual (that is, the decision strategy will vary with the context) or political (reflecting compromise among disputed goals and methods). Finally, the perceived uniformity of enabling laws will affect the personnel agency's judicial function. If laws are viewed as uniform and explicit, the agency's function will be viewed as that of enforcing them. If laws are seen as complex and controversial, the agency will be expected to balance conflicting objectives through compromise and interpretation.

These three environmental factors (laws, subgroup power, and perceptions of the personnel agency's function) interact to channel the behavior of different types of professionals who perform personnel functions into four predictable patterns:

1. *Supervisors* are oriented primarily toward meeting work unit objectives. They are unlikely to support costly or cumbersome personnel procedures required by laws or regulations.
2. *Centralized staff agency personnel* are likely to support "merit system" rules and regulations and to advocate centralization of personnel functions in the name of efficiency and uniformity.
3. *Agency personnel managers* will have loyalties divided between merit system protection and service to supervisors. They are also subject to influence by employees and unions.
4. *Regulatory employees* are likely to favor increased oversight or judiciary

powers for their agency. Their values support the apolitical applications of "merit system" guidelines to individual cases involving employee rights.

These four behavior patterns are expected roles followed by four types of personnel practitioners. Because supervisors are responsible for implementing most personnel systems, they have great impact on employees' cumulative perception of personnel management. However, they are frequently not considered personnel practitioners because their major responsibilities are for direct production activities by line units of the organization.

The behavior of each of these types of personnel practitioners is regulated by enabling laws and resource allocations. Supervisors are concerned primarily with maintenance of short-term work unit productivity: central personnelists with maintaining efficiency and systemic control, decentralized personnelists with maintaining timely and effective service to field agencies, and regulatory agency staff with preserving equity between organizations and employees. While the behavior of such agencies may have been established originally by law and sanctified by historical practice, their operating practices are also reinforced by decision makers' internalized role expectations and perceptions of the agency's task environment.[8]

In sum, the preceding analysis has demonstrated that three environmental factors (the relative power of subgroups, the contradictory functions of laws, and conflicting assumptions about the objectives and the environment of public personnel management) affect the design of personnel agencies.

EFFECTS OF ENVIRONMENTAL FORCES ON PERSONNEL AGENCY OBJECTIVES, STRUCTURE, AND FUNCTION

Environmental forces have influenced the design of state and local personnel agencies in three respects: the nature of their objectives, their structure, and their relationships with other public agencies. Three basic personnel agency objectives have emerged out of the controversy over the expected roles of personnel management: increased efficiency and centralized control, local flexibility and effectiveness, and protection of agency or employee rights.

The first objective, increased efficiency and centralized control, is usually achieved by creating a central personnel department to enhance central control of personnel policy, compliance with merit system regulations, or administrative efficiency. Centralization is also increased to ensure compliance with affirmative action objectives in the event of a court order or consent decree. In many state governments, such as Indiana, centralization occurred in 1972–1975 because of the need to comply with the affirmative action planning and record-keeping requirements of the 1972 Equal Employment Opportunity Act. Elsewhere, in the City of

Miami, for example, the government has been operating under a consent decree since 1977, and its police department has come under a succession of consent decrees since 1975. To comply with the terms of the 1977 decree, the city has centralized control of personnel policies and practices in a human resources department and thereby decreased the power of municipal departments and employee unions. While it would be inaccurate to say that affirmative action compliance was not the primary objective of the centralization, local officials and union leaders are also aware that its unintended consequences have been equally significant for municipal personnel system design.

The second possible objective, increased local flexibility and effectiveness, is usually recognized as primary in situations where environmental factors are so complex or variable that uniform personnel management policies or procedures are ineffective. For example, shortages of trained law enforcement personnel have led many police departments to offer cash bonuses to personnel who recruit new members. Multijurisdictional recruitment teams travel to cities undergoing cutbacks in police funding in hopes of attracting police officers to their communities. Or state personnel departments allow mental hospitals to conduct decentralized recruitment and selection programs targeted toward shortage-category professionals such as psychiatrists, psychiatric nurses, and pharmacists. In these situations, staffing needs are specialized, and selections must be prompt if candidates are to remain available. Structurally, this leads to a decentralization of personnel decision making in state or local government. This model recognizes that they are often more effective than a centralized system at meeting the specialized hiring needs of particular agencies, whereas decentralized recruitment and selection may be less efficient on a unit cost basis. However, decentralization also necessarily leads to less central control over such personnel activities as recruitment, selection, and record keeping. It may also worsen affirmative action compliance problems by favoring practices such as word-of-mouth recruitment.

The third objective, increased protection of agency or employee rights, is served best by the establishment of an independent commission that mediates disputes that occur over personnel policies and practices between public agencies and their employees. Examples of this include the grievance arbitration model followed by public sector labor relations agencies, the affirmative action complaint resolution process followed by affirmative action compliance agencies, or the complaint resolution functions of a municipal merit systems review board. In each case, the personnel agency is established as a neutral arbitrator to investigate and mediate complaints of personnel policy violations by labor or management on a case-by-case basis. In Indiana, the Education Employment Relations Board oversees unit recognition elections and mediates contract disputes. In Ohio, both the state's fair employment practice committee (the Ohio Civil Rights Commission) and the EEOC are empowered to investigate employee allegations that state and local agencies have violated their rights under Title VII of the 1964 Civil Rights Act. Many municipal governments have a merit system review board (with a function similar to the Merit Systems Protection Board at the federal level) that is

TABLE 2 Relationship of Personnel Agencies to Their Intended Objectives

INTENDED OBJECTIVE	TYPE OF PERSONNEL AGENCY
1. Centralized control and increased efficiency ⟶	Centralized personnel agency
2. Effective response to environmental diversity/change ⟶	Decentralized personnel agency or line management
3. Specialized case adjudication ⟶	Investigatory and judicial agency affirmative action, labor management relations, merit system protection)

responsible for investigating complaints of merit system violations by public agencies and serves as appellate body for both employees and management for decisions reached previously in the disciplinary action and grievance process. In all these cases, the independence of the regulatory agency is established by statute as is its investigative process of subpoena and discovery.

The point here is that the decision of each of these three types of personnel agencies is related directly to their intended objectives as summarized in Table 2.

INFLUENCING THE DESIGN OF PERSONNEL AGENCIES

The preceding analysis has shown that it is possible to (1) identify the environmental variables that affect public personnel systems and (2) predict the ways in which these factors will influence agency structure and function. Since the prospect of controlling the behavior of organizations is always more enticing than the mere ability to predict their behavior, personnel practitioners inevitably ask a third question: "What can be done to influence the design of personnel systems?"

Yet this question cannot be answered in a vacuum. As with the other human activities, what *can* be done is affected by what one *wants* to do. In such cases, the most obvious strategy for a personnel practitioner is to emphasize those environmental factors that support the personnel system objectives that he or she favors. For example, the director of a fledgling central personnel agency will probably seek to increase his or her authority by persuading elected officials in favor of the advantages of centralization—greater uniformity of policy and more efficient performance of routine functions.

The wise director will move slowly, beginning with those personnel functions that are least contentious (such as personnel record keeping or recruitment) and least capable of successful performance by line managers (such as general skills training) or most burdensome (affirmative action or OSHA compliance). These will enable the central personnel department to increase its staff, budget, and influence gradually, without risking a premature "showdown" with an irate line manager or agency personnel office. On the other hand, line managers or agency personnel officers will probably seek to maintain their autonomy by insisting that control over management "rights," such as the authority to determine pay, promotions, and performance evaluation criteria, is vested most properly in individual agencies. Or they may argue that their specialized functions are not suitable to centralized personnel management. At a clandestine level, they may develop personnel record-keeping systems and personnel procedures that are too complex or diverse to be assimilated easily into a central personnel system.

Personnel directors who believe that labor relations and affirmative action are troublesome activities that reduce management effectiveness will be likely to work for the establishment of separate organizations for these activities, yet insist that such organization directors report directly to the personnel director. In this fashion, their effect on other personnel activities can be monitored and (it is hoped) controlled. Conversely, affirmative action or labor relations directors are likely to (1) support the integration of these functions with more traditional personnel activities or (2) seek direct access to elected officials rather than rely on the personnel director to support them with top management.

SUMMARY

The functions, structures, and relationships of local personnel agencies are influenced in predictable directions by environmental variables (laws, expectations, and the relative power of competing groups). Specifically, environmental variables affect a personnel agency's objectives, structure, and relationship with other organizations. The predictability of these influences makes it possible for personnel managers to utilize deliberately these variables to change their agencies in desired directions. All these conclusions contradict more traditional assumptions about public personnel management.

NOTES

1. See, for example, Jay M. Shafritz, *Public Personnel Management: The Heritage of Civil Service Reform* (New York: Praeger, 1975), or Donald E. Klingner and John Nalbandian, "Personnel Management by Whose Objectives?" *Public Administration Review*, Vol. 38 (July-August 1978), 366-372.

2. Reorganization Plan No. 1 (43 *Fed. Ref.* 19807, 1977) divided the U.S. Civil Service Commission into two separate agencies: the Office of Personnel Management (responsible for federal agency personnel policymaking and administrations) and the Merit Systems Protection Board (responsible for judicial functions). Reorganization Plan No. 2 (24 *Cong. Rec.* H4464, Doc. No. 95-990, 1977) gave the EEOC control over federal agency affirmative action enforcement.

3. For a general discussion of the political nature of "routine" personnel functions, see Charles Milton, *Ethics and Expediency in Personnel Management* (Columbia: University of South Carolina Press, 1970); or Michael T. Monroe, "The Position Classifier's Dilemma, "

The Bureaucrat, Vol. 4 (July 1975), 204–206; or Frank J. Thompson, "Classification as Politics," in Robert T. Golembiewski and Michael T. Cohen, eds., *People in Public Service: Readings in Public Personnel Administration*, 2nd ed. (Itasca, Ill: F. E. Peacock, 1976), pp. 515–529.

4. In *Organizations in Action* (New York: McGraw-Hill, 1967), p. 124, James Thompson hypothesized that all decision issues can be categorized depending upon the extent to which protagonists agree or disagree on objectives and methods. Each of these four decision contexts has an appropriate decision strategy, as indicated:

EXTENT OF AGREEMENT ON OBJECTIVES

		+	−
EXTENT OF AGREEMENT ON METHODS	+	Computation	Negotiation
	−	Judgment	Inspiration

To some extent, the validity of this decision model has been confirmed by exploratory research: see John Nalbandian and Donald E. Klingner, "Integrating Context and Strategy in Personnel Management," *Administration and Society*, forthcoming.

5. See Donald E. Klingner and Daniel B. Smith, "The Erosion of Home Rule in Public Personnel Management," *National Civic Review*, forthcoming; or Ray Shapek, "Federal Influences in State and Local Personnel Management: The System in Transition," *Public Personnel Management*, Vol. 5 (January–February 1976), 41–51.

6. For examples of conflicts among laws affecting public personnel management, see Jean J. Couturier, "The Quiet Revolution in Public Personnel Laws," *Public Personnel Management*, Vol. 5 (May–June 1976), 150–167; or Richard H. Allen, "Collective Bargaining in the Public Sector," *Barrister*, Vol. 3 (Fall 1976), 65–70; or David E. Robertson, "New Directions in EEO Guidelines," *Personnel Journal*, Vol. 1 (July 1978), 360–363ff.

7. For representative discussions of the scope of the public personnel management function, see Donald E. Klingner, *Public Personnel Management: Contexts and Strategies* (Englewood Cliffs, N.J.: Prentice-Hall, 1980), Chap. 6.

8. For further discussion of the types of public personnel professionals and their respective values, see Donald E. Klingner, *Public Personnel Management: Contexts and Strategies* (Englewood Cliffs, N.J.: Prentice-Hall, 1980), Chap. 6.

David H. Rosenbloom

Syracuse University

CHAPTER THREE
WHAT EVERY PUBLIC PERSONNEL MANAGER SHOULD KNOW ABOUT THE CONSTITUTION

Until relatively recently, American public personnel managers needed to know very little about the Constitution. For the most part it was not viewed as a constraint upon the treatment of public employees. Since the 1950s, however, the courts have played a far larger role in public personnel administration and have left their stamp upon it (Rosenbloom, 1971, 1977). Consequently, nowadays public personnel managers can be oblivious to constitutional considerations only at the risk of having important aspects of their programs, including examinations and affirmative action, overturned in court. This chapter investigates the evolution of constitutional doctrines affecting the rights of public employees and reviews the leading cases in areas of major concern to contemporary public personnel administration. Its purpose is to familiarize public personnel managers with constitutional concepts and to provide an up-to-date survey of the relevant constitutional law.

CONSTITUTIONAL DOCTRINES

Until the 1950s, the rights of public employees were governed by what has become known as the "doctrine of privilege." This approach relied on the tenet that public employment was a privilege rather than a right or coerced obligation such as military service. Consequently, it was thought that it could be withheld for any reason that the governmental employer saw fit, however arbitrary. Not having a right to a position in the public service, upon dismissal the employee lost nothing to which he or she was entitled. As Justice Oliver Wendell Holmes once expressed it, "The petitioner may have a constitutional right to talk politics, but he has no constitutional right to be a policeman" (*McAuliffe* v. *New Bedford*, 1892: 220). The precise nature of this doctrine was identified by Dotson (1955: 77), as follows:

> Its central tenet is that office is held at the pleasure of the government. Its general effect is that the government may impose upon the public employee any requirement it sees fit as conditional to employment. From the point of view of the state, public employment is maintained as an indulgence; from the position of the citizen, his job is a grant concerning which he has no independent rights.

While the doctrine of privilege contained a certain logic, it also ignored the realities of citizens' interaction with government in the administrative state. Thus, if a public employee could be denied his or her job for virtually any reason without violating the individual's constitutional rights, would not the same principle apply to other kinds of privileges, such as welfare benefits, government contracts, passports, and licenses? Could these be denied, as public employment was, for such reasons as the individual favored racial integration, read Tom Paine, or even *The New York Times*, failed to attend church services, or engaged in a host of non-conformist and unconventional activities (Rosenbloom, 1971: 160–168)? Obviously, to the extent that big government creates a dependency between the people and government services (privileges), strict adherence to the doctrine of privilege could easily lead to tyrannical circumvention of the Bill of Rights.

By the 1960s, the Supreme Court disregarded the long-standing distinction between rights and privileges (Van Alstync, 1968), in substantial part on the grounds that it was no longer viable public policy. Thus, in *Sherbert* v. *Verner* (1963), the Supreme Court proclaimed that "It is too late in the day to doubt that the liberties of religion and expression may be infringed by the denial of or placing of conditions upon a benefit or privilege" (404). Although the demise of the distinction between rights and privileges has been uneven, by the early 1970s, the Court left no doubt that in the realm of public employment, which by that time encompassed about 20 percent of the work force, it had "fully and finally rejected the wooden distinction between 'rights' and 'privileges' that once seemed to govern the applicability of procedural due process rights" (*Board of Regents* v. *Roth*, 1972: 571) and "rejected the concept that constitutional rights turn upon whether a governmental benefit is characterized as a 'right' or as a 'privilege' " (*Sugarman* v. *Dougall*, 1973: 644).

Yet rejecting the doctrine of privilege has been easier than replacing it with a coherent alternative approach. Indeed, in the 1970s, the Supreme Court engaged in three marked doctrinal shifts on the questions posed by the constitutional relationship between the government and the citizen in public employment.

The doctrine of privilege was replaced initially by the "doctrine of substantial interest," which held that "whenever there is a substantial interest, other than employment by the state, involved in the discharge of a public employee, he can be removed neither on arbitrary grounds nor without a procedure calculated to determine whether legitimate grounds do exist" (*Birnbaum* v. *Trussell*, 1966: 678). This doctrine had the effect of "constitutionalizing" public employment and forcing public personnel managers to be cognizant of the constitutional rights of employees and applicants in a wide variety of personnel activities. It also led to an increase in the number of public employment cases reaching the Supreme Court and posed difficult questions concerning the definition of "substantial interest."

Indeed, so complex were the issues involved that the Court was unable to formulate a general approach to the application of the concept. Instead, it was compelled to treat each case individually on the specifics of its own merits. This circumstance was exacerbated by the Court's changing membership and marked ideological divisions (*The New York Times*, 1974: 10). The resulting doctrinal change, which has been referred to as the "idiographic approach" (Rosenbloom, 1975), required that, in applying general personnel regulations and principles to individual employees, public employers address the specific sets of facts and circumstances involved. Thus, a large measure of individualized treatment of public employees was necessary constitutionally in terms of such questions as mandatory maternity leave, assignment of personnel by race, and the exclusion of aliens from specific positions.

The major limitations of the idiographic approach were that, because it stressed individualized treatment, rather than broad definitions of rights, it led inevitably to an ever-increasing amount of litigation, and by providing little guidance on the nature of the constitutional aspects of the public employment relationship, it made public personnel management more difficult. By the mid-1970s, these drawbacks had become clear, and the Supreme Court, having been unable to develop a useful general doctrine or approach, sought to "deconstitutionalize" the relationship between governments and their employees.

While deconstitutionalization may presage a return to concepts similar to those contained in the doctrine of privilege, to date the circle is hardly complete; deconstitutionalization has not been applied forcefully in a wide variety of circumstances. The Supreme Court articulated the deconstitutionalization approach in *Bishop* v. *Wood* (1976: 693):

> The federal court is not the appropriate forum in which to review the multitude of personnel decisions that are made daily by public agencies. We must accept the harsh fact that numerous individual mistakes are inevitable in the day-to-day administration of our affairs. The United States Constitution cannot feasibly be construed to require federal judicial review for every such error.

To the extent that deconstitutionalization occurs, it will tend to remove the judiciary from public personnel administration. In the future, therefore, public personnel managers may be less constrained by the Constitution in their treatment of employees and in the development and implementation of personnel policy.

FREEDOM OF SPEECH

Under prevailing constitutional interpretations, the public employee's right of freedom of speech is broadly protected, except where its exercise is in conjunction with a partisan political activity. In *Pickering* v. *Board of Education* (1968), the Supreme Court held that the special duties and obligations of public employees notwithstanding, the proper test for the regulation of their speech is whether the government's interest in limiting their "opportunities to contribute to public debate is . . . significantly greater than its interest in limiting a similar contribution by any member of the general public" (573). Its interest would be presumptively greater when

> There was a need for maintaining discipline and harmony in the work force.
> There was a need for confidentiality.
> The employee's statements would be hard to counter due to his or her presumed greater access to factual information.
> The employee's statements impeded the proper performance of work.
> The employee's statements were so unfounded that his or her competence was called into question.

The employee's remarks jeopardized a close and personal loyalty or confidence.

In applying *Pickering*, the lower courts have held that the Constitution does not protect public speech concerning matters not of public concern, bickering and running disputes among employees, intermeddling, disruptive speech, and "extremely disrespectful and grossly offensive remarks" (Rosenbloom and Gille, 1975: 260). On the other hand, public criticism of an employer has been held to be within the ambit of constitutional protection.

Public personnal managers should also be aware that remarks made in private by public employees may be afforded constitutional protection, depending upon their content. In *Givhan* v. *Western Line Consolidated School District* (1979: 695-696), the Supreme Court reasoned that "this Court's decisions . . . do not support the conclusion that a public employee forfeits his protection against governmental abridgment of freedom of speech if he decides to express his views privately rather than publicly."

The *Pickering* case laid the constitutional groundwork for the protection of "whistleblowers." Indeed, the Supreme Court reasoned there (571-572) that

> free and open debate is vital to informed decision-making by the electorate. Teachers are, as a class, the members of the community most likely to have informed and definite opinions as to how funds allotted to the operation of the schools should be spent. Accordingly, it is essential that they be able to speak out freely on such questions without fear of retaliatory dismissal.

But what is true of teachers in the realm of education is also true of other public employees in other areas of public policy. Consequently, even in the absence of specific protections for "whistleblowers," such as those contained in the 1978 Federal Civil Service Reform Act, public employees who expose inefficiencies, fraud, or other shortcomings of their agencies or co-workers are generally protected by the Constitution from retaliatory adverse actions. Thus, public personnel managers should remain cognizant of the benefits of "whistleblowing" and be willing to protect those employees who engage in it.

Although *Pickering* guarantees broad freedom of expression to public employees, its protection does not extend to the area of partisan speech and activity. In the early 1970s, there was sound reason to speculate that the Supreme Court would hold that regulations for political neutrality in the public service, such as those contained in the Hatch Acts, were unconstitutional. While these were upheld originally by a 4-to-3 margin in *United Public Workers* v. *Mitchell* (1947), both the scope of public employment and the content of constitutional law had changed sufficiently to cast great doubt upon the continuing validity of that decision. Indeed, in *National Association of Letter Carriers* v. *Civil Service Commission* (1972), a federal district court held that past decisions "coupled with changes in the size and complexity of public service, place *Mitchell* among other decisions outmoded by passage of time" (585). On appeal, however, the Supreme Court reversed this decision in no uncertain terms (*Civil Service Commission* v. *National Association of Letter Carriers*, 1973: 556):

> We unhesitatingly reaffirm the *Mitchell* holding that Congress had, and has, the power to prevent [federal employees] from holding a party office, working at the polls and acting as party paymaster for other party workers. An Act of Congress going no further would, in our view, unquestionably be valid. So would it be if, in plain and understandable language, the statute forbade activities such as organizing a political party or club; actively participating in fund-raising activities for a partisan candidate or political party; becoming a partisan candidate for, or campaigning for, an elective public office; actively managing the campaign of a partisan candidate for public office; initiating or circulating a partisan nominating petition or soliciting votes for a partisan candidate for public office; or serving as a delegate, alternate, or proxy to a political party convention.

In *Broadrick* v. *Oklahoma* (1973), a companion case, the Court was even willing to uphold political neutrality regulations that were worded so ambiguously that they might inhibit speech unrelated to the objective of maintaining a non-partisan public service. Hence, restrictions on the partisan activities of public employees, unless drawn very poorly or implemented in some discriminatory fashion, are constitutional.

Can "whistleblowing" and related political speech always be distinguished from partisan expression? While the answer is patently "No," the Supreme Court has yet to be confronted with the need to create a distinction between them. In terms of public personnel management, therefore, some uncertainty remains in this area, especially during electoral campaign periods.

FREEDOM OF ASSOCIATION

Contemporary constitutional law regarding public employees' freedom of association is also of great importance to public personnel managers. Here again, however, the law is divided and perplexing questions remain. Although public employees' rights to join organizations voluntarily, including political parties, labor unions, and even subversive groups, is now well established (*AFSCME* v. *Woodward*, 1969; *Elfbrandt* v. *Russell*, 1966; *Shelton* v. *Tucker*, 1960), their right to refrain from associating with or supporting organizations has sharply divided the Supreme Court.

Elrod v. *Burns* (1976) concerned the constitutionality of patronage dismissals in the Cook County, Illinois, sheriff's department. The Court held that such dismissals constituted an unconstitutional infringement on public employees' freedoms of belief and association, but it was unable to develop a majority opinion on the issue. Justice Brennan, joined by Justices White and Marshall, reasoned that (554-555):

The cost of the practice of patronage is the restraint it places on freedoms of belief and association. In order to maintain their jobs, respondents were required to pledge their political allegiance to the Democratic Party, work for the election of other candidates of the Democratic Party, contribute a portion of their wages to the Party, or obtain the sponsorship of a member of the Party, usually at the price of one of the first three alternatives. Regardless of the incumbent party's identity, Democratic or otherwise, the consequences for association and belief are the same.

He concluded that patronage dismissals were unconstitutional because they were "not the least restrictive means for fostering" legitimate governmental ends, such as the promotion of efficiency and effectiveness (565).

Justice Stewart, joined by Justice Blackmun, concurred, although he viewed the case in a more restrictive light (566):

> The single substantive question involved in this case is whether a nonpolicy-making, nonconfidential government employee can be discharged from a job that he is satisfactorily performing upon the sole ground of his political beliefs. I agree with the Court that he cannot.

Thus, while there was a majority of the Court in favor of the proposition that the patronage dismissals of the employees in question were unconstitutional, there was no majority consensus on precisely why. However, the issue was clarified further in *Branti* v. *Finkel* (1980).

Branti involved the patronage dismissal of two county assistant public defenders. In holding that their dismissals were unconstitutional, the Supreme Court established the principle that "the ultimate inquiry is not whether the label 'policy-maker' or 'confidential' fits a particular position; rather, the question is whether the hiring authority can demonstrate that party affiliation is an appropriate requirement for the effective performance of the public office involved" (1980: 518). It is evident that, under this standard, patronage dismissals in the public service will be extremely limited.

Several members of the Court joined in dissents protesting what can be construed as a kind of constitutionalization of the merit system. In *Elrod*, Justice Powell's dissent was joined by the Chief Justice and Justice Rehnquist. In his view (574),

> History and long-prevailing practice across the country support the view that patronage hiring practices make a sufficiently substantial contribution to the practical functioning of our democratic system to support their relatively modest intrusion on First Amendment interests. The judgment today unnecessarily constitutionalizes another element of American life—an element certainly not without its faults but one which generations have accepted on balance as having merit.

In a similar dissent in *Branti*, Powell was joined by Justice Rehnquist, and to a more limited extent by Justice Stewart.

Elrod v. *Burns* and *Branti* v. *Finkel* protect most public employees from demands that they join or support political parties. At the same time, however, public employees may be compelled to support some of the activities of labor unions. *Abood* v. *Detroit Board of Education* (1977) involved a Michigan "agency shop" arrangement "whereby every employee represented by a union—even though not a union member—must pay to the union, as a condition of employment, a service fee equal in amount to union dues" (269). The issue before the Supreme Court was "whether this arrangement violates the constitutional rights of government employees who object to public sector unions as such or to various union activities financed by the compulsory service fees" (269).

The Court, per Justice Stewart, reasoned that (269):

> To compel employees financially to support their collective bargaining representative has an impact upon their First Amendment interests. An employee may very well have ideological objections to a wide variety of activities undertaken by the union in its role as exclusive representative . . . . To be required to help finance the union as a collective-bargaining agent might well be thought, therefore, to interfere in some way with an employee's freedom to associate for the advancement of ideas, or to refrain from doing so, as he sees fit. But . . . such interference as exists is constitutionally justified by the legislative assessment of the important contribution of the union shop to the system of labor relations established by [legislature].

Consequently, even where a union's *bargaining activities* may run counter to the deeply held moral, religious, social, or political views of an employee, the employee can be compelled to pay the bill.

But what about union activities outside the sphere of collective bargaining? In *Abood*, the teachers argued "that they may constitutionally prevent the Union's spending a part of their required service fees to contribute to political candidates and to express political views unrelated to its duties as exclusive bargaining representative" (283). In upholding the teachers on this point, the Court stated (284-285) that:

> We do not hold that a union cannot constitutionally spend funds for the expression of political views, on behalf of political candidates, or towards the advancement of other ideological causes not germane to its duties as collective bargaining representative. Rather, the Constitution requires only that such expenditures be financed from charges, dues, or assessments paid by employees who do not object to advancing those ideas and who are not coerced into doing so against their will by the threat of loss of governmental employment.

The protection of employees from compulsory contributions to nonbargaining activities poses an especially sensitive problem for public personnel managers. Indeed, the Supreme Court recognized that "there will, of course, be difficult problems in drawing lines between collective bargaining activities, for which contributions may be compelled, and ideological activities unrelated to collective bargaining, for which such compulsion is prohibited" (285). Aside from the problem of establishing mechanisms by which public employees can register their protest against financially supporting specific union activities unrelated to collective bargaining, there is the difficulty of assessing the amount of the individual employee's contribution to these activities. Thus, the *Abood* decision may require some unions to change the nature of their financial record keeping and reporting. In any event, public personnel managers are likely to be compelled to assess the character of union activities and their costs more frequently in the future. All in all, therefore, the situation left in the wake of *Abood* is likely to engender considerable strife and litigation.

LIBERTY

The broad issue of public employees' "liberty" has also been the subject of substantial litigation. Over the years, public employees have been exposed to various types of coercion by their employers. For instance, in the 1960s, Senator Ervin found that public employees had been requested "to lobby in local city councils for fair housing ordinances, to go out and make speeches on any number of subjects, to supply flower and grass seed for beautification projects and to paint other people's houses" (U.S. Senate, 1967: 9). In the 1970s, the Supreme Court addressed three important areas of restriction of public employees' liberty: mandatory maternity leaves, grooming standards, and residency.

    Cleveland Board of Education v. *La Fleur* (1974) and *Cohen* v. *Chesterfield County School Board* (1974), which were argued and decided together, involved issues posed by mandatory maternity leaves. The regulations being challenged forced teachers to leave their jobs, without pay, several months before the expected date of birth of their children. The Supreme Court, per Justice Stewart, elected to decide the case on the basis of "liberty" rather than equal protection. The Court held that "by acting to penalize the pregnant teacher for deciding to bear a child overly restrictive maternity leave regulations can constitute a heavy burden on the exercise of . . . protected freedoms" (640). The regulations were found unconstitutional because they infringed on the teacher's free choice in matters of marriage and family life without advancing any valid state interest: "the provisions amount to a conclusive presumption that every pregnant teacher who reaches the fifth or sixth month of pregnancy is physically incapable of continuing. There is no individualized determination . . . to any particular teacher's ability to continue at her job" (644). For such general regulations to be constitutionally valid, they must not require leave in the absence of an individual physical examination except very late in the normal term of a pregnancy. Similarly, a regulation barring a teacher from returning to work within three months after the birth of her child was held unconstitutional.

In the Court's view, the liberty to bear children must remain free of undue and purposeless governmental interference. Other liberties, however, have been considered less fundamental. Thus, in *Kelley* v. *Johnson* (1976), the Court found no constitutional barrier to grooming regulations applying to male police officers. Although a lower court held that "choice of personal appearance is an ingredient of an individual's personal liberty" (712), the Supreme Court reasoned that the burden of proof should be on the employee challenging the regulation to "demonstrate that there is no rational connection between the regulation . . . and the promotion of safety of persons and property" (716). Since the Court thought that such regulations might enhance the public's ability to identify police officers and contribute to an *esprit de corps* within the police department, it found the challenge to the grooming standards inadequate. In view of the fact that these justifications were exceedingly weak—after all, police wear uniforms to facilitate identification and at least some of them were opposed to the regulations enough to support the suit—it is unlikely that the Supreme Court will overturn similar kinds of restrictions unless they are utterly arbitrary, capricious, or unfairly enforced.

Finally, in *McCarthy* v. *Philadelphia Civil Service Commission* (1976), the Supreme Court upheld the constitutionality of a residency requirement for firefighters. However, it did so without much discussion of the issues involved, and, therefore, it remains unclear whether there are constitutional limits to a public employer's ability to require that its employees live within its jurisdictional boundaries.

EQUAL PROTECTION

The Supreme Court's decisions concerning grooming and residency indicate that public employers have substantial leeway in dealing with aspects of their employees' lives. Its decisions in the 1970s concerning equal protection of the laws also serve to reduce the likelihood that public personnel administrative actions will infringe unconstitutionally upon fundamental rights. Thus, the Court firmly established the principle that public personnel practices having a harsh racial or gender impact will nevertheless be upheld constitutionally unless they manifest a discriminatory *purpose*.

This line of constitutional interpretation was developed first in *Washington* v. *Davis* (1976). The case involved a challenge to the constitutionality of a written qualifying examination given to applicants for positions as police officers in the District of Columbia. The exam had a disproportionately harsh racial impact by disqualifying four times as many blacks as whites. Several lower court decisions held that such a disparity required the governmental employer to demonstrate that the exam in question served a compelling state interest. This generally entailed a demonstration of the test's validity (Rosenbloom and Obuchowski, 1977). However, the Supreme Court rejected this approach in favor of one requiring that "an invidious discriminatory purpose" (*Washington* v. *Davis*, 1976: 4792) be shown to overturn a public personnel practice on the grounds that it violates the Equal Protection Clause (4792):

> This is not to say that the necessary discriminatory racial purpose must be express or appear on the face of the statute, or that a law's disproportionate impact is irrelevant in cases involving Constitution-based claims of racial discrimination . . . .
>
> Necessarily, an invidious discriminatory purpose may often be inferred from the totality of the relevant facts, including the fact, if it is true, that the law bears more heavily on one race than another.

At the time it was decided, it appeared that the impact of *Washington* v. *Davis* on public personnel management would be limited because identical issues can be litigated under federal equal employment opportunity statutes that, unlike the Constitution, do not require that a discriminatory purpose be shown to invalidate a public personnel practice having a harsh racial impact (4794). However, the significance of the *Washington* v. *Davis* decision was made evident in *Massachusetts* v. *Feeny* (1979), which involved a challenge to the constitutionality of Massachusetts' veterans preference law on the grounds that it violated the equal protection clause by disproportionately excluding women from public employment. The Equal Employment Opportunity Act of 1972 foreclosed the possibility of challenging such regulations on statutory grounds by providing that "nothing contained in this title [VII] shall be construed to repeal or modify any Federal, State, territorial, or local law creating special rights or preference for veterans" (EEO Act, 1972: sec. 712). The Supreme Court agreed with the challengers that the impact of the Massachusetts law on the "public employment opportunities of women has . . . been severe" (*Massachusetts* v. *Feeny*, 1979: 4654). Nevertheless, it upheld the constitutionality of the "absolute" preferential scheme on the basis that not impact, but rather "purposeful discrimination is the condition that offends the Constitution" (4655).

The importance of the *Washington* v. *Davis* approach may also be manifested in future public sector affirmative action cases. It is evident that, if purposeful discrimination against minorities is unconstitutional, such discrimination against nonminorities might also violate the Constitution. This appears to be especially likely where a personnel practice resembles the creation of a quota system. Although not an employment case, this was the thrust of the Court's position in *Regents* v. *Bakke* (1978). And, in upholding private sector affirmative action quotas in *Kaiser* v. *Weber* (1979), the Supreme Court stressed that "since the . . . plan does not state action, this case does not present an alleged violation of the Equal Protection Clause of the Constitution" (4853). Indeed, to date the Supreme Court has explicitly endorsed quotalike racial preferences in public employment only in the case of *Morton* v. *Mancari* (1974), which concerned the constitutionality of an Indian preference scheme in the Bureau of Indian Affairs. In upholding the system, the Court stressed the unique status of Indians as "quasi-sovereign tribal entities" (554).

DUE PROCESS

The Constitution protects citizens against governmental denial of their "life, liberty, or property, without due process of law" (Fifth and Fourteenth Amendments). Although perplexing to define in a technical sense, due process generally refers to fundamental fairness (*Hannah* v. *Larche*, 1960). In the realm of public employment it raises the question of when an adverse action constitutionally requires that a hearing be held and the issue of what form such a hearing must take. Here, as in the areas of liberty and equal protection, toward the end of the 1970s, the Supreme Court moved to diminish the relevance of the Constitution as a constraint on public personnel management.

In *Board of Regents* v. *Roth* (1972), the Court clearly established the potential applicability of the Constitution in adverse actions in the public sector. It identified four situations in which public employees would have a constitutional right to a hearing in dismissal actions: (1) where the dismissal was in retaliation for the exercise of protected rights, such as freedom of speech; (2) "where a person's good name, reputation, honor or integrity is at stake because of what the government is doing to him, notice and an opportunity to be heard are essential" (573); (3) where a dismissal diminished a public employee's future employability; and (4) where the employee has a property right or interest in a position, such as tenure or a contract.

In *Arnett* v. *Kennedy* (1974), however, the Court was unable to reach a majority opinion on the issue of whether a federal employee could be dismissed, without a pretermination hearing, for publicly accusing his supervisor of seeking to bribe a third party. Although six justices agreed that the Constitution was a relevant constraint in such circumstances, two of these believed that its requirements would be met by a posttermination hearing. On the other hand, the three remaining justices argued that the case should be governed solely by the prevailing statute (the Lloyd–LaFollette Act of 1912) rather than the Due Process Clause of the Fifth Amendment. (These were Justices Rehnquist and Stewart and Chief Justice Burger). Consequently, a majority of five justices found no constitutional infirmity in the employee's dismissal.

By 1976, a majority of the Court seemed determined to limit the constitutional requirement of due process even further. In *Bishop* v. *Wood*, it found that a police officer who was defined as a "permanent employee" by a city ordinance nevertheless had no constitutionally cognizable property interest in his position and therefore (693):

> In the absence of any claim that the public employer was motivated by a desire to curtail or to penalize the exercise of an employee's constitutionally

protected rights, we must presume that official action was regular and, if erroneous, can best be corrected in other ways. The Due Process Clause of the Fourteenth Amendment is not a guarantee against incorrect or ill-advised personnel decisions.

Thus, *Bishop* v. *Wood* provided public personnel managers with greater freedom in the realm of adverse actions without running the risk of violating constitutional requirements of due process. In *Codd* v. *Velger* (1977), the Supreme Court reduced the applicability of due process even further by noting that "if the hearing mandated by the Due Process Clause is to serve any useful purpose, there must be some factual dispute between an employer and a discharged employee which has some significant bearing on the employee's reputation" (627). Consequently, in the absence of such a factual dispute, no hearing is required by the Constitution.

It should be borne in mind, however, that several lower court decisions have held that when hearings are constitutionally required they must include cross-examination, confrontation, impartiality, and perhaps be open to the public (Rosenbloom and Gille, 1975: 254-258). In addition, where an adverse action is taken against an employee who has engaged in constitutionally protected conduct, such as free speech, the employer may have to show "by a preponderance of the evidence that it would have reached the same decision . . . even in the absence of the protected conduct" (*Mt. Healthy City School District Board of Education* v. *Doyle*, 1977: 287).

LIABILITY

It is important to stress that for the public personnel manager knowledge of the constitutional rights of public employees is anything but academic. Indeed, as a result of several Supreme Court decisions over the past decade, such knowledge has become a positive job requirement. Today, the public personnel manager is likely to be *personally* liable for infringing upon the constitutional rights of public employees and applicants if he or she (1) acts in bad faith, that is, intends to abridge such rights, (2) acts unreasonably in the light of the circumstances prevailing at the time, or (3) knew or reasonably should have known that the action taken would be in violation of protected constitutional rights (Rosenbloom, 1980). Where such liability obtains, the personnel manager may be sued for damages under state statutes, federal statutes, or the Constitution. If the breach of constitutional rights is caused by a political subdivision, that unit may be sued directly and is not entitled to attempt to raise a "good faith" defense (*Owen* v. *City of Independence*, 1980). In such a case, the sole question will be whether a violation of constitutional rights was actually caused by the subdivision's actions or policies. In sum, the personnel manager who seeks to protect his or her pocketbook or agency from civil suits for damages must be scrupulous in avoiding infringements upon the constitutional rights of public employees.

CONCLUSION

Discussions of the constitutional rights of individuals often have an air of unreality about them. There is no doubt that attempting to vindicate one's rights through a lawsuit that turns on matters of constitutional interpretation is generally an arduous process. It is time consuming, expensive, and psychologically burdensome. Thus, it would come as no surprise if there were a substantial gap between the constitutional rights of public employees in theory and in practice. Nevertheless, the public personnel manager should always remain watchful of judicial decisions for several reasons.

First, such decisions signal the degree of judicial intervention in public personnel administration. For instance, whereas in the 1960s the public employment relationship became substantially governed by the Constitution, the record of relevant Supreme Court decisions in the 1970s reveals a diminution of the extent to which public personnel management is constrained by that document. At the Supreme Court level during the latter decade, public employees were clear victors over their employers in only two areas: patronage dismissals and mandatory maternity leaves. This shift is indicative of a changing outlook on the Supreme Court that favors allowing governments more leeway in dealing with their employees. It is a change that will be welcomed by many public personnel managers who would prefer to do their jobs with less judicial intervention. However, the constitutional foundation has been laid for a shift back in the other direction as well. And presumably such a change in judicial outlook could be brought about by a callous disregard of public employees' constitutional rights by public personnel managers.

Second, it is evident that citizens do still enjoy considerable constitutional rights while in public employment, including those in the realm of nonpartisan speech, association, liberty, and protection from intentional discrimination based on unconstitutional factors such as race or religion. Regardless of the overall trend of judicial decisions, some of these rights will be expanded over the next decade. Given public personnel managers' liability for breaches of constitutional rights that they may inflict, personnelists must always remain cognizant and up to date with respect to such legal developments.

Finally, it should be noted that judicial decisions concerning the public employment relationship generally seek to establish a balance between the constitutional rights of public employees and the needs of public employers. Their efforts can provide public personnel managers with guidance as to how public personnel policy can create a greater harmony between the needs of the administrative state for productive, efficient employees and those of constitutional democracy for free citizens.

In sum, the constitutional status of public employees is likely to remain a problematic area for public personnel managers and one that will present public personnel administration with great challenges and opportunities in the years to come.

REFERENCES

Abood v. *Detroit Board of Education.* 1977. 52 L.Ed.2d 261.
AFSCME v. *Woodward.* 1969. 406 F.2d 137.
Arnett v. *Kennedy.* 1974. 416 U.S. 134.
Birnbaum v. *Trussell.* 1966. 371 F.2d 672.
Bishop v. *Wood.* 1976. 48 L.Ed.2d 684.
Board of Regents v. *Roth.* 1972. 408 U.S. 564.
Branti v. *Finkel.* 1980. 445 U.S. 507.
Broadrick v. *Oklahoma.* 1973. 413 U.S. 601.
Civil Service Commission v. *NALC.* 1973. 413 U.S. 548.
Cleveland Board of Education v. *La Fleur.* 1974. 414 U.S. 632.
Codd v. *Velger.* 1977. 429 U.S. 624.
Cohen v. *Chesterfield County School Board.* 1974. 414 U.S. 632.
DOTSON, A. 1955. "The Emerging Doctrine of Privilege in Public Employment."
    Public Administration Review 15 (Spring): 77–88.
Elfbrandt v. *Russell.* 1966. 384 U.S. 11.
Elrod v. *Burns.* 1976. 49 L.Ed.2d 547.
EQUAL EMPLOYMENT OPPORTUNITY ACT. 1972. 86 Stat. 103, March 24.
Givhan v. *Western Line Consolidated School District.* 1979. 99 S.Ct. 693.
Hannah v. *Larche.* 1960. 363 U.S. 420.
Kelley v. *Johnson.* 1976. 47 L.Ed.2d 708.
McAuliffe v. *New Bedford.* 1892. 155 Mass. 216.
McCarthy v. *Philadelphia CSC.* 1976. 47 L.Ed.2d 366.
Massachusetts v. *Feeny.* 1979. 47 Law Week 4650.
Morton v. *Mancari.* 1974. 417 U.S. 535.
Mount Healthy City School District Board of Education v. *Doyle.* 1977. 429 U.S.
    274.
NALC v. *CSC.* 1972. 346 F. Supp. 578.
New York Times, The. 1974. July 1, p. 10.
Owen v. *City of Independence.* 1980. 445 U.S. 622.
Pickering v. *Board of Education.* 1968. 391 U.S. 563.
Regents v. *Bakke.* 1978. 46 Law Week 4896.
ROSENBLOOM, D. 1971. *Federal Service and the Constitution.* Ithaca, N.Y.:
    Cornell University Press.
——. 1975. "Public Personnel Administration and the Constitution." *Public
    Administration Review* 35 (Jan/Feb): 52–60.
——. 1977. "The Public Employee in Court," in C. Levine, ed., *Managing Human
    Resources.* Beverly Hills, Calif.: Sage.
——. 1980. "Public Administrators' Official Immunity and the Supreme Court:
    Developments During the 1970s." *Public Administration Review* 40. 166–
    173.
ROSENBLOOM, D. and J. GILLE. 1975. "The Current Constitutional Approach
    to Public Employment." *University of Kansas Law Review* 23: 839–869.
ROSENBLOOM, D. and C. OBUCHOWSKI. 1977. "Public Personnel Examina-
    tions and the Constitution." *Public Administration Review* 37 (Jan/Feb):
    9–18.
Shelton v. *Tucker.* 1960. 364 U.S. 479.
Sherbert v. *Verner.* 1963. 374 U.S. 398.
Sugarman v. *Dougall.* 1973. 413 U.S. 634.
United Public Workers v. *Mitchell.* 1947. 330 U.S. 75.

U.S. SENATE. 1967. "Protecting Privacy and the Rights of Federal Employees."
      Report 519. 90th Cong., 1st sess., August 21.
VAN ALSTYNE, W. 1968. "The Demise of the Right-Privilege Distinction in
      Constitutional Law." *Harvard Law Review* 81: 1439–1464.
Washington v. *Davis.* 1976.   44 Law Week 4789.

T. Zane Reeves

University of New Mexico

CHAPTER FOUR
INTERGOVERNMENTAL PERSONNEL RELATIONS: THE PROSPECTS FOR "RENEWED FEDERALISM"

Since the founding of the Republic, intergovernmental relations in the United States have been conducted on the theoretical basis of federalism. Uniquely American in its origins, federalism ordained separate and coequal spheres of sovereignty for state and national governments.[1] Neither party would dominate or encroach upon the other's domain. Yet the dualism of federalism was not to endure.

The New Deal era of the 1930s ushered in what David Walker (1981) describes as *Cooperative Federalism,* wherein Washington and the states acted together in addressing problems. By the 1960s and 1970s a "New Federalism" reigned, based on an interlocking, interdependent network of governments and a new, direct relationship between Washington and local governments (Reagan, 1972). New Federalism was based on a recognition that there is a lack of sufficient resources at the state and local levels to solve important social and economic problems. Because of this, the federal government addressed policy issues reserved historically for the states.

By the 1980s, the prevailing ethos of New Federalism had come under attack by those, among them President Reagan, who wished to revitalize what they believed to be the dual federal relationship of an earlier era. They contended that New Federalism had failed to solve the social problems that it sought to cure, and at an enormous budgetary cost. President Reagan and his supporters proposed to return to the federalist principle of separation of powers so that states could solve their own problems, at much less cost. For purposes of discussion, this approach may be characterized appropriately as *Renewed Federalism.*

The evolution of intergovernmental relations and debate over federalism has direct consequences for personnel policymaking. Personnel issues, once the exclusive concern of state and local officials, came under review by Washington during the period of New Federalism. Federal access to state and local personnel policymaking was accomplished through two avenues: congressional legislation and grants-in-aid. How this intervention occurred and the resulting consequences for personnel administration in states and communities are issues of debate for the 1980s.

IMPACT OF FEDERAL LEGISLATION ON STATE AND LOCAL PERSONNEL PRACTICES

Throughout the era of New Federalism, Congress passed legislation that indirectly affected state and local personnel practices. Major social legislation, such as the Occupational Safety and Health Act of 1970 (OSHA), the Equal Employment Opportunity Act of 1972, the Fair Labor Standards Act of 1975, and the Federal Election Campaign Act of 1974, changed particular personnel practices among state and local governments. In a more direct fashion the Intergovernmental Personnel Act of 1970 provided categorical grants to assist state and local governments that were willing to upgrade their personnel system.

Despite this far-reaching legislation, the ability of Congress to mandate state and local personnel practices directly is somewhat restricted. In 1975, the U.S. Supreme Court upheld the right of state and local jurisdictions to set their own wage scales. In *National League of Cities et al.* v. *Usery* (1976), the Court held that the federal government lacked authority under the Constitution's commerce clause to interfere in the wage-and-hour-setting process in that it was a power reserved to the states by the Tenth Amendment.

The *League* decision does not prohibit Congress from regulating all aspects of state or local employment. Federal regulation is still possible under certain conditions. For instance, Congress may still impose a wage freeze on state and local employees during an emergency.

Thus, the question of which state and local activities may be legislated constitutionally by Congress is raised. As a guideline, the Fair Labor Standards Act's minimum wage and overtime provisions are not applicable to "integral operation of States and their political subdivisions in areas of traditional government functions." This means that employees in schools, hospitals, fire prevention, police, sanitation, public health, parks and recreation, and other traditional governmental functions are not covered by the minimum wage and overtime provisions.

As Rubin (1978) observes, the general directive of the *League* decision is clear: to allow state and local government to develop their own minimum wage and overtime standards and to continue such practices as

1. Giving employees compensatory time off for overtime worked rather than paying them time and a half for overtime.
2. Hiring teenagers at lower salaries than the federal minimum wage for summer work.
3. Using volunteers in fire departments.

The *League* decision does not mean that the federal government can no longer regulate any aspect of state and city employment. Although the *League* decision invigorated state sovereignty over employment practices, recent court decisions limit this power in two ways.

1. Congress may still extend the Civil Rights Act (Title VII) to state and local government employees despite the states' claim to sovereign immunity under the Eleventh Amendment.
2. The Equal Pay Act and the Age Discrimination in Employment Act still apply to state and local government employees according to recent federal court decisions.

Not the least important implication of the *League* decision may have been to prevent Congress, as it was periodically so inclined, from passing a national collective bargaining law for state and local workers. Nor does the *League* decision prevent Congress from legislating restrictions against poor working conditions for state and local employees under the Fourteenth Amendment. But, as a matter of course, the Supreme Court has warned Congress against intervening in day-to-day personnel policymaking among state and local governments.

The Intergovernmental Personnel Act of 1970 (IPA) provided the carrot for federal efforts to bring about personnel reform in state and local jurisdictions. Its purpose was to help improve personnel management, productivity, and management capacity in state, local, and tribal governments. Officials estimate that, in the ten years of its existence, IPA granted more than $160 million in "seed money" for more than 5,000 grant projects.

How well did IPA succeed in accomplishing personnel changes? It depends on whom you ask. In 1981, OPM spokespersons lauded IPA assistance because it helped state and local governments to manage their resources effectively (OPM, 1981a). A National Governors' Association survey attributed IPA assistance as playing a major role in improving state training capabilities (Beckman, 1980). Yet President Reagan's 1981 and 1982 budgets called for a reduction and later elimination of IPA. Why, one might reasonably ask, were successful IPA programs axed?

Seemingly, IPA's budget cut was not based on a perceived failure but on a desire to "eliminate Federal involvement in areas that are essentially state and local concerns" (OPM, 1981a). Or as one OPM official explained IPA's demise, "Now that IPA has completed its job, state and local government resources can carry on those efforts" (OPM, 1981a). For whatever reasons, IPA was not a budgetary priority of Renewed Federalism.

Federal legislation such as IPA and the Fair Employment Practices Act changed certain state and local personnel practices. Yet they were less influential than another federal strategy, the grant-in-aid. During the era of New Federalism, over 39,000 local governments and fifty states were federal grantees. How did these federal grants affect personnel decisions? "Almost every grant program passed by Congress has been subject to administrative rules and regulations promulgating federal intervention in state and local personnel management practices" (Shapek, 1976). During the 1960s and 1970s, federal requirements as a condition for grant acceptance became the primary vehicle in changing state and local personnel practices.

Grants as "Glue" in Intergovernmental Relations

Agencies of the federal government award thousands of grants, contracts, loans, and revenue sharing annually to a variety of organizations, including numerous state and local governments as well as other organizations. Consequently, a bewildering array of legal and fiscal arrangements proliferated during the 1960s with a frequent confusion over rights, responsibilities, and accountability among the involved parties (OMB, 1980).

Briefly, a few fundamental distinctions of how federal money is distributed are worth remembering:

Grants and *contracts* impose quite different legal relationships. Contracts essentially are agreements between two parties, legally responsible to each other for providing goods or services, whereas grants are a financial award by one jurisdiction (the federal government) to another (state or local government). The "grantee" agrees to perform certain services at the behest of the "grantor." Although seemingly obvious, the dependent relationship of grantee to grantor is sometimes ignored by state and local governments, which in frustration may later attempt to ignore federal grant guidelines.

Categorical and *block grants* reflect separate approaches to federal funding (even though they are occasionally consolidated in programs, e.g., CETA). *Categorical grants* are targeted specifically to accomplish certain federal objectives. Guidelines are usually defined narrowly by the federal agency and may be revised each budgetary cycle by either Congress or administrative order. Procedures and Request for Proposal (RFP) application deadlines are also determined by the federal agency. Although proposed changes in agency regulations and grant administration must be published in the *Federal Register* to solicit comments from recipients, the administering agency usually views such comments as advisory only.

Block grant programs, such as Title XX of the Social Security Act and the Omnibus Crime Control and Safe Streets Act, have much broader objectives whose parameters are set by congressional action. There are fewer block grants, but they usually involve larger sums of money than do categorical programs. The amount awarded in a block grant is generally set by a *formula* based on the number of eligible individuals within the grantee's jurisdiction.

General revenue sharing, initiated by President Nixon and passed by Congress in 1972, allowed federal tax revenues to be redistributed by formula to over 39,000 general-purpose units of government. Few restrictions were placed on how the money could be used.

Thus, the degree to which federal grants affect state or local personnel practices is set initially by the type of grant. Block grants, such as those in health planning, community development, and other areas, are much less restrictive than are categorical grants because the former allow grantees more autonomy in deciding priorities and personnel procedures. Local and state employees whose wages are paid through block grants are minimally affected by federal personnel policies except for affirmative action provisions. In most cases, they are indistinguishable in the work place from their co-workers and subject to the same personnel policies.

By comparison, categorical grant programs awarded for specific purposes often impose federal guidelines for many facets of personnel management such as compensation levels, employee benefits, position classification, affirmative action, adverse action, and grievance procedures. Some observers believe that, left undeterred, federal categorical grant guidelines would eventually expand to include areas of personnel decision making such as collective bargaining and pension fund management (Stenberg, 1981).

To appreciate how effective grants were as a personnel "change agent," one must first understand certain myths and realities of the grantee-grantor relationship. A widely held illusion among many uninitiated state and local officials is that federal grants need not change personnel practices or decision-making autonomy. Quite the opposite is often true. Federal grants can significantly affect state and local personnel practices, often in ways quite unanticipated.

That grants became so crucial in personnel management was due to a major restructuring in fiscal relations among federal and state governments. Beginning in the 1960s, state and local governments moved from relative autonomy in fiscal decision making to dependence on federal funds. Prior to this period, few had received significant federal funding. By the 1980s, federal grants accounted for a substantial portion of many state and local budgets. In many older cities, federal aid constituted a majority of annual expenditures. On a national average, more than $1 of every $3 spent by state and local governments was a revenue transfer from the federal treasury. Few local jurisdictions refused some form of federal aid, and most were dependent on it to provide a wide range of mandated public services so that many became "creatures of the state and fiscal wards to the federal government" (ACIR, 1978: 6).

Quite simply, many local governments are caught in the growing gap between dwindling local revenues and rising expenditures. They pursue federal grants as a last resort for survival. To many, acceptance of federal money is an easier pill to swallow than facing options of fiscal cutbacks and employee layoffs. Other state and local governments view federal monies as a viable means of financing non-essential "frills" or highly visible programs such as urban beautification or bicycle paths. Regardless of their motives, few local jurisdictions are prepared financially to go it alone and ignore federal aid.

During New Federalism (1960 to 1980), the modus operandi of federal spending for social programs was transformed from a direct to an indirect mode. At the same time, federal agencies expended grant contributions to state and local officers over tenfold, from $7 billion to $73 billion (Austerman, 1978). By fiscal 1981, over 58 percent of the federal budget went for direct benefit payments to individuals, usually distributed by formula grants to states and communities. Yet the federal government's own budget as a percentage of total gross national product remained relatively stable as did the size of the federal bureaucracy.

These trends reflect a fundamental change in the method of accomplishing federal program objectives. Rather than funding social welfare programs directly, Washington sought increasingly to support them indirectly, by granting monies to state and local governments for that purpose. This "law of appropriateness" holds that the level of government most appropriate to provide a service is the one closest to the problem while some other jurisdiction may be more appropriate to finance the activity (Kennedy, 1972).

Both grantee and grantor needed each other. The intricate grants-in-aid network that developed during this era allowed the federal government to deliver social welfare assistance to financially strapped states and communities. Even though federal agencies had responsibility for monitoring grant programs, the interrelated interests of both parties made strict regulation rare. Hale and Paley (1981) suggest that the federal grantor and its grantees behaved analogously to regulatory agencies and their "regulated" industries: neither wished to rock the boat.

Bringing About Uniform
Personnel Procedures

The interdependent grants system also proved a tempting conduit for imposing personnel standards on state and local recipients. By the 1980s, every state and thousands of local governments were administering federal grant programs that required grantee personnel systems to follow Federal Merit System Standards (FMSS) as administered by the Office of Personnel Management (OPM, 1979). Approximately half the grant programs, involving more than $30 billion, mandated grantee personnel systems to be in conformity with federally defined personnel practices.

Federal Merit System Standards embody six "merit principles," first stated formally in the Intergovernmental Personnel Act of 1970 and subsequently revised, which serve as a "bible" of federal personnel values.

1. Open *recruitment* of employees with special emphasis on attracting ethnic minorities and women. *Selection* procedures that are job related, objective, and provide open competition; *appointments* made from qualified persons on eligibility lists; defined *career advancement* or promotional systems.
2. Update *compensation* and *classification plans* that incorporate goals of (a) equal compensation for equal work, (b) commensurate levels of responsibility and difficulty, and (c) wages that are competitive in the marketplace.
3. Systematic *training* programs for employee development.
4. *Layoff* of permanent employees only for cause, curtailment of work, or lack of funds; *separation* of employees for inadequate performance only after corrective efforts; *reduction in force* with systematic consideration of types of appointment, quality of performance and other factors. *Employee evaluations* on a systematic job-related basis is highly recommended although not required.
5. *Affirmative action* programs to achieve equal employment opportunity with specific requirements to (a) collect applicant and employee data for determining "adverse impact" and (b) select guidelines whenever adverse impact exists.
6. Limited political activities of public employees through Hatch Act-type legislation.

To what extent were merit principle guidelines successful in restructuring state and local personnel procedures? It would appear that their impact was significant.

A 1976 Civil Service Commission (CSC) report compared personnel systems in 172 selected CETA grantees who were not subject to FMSS with grant programs that were covered in 119 counties and 53 cities. Of those not in conformity, only 48 percent required open, competitive exams in hiring based on applicant ability.

Many restricted competitive exams to certain entry-level positions, and less than half had any written promotional policy. Only 42 percent had formulated affirmative action plans, and less than 40 percent had written restrictions against partisan political activity by their employees.

One cannot reasonably assume that without federal prodding state and local governments would totally reject merit principles as the basis of personnel systems. The same CSC survey showed that most CETA sponsors provided a comprehensive compensation plan and a position classification plan (75 and 66 percent, respectively). This suggests that the federal carrot is, at best, an incentive to personnel policymakers at the state and local levels. Connecticut's personnel commissioner believes that federal merit standards "have been a powerful impetus in state and local governments," because their personnel specialists could invoke the federal merit standards as a sword of Damocles "to deal with various pressures which would not be in the interest of good personnel and program administration" (Biloon, 1978: 29). Shapek (1978: 328) feels that federal intervention forced state and local administrators to "improve personnel selection techniques, personnel classifications, pay plans, and employee training."

Others, notably President Reagan, contend that state and local autonomy was seriously eroded by the federal government.

Were Washington's Uniform Selection Guidelines, however well intended, yet another avenue for federal domination of intergovernmental personnel relations? Former OPM Chairman Alan Campbell (1978) decries the "common presumption" that personnel policy making "begins in Washington, moves to the state level, and trickles down to local government." Campbell believes that a more accurate picture would acknowledge the innovative and cutting edge played by the states that "are in many cases, charting the direction in which I believe the Federal Government must move."

Despite specific cases of personnel policy experimentation among the states, there has been no widespread rash of such activity. The personnel policymaking relationship between Washington and its grantees is analogous to a parent-child interaction. The child is "free" to develop and grow within certain prescribed boundaries. Good or bad behavior is appropriately punished or rewarded through the gift of grants.

In its parental role, OPM monitored an honor roll of states to track their progress in adopting elements of the Federal Merit System Standards (OPM, 1980). Four states (Colorado, Illinois, Massachusetts, and Oregon) were commended for reform efforts, and Utah was singled out for its personnel management reforms (OPM, 1981). During the first year of the Civil Service Reform Act, thirty-two states debated or adopted elements of the Act's restructured civil service system (*The Wall Street Journal*, 1980). Once again, state grantees responded to the federal carrot in personnel policymaking.

Consistency, never the trademark of federal policy making, is also lacking in federal personnel priorities. This ambivalence was exemplified by the Civil Service Reform Act of 1978 (CSRA), which included revisions to Federal Merit System

Standards. These changes were in response to criticisms that merit systems had become barriers to effective management by restricting managerial discretion in motivating workers. Implemented in 1979, the FMSS allowed less rigorous applicant selection criteria and simplified grievance-handling procedures for grantees.

Despite shifting guidelines, grant provisions have caused substantial conformity in personnel practice by many jurisdictions. Even so, federal personnel procedures are generally more detailed and restrictive than are those of grantees, particularly smaller jurisdictions. As a result, a potential for conflict exists.

Federal versus Grantee Personnel Policies

Preeminence of federal personnel practices over state and local practices is long established. The Social Security Act of 1935 requires "substantial compliance" by state recipients with federal merit principles and uniform state planning for program administration. Adherence to federal personnel practices was strengthened in 1971 when the Intergovernmental Personnel Act transferred responsibility for enforcement from Health, Education, and Welfare to the Civil Service Commission, a move called by one observer a "most significant merit enactment" (Shapek, 1976). It became the commission's mandate to upgrade personnel systems at the grantee level by enforcing federal merit standards. It proved to be a mandate accompanied by conflict.

This conflict is corroborated by an OMB review (1980) of the Federal Grant and Cooperative Agreement Act of 1977, which laments "the increasing frequency of assistance-related disputes" between federal agencies and their grant recipients. As a result, a new body of assistance law is being developed in the courts. Much of this intergovernmental friction is due to the basic differences in the way in which federal government and grantees operate. Congress and the federal agencies appropriate and evaluate programs separately, whereas grantees usually receive grants from a variety of federal sources and frequently find themselves administering federal programs with a plethora of personnel guidelines and confusing regulations.

The Comprehensive Employment and Training Act of 1973 exemplified federal grants that required changes or adaptation of recipient personnel systems. This occurred despite CETA's avowed emphasis on equal treatment for both CETA employees and permanent employees. Its eight titles included a variety of employment programs administered by the Department of Labor. Two programs supported transitional employment in public sector jobs for the *un*employed and the *under*employed. These were used widely by states and local communities during the 1960s and 1970s. As "prime sponsors," urban jurisdictions seized upon CETA money as a means of gaining additional workers, inexpensively, without long-range personnel costs of regular employment such as pensions and health plans. In numerous instances, conflict between CETA personnel regulations and grantee personnel procedures undermined the program's effectiveness and encouraged its demise during the Reagan administration.

Five areas of personnel management caused frequent conflict between CETA prime sponsors and "the feds":

1. *Recruitment and selection.*   CETA guidelines mandated that hiring preferences be given to women, ethnic minorities, veterans, physically handicapped, those under 18 and over 45 years of age, and the unemployed or underemployed. CETA applicants were not screened by standardized testing or selection techniques. This meant that a dual hiring process was created, one that resulted in regularly hired employees and CETA-selected workers being placed side by side on the same job.

2. *Employee compensation.*   Tension sometimes arose over wage rates paid to CETA workers, especially because contradictory CETA regulations set a maximum wage for CETA employees that was often lower than entry-level wages for many jurisdictions (Indiana, 1980), even though CETA guidelines also specified that CETA participants receive regular entry-level wages.

Employee benefits for CETA participants and their co-workers also differed. Benefits allowable to CETA workers varied from jurisdiction to jurisdiction. Again, two compensation packages were usually necessary for each CETA sponsor, one for regularly hired workers and one for CETA-selected workers.

3. *Job security.*   Although CETA regulations set forth a uniform approach to layoffs, such was not the practice in reality. This happened because federal regulations prohibited CETA employees from entering or keeping a job vacated by a non-CETA worker; neither could a CETA worker keep or enter a position that had been left vacant by a laid-off permanent employee. This "rule of concurrent discharge and layoff" meant that employers could only lay off CETA workers if they also discharged regular workers in the same position classes. Only if a non-CETA tree trimmer were laid off, for example, could a CETA tree trimmer also be discharged. This practice was followed so that CETA employers would not lay off CETA workers unilaterally.

4. *Grievance procedures.*   Federal regulations required that CETA employees be given a grievance resolution process separate from that of permanent workers, one that proved more complex. It allowed CETA workers access to a grievance procedure unavailable to other employees. Federal legislation mandated that employers set up a separate grievance system and inform CETA workers of their right to file job-related complaints. To make the process easier, employers were required to assign personnel specialists to assist CETA workers wishing to file grievances.

Grievance procedures required for CETA employees are far too complex to describe here. Suffice it to note that, if the CETA worker remained dissatisfied with the employer's efforts to resolve his or her complaint, then a higher regional grant officer might hear the case. At a higher level, if the CETA employee still grieved, an administrative law judge could even adjudicate the issue. These grievance resolution steps were obligatory regardless of whether a grievance impasse resolution process for employees already existed.

5. *Collective bargaining.* CETA funds were not to be used in either promoting or opposing unionization. At the same time, CETA workers appeared to be "neither fish nor fowl" in regard to labor law. CETA workers could not be compelled to join a union in programs providing institutional training only. On the other hand, federal guidelines allowed employers to have "dues check-off" if required by a labor contract or state law.

The issue of including CETA workers within existing bargaining units was particularly perplexing. Individual states might allow CETA employees to be grouped within municipal bargaining units if they so desired. As with many personnel issues, there was no consistent response among the states.

Thus in a number of personnel areas CETA guidelines were in conflict with grantee practices. By enforcing dual personnel systems, CETA regulations undermined merit-based personnel practices at the state and local levels.

CETA was not alone in dictating contradictory personnel systems for grantees. Under the Davis-Bacon Act, employee wage scales for federally subsidized construction projects were set by the Department of Labor. This usually meant that construction union scales in a local area were adopted as guidelines. Utilization of union scales for Davis-Bacon projects produced widely varying results depending on the strength of unions in a particular geographic area. In Vermont, Davis-Bacon wages for carpenters were 16.4 percent higher than were those on a nonfederal work; in Dallas, the difference averaged 20 percent (Muller and Fox, 1981). In contrast, in Newark and Seattle, where unions were much stronger, workers on federal and nonfederally subsidized projects received comparable wages.

Not surprisingly, Davis-Bacon and CETA were criticized by the Reagan administration as inflationary and examples of Washington's imposition of personnel practices upon grantees. Both programs implement personnel guidelines set in Washington and imposed upon nonfederal jurisdictions. For these reasons they are attacked as an erosion of federalism.

GRANTS MANAGEMENT
AND EMPLOYEE RESPONSIBILITY

Mismanagement of some federal grants and increasing litigation against state and local grantees have focused attention on a heretofore vaguely defined point—whose responsibility is grants management: the federal grantor, the local grantee, or both?

Increasingly, the courts have placed tort liability upon grantee jurisdictions and their employees.

Grant Monitoring: Slipping
Through the Cracks

Numerous media accounts have documented mismanagement and poor personnel practices among grantees. Perhaps the most notorious revelations center on CETA and HUD community block and community action grant projects. One community action agency, even though administered jointly by a city and county with reputations for governmental honesty, allowed the following personnel abuses (Fertig, 1978):

> Staff members were fired without regard to their right to due process. Many were awarded back wages through costly legal action.
>
> Federal audits determined that personal friends of the agency's management were hired, often at salaries that violated federal guidelines.
>
> Large and wasteful purchases were made without competitive bidding, and personal trips were charged to agency accounts.

A federal administrator in the regional office belatedly observed, "We should have been in there with tighter monitoring" (Rodrigues, 1978).

Publicized personnel abuses among federal grantees may be only the tip of the iceberg. The General Accounting Office (GAO) estimated that $4.3 billion was unaccounted for in "unsolved audit findings" from federal grants and contracts. Although 80 percent of these funds from 34 agencies were "potentially returnable," observers speculated that only minimal amounts would be retrieved (GAO, 1979). The GAO reports that few federal agencies have adequate systems for tracking and collecting audit-determined discrepancies. This situation is compounded by the fact that many federal grant administrators consider audit recovery to be an "onerous and low-priority task." Few cherish the role of federal bill collector to state and local agencies. Whenever possible, federal administrators want state and local administrators to monitor their own federal grants.

Grantees are also reluctant to enforce strict standards of program accountability. Politically, local officials often have little motivation to check for grant abuses. Violations are frequently perceived as misuses of federal rather than local money. Even honest politicians might hesitate to carry out purges against constituents or politically influential persons.

Accountability in grants management is blurred further by confusing personnel guidelines. At times, grantee jurisdictions are prevented from applying existing personnel procedures to grant-supported workers. Grant-mandated exemptions from merit system hiring or noncompetitive bidding for purchasing means that dual standards of accountability are employed. Joint accountability by federal and grantee managers for personnel practices has simply meant no accountability in many instances, leading to a deterioration of existing personnel systems in state and local governments.

Litigation and Grantee Immunity

Prior to 1979, recipients of federal grants generally were protected from tort liability because of their grantee status. However, a series of court decisions left little doubt that private citizens have the right to file discrimination suits against grantee jurisdictions. The Supreme Court rejected the argument that only the federal government, not individuals, might litigate to enforce Titles VII and IX of the 1964 Civil Rights Act.

In *Cannon* v. *University of Chicago* (1979), a woman denied admission to two medical schools filed suit against the universities, charging discrimination in violation of Title IX. The universities argued that only the federal government (by shutting off federal funds), not individuals, could seek legal remedy under this act. The Supreme Court disagreed, thereby implicitly opening the door for anyone denied admission (or conceivably employment) to sue federal grantees.

The Court also expanded citizen rights to sue state and local grantees who failed to provide adequate public services. In *Maine* v. *Thiboutot* (1980), the justices upheld an individual's right to sue state or local administrators if violations, even unknowingly, of federal law could be proven in court. The decision meant that infringement of civil rights is no longer the sole criterion for tort liability.

Specifically, the Court concurred with a family who charged that its welfare benefits under AFDC had been computed incorrectly by the Maine Department of Human Services. In dissent, Justice Powell called the case a "landmark" with "far-reaching consequences" and warned that local officials might be sued for failing to administer federal grant programs properly. Other observers concur that "the consequences of *Thiboutot* are indeed immense" (Groszyk, 1981).

As if *Maine* v. *Thiboutot* were not menacing enough to local officials, the Court seemingly removed any remaining immunity in two related cases: *Maher* v. *Gagne* (1980) and *Owen* v. *City of Independence* (1980). In *Maher* v. *Gagne*, the Court held that attorney fees could be awarded to successful litigants in cases such as *Thiboutot*, a decision that one observer predicted would "lead to an even greater increase of these cases" (Groszyk, 1981). In *Owen*, the City of Independence, Missouri, was found liable because its city manager had improperly fired the police chief in violation of certain constitutional rights.

The "vanishing immunity" of state and local grantees is not likely to be reversed by the court. Even though state and local managers are strained to the breaking point by cutback management, they must now be accountable for grant programs that they neither designed nor, from a practical standpoint, can refuse.

President Reagan's effort to return federal programs back to state and local governments was not helped by the *Thiboutot, Maher,* and *Owen* decisions. His "devolution" strategy hinged on reducing duplication of federal and nonfederal programs. He believed that federalism's renewal was predicated, in large part, on the willingness of states and communities to play major roles in administering federal monies to block grant programs. This prospect is diminished, however, if grantees may be sued at "the drop of a hat" in the course of administering federal grants.

REAGAN'S RENEWED FEDERALISM:
PROBLEMS AND PROSPECTS

Federal grants have long been used by presidents from both political parties as a device for influencing state and local policy making. In that regard, grants have been notably successful. However, in an important departure from his predecessors, President Reagan embarked upon a strategy that may be termed "Renewed Federalism" in that it proposed to a far greater extent than ever before, to restore state autonomy and fiscal responsibility in federalist decision making.

As key components of this plan, the Reagan administration proposed a federal budget (fiscal 1982) that would (1) reduce by 25 percent the total amount of federal aid to states and communities, (2) consolidate a number of categorical grants into five block grants that would be administered by the states and (3) shift more than 40 federal programs back to the states as the federal government assumed responsibility for Medicaid health insurance. These proposals would supposedly renew the federal equilibrium.

Cutting Federal Assistance

President Reagan's self-termed "New Federalism" efforts included an overall budgetary cutback of 25 percent *before* transferring grant programs to the states. As noted in Table 1, federal aid to states and localities *rose* by an average annual rate of 16 percent from 1974 to 1978. By comparison, the fiscal 1982 budget projected an absolute *decline* of federal assistance by 8.5 percent.

This severe cutback in the federal program was justifiable to the Reagan administration because, as the President charged in his second state of the union address, "Many welfare programs are poorly administered and rife with waste and fraud." Furthermore, President Reagan believed that "virtually every American who shops in a local supermarket is aware of the daily abuses that take place in the food stamp program." Thus, the 25 percent reduction in social programs would be achieved by improved management and accounting procedures in programs such as the following:

1. *Social Security Disability Insurance* was to be cut about $600 million in fiscal 1982 by tightening up on administration and providing for reexamination of beneficiaries to see if they are still disabled along with other actions.
2. *Aid to Families with Dependent Children.* Changes were projected to save $671 million in 1982 and $845 million in a year by 1985 through such strategies as retrospective accounting, elimination of payments below $10, tougher reporting requirements, inclusion of step-parent income in eligibility determination, and limiting deductions for work expenses when determining income of an applicant.
3. *Federal jobs program* under the Comprehensive Employment and Training Act (CETA) was to be eliminated to save nearly $3.8 billion in fiscal 1982.
4. *Medicaid.* Federal outlays for the Medicaid program were "capped" at about $16.3 billion for fiscal 1981 and could rise only 5 percent in fiscal 1982,

TABLE 1 Federal Grants-in-Aid as a Percentage of State-Local Receipts From Own Sources, 1960-1980, Estimated for 1981 and Projected for 1982 (dollar amounts in billions)

FISCAL YEAR[1]	FEDERAL GRANTS		STATE-LOCAL RECEIPTS FROM OWN SOURCES[2]		FEDERAL GRANTS AS A PERCENT OF STATE-LOCAL RECEIPTS FROM OWN SOURCES
	AMOUNT	PERCENT INCREASE	AMOUNT	PERCENT INCREASE	
1960	$ 7.0	5.3%	$ 41.6	10.1%	16.8%
1961	7.1	1.3	44.9	7.9	15.8
1962	7.9	11.0	48.7	8.5	16.2
1963	8.6	9.4	52.2	7.2	16.5
1964	10.1	17.5	56.5	8.2	17.9
1965	10.9	7.5	61.6	9.0	17.7
1966	13.0	18.9	67.0	8.8	19.3
1967	15.2	17.6	73.9	10.3	20.6
1968	18.6	22.0	82.9	12.2	22.4
1969	20.3	8.9	93.9	13.3	21.6
1970	24.0	18.6	105.0	11.8	22.9
1971	28.1	17.0	116.6	11.0	24.1
1972	34.4	22.3	131.6	12.9	26.1
1973	41.8	21.7	146.9	11.6	27.2
1974	43.4	3.6	158.9	8.2	28.5
1975	49.8	14.9	171.4	7.9	29.0
1976	59.1	18.6	190.2	11.0	31.0
1977	68.4	15.8	221.0	16.2	31.0
1978	77.9	13.8	245.4	10.9	31.7
1979	82.9	6.4	270.8	10.4	30.6
1980	91.5	10.4	295.7	9.2	30.9
1981 est.	94.4	3.2	N.A.	N.A.	N.A.
1982 proj.	86.4	-8.5	N.A.	N.A.	N.A.

[1] Data for 1960 through 1976 are for fiscal years ending June 30; for 1977 through 1982, for fiscal years ending September 30.

[2] As defined in the national income accounts.

N.A.: Not available.

SOURCE: Advisory Commission on Intergovernmental Relations staff computations; *Public Administration Times* (May 1, 1980), 12.

which would save $1 billion in fiscal 1982 as compared with currently anticipated outlays.

5. *Food stamp* eligibility was tightened sharply by raising income limits, reducing benefits for children getting school lunch, benefits, cutting benefits 35 cents instead of 30 cents for each dollar a recipient earns, and retrospective accounting. Anticipated savings were $2.6 billion in fiscal 1982 and $3.6 billion a year by 1986.

Although the Reagan strategy to reinstate federalism is not an issue here, a potential consequence is worth noting. Block grants do not carry extensive restrictions on how money may be spent as do narrowly defined categorical grants. However, categorical grants which are allocated on a formula of need basis are a different story. Formula grant programs such as Food Stamps and Aid to Dependent Children are to be made more effective through stricter eligibility requirements for recipients. That tighter restrictions and monitoring by state and local jurisdictions can occur at present staffing levels would seem unlikely.

Consolidating into Block Grants

Not only does Renewed Federalism drastically decrease the total grant amount given to states, but it also shifts away from categorical to block grants. President Reagan promised National League of Cities members that, "We're giving local government the power to decide what will be done with the money, you will set your own priorities." A second strategy for revitalizing federalism centered on replacing categorical with consolidated block grants so that states would be free of Washington's domination.

An underlying assumption is that thousands of categorical grants restrict centralized planning. They are also viewed as requiring excessive overhead for administration. In education, for example, the federal government had supported several hundred categorical programs for state and local school districts. These ranged from ethnic studies and vocational education to drug abuse prevention. Quite simply, the Reagan administration proposed to consolidate thirty of these programs into a single block grant, albeit at a reduced amount, thereby letting grantees decide how to use the funds.

Shifting Responsibility to the States

In addition to consolidating categorical programs into block grants, the Reagan administration advocated turning over to the states control of 43 other programs. These included such diverse programs as black-lung clinics, virtually all education projects, and food stamps. Several block grants, each involving consolidation of other programs were also slated for transfer to the states. The major block grant programs were mandated to the states with few strings attached: social services ($2.4 billion); community services ($348 million); prevention ($81.6 million); alcohol, drug abuse, and mental health ($432.1 million); primary care ($247.4 million); and maternal and child care health ($347.5 million).

The "turnback" programs also carried with them revenue authority as well. During an eight-year transition period, starting in 1984, a special $28 billion trust fund using revenues from federal excise taxes and the windfall oil tax would be available to the states. At the end of 1991, the trust fund would expire and the states could either assume full financial authority for the former federal programs or discontinue them.

Those who opposed the Reagan strategy did so for a variety of reasons. Most urban interests opposed grant consolidation as a threat to their direct funding pipelines to Washington (Peirce, 1981). They felt that their particular needs would be submerged in block grants given to rural areas that dominated state capitols. Interest groups representing the disabled, mental health, minority groups, or the poor feared that state officials would respond to "political" priorities while ignoring their needs.

Perhaps surprisingly, Renewed Federalism was also an approach criticized by most state governors as well. This happened even though a wide range of state and national organizations had long supported grant consolidation as a much needed reform (OMB, 1980; ACIR, 1981; and National Academy for Public Administration, 1981). Hostility of state officials to the Reagan plan stems from the proposed reduction of 25 percent in total grant allocation, a sum that they would have to make up or face the political repercussions.

What, then, of federalism's future and that of intergovernmental personnel relations? Three trends have emerged in our discussion. First, there is little indication that the interrelated intergovernmental system will go the way of tyrannosaurus rex. Despite the challenge and possible inroads of Renewed Federalism in the 1980s, the days are irretrievably gone when state and local jurisdictions can survive (let alone prosper) without Washington's assistance. The inadequate taxing resources of most states and communities limit their ability to solve most of the complex problems confronting them.

Second, future decades will undoubtedly find substantial experimentation with both *how* grants are distributed and to *whom*. Both issues raise questions of federalism's separation of powers as old as *The Federalist Papers* (No. 51). Finding an appropriate mechanism for distributing federal funds to the states and communities, without overly compromising their political sovereignty remains an on-going quest for policy makers. With New Federalism, the Republic experimented with a multitude of categorical and block-grant programs. Categorical grants had the appeal of assuring potentially forgotten groups of access to federal monies. On the other hand, block grants could funnel large sums of federal money to grantees without restrictions, thus allowing them to set their own priorities. In a larger sense, the block-categorical grant debate reflects a continuing tension between preserving minority rights (states) while allowing for majority rule (the national government).

Finally, the history of federalism in the 1960s and 1970s is one that relegated the state's role to a secondary status. Categorical grant monies were funneled directly to local governments and community groups (Lowi, 1969). States had little voice in how categorical funds were to be used. As Vermont's Governor Snelling (1980) observes, "The states and municipalities . . . were not capable or sophisticated enough to implement federal goals by themselves, without the firm leadership of the Washington bureaucracy." But, as the governor also notes about the federal attitude toward "lesser" forms of government, "Their lack of confidence has always seemed ill-founded." Renewed Federalism of the 1980s proposed a reevaluation of the states' role in grants programs; it proposed nothing less than restoring states to the original federal-state partnership.

Whether or not states become full-fledged partners in federalism is open to debate. But their increased status and role as policy makers seem secure. In the 1960s and 1970s the states were not trusted to set their own personnel policies. The federal grant used a carrot and stick approach to enforce personnel standards set in Washington. It appears now that the states will be encouraged to set their own personnel systems and procedures, a prospect that could create a hotbed of experimentation in personnel policy making. In such a scenario, personnel practices developed and tested in Utah might be tried in other states. A less happy prospect is that truly merit-oriented personnel procedures will be abandoned or never adopted without the pressure of grant guidelines.

As the states take a more independent role in setting personnel procedures, they will assume a greater burden of defending these same policies from litigation. With vanishing immunity will likely come direct responsibility for personnel policies and their enforcement as well.

NOTES

1. In addition to Michael Reagan, several observers in the late 1960s drew attention to the radically altered nature of American intergovernmental relations: Daniel Elazar, *American Federalism: A View from the States* 2nd ed. (New York: Harper & Row, 1972); Robert L. Merriam, *Federalism Today* (Washington, D.C.: Graduate School Press, U.S. Department of Agriculture, 1969); Richard Leach, *American Federalism* (New York: W. W. Norton, 1970); James L. Sundquist and David Davis, *Making Federalism Work* (Washington, D.C.: Brookings Institution, 1969).

REFERENCES

ADVISORY COMMISSION ON INTERGOVERNMENTAL AFFAIRS. 1977. *The Comprehensive Employment and Training Act: Early Readings from a Hybrid Block Grant.* Washington, D.C.: G.P.O., June.

ADVISORY COMMISSION ON INTERGOVERNMENTAL RELATIONS. 1978. "A Tilt Toward Washington: Federalism in 1977." *Intergovernmental Perspective* 4 (Winter): 4-14.

ADVISORY COMMISSION ON INTERGOVERNMENTAL RELATIONS. 1981. "An Agenda for the Eighties." *Intergovernmental Perspective* 7 (Winter).

AUSTERMAN, WINNIE. 1978. "Can Legislatures Control Federal Funds?" *State Legislatures* 4 (January, February).

BECKMAN, NORMAN. 1980. "Training Under the IPA: Succeeding at the Art of the Possible." *Intergovernmental Personnel Notes* (November–December): 13, 21.

BILOON, SANDRA. 1978. In *Conference Report on Public Personnel Reform.* Washington, D.C.: Civil Service Commission, p. 29.

CAMPBELL, ALAN K. 1978. "The Not-So-Quiet Revolution in Civil Service," address delivered to the Conference on Public Personnel Management Reform, Hall of States, Washington, D.C., (January 23).

Cannon v. University of Chicago and Northwestern University. 1979. 77-926.

CIVIL SERVICE COMMISSION, Bureau of Intergovernmental Personnel Programs. 1976. *A Graphic Presentation of Public Personnel Systems in 172 Large Cities and Counties.* Washington, D.C.: CSC.

FERTIG, RALPH. 1978. "Noble Funds for Ignoble Ends," editorial in *The Los Angeles Times,* (November 9) II, 4.

GENERAL ACCOUNTING OFFICE. 1979. *Perspectives on Intergovernmental Policy and Fiscal Relations.* Washington, D.C.: G.P.O. (June 28).

GROSZYK, WALTER S. JR. and THOMAS J. MADDEN. 1981. "Managing Without Immunity: The Challenge for State and Local Government Officials in the 1980's." *Public Administration Review* 41 (March–April): 268–278.

HALE, GEORGE E. and MARIAN LIEF PALLEY. 1981. *The Politics of Federal Grants.* Washington, D.C.: Congressional Quarterly Press.

INDIANA UNIVERSITY. 1980. "CETA and Public Sector Labor Relations." *Midwest Monitor* (March, April): 3.

KENNEDY, DAVID J. 1972. "The Law of Appropriateness: An Approach to a General Theory of Intergovernmental Relations." *Public Administration Review* 32 (March–April): 135–143.

Los Angles Times, The. 1978. "Urban Aid Often Aids Abuses Instead," (October 14).

LOWI, THEODORE. 1969. *The End of Liberalism* (Chicago: W. W. Norton).

Maher v. Gagne. 1980. 10 S.Ct. 2570 U.S. 622.

Maine v. Thiboutot, 1980. 100 S.Ct. 2502.

MULLER, THOMAS and MICHAEL FOX. 1981. "Federal Rules, Local Costs," in *Policy and Research Report.* Washington, D.C.: The Urban Institute, 2 (Spring): 1–7.

NATIONAL ACADEMY FOR PUBLIC ADMINISTRATION. 1981. "Academy Advises Roth on Grants," *National Academy Reporter* 8 (April): 1–2.

National League of Cities et al. v. W. J. Usery, Jr., Secretary of Labor. 1976. 96 S.Ct. 2465.

OFFICE OF MANAGEMENT AND BUDGET. 1980. *Managing Federal Assistance in the 1980's.* Washington, D.C.: G.P.O. (March).

OFFICE OF PERSONNEL MANAGEMENT. 1979. "OPM Publishes Revised Merit Systems Standards for State and Local Governments." *OPM News* (February 23).

OFFICE OF PERSONNEL MANAGEMENT. 1980. *State Government Personnel Management Project and Programs: A Review of Recent Developments.* Washington, D.C.: Office of Intergovernmental Programs (November).

OFFICE OF PERSONNEL MANAGEMENT. 1981a. "OPM Marks Tenth Anniversary of IPA." *OPM Notes* (January–February): 4–5.

OFFICE OF PERSONNEL MANAGEMENT. 1981b. "Update Highlights: Utah." *Intergovernmental Personnel Notes* (March–April).

Owen v. City of Independence. 1980. 445 U.S. 622.

PEIRCE, NEAL R. 1981. "Block-Grant Shift May Be Too Fast," *The Los Angeles Times* (May 29): 7.

REAGAN, MICHAEL. 1972. *The New Federalism.* New York: Oxford University Press.

REAGAN, RONALD R. 1981. Address delivered to the National League of Cities, Detroit (March 2).

RODRIGUES, ALPHONSE. 1978. "LACAC Scandal Continues." *The Los Angeles Times* (October 14): I,13.

RUBIN, RICHARD S. 1978. "States Rights and Public Employees." *Civil Service Journal* (July–September): 24–26.

SHAPEK, RAYMOND A. 1976. "Federal Influences in State and Local Personnel Management: The System in Transition." *Public Personnel Management* 5 (January–February): 41–51.

SNELLING, RICHARD A. 1980. "American Federalism in the Eighties." *State Government* (Autumn): 168–170.

STENBERG, CARL W. 1981. "Beyond the Days of Wine and Roses: Intergovernmental Management in a Cutback Environment." *Public Administration Review* 41 (January–February): 10–20.

WALKER, DAVID B. 1981. *Toward a Functioning Federalism*. Cambridge, Mass.: Winthrop.

Wall Street Journal, The. 1980. "Looking to the Feds, Many States Scrutinize Their Civil Service Systems." (February 12).

Steven M. Neuse

University of Arkansas at Fayetteville

CHAPTER FIVE
DIVERSITY IN THE PUBLIC SERVICE: PROFESSIONAL PERSONNEL IN STATE EMPLOYMENT

PROFESSIONALS
IN THE PUBLIC SERVICE

In the last few decades, considerable attention has focused on the increasing importance of professionalism in modern employment sectors. Writers from widely varying fields have coined such phrases as "technocracy," "the managerial society," "the scientific estate," and "the professional state" to describe an era in which professional knowledge is linked closely with decision making in both private and public organizations.

In the public realm, between 1960 and 1976, there has been a twofold increase in the number of "professional, technical, and kindred" ("PKT" workers) personnel, so much so that in the latter year "two of every five PKT workers in the employed civilian labor force in the United States worked for federal, state or local government" (Mosher and Stillman, 1977: 631). In observing this growth, scholars have noted two points regarding such "professionalization." On one hand, full-time professional expertise has become an essential aspect of the public organization because of the demands of complex policy formulation and execution. No longer are governments able to operate with many clerks, a few general administrators, and a small contingent of traditional professionals such as attorneys, public health physicians, and civil engineers.

On the other hand, the public service has become "professionalized" or stabilized and removed from inordinate political influences to meet the needs of increasingly complex and large bureaucratic organizations. Neither transient patronage employees nor "mindless" clerks are able to deal effectively "with the formulation policy, with the coordination and improvement of government machinery, and with the general management and control of the departments of the public service" (White, 1948: 344). Essentially, then, the responsible official is one who is prepared, capable, and qualified—in a word, a professional. Without certain expertise, the civil servant cannot do his or her job and thus cannot act responsibly.

Despite this recognition of the necessary and, indeed, beneficial role of professional and technical expertise in public organizations, there has been a consistent sense of apprehension among those involved with policy and personnel management over increasing "professionalism," or domination by persons in "clear cut occupational fields[s], . . . requir[ing] higher education . . . [and] offer[ing] a lifetime career to [their] members" (Mosher, 1968: 106). In general, the argument posits that professionals tend to bring attitudes and modes of behavior to the public service that make management and personnel tasks more difficult. Professional education experiences tend to socialize the individual into an insulated occupational system. The professional, it is suggested, is suspicious of organizational activities of other occupational groups and is more likely to respect the authoritative norms of his or her occupation than of the organization (Blau and Scott, 1962: 67-68; Gouldner, 1957-58; Reissman, 1949).

Sometimes the professionalization process results in the capture of public agencies by "elite" professions that extend their control over employment and personnel policies, develop insulated career systems, and foster an attitude toward public service stressing peer control rather than hierarchical or public participation authority. The consequence is either the formation of total elitist administrative systems comprised of firmly entrenched professionals (Mosher, 1968: 198–211) or "pockets" within the public service unduly identified with professional interests or special clienteles (Willburn, 1954: 19).

Obviously, the professionalization process has significant consequences for the personnel administrator. Manpower development and procurement and people management activities (such as classification and pay) become increasingly onerous as occupational diversity becomes a fact of organizational life. Too, the personnel manager is faced with the difficult tasks of (1) maintaining the integrity of the personnel function among other "experts" who "know better" or who see personnel as obstructionist or irrelevant and (2) simply maintaining lines of communication and service within complex and often fragmented organizations.

This chapter introduces the student concerned with personnel issues to the world of the professional public servant. Drawing upon data gathered from a large sample of state employees, we will examine the range and distribution of professions in public agencies, the personal characteristics of individual professionals, and some of their attitudes toward their jobs. This assignment will help to familiarize the reader with the diverse occupational structure of a typical civil service system, enabling a better understanding and possibly improved execution of personnel functions.

The study is based on a comprehensive statewide survey of administrative, professional, and technical (APT) personnel in eight of the largest and most important agencies (see Table 1) in the State of Texas. The survey, conducted in late 1975, was drawn from a stratified random sample of personnel at or above a certain level in the salary classification plan.[1] Between 105 and 132 questionnaires were mailed to employees in each of the eight agencies for a total of 923. Seven hundred and twenty-two usable responses were received for a return rate of 78 percent.

While the study does not claim to be representative of all APT personnel in all jurisdictions, the responses probably are indicative of patterns in many other states and in the federal government. All the Texas agencies sampled have counterparts in the remaining forty-nine states and in the federal government. Moreover, Texas is a complex, highly industrialized American state, one that has come to require an equally complex administrative system. From time to time, the Texas findings will be compared with data gathered from other studies focusing on state and federal employees. Regrettably, however, most of these studies were completed before 1970 and thus are only of limited comparative value.

THE PROFESSIONS
AND PROFESSIONAL
CHARACTERISTICS

The survey findings indicate clearly that professional diversification is an organizational fact of life (Table 1). The seven-hundred-odd APT respondents reported seventy-seven different occupational categories. As expected, many respondents

TABLE 1 Professional Diversification in State Agencies

AGENCY (*n*)	NUMBER OF PROFESSIONS IN AGENCY SAMPLE	MOST NUMEROUS PROFESSIONS REPORTED[1]	GENERAL ADMINISTRATORS IN SAMPLE[1]
Comptroller of Public Accounts (90)	11	Accountant (55%) Tax specialist (16%) Compliance officer (8%)	7%
Department of Mental Health and Retardation (104)	23	Registered nurse (22%) Physician (18%) Psychologist (13%)	15
Parks and Wildlife Department (86)	23	Biologist (31%) Law enforcement officer (11%) Accountant (6%)	11
State Department of Health (82)	29	Registered nurse (26%) Sanitarian (7%) Engineer and accountant (6%)	9
Department of Human Resources (90)	17	Social worker (41%) Accountant (13%)	25
Highway Department (103)	18	Engineer (46%) Engineering technician (26%) Accountant (5%)	5
Texas Education Agency (78)	15	Educator (43%) Accountant (16%) Consultant (16%)	9
Texas Rehabilitation Commission (89)	13	Rehabilitation counselor (58%) Disability examiner (11%)	9

[1] Percentage of total agency sample. Only those occupational groups with 5 percent or more of the total agency sample were reported.

represented traditional professions such as accounting, engineering, and social work. The occupational enumeration went far beyond these groups, however, and included such specializations as archaeology, computer analysis, economics, epidemiology, music, psychophysiology, and wildlife management.

Table 1 shows the degree of occupational diversification within each agency. The two health agencies and Parks and Wildlife reflect the greatest diversity, with well over twenty professions reported in each. Such diversity is occasioned in Parks and Wildlife by the multiple goals of that organization that include recreation, conservation, and public order maintenance. The proliferation of occupations in both health agencies is indicative of the highly complex occupational system that has developed in health care sciences (Krause, 1971: 6). Twentieth-century health care has expanded far beyond the traditional triad of physician, lay assistant or practitioner (nurse or midwife), and chemist.

At the extreme, certain agencies seem to reflect more narrow occupational distributions. The comptroller's office reports only eleven professions, and the three reported most frequently comprised nearly 80 percent of the total sample. In a like manner, over 70 percent of the Highway Department sample is in two engineering categories, and in Rehabilitation about that proportion is involved in rehabilitation counseling or investigation. Only one professional group, accounting, is substantially represented in as many as five agencies and only engineering (in Highway and Health) and nursing (in Mental Health and Health) have significant representation in two agencies.

Needless to say, each of these situations poses different challenges for the personnel administrator. On one hand, the more kaleidoscopic the occupational structure in an organization, the more attention personnel must direct to meeting the varied needs of different occupational groups (e.g., career and organizational development) and to balancing the interests of these groups (e.g., comparable pay for comparable work). On the other hand, in an organization with fewer occupational groups and/or one dominated by a single professional focus, the personnel specialist must be aware of the possibility of an elite profession controlling the agency and the subsequent diminution of his or her own professional influence. Such domination is a reality in the Texas Highway Department and is reflected in a statement by an accountant in that agency (it just as easily could have been from a personnel professional) who complained that "employees with a comparable amount of responsibility are not able to progress to the level which can be attained by individuals in the engineering related fields."

The ten most numerous professions made up a little more than two-thirds of the total sample (Table 2). By and large, most of these groups were concentrated in one or two agencies. Only accountants and administrators were spread throughout most agencies, and only administrators were reported with any regularity (more than 5 percent) in all the agencies (Table 1).

Five of the ten groups can be classified as technical and four as human relations professions. Nursing has characteristics of both groups, although some observers argue that human relations functions predominate (Johnson and Martin, 1958;

TABLE 2 Characteristics of Dominant Professions

PROFESSION[1]	TYPE OF PROFESSION	MALES IN SAMPLE	AVERAGE EDUCATIONAL LEVEL	SALARY RANK COMPARISON (1 = HIGHEST)
Accountant (92)	Technical	95%	Some college	6
Administrator (79)	Human relations	83	College graduate	3
Engineer (53)	Technical	100	Some college	2
Rehabilitation counselor (52)	Human relations	75	Graduate work	5
Educator (46)	Human relations	77	Graduate work	4
Registered nurse (45)	Both	2	Some college	10
Social worker (44)	Human relations	40	College graduate	8
Biologist (29)	Technical	96	College graduate	7
Engineering technician (23)	Technical	100	High school graduate	9
Physician (23)	Technical	95	Graduate degree	1

[1] Other professional groups with ten or more in the sample include psychologists (17), consultants (17), tax specialists (14), and law enforcement officers (10).

Vollmer and Mills, 1966: 207). All occupations but one report average education levels indicating some degree of college training. All physicians (naturally) possessed graduate degrees, and most of the rehabilitation counselors and educators had some graduate schooling. Only the engineering technicians had less than a college education. Indeed, this was the only group in the top ten whose job description did not require at least some college training or its equivalent.

Table 2 also reveals an obvious male dominance in these top occupations. In all but nursing and social work, traditional female professions, males predominated by an overwhelming majority. In fact, neither engineering group boasted a single female, and 95 percent of the physicians and accountants were men. Salary levels, too, seemed to reflect certain disparities between the sexes: on the average, social worker and nurse salary levels were lower than were those of any of the other groups except the aforementioned "semiprofessional" engineering technicians.

These characteristics continue to be reflected when one moves from a consideration of the individual groups to the entire sample. Clearly, civil servants at these levels are well educated and are becoming better educated. Nearly a third of the sample reported graduate degrees and over 70 percent had earned at least a bachelor's education. (Table 3). In comparison with other states and the federal government, the Texas sample seems to lag a bit in attained education levels. However, it should be noted that the Texas survey is somewhat broader and more inclusive than the others. In any case, in every study, a large majority of the respondents report holding undergraduate degrees or better.

Comparing educational achievement with year of entry into state employment, one notes a significant rise in educational levels attained. Among those persons recruited before 1960, only 10 percent had advanced education beyond the bachelor's level. After that date, however, about 40 percent of those entering state service had some graduate education. This trend was especially obvious in the period after 1969. More than 40 percent of those recruited after 1969 held one or more graduate degrees.

Table 4 also shows that, as with the individual professions, the entire Texas APT work force was dominated by males *and* whites: over three-fourths of the respondents were male and about 90 percent were white. Considering the proportion of females and minority group members in the work force, the overrepresentation of white males is dramatic. Too, white males generally reported higher salaries than did blacks or women (but not Spanish-surnamed respondents). For example, 28 percent of the male and only 15 percent of the female subsample were located in the top three levels of the salary classification system or in the highest salary level, the exempt position category.[2] Interestingly, both minority groups and women ranked slightly higher than did whites and males, respectively, in terms of educational levels attained. It is interesting to note, too, that the same sexual and racial patterns prevail in other states and in the federal sector. Minority representation is almost identical in each sample or population. With regard to female employment, Texas ranks a bit behind the other states and a bit ahead of the federal government at comparable levels.

These summary statistics do a great deal to highlight some of the dilemmas and problems facing the modern personnel administrator. In the first place, it is obvious that the current APT work force is well educated, at least in terms of formal requisites. Furthermore, it stands to reason that they also have developed critical faculties that allow them to evaluate and assess many other organizational issues, including those concerned with employee management and development. At the very least, the personnel officer has to develop finely honed skills to maintain a respected peer position among the influential professionals carrying out the agency's mission.

The absence of sexual and racial balance also presents a challenge to the personnel specialist. Indeed, this is perhaps the most perplexing issue this person may have to face, torn between the legitimate pressures of officially mandated affirmative action plans demanding more jobs for minorities and women and the realities of the labor market that produces few minority or female accountants, engineers, or biologists. These pressures are accentuated, too, because of personnel policies designed to enhance organizational efficiency and fairness such as pay comparability and the discouragement of lateral entry of personnel in some agencies. If public sector salaries continue to be pegged to those in the private sector, and if women continue to concentrate in lower-paying occupations (nursing as opposed to medicine, social work as opposed to engineering), sexual salary disparities will continue to exist. Of course, recent court decisions suggesting that "comparable" (not equal or the same) work experiences should be the measure of salary differentiation will make the personnel function incredibly more complicated. Finally,

TABLE 3 Education Characteristics

A. Highest Level of Education: State and Federal Employees[1]

	TEXAS	CALIFORNIA[2]	ILLINOIS[3]	PENNSYLVANIA[4]	TENNESSEE[5]	FEDERAL[6]
High School and below	8.7%	4.8%	6.0%	21.8%	8.0%	9.6%
Some college	19.1	18.8	10.0	15.3	22.0	
Undergraduate degree	32.3	41.3	34.0	28.8	20.0	32.7
Some graduate	8.0		50.0	7.3	11.0	
Graduate degree	31.8	35.0		26.1	39.0	57.7
Total	99.9%	99.9%	100.0%	99.3%	100.0%	100.0%
(n)	(721)	(857)	(927)	(400)	(284)	(33,000)

B. Highest level of Education and Year of Entry Into State Employment: Texas Sample[1]

HIGHEST LEVEL OF EDUCATIONAL ATTAINMENT,	TOTAL SAMPLE	1939 AND BEFORE	1940–1949	1950–1959	1960–1969	1970 AND AFTER
Less than high school	1.1%	—	5.3%	2.8%	1.2%	—
High school	7.6	—	23.7	23.1	6.6	1.5%
Some college	19.1	66.7%	21.1	34.3	22.1	11.3
Undergraduate degree	32.2	33.3	44.7	26.9	29.9	34.5
Some graduate school	8.0	—	5.3	—	10.2	9.5
Graduate degree	31.8	—	—	13.0	29.9	43.3
(n)	(721)	(3)	(38)	(108)	(244)	(320)[7]

[1] Totals may not add to 100 percent because of rounding.

[2] This study sampled from appointed administrators and all civil servants at approximately director, deputy director, division head, and bureau chief levels (Hackett, 1968: 5).

[3] This study sampled from noneducational personnel engaged in "executive" functions (Pisciotte and Anton, 1968: 50).

[4] This study sampled from "the 5,900 highest ranking APT state employees" (Lee, Crawford, and Rabena, 1970: 602).

[5] This study sampled from "officials who rank just below the appointed heads of each of the state agencies . . . [and] . . . who make or contribute to policy . . . despite changing political administrations" (Kelley and Patterson, 1970: viii).

[6] A survey of all federal employees at GS levels 15–18 or their equivalents (CSC, 1977: 38).

[7] Subtotals on this side of table add to 713 because of missing information on "year of entry."

TABLE 4 APT Employee Characteristics: Race and Sex

A. Race

	TEXAS	OTHER STATES[1]	FEDERAL[2]
White	90.5%	90.6%	90.5%
Minority	9.5	9.4	9.5
(n)	(721)	(378,172)	(665,611)

B. Sex

	TEXAS	OTHER STATES[1]	FEDERAL[3]
Male	78.0%	70.0%	17.1%
Female	22.0	30.0	82.9
(n)	(721)	(378,172)	(710,305)

C. Sexual Distribution in Salary Classification System (Texas Sample Only)

CLASSIFICATION LEVEL	MALES IN LEVEL (WITHIN SEX)	FEMALES IN LEVEL (WITHIN SEX)
13–14 (lower-middle)	18%	27%
15–18 (middle)	55	58
19–21 (middle-upper)	17	8
Exempt (upper)	11	7
(n)	(564, 78%)	(157, 22%)

[1] This category consists of all "full-time officials/administrators" and "full-time professionals" in all states at annual salary levels of $10,000 or more. This level is comparable to the beginning level for the Texas sample (EEOC, 1977: 3–4).
[2] Federal employees in GS grades 9–18 (CSC, 1976: xi, 35, 43, 44, 49).
[3] Federal employees in GS grades 8–18 (CSC, 1975: 6, 40, 52, 54, 62, 66).

as long as organizations develop career systems that (for very good organizational reasons) discourage lateral entry from the outside (the Texas Highway Department is very much like this), it will be very difficult to achieve racial and sexual balance at professional levels throughout the organization.

In summary, the job of developing a fair and just personnel system, *in light of existing economic and social realities*, poses very difficult questions for the personnel administrator. Essentially, the problem of overt or deliberate discrimination is but one factor (but it does continue to exist, make no mistake) in the calculus of the personnel officer's attempts to develop plans for recruitment, hiring, promotion, and development.

PROFESSIONAL PERSPECTIVES: JOB VALUES, CRITICISMS, AND PUBLIC SERVICE NORMS

In addition to being familiar with the demographic and sociological characteristics of the professional work force, it is equally important for the personnel administrator to be aware of the values, frustrations, and aspirations of people in APT positions. Indeed, before this person can assist line managers in developing motivation strategies or development plans, he or she must understand those fundamental values to which professionals aspire. To this end the following discussion will consider three questions:

1. What values are held most dearly by APT employees?
2. What kinds of job-related issues most disturb this group?
3. How do professionals feel about the public service?

One of the first tasks the personnel administrator will face is that of motivating employees to do the organization's work. This responsibility is of critical importance because it is costly, complex, and essential to organizational goals (Barnard, 1938: Ch. 9). The problem, however, is costs to the organization and to the individual: the organization must offer the individual certain incentives or inducements to make it worthwhile for that individual to contribute his or her energies to the pursuit of organizational goals (Barnard, 1938: 9). The problem, however, is that there are many incentives relevant to the motivation process. For example, research over the past four or five decades has shown that money (the easy answer to the incentive problem) is only one of many values or valued objects sought by people in their "work" role or capacity. In fact, it is widely held that money and other "extrinsic" rewards (rewards originating from outside the individual) are secondary to the professional work value structure. This occupational structure has developed a value or reward system that stresses self-satisfaction for effective performance, peer respect, pride in service, and other nonmaterial factors. The most highly held professional values, in a sense, come from within and are "intrinsic" to the person holding them.

Table 5 appears to confirm these observations. The five highest reported occupational norms are "intrinsic values." Self-satisfaction, creativity, independence, service, and peer awareness are the kinds of values, it is suggested, most likely to be rated highly by professionally oriented persons. Clearly, extrinsic, or external, reward values (6-9) are subordinate to intrinsic norms in the entire sample.

However, there is considerable variation among the different professions on job values. Physicians, rehabilitation counselors, and biologists rated extrinsic values lowest; engineering technicians, nurses, and accountants ranked them highest. On the other hand, educators and nurses ranked highest and accountants and engineering technicians lowest on intrinsic values.

TABLE 5   Occupational Value Rankings of APT Employees

A. Occupational Scores

INDIVIDUAL OCCUPATIONAL VALUES[1]	AVERAGE SCORE
1. Satisfaction in doing a job well	4.57
2. Chance to use professional skills in creative manner	4.30
3. Freedom to act and think independently on the job	4.22
4. Chance to be of service to people	4.11
5. Chance to work with highly qualified and motivated people	3.83
6. Job security	3.81
7. Good working conditions	3.78
8. Good salary	3.71
9. Good fringe benefits	3.57
10. Opportunity to advance to positions of greater personal advantage	3.55
11. Chance to look out for the public interest	3.50
12. Being a public servant	2.81
13. High prestige in the public eye	2.69
14. Chance to work for the state government	2.62
15. Opportunity to meet important people	2.52

B. Ranking on Extrinsic and Intrinsic Values

OCCUPATIONAL RANKING ON EXTRINSIC VALUES[2]	OCCUPATIONAL RANKING ON INTRINSIC VALUES[3]
1. Engineering technicians	1. Educators
2. Registered nurses	2. Registered nurses
3. Accountants	3-4-5. Administrators
4. Engineers	3-4-5. Biologists
5. Administrators	3-4-5. Social workers
6-7. Educators	6. Physicians
6-7. Social workers	7-8. Engineers
8. Biologists	7-8. Rehabilitation counselors
9. Rehabilitation counselors	9. Engineering technicians
10. Physicians	10. Accountants

[1] Each respondent was asked to rate these values on a one- to five-point scale, from "of little or no importance" to "of very great importance." The scores reported here are the average scores of all respondents.

[2] This occupational ranking was compiled by calculating the scores of each member of the group on items 6, 7, 8, and 9, summing the scores of all group members, and averaging. The differences between the group scores are statistically significant ($p < 0.000$).

[3] This occupational ranking was compiled by calculating the scores of each member of the group on items 1, 2, 3, 4, and 5, summing the scores of all group members, and averaging. The differences between the group scores are statistically significant ($p < 0.004$).

Personnel officials, then, must pay close attention to the kinds of inducements that are offered to APT employees. Obviously, in a highly professionalized agency, it well may be wasteful, or perhaps even counterproductive to recommend better working conditions or fringe benefits when the problem really lies in feelings of constraint, regarding the use of professional skills or the failure of the organization to provide an atmosphere allowing professional self-actualization. Too, it should be stressed that job-related values vary from profession to profession and even within single professions over time. A constant monitoring of and sensitivity to employee needs will eventually pay rich benefits in terms of overall organizational performance and individual development.

It is just as important for the personnel administrator to be aware of negative perceptions of the organizational ambiance. There are several reasons for cultivating this sensitivity. First, unanswered or unconsidered criticism in an agency can have a significant negative effect on employee morale and efficiency, particularly if employees sense that the organization is really not listening. Second, the critical perspectives of APT staff often are well worth seeking and hearing: the professional is well trained in problem-solving techniques and may have a great deal to offer personnel administrators concerned with organizational maintenance. Third, where critical attitudes are based on faulty perceptions, or where it is not feasible (or even good policy) to eliminate a source of frustration, it would be wise to explain to the professional staff precisely why nothing can (or should) be done to relieve the source of frustration.

Perhaps more than any of the other indicators or measures considered so far, job criticism attitudes may be particularly sensitive to local conditions. Nevertheless, keeping this caution in mind, it is instructive to note the kinds of critical concerns raised by this sample. First, one observes that neither extrinsic nor intrinsic job value criticisms are voiced very strongly (Table 6). Complaints about salaries rank sixth and those related to fringe benefits and working conditions rank last. This lack of criticism in Texas, which traditionally has lagged other states in employee benefits (Office of the Governor, 1975: 50-52), is significant. Perhaps it reflects, again, the relative lack of concern for such values among professionals. In a like manner, complaints about the quality of the professional work setting are muted. Four criticisms touching intrinsic job values (7-10) are ranked low in the overall list of criticisms. Thus, one might assume that the professional work setting in the state generally was satisfactory.

Turning to the strongest criticisms, one can make two observations. On one hand, these professional "bureaucrats" seem to reflect the same critical attitudes that outsiders have of public bureaucracies. "Red tape" and "politics" are just as worrisome to this group of professionals as they are to the general population. The red-tape concern is engendered in part by an increasing frustration in meeting federal mandates. The criticism regarding too much "political influence" may relate to a natural "built-in aversion between the professions and politics" (Mosher, 1968: 108). Professional education tends to inculcate a strong faith in impartial and

TABLE 6   Job Criticism Rankings of APT Employees[1]

JOB CRITICISMS	AVERAGE SCORE
1. Hard to get things done (too much "red tape")	3.5
2. Difficult to obtain personal recognition	3.3
3. Too much political influence in agency	3.3
4. Little prestige in being a public employee	3.1
5. Poor career advancement opportunities	3.1
6. Low salaries	3.0
7. Agency has little sense of concern for employees	2.6
8. Inadequate sense of professional pride in agency	2.6
9. Difficult to use skills creatively	2.6
10. Difficult to exercise initiative	2.6
11. Poor fringe benefits	2.5
12. Poor working conditions	2.2

[1] Each respondent was asked to rate these criticisms on a one- to five-point scale, from "totally invalid" to "highly valid." The scores reported here are the average scores of all respondents.

impersonal decision making, which in turn often leads to a general disdain for political decisions that are anything but impartial and impersonal.

On the other hand, the two other highly rated criticisms (those ranked 2 and 4 in Table 6) point to the curious lack of status that has plagued the public service generally in the United States. Despite the increasing professionalization of the work force, the gravity of issues handled in the public sector, and the overall improvement of working conditions in public organizations, there still remains a strong prejudice against "bureaucrats." One can hardly pick up a newspaper or listen to a major speech or press conference by an influential political leader without hearing negative remarks about government employees. Obviously, this group of professionals was aware of this sentiment, complaining about lack of "personal recognition" and "prestige in being a public employee." In this situation the personnel specialist has a strong responsibility to build a sense of occupational self-worth into the career development process to help offset potentially demoralizing consequences.

A final dimension of some importance is the attitude of APT employees toward the public service ethic. Since the civil service reforms of the late nineteenth century, the notion has developed that there is something special about the public service and that public employees are expected to develop a unique ethic regarding their employment. Public employees are "servants" to and guardians on behalf of their masters, the taxpaying public. As such, they are charged with recognizing that public employment is a "privilege," not a right, and that public employees are expected to comport themselves in a special manner. Indeed, the service and privilege norms have been used time and time again to justify low salaries and paternalistic personnel systems throughout the land. Previously, all the personnel administrator had to do was appeal to the "public-regarding" belief system of the civil servant to achieve appropriate responses from the employee.

But is this the case anymore? The public service at all levels has been changed dramatically in the last fifty years. Its size has increased rapidly, it has become highly professionalized, and it has come to be peopled by a new brand of person, no longer pliant or deferential to the "doctrine of privilege." All these factors, it is suggested, work against the development of a special public service work ethic. The rapid expansion of public employment has diluted a strong sense of publicness and service among public employees. Professionalization tends to divide the loyalties of the employee who now often looks to occupational rather than to public service organizational norms. Finally, it appears that public employees, increasingly unionized and vocal about working rights, are no longer willing to accede to servant status—for anyone.

At first glance, it appears that this group of professionals does indeed sense something unique about the public service. In response to the question, "Do you feel that there is anything special about being a public employee?" nearly two-thirds of these employees answered "Yes." However, in a follow-up asking the respondents to elaborate on their answers, the findings were not so clear cut. (see Table 7).

Little more than 60 percent of the affirmative answers emphasized that public employment was a special responsibility and that the employee must be accountable to the public. Most of the other "yes" answers indicated that the public service was special because of personal reasons (good opportunity for professional development, job security, etc.) or for negative reasons. A majority of these negative responses stressed that the job was "special" because state employees were discriminated against by both the public and their employers. Other negative

TABLE 7 Public Service Values of APT Employees

Do you feel that there is anything special about being a public employee?

RESPONSE	%	(n)
Yes	64.7%	(448)
No	35.3	(244)

REASONS FOR AFFIRMING SPECIAL NATURE OF PUBLIC EMPLOYMENT	%	(n)
Public service work ethic answer	61.2%	(257)
Negative reflection on public service	16.9	(71)
Personal reasons given for public service	14.0	(59)
Other	7.9	(33)

reasons included poor quality of co-workers, an inept state government, and extra-ordinary job pressures.

Of those persons who commented on their "no" answers to the original question, about one-half said that there was no difference between public and private employment. Other comments following "no" responses were generally either critical of state employment, for the reasons discussed, or stressed that personal satisfaction was important but that public employment was not essential to attain such satisfaction.

Thus, when one examines the reasons why public employees think of the public service as special, it appears that far fewer than two-thirds give traditional "service to the people" or "guardian of the public interest" answers. In fact, considering the comments offered by the sample, only half the respondents described their jobs in terms of a special ethic. Other comments following answers were divided about equally between critical remarks, statements stressing personal satisfaction, and those emphasizing the lack of differences between public and private employment.[3]

These responses are suggestive for personnel strategies. Most obviously, the personnel specialist must realize that many public employees do not feel that their jobs require fealty to a special public service ethic. People work for the government for many reasons, and only some of them hold a special responsibility as a universal motivating factor in the public organization. Too, these responses show that a fairly large minority of this APT sample reflects negative attitudes toward work or occupational self-images. Again, the personnel specialist must utilize his or her skills to develop a more congenial workplace and to do as much as possible to develop positive self-images within these essential occupational groups.

CONCLUSION

The most obvious summary statement is that the public service at middle and upper levels is extremely complex. The exigencies of modern government have made it necessary to employ a large and diverse group of administrative, professional, and technical specialists. Within and among these groups, there appears to be an almost endless variety of characteristics and attitudes, so much so that one wonders if effective management is possible.

In terms of the personnel function, it is absolutely necessary to be aware of two factors. First, personnel management no longer can be understood (if ever it could) as a process of applying simple and sure rules and regulations to a docile and homogeneous work force. Increasingly, public employees are highly educated, diverse in their backgrounds, and of discriminating and critical mentalities. The personnel manager must be aware of this reality and sensitive to this diversity, particularly as it relates to the idiosyncrasies of APT employees. But, more than this, personnel administrators must be as well educated as their professional peers and flexible enough to apply a wide range of techniques and methods to the task of meeting both organizational and individual development needs.

Needless to say, fitting the personnel function to the professional work force will not be easy. However, the job will be facilitated to the extent that the specialist in this area knows "the lay of the land," including an intimate awareness of the organization's most valuable resource, its educated and professional staff.

NOTES

1. The state classification officer assisted the author in selecting the level that could be described best as "entry level" for most APT personnel.

2. There were too few minority group employees to make meaningful comparisons here.

3. A more complete discussion of public service norms can be found in the author's article, "The Public Service Ethic and the Professions in State Government," *Southern Review of Public Administration*, Vol. 1 (March 1978),: 510-528.

REFERENCES

BARNARD, C. 1938. *The Functions of the Executive*. Cambridge, Mass.: Harvard University Press.

BLAU, P. M. and W. R. SCOTT. 1962. *Formal Organizations*. Scranton, Pa.: Chandler.

CIVIL SERVICE COMMISSION. Manpower Statistics Division. 1975. *Study of Employment of Women in the Federal Government*. Washington, D.C.: G.P.O.

——. Bureau of Personnel Management Information Systems. 1976. *Minority Group Employment in the Federal Government*. Washington, D.C.: G.P.O.

——. Bureau of Executive Personnel. 1977. *Executive Personnel in the Federal Service*. Washington, D.C.: G.P.O.

——. Equal Employment Opportunity Commission. 1977. *Minorities and Women in State and Local Government*. Washington, D.C.: G.P.O.

GOULDNER, A. 1957-1958. "Cosmopolitans and Locals." *Administrative Science Quarterly* 2 (December–March): 281-306.

HACKETT, BRUCE. 1968. *Higher Civil Servants in California*. Berkeley, Calif.: Institute of Governmental Studies.

JOHNSON, M. M. and H. W. MARTIN. 1958. "A Sociological Analysis of the Nurse Role." *American Journal of Nursing* 58 (March): 373-377.

KELLEY, HARRY F., JR. and CHARLES E. PATTERSON, JR. 1970. *The Tennessee Bureaucrat*. Knoxville: Bureau of Public Administration, University of Tennessee.

KRAUSE, E. A. 1971. *The Sociology of Occupations*. Boston: Little, Brown.

LEE, ROBERT D., CHARLES CRAWFORD, and KATHLEEN RABENA. 1970. "A Profile of State APT Manpower Resources: Preliminary Findings." *Public Administration Review* 30 (November–December): 602-610.

MOSHER, F. C. 1968. *Democracy and the Public Service*. New York: Oxford University Press.

MOSHER, F. C. and R. STILLMAN. 1977. "Introduction: The Professions in Government." *Public Administration Review* 37 (November–December): 631–633.

OFFICE OF THE GOVERNOR (ca. 1974). *Quality Texas Government: People Make the Difference*. Austin, Texas.

PISCIOTTE, JOSEPH P. and THOMAS J. ANTON. 1968. "Provincial Administrators: Profile and Career Patterns of Illinois State Officials." In Joseph Pisciotte, ed., *Manpower for Illinois Governments*. Urbana: Institute of Government and Public Affairs, University of Illinois.

REISSMAN, L. 1949. "A Study of Role Conceptions in Bureaucracy." *Social Forces* 27 (March): 305–310.

VOLLMER, H. W. and D. L. MILLS. 1966. *Professionalization*. Englewood Cliffs, N.J.: Prentice-Hall.

WHITE, L. D. 1948. *Introduction to the Study of Public Administration*. 3rd ed. New York: Macmillan.

WILLBURN, Y. 1954. "Professionalization in the Public Service: Too Little or Too Much?" *Public Administration Review* 14 (Winter): 13–21.

PART TWO
TECHNIQUES OF PERSONNEL ADMINISTRATION

One of the first thoughts that comes to mind when personnel "techniques" are mentioned is Wallace Sayre's classic observation that personnel administration represents the "triumph of technique over purpose." This phrase refers to the past tendency of public personnel administration to give exclusive attention to the means of the personnel function, thereby losing sight of the organizational and societal goals that were entrusted to it. In a fruitless search for the "one best way" in which to perform their functions, personnelists became unresponsive to both organizational and extraorganizational interests. As a result, the profession remained static while its environment became increasingly turbulent and dynamic.

Although vestiges of public personnel administration's technical preoccupation still exist, Sayre's comment has lost much of its original validity. In response to an avalanche of social, political, and organizational changes over the past three decades (many of which are mentioned in Part II), public personnel administration has emerged from its slumber to assume a leadership role in assisting public organizations in buffering the effects of environmental change. An important aspect of this evolving role is the now prevalent tendency of personnelists to reexamine and revitalize the tried-and-true techniques of an earlier era.

The chapters in Part II discuss the ways in which several of the most important personnel techniques have been affected by the enhanced organizational role of public personnel administration. Thomas and Heisel, for example, describe how the recruitment, selection, and promotion processes have been altered to accommodate the pressing demands for social equity and improved personnel professionalism. Hyde and Shafritz discuss the ways in which position classification and staffing practices are being revised in response to the changing nature of work in the public sector. Similarly, Tyer and Sylvia chronicle changes in performance appraisal strategies and training and development techniques, respectively. Central to all these discussions is the theme that personnelists are engaged in a process of reassessing these techniques to improve their utility in assisting public organizations to achieve desired goals.

March, conversely, emphasizes the problems rather than the prospects of an old yet widely ignored personnel function: retirement and pension management. After presenting a thorough discussion of the history and philosophy of employee retirement benefits, March analyzes a series of financial and motivational dilemmas that are tied to current pension practices. His conclusions regarding the prospects of pension reform are especially troublesome. Yet, for those accustomed to the traditional reluctance of public personnel administration to address the "hard questions," his discussion exemplifies an encouraging and enlightening trend.

John Clayton Thomas
University of Missouri, Kansas City
and
W. Donald Heisel
University of Cincinnati

CHAPTER SIX
THE MODERNIZATION OF RECRUITMENT AND SELECTION IN LOCAL GOVERNMENTS

The processes of employee recruitment and selection in local governments have been undergoing extensive change in recent decades. The purpose of this chapter is to describe some of those changes and to offer some guidelines for desirable recruitment and selection practices at the local level.

In general terms, the change has been from a traditional civil service model toward a modern professional personnel model. The traditional civil service model was a product of the urban reform politics of the first third of this century. That model reflected a desire to eliminate politics from personnel practices, either by insulating personnel officials from elective officials (e.g., through the establishment of independent civil service commissions to manage the personnel function) or by stipulating in detail how recruitment and selection would be conducted (e.g., the frequent requirement that selection be based on written tests).

While the traditional civil service techniques may have succeeded in insulating employee selection from partisan political considerations, at the same time they may have made the local public service less responsive. That at least was increasingly the perception in the 1960s of key figures both inside and outside local government. Professional administrators in local governments complained that the civil service model was severely limiting the responsiveness of municipal employees to management concerns. Others outside local government—minority group representatives, in particular—argued that civil service contributed to a lack of responsiveness by local governments to minority concerns. Sparked by these complaints, changes began to occur in local government recruitment and selection practices.

RECRUITMENT

Recruitment, the first step in the employment process, has traditionally been a rather simple task for local governments. Civil service rules typically required that job openings be announced for some period (e.g., thirty days) in advance of testing for the positions. There was no requirement of active recruitment beyond that public announcement, and active recruitment seldom occurred unless the expertise required for a position was sufficient to require recruitment from specialized audiences.

The Recruitment Problem

This lack of active recruitment had a definite economic logic to it. Why spend money on recruitment if sufficient qualified candidates could be found without spending the money? The answer to that question came only recently in the form of two arguments. First, minority representatives argued that the lack of recruitment effort meant that those coming into local public service often were friends or relatives of those already employed by local governments. This recruitment pattern—essentially, likes attracting—made for minority underrepresentation rather than for "representative bureaucracy" (Krislov, 1974) in local governments. Second, municipal government professionals argued that this recruitment pattern might also mean that local governments were not always getting the best employees they could attract. They might be getting less than the best because they were not attempting to attract the best.

Much of the change in response to these arguments has come through *affirmative action* programs. Affirmative action usually affects all phases of the employment process but may have had its greatest effects on recruitment practices. Where the traditional civil service model and the policy of *equal employment opportunity* (the policy preceding affirmative action) hold that jobs are equally available to all who are interested, usually no special effort would be made to find those who might be interested. Affirmative action goes beyond that passive offering of equal opportunity to an active solicitation of minority applicants, those who have traditionally been underrepresented in local government employment. Thus, local governments under affirmative action seek out black applicants, where under traditional civil service and equal employment opportunity they said only that black applicants were welcomed.

Perhaps nowhere in local government employment is active recruitment of minority applicants more desirable than in police and fire employment. The police and fire services often have a strong "in-group" identification that resists and discourages minority elements from joining those services (Wilson, 1970: 48–49). That resistance to change only increased in the 1960s with the many urban conflicts between minorities and the police. The two groups increasingly perceived each other as "the enemy," and few on either side wanted to be perceived as defecting to the enemy.

Yet the police and fire services have several advantages for minority applicants. First, since they are two of the largest employment areas in local government, they can be routes for relatively rapid change in the extent of minority representation in local government. Second, police and fire work can be a relatively lucrative option for minority applicants, as police and fire employees tend to be relatively well paid. The in-group identification has contributed to the development of strong organizations (e.g., the Fraternal Order of Police, the International Association of Firefighters) that have produced good wages for police and fire personnel in many locales. Finally, since entry-level police and fire positions require no prior training, the positions can be ideal for minorities who tend to be disadvantaged in educational and training credentials. For these reasons, the police and fire services should be and often are among the first employment areas attacked in municipal government affirmative action efforts (Thompson, 1974).

Recruitment Techniques

The techniques for successful minority recruitment must be adapted to each local situation and to each minority to whom appeal is being made. Normally, the recruiter can locate minority organizations in the community and work through them to seek applicants. For example, there may be a black ministerial alliance that is influential in the black community. Urban leagues are often active in seeking employment opportunities for blacks. Some chapters of the National Association for the Advancement of Colored People include employment among their objectives.

Taking at least part of the selection process to the minority community, rather than requiring applicants to visit the oft-tainted city hall, can be useful. A mobile van parked in a shopping center frequented by minorities is likely to bring in more applicants than is an office in a city hall. When written tests are going to be used as part of the selection process, training in how to take such tests can be helpful, both in reducing cultural bias and in persuading minorities that the jurisdiction is sincere in seeking minority applicants. Some people have a deep-seated fear of any kind of written test, a fear based at least in part on the fear of failure. Building the confidence of such candidates helps them to show more accurately their potential for job success.

In some communities the level of hostility between the minority community and "the establishment" (particularly the police department) is so high that male white recruiters are doomed to failure. Some cities have achieved success in minority recruitment by first hiring a minority to develop and carry out the campaign. Not only does such a person have a higher trust level among his fellow minorities, but he or she is also sensitive to the principal roadblocks to success. In one campaign, for example, the jurisdiction used a picture of a black patrol officer on a poster designed to attract black candidates to apply. What the agency did not catch was the fact that the chosen officer had several hash marks on his sleeve, indicating considerable seniority. The message received by the blacks was that they would be welcome as patrol officers but would not get a fair crack at promotion.

The recruitment of women for traditionally male jobs poses different types of problems. Women typically read the same mass media as the men. The problem becomes how to use the media to overcome a socialization process that started when they were in their cribs. Women are often very sensitive to what men perceive as minor sexual discrimination. When a police chief is quoted as saying, "Okay, we'll take any woman who can do what a man can do," he is telling women not to apply, as they will be judged on male criteria.

A similar problem has arisen where jurisdictions have tried to meet federal requirements for the employment of more Spanish-surnamed minorities. Until recently, for example, police and fire agencies commonly established minimum height requirements; yet Latins are typically shorter than Anglos. Such requirements are obviously discriminatory.

Some Cautions

None of these techniques will work if the total selection process contains bias. An examination of the entire process is therefore necessary. Otherwise, there is the possibility that minorities, once recruited, would be screened out by discriminatory practices at other stages in the selection process. (These will be discussed in detail in the next section.)

Finally, employers should recognize that minority recruitment efforts will need time to develop measurable success. The frequent reputation of local governments as antiminority, whether valid or invalid, takes time to change. A single recruitment campaign in the minority community is seldom sufficient to produce this change.

There are at least two other cautions worth keeping in mind in these accelerated efforts to recruit minorities. First, the efforts should focus on recruiting *qualified* minority applicants. Neither the status of minorities nor the caliber of municipal services will be improved by hiring unqualified minority applicants. If they lose their jobs or are unhappy with those jobs, their feelings may affect the attitudes of other minorities toward municipal jobs, making more difficult subsequent minority recruitment, while at the same time perhaps lowering the quality of municipal services.

Second, the recruitment efforts either should not be made or should be accompanied by cautions to potential minority applicants if the jobs are not secure in the near future. The security of public jobs has generally not been a concern in the past, but we are now in an era of public sector retrenchment. Affirmative action recruitment becomes a sham if minorities are hired under special recruitment programs, only to be laid off shortly thereafter, as has happened already in more than one financially pressed large city (Thomas, 1978).

SELECTION

Where the traditional civil service model said little about recruitment, it spoke at length about the selection process. The model specified detailed guidelines for who would be responsible for selection, what techniques could be used in selection, the precise steps in the selection process, and how much choice would be available for the appointing officials. In so doing it created a rigid selection process that has been relaxed only gradually in recent years.

The Selection Powers

Under the typical civil service law, authority over the selection process is divided. The civil service commission, or its equivalent, conducts or oversees the examination phase of the process. The administration—department head, supervisor, or other responsible official needing additional employees—does the actual selection from the results of the civil service examination.

The historic purpose of this division of authority was to eliminate partisanship from the process. Under the Jacksonian model of political spoilsmanship, the chief executive—mayor, governor, or principal department head—was able to select whoever he pleased; in many instances this broad authority was used to develop political bases.

Reformers desiring to end political partisanship developed the concept of the independent civil service commission, with authority to limit appointing officials' discretion. The civil service commission itself was to consist of a small number—usually three or five—upright citizens, appointed by the mayor or governor for lengthy terms to insulate them from political influence.

Their role was to conduct examinations, the results of which would be used in the selection process. The appointing official could choose from only a limited number of those who passed the examination. The commission would certify the top three or five names from those passing the examination, and the appointing official had to choose one of the three or five or else keep the job vacant for a lengthy period.

While some officials used partisan considerations in choosing from among those certified, their hands were tied rather effectively; if no one from their political party was among the number certified, they had to appoint on a nonpartisan basis. Some laws, in fact, went so far as to mandate the appointment of the number one eligible, with no discretion allowed.

However, in their efforts to minimize the role of politics in selection, the civil service reformers also minimized the role of expertise. Civil service commissioners were usually amateurs in personnel matters, and, since they were also usually unpaid, the commissioners could not be expected to run a professional selection process.

That lack of professionalism in the selection process became increasingly intolerable to city administrators as both those administrators and personnel practices generally became professionalized. The result has been an evolution toward transfer of the selection powers from the amateur commissioners to personnel professionals. This is, to be sure, a long-term evolution that has only gained additional impetus from the recent increased criticisms of selection procedures. In some jurisdictions the evolution has moved through statutory or charter changes, transferring selection responsibilities to a professional personnel department. In other jurisdictions the changes have come without changes in the law—or after unsuccessful efforts to change the law—as personnel professionals, serving as commission staff, have gradually assumed powers that commissions, for lack of time or expertise, were unable to exercise. The civil service commission as the central authority in personnel selection now survives primarily in smaller communities where personnel tasks have not yet reached the magnitude to warrant the hiring of personnel professionals.

Selection Techniques

The civil service reformers were not satisfied with taking most control over selection away from city employees. To be doubly safe, they also stipulated in some detail the techniques that could be used as selection devices, in particular placing a heavy emphasis on measurable standards. The measurable standards were intended to be indicative of merit, but they were in any event—and more important then—unlikely to reflect partisan political influences, which the reformers were anxious to eliminate.

One example of this emphasis on measurable standards is the frequent requirement of a particular level of educational achievement as a minimum for a public job, as when city governments have required a high school degree for all municipal civil service jobs. An even more common example is the requirement, which persists today in many jurisdictions, that written examinations be used as the primary selection technique. With both these examples, the interest has not always been in a job-relevant requirement, but only in a requirement that is almost certainly politically neutral, at least in partisan terms.

Actually, the detailed specification of selection procedures may have been welcomed by many civil service commissioners. Lacking background in personnel procedures, they may have appreciated a precise delineation of how to execute their responsibilities.

Moreover, as the model's durability suggests, it had other advantages. For one, it reduced the role of partisan politics in employee selection by basing selection on measurable standards unrelated to partisanship. And it probably did generally produce acceptable employees; those applicants who could satisfy the measurable standards did in the process demonstrate some abilities.

But it was not clear that those abilities were always necessary for the particular job or, if they were necessary, that they were the only abilities necessary. Complaints focusing on these issues came from two by now familiar sources. First, minorities (and others concerned about minority underrepresentation in the public sector) disputed whether the selection techniques were measuring abilities necessary for the jobs. In many cases, they contended, the techniques might be discriminating between applicants on grounds unrelated to potential job performance, and, even if those grounds were neutral in partisan political terms, they were often not racially neutral. This argument was persuasive to the U.S. Supreme Court, which ruled in 1971 in *Griggs* v. *Duke Power Company* (National Civil Service League, 1973) that an employer could not use a selection technique having an adverse impact on minorities unless that technique had been shown to measure job-related skills.

Second, urban administrators complained that the selection techniques often were not measuring all the necessary abilities. The emphasis on objective measurable standards, they argued, was hindering the use of other perhaps less objective, but still important, selection techniques (such as oral interviews). As a result, the employees eventually hired might not be able to perform as desired.

These complaints resulted in a movement to increase the flexibility available in choosing selection procedures. The primary route for the movement has been through changes in the law, changes to delete precise delineations of how the selection process would operate. Decisions on that operation would be left instead to personnel professionals.

A typical selection process should begin with the performance of a job analysis—an analysis of the knowledge, skills, and abilities necessary for the position. If the position is currently filled, as in the case of a resigning employee, that employee should be asked to list all his or her duties. This list, analyzed by a personnel technician, provides the basis for both the job description and for decisions on the selection techniques for the job.

This job analysis can be useful in establishing, or at least building a case for, the validity of particular selection techniques. The preferred kind of validity is criterion related, namely, *predictive validity* (i.e., statistical evidence that those who do better on the selection technique also perform better on the job). A good job analysis provides the basis for the choice of selection techniques that are more likely to have predictive validity.

Predictive validity, however, is difficult to establish. It requires that a large number of applicants be processed with the selection techniques and then tested for on-the-job performance. Obviously, this takes time, something employers often lack. Perhaps more important, smaller jurisdictions—and smaller job classes in larger jurisdictions—may never have numbers of employees sufficient to establish predictive validity for most job classes.

These problems have led many jurisdictions to seek, at least in the short term, *content validity* rather than predictive validity. Content validity is evidence that the selection techniques measure the content of the job in question, the knowledge, skills, and abilities necessary in the job. A professionally performed job analysis, linked to the choice of selection techniques, can furnish a persuasive argument for content validity.

Each of the many kinds of selection techniques has its advantages and disadvantages. Space is not available to discuss those in detail, but a few comments are possible on each type of selection technique.

Minimum requirements. Publicly advertised statements of minimum requirements are important from at least two viewpoints: (1) they tend to reduce the number of applicants who need to be processed in the examination, and (2) they help to describe the kind and level of work to be performed, so that potential applicants can in many cases screen themselves out. In the past, however, they have been used too often to screen out applicants who may be well qualified. Too often they were established without any apparent validity other than that it seemed like a good idea. For example, requiring all applicants to have a college degree or a high school diploma may produce a sufficient number of qualified candidates, but it also tends to keep out a number who could do well on both the examination and the job. Further, educational qualifications have been proven to have a discriminatory impact, in that some ethnic and racial groups typically have less formal education than does the Caucasian majority. Similarly, minimum height requirements for police work are discriminatory against women and the Latin minority, yet they have not been demonstrated to be necessary in the performance of police duties. Since the *Griggs* v. *Duke Power* case, no such minimum requirement can be imposed, if it has a disparate impact, unless it can be demonstrated to be necessary for the satisfactory performance of job duties.

This history of discriminatory minimum requirements does not mean that they should be rejected in all cases, but it does suggest that their validity and possible adverse impact on minorities should be evaluated carefully beforehand. This is among the functions of job analysis.

However, some types of minimum qualifications used widely in the past are, for all practical purposes, prima facie illegal. For example, limiting applications to males and thus excluding females is illegal unless sex can be shown to be a *bona fide occupational qualification* (BFOQ). Maximum age limits are likely to run afoul of the Age Discrimination Act. Likewise, it is virtually impossible to establish a particular race as a BFOQ. Any employer who attempts to make a case for any of these requirements as a BFOQ bears the burden of legal proof.

Parenthetically, it should be noted that, in the absence of an established BFOQ, it is illegal even to provide a place on an application form for a number of items that could be used in a discriminatory way. In addition to the obvious restrictions on sex, race, and age, it is illegal to ask a female about her marital status, pregnancy, number of children, or arrangements for their care. Questions about national origin, religion, physical condition, and height or weight are not allowed unless the employer can defend the subject as a BFOQ.

Evaluation of training and experience. This subject can be used in either of two ways: (1) it may be a part of a more comprehensive examination, with the grade averaged, according to preestablished weighting, with grades from other tests such as a written or a practical demonstration test; or (2) it may be the only test (usually called an "unassembled" test) used to determine relative ranking for appointment. Evaluations of training and experience are most useful for advanced positions where prior training and/or experience is required for quality job performance. Normally, the grade is based upon a personnel technician's evaluation of information furnished on the application form. However, it is not unusual for the agency to require candidates to furnish supplemental statements, or to answer a more extensive questionnaire, where space on the application form is too limited for detailed information to be set forth clearly.

It is frequently recognized that persons can acquire knowledge in a variety of ways. Usually, job experience is considered the best preparation. However, determining how much education can be substituted for experience is a problem in these evaluations.

Written examinations. As with minimum requirements, written examinations have a bad track record for discrimination. Yet they remain potentially the most useful of the selection techniques available since they can be objective, valid, and often relatively inexpensive. There are at least two keys to their proper usage. First, they must be used where they are valid, which is to say, where an aptitude or knowledge necessary for the job can be measured on a written examination. Second, they should not be relied upon as the *only* selection technique unless, in fact, they measure the *only* qualification necessary for the job.

Performance examinations. Examinations requiring the applicant to perform some task (e.g., typing or running manual equipment) can be very useful. But they can also be relatively expensive, as they sometimes require (as with large manual equipment) one employee to supervise each applicant as the examination is taken. That contrasts to a written examination where one employee may supervise a large number of applicants in a testing room.

Furthermore, performance examinations can be very expensive in terms of equipment, materials, and supplies consumed and (often) wasted. For example, if a truck driver candidate wrecks the truck in an accident, it is the agency, not the candidate, who pays for its repair and bears the liability for personal injury or other property damage.

While the costs are high, these expenditures may prevent even greater costs of a poor selection later. A well-constructed performance test is not only valid from a legal standpoint, but it also has *face validity*—the appearance of validity that makes it acceptable to candidates, regardless of their race or sex. In this sense it meets equal employment guidelines extremely well.

Oral examinations. Oral examinations (i.e., interviews) have often been criticized because their subjectivity may undermine the potential validity of the results; the interviewers' discretion can be abused. That criticism may be harsher than is justified. Subjectivity can be reduced considerably by using more than one interviewer and pooling their judgments. If race or sex is a possible source of bias, it is advisable to establish interview panels containing blacks and whites or males and females. It is also possible to reduce subjectivity by structuring the interview so that the same questions are asked and the same qualifications are rated on all candidates.

Oral examinations are useful in measuring qualifications where other techniques are not available. For example, if a position requires ability to deal with the public, no written instrument yet developed will measure this ability.

Background checks. Previous employers often can provide valuable assessments of an applicant's prior work performance. Normally, however, previous employers will limit written reports to factual data—dates of employment, job title, pay rates, official reason for termination. Qualitative aspects of job performance will seldom be reported (unless it is favorable) unless the prior employer is assured confidentiality. This is sometimes a problem in public agencies.

Background checks are not used in competitive and relative ranking of candidates. Ordinarily, this information is used only in the interview of those certified for consideration by the appointing official. At that time, it is possible to get information from prior employers by telephone, on a confidential basis, that can assist in deciding which of the three or so certified should be selected.

Another aspect of background checks is the problem of arrest and conviction records. For most jobs, the rule is: never inquire about arrest records; use conviction records only when the offense for which the candidate was convicted bears some relationship to the job for which he or she is being considered. Admittedly, this is a broad standard; there can be honest differences of opinion as to whether a given offense is or is not job related. Generally, the more sensitive the work (e.g., police work), the broader the discretion allowed.

Steps in the Selection Process

Another part of the civil service effort to restrain political influence was the frequent prescription in law of the exact sequence of steps in the local government selection process. It was not uncommon, for example, for the law to specify when tests will be given, perhaps restricting them to a particular month of the year (with some contingency for the possibility that additional employees might be needed at a later date).

Frequently, this detailed specification has meant that applicants must go through a number of steps—and a number of visits to municipal offices—to remain in the running for a city job. The first step is to apply, probably learning then that examinations will not be given until a later date. The second step is to return to take the actual examination. Additional return visits may then be required for oral interviews or other screening procedures.

This attenuated process has been criticized because it may discourage applicants from seeking public jobs. Urban administrators complain that the process discourages some of the better applicants, who may conclude that municipal jobs are not worth the wait. And minority group leaders complain that the process may discourage minority applicants, whose expectations of discrimination may lead them to view the extended selection process as a runaround.

The major defense for this sequence of steps in the selection process has been that each successive selection technique can serve to narrow—or filter—the field of applicants. This filtering has been especially desirable for positions where the applicant pool is large (e.g., clerical workers, entry-level police officers, and fire-fighters).

The cost advantages of this filtering process are obvious and recommend its continued use (assuming that the filtering devices can be shown to be both valid and nondiscriminatory). However, filtering need not require several trips to city hall for the prospective employee on a schedule perhaps set decades ago by local or state law. Recognizing this fact, many jurisdictions, when permitted by law, have moved to a continuous testing system where an applicant can apply and be tested (and perhaps even be hired) on the same visit to municipal offices. This technique does not preclude use of any particular selection technique as a filtering device, but it does eliminate much of the apparent runaround for the applicant, thus probably making the selection process less discouraging to prospective employees and more responsive to governmental needs.

Certification and Final Selection

As noted, the traditional civil service model has emphasized the certification of a limited list of eligibles for jobs. Commonly, only three candidates might be certified as eligible for appointment to the public job in question. The idea, once again, was to decrease the likelihood of politics playing any role in employee selection by limiting the choice of the appointing officer (e.g., city manager, department head).

This limitation on managerial discretion might be acceptable if the selection techniques were strong predictors of on-the-job performance. They seldom are, of course. Moreover, the civil service fondness for written tests has meant that frequently the results of those tests were the sole basis for certification. This restriction further undermined the rationale for a limited list of eligibles.

The concept of ranking of civil service eligibles has been carried to an unreasonable extreme in some jurisdictions. Grades are computed to the thousandth of a decimal point in some agencies; in others, computations may go "only" to the hundredths of a point. These fractions were not defended on the basis that they made any sense, that someone with a grade of 83.535 was any better than someone with a grade of 83.534; the reason was simply that each name had to have a distinct rank because rank determined whether and when the candidate would be certified for consideration. If these fractions were not used, some other equally meaningless formula was needed, such as date of application.

The problem, then, in the certification process was the attention to rank. At one stage of history, this made no difference, but when an appointing official needed to improve his or her affirmative action performance, the slavish attention to rank often was a hindrance. The official might be required to choose one of three white males when the fourth-ranking candidate, a black or woman, was only a small percentage away and therefore probably just as qualified. If affirmative action was to be an effective national policy, it was essential that the appointing official have wider discretion to reach down the list for minorities and females.

While many civil service agencies still retain the narrow certification (three or perhaps five), the evolution has been toward increasing the number of eligibles. Where three may have been the modal number certified in the past, five is now the mode (Institute of Governmental Research, 1979: 26). Further, it is more and more common to include on a certification any candidate whose score is tied with the third (or fifth) name. When this is done, it is also increasingly common to use "whole" scores, meaning that the grades are reported only to the nearest whole number. This obviously increases the number of ties and thus increases the number of names certified when ties are included. Thus appointing officials are in many jurisdictions getting a wider selection, usually to improve their performance under affirmative action plans. Unfortunately, we are not aware of any research that links broader certification policies with affirmative action success.

In addition, where jurisdictions employ continuous testing, they are likely to have an "open-register" system of certification, where an applicant can be tested at any time and, if successful, be added to the certified list with a ranking reflecting the test performance.

PROMOTION

When we reach the point of promotions in the local public service, it is perhaps less civil service principles and more the wishes of public employees that have shaped the guidelines that local governments follow. Two guidelines may be particularly important.

The first is that local governments should hire from within, wherever possible. The thrust of this rule, a rule often embodied in law, is that a position should be declared promotional, rather than entry level, if at all possible. With that declaration, the position becomes available first to existing public employees. Those employees have an obvious interest in the rule as it increases their possibilities for advancement. Thus, those employees have often been responsible for the rule's adoption.

The rule is not a bad one for the most part. By requiring promotion from within rather than hiring from without, the rule creates the potential for career ladders in the local public service, and that potential may increase the motivation of public employees. The major problem with the rule is that it often applies to even the highest public service positions, positions sufficiently close to policymaking that they should be subject to turnover when the actual policymakers change. The result of applying the rule to these positions is a diminished responsiveness by local government to political changes. Consequently, local governments are wise to seek the exemption of these higher-level positions from civil service coverage or at least from the career ladders.

The second common guideline for promotion is that the promotional decision be based solely on a particular selection device—predictably, often a written examination—with the appointing officer required to appoint the top scorer on the test (i.e., the "rule of one"). Employees have sought this rule apparently to reduce the subjectivity in the promotional process, usually from fear more of personal politics (such as the dislike of a superior) than partisan politics. Sometimes the rule is part of the law, sometimes a result of collective bargaining. In Cincinnati, for example, the rule of one in promotions is based on state law for police and fire employees but on union contracts for the nonuniformed employees.

This rule obviously has its shortcomings as it reflects some of the problems already described with entry-level civil service procedures, but the strength of public employee organizations and their belief in the rule makes its demise unlikely. If the rule cannot be eliminated, it perhaps could be modified by increasing the flexibility in the types of measurement devices available for promotional decisions. Basing promotional decisions solely on written examinations is ludicrous since personal skills unmeasurable through written examinations are often the skills most necessary for quality performance in supervisory positions. Public employee organizations might be willing to accept more flexibility in promotional techniques if they are persuaded that the flexibility will not mean an increased role for personal politics in promotional decisions. Local governments might accomplish that persuasion with the interview technique, for example, if they used outsiders, rather than departmental officials, as the interviewers.

CONCLUSIONS

The movement toward civil service in the first half of this century represented an understandable reaction to and rejection of patronage politics. Patronage politics had produced both inefficiency and partisan bias, neither of which belonged in the public service.

But the movement toward civil service created its own problems. In their zeal to eliminate politics from employee recruitment and selection, civil service reformers often bound local governments to a set of rigidly defined recruitment and selection procedures. Those procedures, while perhaps insulating employee selection from partisan politics, eventually reduced the responsiveness of the public service to both managerial mandates and legitimate minority group demands.

Recognition of that loss of responsiveness has in the last decade brought its own reform initiatives, initiatives outlined earlier. What may be worth underscoring, by way of conclusion, are the three principles that the initiatives suggest should be central to the contemporary reshaping of public sector recruitment and selection practices.

Validity. The paramount concern has to be selecting the best employee for the job, and that means that the techniques for selection—including recruitment and promotional techniques—must be designed to produce the employees who best fit the demands of the job.

Responsiveness. Public sector recruitment and selection must be responsive to the varying needs of different publics and to the changing needs of the public, in general. For one thing, recruitment and selection techniques must be adapted to the different backgrounds of minorities. Discrimination can no longer be justified on grounds of needs for uniformity and partisan political neutrality. In addition, those techniques should be capable of adapting as the general public's needs for civil servants may change in the future.

Flexibility and discretion. If the previous two goals and other public sector goals are to be achieved, there must be flexibility in recruitment and selection procedures. Moreover, that flexibility must be available as discretion for personnel professionals so that they can shape the recruitment and selection process to meet the needs of the public service and of the public.

Critics of these recommended relaxations of civil service strictures have sometimes argued that the result may be a new era of patronage politics. That seems unlikely. In most cities there is considerably less interest in patronage jobs than there was historically; and the growing contemporary influence of professionalism in local governments seems unlikely to be reversed by any pressures that might develop for patronage.

REFERENCES

INSTITUTE OF GOVERNMENTAL RESEARCH. 1979. "Civil Service and Personnel Administration: A Report to the City of Dayton, Ohio." University of Cincinnati.

KRISLOV, S. 1974. *Representative Bureaucracy*. Englewood Cliffs, N.J.:Prentice-Hall.

NATIONAL CIVIL SERVICE LEAGUE. 1973. *Judicial Mandates for Affirmative Action*. Washington, D.C.: NCSL.

THOMAS, J. C. 1978. "Budget-Cutting and Minority Employment in City Governments: Lessons from Cincinnati." *Public Personnel Management* 7 (May–June): 155–161.

THOMPSON, F. J. 1974. "Bureaucratic Responsiveness in the Cities: The Problem of Minority Hiring." *Urban Affairs Quarterly* 10 (September): 41–68.

WILSON, J. Q. 1970. *Varieties of Police Behavior*. New York: Atheneum.

Albert C. Hyde

University of Houston at Clear Lake City

and

Jay M. Shafritz

University of Colorado at Denver

CHAPTER SEVEN
POSITION CLASSIFICATION AND STAFFING

Few areas of personnel administration will experience more tension and stress in the future than will position classification and staffing. In nearly eighty years of development, proponents of position classification have stressed its continuity and stability, even though other personnel functions, in marked contrast, have been more responsive to the changing demands of the work environment. This is not to say that classification has not undergone major changes but, rather, that classification has stood fast in maintaining its original objectives, role, and "style."

The perennial problem is the insistence that classification must service the organization first and directly and the individual second and only indirectly. This occurs despite the fact that there is a considerable reversal of individual and organizational roles in modern work environments. Today's trends, organized loosely under the heading of "changing nature of work," include:

Faster appearance of new work technologies
Increasing obsolescence of worker skills/capabilities
More individualized work-life patterns
Wider variation in models of work behavior
Development of new management styles with rapidly adjusting organizational structures

It is not readily apparent how classification, as part of the overall staffing process, will function in today's emerging work environment. The practice of classification in the past provides some clues as to how it will meet the challenge of the "changing nature of work," but its future is highly speculative. This chapter provides an overview of position classification theory and practice and concludes with some preliminary assessments of how classification is preparing to meet the first real wave of change—the work redesign movement. The overview necessarily begins with an examination of the staffing function, which provides the context for classification.

One caveat is in order. Classification is a topic that arouses a certain amount of passion. Classification advocates will undoubtedly feel that this brief overview gives insufficient attention to the underlying premises, continuing objectives, and high level of task difficulty that are essential elements of the classification process. Critics, on the other hand, may feel that what is provided is insufficient documentation of decades of rigidity, dysfunctionality, and abuses and subsequent impacts. Our own views, while rather clear, are split: one advocate and one critic. While our attempt is to cover the middle ground by explaining objectives, the readers must also be wary of their own preconceptions.

STAFFING AND POSITION
MANAGEMENT: THE CONTEXT

In one sense, staffing is considered to be synonymous with employment, that is, the process of integrating people into organizations to perform work. It could be said that the employees constitute one definition of the organization. A more management-oriented definition, however, would state that the organization is the collective body of functional work assignments or positions (in effect, a staffing blueprint). This is in fact one valid representation of the staffing process, but it is not an application derived by accident. The selection and promotion of employees should be based on some rational process, and staffing is intended to be that process. It provides a definition for the organization by translating its objectives, its formal or informal goals, into a specific work plan that should realistically reflect the characteristics of its membership (the employees). Staffing is the structuring of responsibilities for the organization's human resources into such a work system since it attempts to define who will do what and who will have responsibility and authority for which organizational activities. Finally, as a personnel process, staffing is constructed and documented in sufficient detail to provide an information base for compensation decisions.

In the public sector, staffing takes on additional complexity. It must encompass formal elements for making the employment, advancement, and compensation processes satisfy equity and due process criteria yet relate these processes to the organizational structure to ensure relevance. Each of these processes is linked accordingly:

1. *Employment*—By specifying work responsibilities to be performed and essential professional qualifications needed to perform work responsibilities.
2. *Advancement or promotion*—By specifying relevant criteria for work requirements at various levels throughout the organization and structuring the number of positions in the organizational hierarchy to provide a balance between employee advancement and organizational development needs.
3. *Compensation*—By specifying relationships between the organization's work and similar work performed on the outside to ensure that there is equal pay for equal work and that work levels are defined accurately.

Perhaps staffing seen from this perspective should be called *staffing requirements*, quite simply, the formal process of structuring the organization's work force. In this process, the definitional unit of staffing is the job or the position. While both words often are used interchangeably, this is somewhat regrettable since there are some significant differences.

The U.S. Training and Employment Service makes the following distinction between job and position (U.S. Department of Labor, 1972 a: 1):

A position is a collection of tasks constituting the total work assignment of a single worker. There are as many positions as there are workers.
A job is a group of positions which are identical with respect to their major or significant tasks and sufficiently alike to justify their being covered by a single analysis. There may be one or many persons employed in the same job.

Whereas a position represents a single unit, a job is an aggregate concept; each should be construed and used separately. As Yoder notes, "the job is impersonal, the position is personal" (1970: 210). One further distinction is in order. Job is still an organizationally unique term in that it refers to types of similar work being performed in that particular organization. Certain jobs will have similar counterparts throughout private sector and public sector organizations. The term "occupation" is generally used as a label for jobs that are so recognized.

STAFFING AND CLASSIFICATION AS INFORMATION SYSTEMS

Staffing has two time-related dimensions: ensuring accountability in the present and planning for needs in the future. When staffing is carried out effectively in an organization, it will link both dimensions, providing all levels of the organization with capabilities for controlling current levels of human resources and implementing future changes. In this sense, staffing is an implementation process for whatever forms of work force-human resources planning that exist in the organization. As an implementation process, it exhibits the same characteristics as an information system and performs a translating process for personnel.

Staffing fulfills two functions in the personnel information process. It defines the current organization by accounting for the numbers of employees and positions currently on hand. And it translates projected changes into specific position definitions that act as authorizations for employment, promotion, and other personnel processes. As these actions are completed, the results are accounted for and entered into the staffing information system, thus updating the system's accountability of its organizational status. The cycle is completed and continues.

As a basis for recording staffing information, personnel organizations generally employ documents called *staffing patterns* or *manning tables*. These documents will list each position by title in the organization, the grade level (and/or salary), and appropriate data about the incumbent. In addition, the document will probably follow suborganizational lines, illustrating various offices and indicating supervisory responsibilities. As an organization reference, much like organization charts with their boxes and solid and dashed lines, staffing patterns will always be used. But their value has diminished considerably with the increasing size and complexity of public organizations. For example, the staffing pattern alone for the approximately 12,000 employees of the U.S. Department of State consists of two volumes of nearly four hundred pages.

Advances in automated personnel information systems represent a further means of integrating staffing data into a management information system. Generally, personnel information systems consist of two types of automated data: records for positions and records for employees. These records contain various types of information that can be used by the organization for various purposes—everything from printing simple phone or address directories to complex career planning or placement matching processes.

When the organization's files on its positions and employees are linked and compared, a requirements-skills inventory can be produced. These documents have come to be the central planning and information tools for organizations. By grouping positions into various job categories and subtotaling numbers of employees into like categories, the organization can produce a document capable of assessing its current human resource balances and imbalances.

Essentially the data for each position (or employee) constitute a "record." All the records for positions (or employees) constitute a "file" that is stored in the computer system. Any particular requirements-skills inventory can demonstrate a number of ways of viewing the organization—for example, by functional skill or grade level. Basically, requirements-skills inventories are designed to provide accurate snapshots of an organization's staffing.

However, as desirable and simplistic as inventories appear to be, they suffer numerous sins. The most grievous is their total reliance on job labels without regard for position specifics. In other words, there is often no assurance that the specific positions that are included in job categories actually belong there. Further, it is difficult to integrate the two dimensions that they are supposed to cover—current accountability and future planning. Some inventories depict the current work force as a form of skills bank illustrating what employees could do. Others show only current requirements and what the work force is doing at present in response to these needs. The former inventory is ideal for planning purposes, the latter for accountability, but each may be ill suited to serving the needs of the other. The problem is compounded further by the wide range of needs to which the inventory is supposed to respond. Organizations expect the inventory to solve all informational needs, and in fact it serves primarily to whet the appetites of managers and show them how much more information they need to have. But the informational problems of staffing inventories are derived from the personnel function that controls and directs the staffing process—namely, position classification. While it is important to understand the critical relationship between staffing and classification, it should be recognized that classification was and is the controlling factor. It can be argued that a new definition and theory of staffing is emerging, but the classification practice remains the dominant force.

POSITION CLASSIFICATION: THE STRUCTURAL FRAMEWORK

Position classification is the *control process* for staffing. It is usually defined through its practices, that is, the series of formal job descriptions that organize all positions in a specific organization into classes on the basis of duties and responsibilities for the purpose of delineating authority, establishing chains of command, and providing equitable salary scales. The original principles and processes of position classification that developed in the public sector trace their origins to the scientific management movement. This school of management, pioneered by Frederick Taylor, was based on the theory that, through extensive "scientific analysis," the "one best way" to perform work could be discovered and used to divide work responsibilities rationally. The concept was based on time and motion study, with the emphasis on increased efficiency, higher productivity, and no duplication of responsibilities.

As a central component of personnel reform in the early 1900s, the first position classification program was established in the City of Chicago in 1912. The State of Illinois followed suit that same year, becoming the first state to implement such a program. Most progressive state and local governmental jurisdictions established some form of classification system over the next two decades. While there was considerable activity to institute classification programs in the federal government as early as 1902, it was not until 1919 and 1920, with the creation of the congressional Joint Commission of Reclassification of Salaries and its subsequent report, that the underlying principles for a classification system were delineated. These principles are worth reiterating (U.S. Congress, 1920):

1. That positions and not individuals should be classified.
2. That the duties and responsibilities pertaining to a position constitute the outstanding characteristics that distinguish it from, or mark its similarity to, other positions.
3. That qualifications in respect to education, experience, knowledge, and skill necessary for the performance of certain duties are determined by the nature of those duties. Therefore, the qualifications for a position are an important factor in the determination of the classification of a position.
4. That the individual characteristics of an employee occupying a position should have no bearing on the classification of the position.
5. That persons holding positions in the same class should be considered equally qualified for any other position in that class.

The transmission of principles into workable practice at the federal level would take another eighty years to accomplish. Although a classification act was passed in 1923, it was at best a skeleton law. The Classification Act of 1949, despite numerous amendments, was the real foundation of the federal classification system and remains the principal legal authority.

The Classification Act of 1949 tied all positions into one compensation plan consisting primarily of eighteen pay grades, with the responsibility for determining actual occupational groupings and evaluation methods delegated to the central personnel authority. The principles to be employed in making these determinations are elaborated further (U.S. *Statutes*, 1949: 954):

1. Work is accomplished through positions; therefore, their control is an essential part of management.
2. Bringing together similar positions into "classes" reduces the numbers of discrete units that must be controlled and facilitates personnel and administrative transactions.
3. The various "classes" of positions will each relate to established "standards." Authority for establishing additional class titles for occupations covered by printed standards is centralized in the central personnel authority.

4. Because of the growing complexity of today's occupations, standards can no longer be catalogs of specific duties and responsibilities. If new standards are to remain usable over a reasonable period of time, they must be written in terms of those elements of difficulty, responsibility, and qualification requirements that capture the essential character of the field of work.

As Table 1 demonstrates, the focus of the traditional classificational system is on classification standards. These are defined best as a set of documents published by the central personnel authority that provide information for distinguishing the duties, responsibilities, and qualification requirements of positions in one class from those of positions in other classes and that, thus, provide the criteria for placing each position in its proper class. These standards are designed to distinguish both level of difficulty and responsibility regarding the kinds of work performed.

Position classification standards have, of course, a definite function in classifying positions according to their appropriate series and grades (Civil Service Commission, 1963). In this respect, they

1. Demonstrate why certain kinds of positions are classified to particular classes, by showing the work factors with respect to kind and level of work that cause positions to fall in one class rather than another.
2. Seek to secure uniformity and coordination in classifying positions, by providing an established standard for common reference and use in the classification of positions in different organizations, locations, or agencies.
3. Seek to expedite the process of classifying positions to schedule, series, and grades by furnishing a comprehensive reference for comparing the work factors of a particular position with those of another position and with those stated in the standards.

Their use, however, goes beyond the procedures of position classification. For example, position classification standards should facilitate recruiting and placement processes since the qualifications statements can be used as guides in recruiting, testing, and selecting employees. In theory, classification standards also augment career development, training, transfer and promotion, and performance evaluation functions by providing commonly understood reference points for understanding work and performance requirements.

Unfortunately, despite its compelling logic, the theory of classification led to retrenchment and isolation in practice. Proponents of classification, in application, became obsessed with control and stability—and fell behind the advocates of new public management practices that increasingly emphasized flexibility and change. As a consequence of long-standing complaints about the technique's lack of touch with political realities, the theory of classification was under siege throughout the 1950s and 1960s. Two events marked a turning point for this conflict in the early 1970s. The first was the application of the behavioral critique to classification, which held that classification theory was flawed and obsolete. The second was the development of a new methodological thrust—the *factor evaluation system—*

TABLE 1 The Traditional Approach to Position Classification

PREPARE POSITION DESCRIPTIONS FOR EACH POSITION	CATEGORIZE POSITIONS INTO CLASSES	DEVELOP STANDARDS FOR EACH CLASS OF POSITIONS	ALLOCATE POSITIONS TO CLASSES, ADMINISTER SYSTEM	DEVELOP CLASSIFICATION PLAN ADMINISTRATION
Describe each position in terms of work assignment, knowledge and skill requisites, autonomy and judgment required	Using position data, group similar positions by classes[1]	Prepare written standards that define and separate classes from each other and guide the placement of positions in the class by level	Using standards, assess grade level of each position by placing it at the appropriate level within its class	Develop classification system capable of monitoring and updating position allocations, maintaining a verification system (i.e., audit), establishing an appeals system or method for incumbents to dispute classification of positions

[1] A class is defined as a number of positions sufficiently alike in respect to duties, authority, responsibility, etc.

Source: Conceptual design by the authors; For discussions of the traditional approach to classification see Ismar Baruch, *Position Classification in the Public Service* (Chicago: Civil Service Assembly, 1941), and O. Glenn Stahl, *Public Personnel Administration* (New York: Harper & Row, 1976), 78–92.

which applied more flexible and accurate measurements techniques for improving the practice.

THE BEHAVIORAL CRITIQUE

According to Shafritz (1973: 3),

> While position classifications are almost universally recognized as essential for the administration of a public personnel program, they are frequently denounced as unreasonable constraints on top management, as sappers of employee morale, and for being little more than polite fictions in substance. The definitive history of the United States Civil Service counts position classifications among the "great institutional curses of the federal service at the present time." As with other aspects of traditional public personnel administration, they often represent what Wallace Sayre has termed the "triumph of techniques over purpose." In seeking to thwart the excesses of spoils politics the reform movement instituted many civil service procedures that have inadvertently had the effect of thwarting effective management practices as well.
>
> Thus the negative role of the public personnel agency in guarding the merit system has commonly been more influential than the positive role of aiding management in the maintenance of a viable personnel system. This contradictory duality of function in public personnel operations is nowhere more evident than with position classification procedures. While position classifications have received substantial criticism, this has not generated a corresponding revision of established classification principles and practices.

The behavioral critique was launched, as the quotation attests, on the premise that position classification had become dysfunctional because it was essentially obsolete. It was argued that, because of advances in the social sciences and radical changes in the nature of the work force, conventional position classification systems were outmoded, not only because they were less efficient than other modes of organization but also because they proved to be counterproductive to the organizational mission. The argument ran that, because of the continual rise in American educational levels, the bulk of the labor force increasingly consisted of highly skilled technical and professional employees. It is questionable whether such workers could be treated as if they were semiskilled laborers, menials, or clerical functionaries. Yet most position classification systems, which were designed to oversee the more routine job functions, were now being imposed upon administrative, professional, and technical employees, where high task ambiguity and high job discretion were prevailing considerations for organizing and motivating a work force.

Unfortunately the behavioral critique was upstaged by two developments: a new methodological thrust in classification, namely, factor evaluations, and the increasing attention being given to work redesign efforts. The behavioral critique advocated turning classification away from a largely negative control and accountability perspective toward a more positive, advisory perspective "specializing in the motivation and optional utilization of human resources" (Shafritz, 1973: 22). Oliver, the principal architect of factor evaluation, saw little incompatibility between the new behavioral science approaches and the expanded technical concept of factor evaluation. In fact, both developments went their separate ways. Factor evaluation would take classification in a comprehensive, formal, and quantitative direction. The behavioral critique presaged the work redesign movement that, at least in the public sector, was to follow a more experimental, informal, and subjective direction. As one might expect, the reform marriage of factor evaluation and the behavioral critique was one based in circumstance and would not endure.

THE FACTOR EVALUATION APPROACH

The behavioral critique was accompanied by a new methodological thrust for classification theory that originated with the federal government. Following a two-year congressional study of job classification systems begun in 1967, a special task force was created in 1970 to survey existing classification systems in the private and public sectors. This task force acknowledged the inadequacies of the current practice and recommended a revised job evaluation system, known now as the *factor ranking benchmark system.*

Factor evaluation attempted to combine some of the best elements of all previous traditional systems. The design emphasizes accuracy and flexibility, yet is to be simple and inexpensive to implement. A critical ingredient is that it plans for the active involvement of operating management with the idea of developing a team approach as opposed to the old combative relationships that came with control-oriented traditional classification methods.

The impact of factor evaluation on the classification practice is only now being assessed. From a methodological standpoint, it certainly has the potential for providing more relative accuracy and flexibility. It also can be said that, despite its complexity, it is generally more understandable for position incumbents and requires less arbitrary judgment from position classifiers.

What then is this new or, rather, renewed methodological approach? The main focus is on evaluating positions by comparing them with each other in terms of essential job elements, called *factors.* Although many specific factors pertain to various jobs, factors can usually be grouped within one of these major categories:

1. *Job requirements*—The knowledge and abilities needed to perform the work of a specific job.
2. *Difficulty of work*—The complexity or intricacy of work and the mental demands required to perform the work of a specific job.
3. *Responsibility*—The degree of freedom to act and the impact of the work performed on the mission of the organization.
4. *Personal relationships*—The nature of interpersonal relationships and the importance to the success of getting the work performed or accomplished.

5. *Other factors*—The additional, specific job-oriented elements that should be considered in the evaluation process, for example,
   a. physical demands (for manual jobs).
   b. working conditions (for manual jobs).
   c. accountability (for supervisory jobs).
   d. workers directed (for supervisory jobs).

The federal government's system uses nine factors, but a jurisdiction can and should use whatever number of factors is deemed appropriate and essential. Once factors have been selected for evaluating positions, the comparison process hinges on a ranking concept.

Ranking then becomes a process of comparing one position with another. Only three answers are possible: is the position higher, lower, or equal to the other position on that factor? Thus, each position is compared with another overall ranking (one of three choices for four to five factors).

The comparative standard for the system is the *benchmark* position. Each series of choices in ranking one position against another results in a composite ranking of all the choices. These, when assigned numeric values, yield a score that assigns position X and position Y to specific points within an array of evaluations. Each time such determinations are made, they add to the array, thereby increasing the number of benchmarks. Each addition to the number of benchmarks facilitates arriving at the ranking choices for other jobs not yet evaluated. Finally, when *all* jobs within an organization are evaluated, they all become benchmarks for future comparisons. This completed, evaluated structure therefore has been obtained from specific comparisons of each position, all of which have been based on higher, lower, or equivalent rankings. This is the essence of the methodology that is now well documented in IPMA's definitive volume, *Job Evaluation and Pay Administration in the Public Sector*, (Suskin, 1977). Table 2 outlines the actual mechanics of the system. Keep in mind that the ranking concept is the mode of comparative evaluation in each stage of the process.

Generally, *guide charts* are the *reference tool* or measuring device used in the ranking process to select one of the three choices required for each factor. Separate guide charts must be developed for each factor and subsequently validated. Basically, the guide charts provide a method by which to determine grade levels for positions outside the existing organization structure. They should be developed to reflect specific organizational values and can be modified or expanded subsequently to comply with appropriate organizational needs.

The development for use by the federal government of the factor evaluation system has been hailed as an advance and as a return to the despised classification principles of the 1920s (Shafritz, Hyde, and Rosenbloom, 1981: 133). Indeed, in its factor components it resembles the factor comparison methods developed by Eugene Benge in the late 1920s. But factor evaluation is a more systematic method of classification and is certainly different from traditional classification methods. As a hybrid system, it does contain some of the "best" concepts of different classification methods. Only time will tell how long it will take to develop some of the "worst" aspects.

TABLE 2 The Factor Evaluation Approach to Classification

JOB CATEGORIZATION	FACTOR SELECTION	KEY JOB EVALUATION	GUIDE CHARTS DEVELOPMENT	PAY EQUIVALENCY	POSITION CLASSIFICATION
Identify positions to be covered in a single evaluation plan: categorize all jobs by functional relevance into homogenous job families	Select factors to measure and/or compare positions: for example, skill requirements, work difficulty, responsibility, interpersonal contacts, physical demands, etc.	Identify a sample of key jobs for comparison and development of benchmark standards: select sample of key jobs, prepare position descriptions of key jobs, rank key jobs,[1] (whole job ranking, factor ranking), identify from ranking alignments levels within each factor	Develop narrative descriptions for each factor level and designate point value equivalent: prepare narrative descriptions for each factor level, weigh each factor in terms of overall position value, assign point values to corresponding degree definitions, assemble a final point-value-degree, definition-factor-level array (a guide chart)	Establish a series of pay grades to relate to factor point values: establish appropriate number of skill levels or grades for pay system, develop conversion table for equating total factor point values for all jobs into pay grades	Evaluate all positions in the organization; classify positions using any of the following—a single benchmark position, two or more benchmark positions, benchmark positions and guide charts, guide charts only

[1] In whole job ranking, each job in the sample is rank ordered as a whole unit, whereas in factor ranking, each factor is rank ordered separately in each job.

Source: Conceptual design by the authors; Referenced in part from Harold Suskin, "The Factor Ranking System" in Harold Suskin (ed.) *Job Evaluation and Pay Administration in the Public Sector* (Chicago: International Personnel Management Associates, 1977), pp. 130–174.

JOB ANALYSIS: REDEFINING
THE DATA UNITS

The context used thus far in discussing classification is that of the information system. As noted, within the organization the position constitutes the definition of any specific individual's work assignment. Since each position consists of a unique series of duties and responsibilities, a separate position definition or "position description" is prepared. Positions involve two other dimensions as well: their location or identity in the organizational structure and the professional requirements necessary for effective performance. Classification is based in part on the premise that position descriptions can provide the information necessary to evaluate the work components of position. The process that accomplishes that "evaluation" (that determines which positions fit into which jobs or job families) is termed *job analysis.*

In the analysis of jobs, it is necessary to determine the jobs and their precise limits; that is, where the jobs begin and where they end. Job analysis must be able to examine a number of positions, determine how the positions should be grouped as jobs, and then determine the exact nature of these jobs. If the data on each position are questionable, then the entire exercise of job analysis is dubious.

In response to this problem, the public sector has undertaken the task of providing methods for uniform categorization of positions. Job analysis is the most significant application developed to date. However, two types of job analysis have been developed: one based on categorizing work content, the other developed to identify requisite knowledge, skills, and abilities. Still a common definition is possible. Job analysis can be described as a systematic process of collecting and

TABLE 3   Structure of Worker Functions

DATA	PEOPLE	THINGS
0 Synthesizing	0 Mentoring	0 Setting up
1 Coordinating	1 Negotiating	1 Precision working
2 Analyzing	2 Instructing	2 Operating, controlling
3 Compiling	3 Supervising	3 Driving, operating
4 Computing	4 Diverting	4 Manipulating
5 Copying	5 Persuading	5 Tending
6 Comparing	6 Speaking, signaling	6 Feeding
	7 Serving	7 Handling
	8 Taking instructions, helping	

Source: U.S. Department of Labor, *Analyzing Your Jobs* (Washington, D.C.: G.P.O., 1976), p. 5.

making certain judgments about all the important information relating to the nature of specific jobs through evaluation of any number of positions within an organization.

Job analysis pertaining to work content has been a major project of the U.S. Department of Labor for some time. The concept here involves developing a taxonomy of work functions that categorizes specific job relationships on the part of the worker to data, people, and things, as illustrated in Table 3.

Work content is thus determined by identifying the function and the related object(s), thereby creating a standardized description method. An example is the set of functions and objects outlined in Table 4.

Developing taxonomies to describe the work functions found in positions allows accurate and systematic assignment of positions into job categories. The taxonomy provides an essential common vocabulary for the analysis and yet is a flexible tool insofar as organizations can develop their own lists of work functions.

The importance of job analysis is the methodological foundation that it provides for many other personnel management functions and decisions, such as recruitment, selection, placement, training, advancement, and performance appraisal, and the way in which it links these functions to classification and compensation. If performed properly, the greater understanding of jobs provided is the basis for ensuring that all personnel actions are job related. For example, selecting qualified people to fill jobs requires knowing clearly what work is performed and the requirements necessary to work effectively. In redesigning or restructuring jobs for various reasons, it is essential to know the job tasks and their related requirements.

As noted, the "structure of worker functions" (adapted from the Department of Labor's *Handbook for Analyzing Jobs*) is one application of the job analysis approach. The origins of job analysis, however, trace back to the development of the *Dictionary of Occupational Titles* (or *DOT*), which was and remains the most complete and authoritative occupation classification system available today (U.S. Department of Labor, 1972b). *DOT* contains over 35,000 occupational entries and provides a base vocabulary for all employment and placement programs, in both the public and private sectors. With the advent of computerized "job bank" systems designed to find jobs for new and old labor force entrants, the use of common occupational titles in all organizations is essential.

TABLE 4 Worker Functions and Objects

WORKER FUNCTION	THINGS[1]
Compares	Gas thermometer, fan controls, equipment action with specifications
Takes instructions from	Supervisor
Operates and controls	Coal drier, auxiliary equipment

[1] Machines, tools, equipment, work aids; data; people.

The other dimension of job analysis involves the fit between task requirements and worker traits (i.e., the employee's aptitudes, general educational development, vocational preparation, physical demands, and personal traits). Task requirements are generally reflected in the following components: (1) training time, (2) aptitudes, (3) temperaments, (4) interest, and (5) physical demands and environmental conditions.

Data relating to these job concerns can provide a sharper focus on the type of work involved and how the individual worker will relate to any specific work assignment. This information can then be used in counseling, job development, training, and other activities directed toward maximum work force utilization and, it is important to add, development.

More sophisticated methods of job analysis are emerging that meld measurements of work functions and worker traits. One such process is termed *functional job analysis* (Fine, 1955). Functional job analysis introduces the concept of effective performance as involving three kinds of skills: adaptive, functional, and specific content. Adaptive skills enable an individual to meet the demands for conformity and change made by the physical, interpersonal, and organizational arrangements and conditions of a job. Functional skills enable individuals to function in relation to things, data, and people with some degree of complexity appropriate to their abilities. Specific content skills enable an individual to perform a specific job according to the specifications and conditions of a particular employer and according to standards required to satisfy the consumer of that employer's product or services.

Functional job analysis has been used primarily to develop *job-relevant criteria* on which to base selection, advancement,and retainment decisions. Such criteria are of increasing value to organizations given the need for better educated and more sophisticated employees and the emergence of more technical and demanding work environments. However, the additional complexity involved begins to strain the capacity of any one method of data collection to provide the necessary information with which to develop a sound data base for job analysis.

What has been lacking to date has been a taxonomy of *worker traits* that will provide a common vocabulary for this second form of job analysis. A landmark work by Primoff (1973) signals the development of such an advancement. Primoff has developed a categorization system involving job elements. His research has shown that the major job elements that constitute superiority in a job may include a wide variety of characteristics, with some depending on specific training and some more general. A *job element* is defined as

A knowledge, such as knowledge of accounting principles.
A skill, such as skill with a machine or tool.
An ability, such as an ability to manage a project.
A willingness, such as willingness to do simple tasks repetitively.
An interest, such as interest in learning new techniques or processes.
A personal characteristic or aptitude, such as reliability or creativity.

Primoff has also developed an elaborate methodology for determining and validating the significance or weights of job elements as they determine the composition of job success. Even more important, however, may be the determination of 137 job elements that he found and has listed as applicable to administrative position, as these job elements constitute the beginnings of a traits classification system. These general elements can be consolidated somewhat to relate to the more commonly known worker characterization concepts of KSAPs: *K*nowledge, *S*kills, *A*ptitudes, and *P*ersonality characteristics. It remains for job analysis techniques to relate traits to functions via valid measurement systems. By linking KSAPs to actual work functions, a rational basis can be established for selection and advancement, which is also grounded in the classification system.

Research in the job analysis area is continuing, especially in performance appraisal, where detailed job analysis and critical job element analysis are being used to develop more accurate and objective evaluation information on individual performance. The analytical focus thus far has been largely micro oriented, that is, in terms of how positions are grouped and evaluated as jobs within a given organization. Current research is being conducted with a macro orientation as well; specifically, how jobs relate to other jobs is a current research focus in the exploration of the *job family*. By identifying interrelationships among jobs, job families can serve as a more refined classification system for the purposes of determining appropriate salary levels, training requirements, task performance, and work requirements across organizational lines. Part of the purpose of job family research seems to be to develop a unified taxonomy of work performance and to incorporate much broader job analysis methods (methods that could group jobs on the basis of work content or structure or human attributes requirements, with only a minimum reference to specific tasks, duties, or work behaviors) (Pearlman, 1980). This kind of information would be pivotal for classification and other personnel functions where work assignments were constantly being changed and individuals were being reassigned on a continuing basis. In fact, the job family concept can be interpreted as a significant step away from more molecular forms of job analysis toward a more organic concept that fits the characteristics of new work environments.

CLASSIFICATION AND WORK REDESIGN

Although the factor evaluation system represents an attempt to make the classification practice more objective and accurate, the current sociotechnical environment of work may be beyond the capabilities of any systemwide reform. Specifically, since the mid-1960s, one of the most significant trends in organizations has been a group of techniques clustered around a concept termed *work redesign*. The techniques are known variously as job rotation, work simplification, job enlargement, job enrichment, and semiautonomous team building. While the literature on job redesign is extensive and well beyond the scope of this review, some discussion of the concepts involved is essential to understand future trends.

Earlier, the point was made that the behavioral critique of classification prophesied the work redesign movement. Technically, that is not so, since work redesign experiments were being reported in the early 1950s. The first job enlargement program is attributed to Thomas Watson and IBM in the early 1940s (see Reif and Monczka, 1974) and was undertaken to alter the work content of the assembly line at IBM to combat boredom and monotony. From that simple experiment, a mountain of change has come.

The purpose of work redesign seems fairly straightforward—changing the work assignments in jobs to make them more rewarding, more satisfying, and therefore, more motivating. Primarily, two approaches are used. The first, job enlargement, which entails increasing the variety of tasks performed at any level, is designed to reduce boredom and repetitive actions. The second, job enrichment, which is attributed to Herzberg, is more qualitative in that it allows employees to plan, control, and begin to manage the work that they are to do. Myers (1976) makes an interesting and useful distinction between the two. Job enrichment and job enlargement are both dimensions of work redesign: the former is vertical change wherein employees participate in planning, organizing, leading, and controlling work functions; the latter is horizontal change wherein the range of actual work being done is increased.

Davis and Taylor (1979) provide a more comprehensive assessment of the work redesign movement. They divide events into four stages of concurrent emphasis.

1. Task and job rationalization or work simplification
2. Changing job content
3. Changing role content
4. Self-maintaining organizations

Task rationalization involves engineering work assignments through the use of scientific management with time and motion study, work physiology, and the study of worker-machine interface. These foci emphasize variables such as simplifying work assignments, reducing industrial fatigue, and improving management and human engineering in work settings.

Davis and Taylor include both job enlargement and enrichment in the *job content stage*. The focus is on intrinsic job satisfaction emanating from the work itself. The variables being changed are task variation and range, planning, regulation, and control activities. The final two phases, *role content* and *self-maintaining organizations*, have a more sociological systems focus in that work redesign is viewed in both an organizational and sociotechnical context. Included in this stage is worker democratization or worker control. Self-maintaining organizations envision only minor dependence on specific jobs, with major emphasis on roles within organizational systems. Davis and Taylor conclude that jobs and job redesign are *not* the fundamental building blocks for modern organizations: "focusing on job revision, job enlargement, job enrichment, etc., will not fundamentally alter the organizational system, the roles of the organization's members and managers, the opportunity for self-regulation, or the flexibility or adaptability of the organization and its members" (1978: xvii).

This rather interesting prediction has not lessened the enthusiasm for the work redesign movement, which is now being considered actively in the public sector. Prevailing work redesign theory has identified the key work variables that are to be changed (variety, task identity, task significance, autonomy, and feedback) and the expected outcomes (experienced meaningfulness of the work, experienced responsibility for work outcomes, and knowledge of actual results of work activity). The work of Hackman and Oldham (1980) and Lawler (1972) have shown how these core dimensions of jobs impact on personal motivation, productivity, and job satisfaction.

Lawler (1972) reports some rather interesting conclusions about work redesign outcomes. Specifically,

1. Work redesign affects work quality more strongly than does productivity.
2. Work redesign strongly affects job satisfaction, involvement, and absenteeism (which are more personal than organizational values).
3. Interpersonal dimensions of work have little impact on worker satisfaction or performance.
4. Many managerial-professional jobs rate low on the core job dimension identified.
5. Supervisors often misperceive the jobs of their subordinates (they rate the existence of the core job dimensions much higher than the employees themselves).
6. Supervisors are often major obstacles to job redesign efforts.

What these conclusions suggest is that there is likely to be considerable misunderstanding about the objectives, outcomes, and mechanics of work redesign efforts when applied in the public sector. These difficulties will be even greater for classification. Thus far, the compensation and classification dimensions of work redesign have received only cursory attention. In one of the few articles available on the subject, Caulkins concludes that, when effective job redesign efforts are carried out, there is less emphasis on compensation or grade reclassification. He adds (1974: 30),

> Or employees are so engrossed in learning to handle their new responsibilities that they tend to be less concerned with matters outside the job itself. It is when jobs are badly redesigned, so that workers fail to get intrinsic satisfaction from the work they are doing, that their minds tend to focus on their pocketbooks. Then, as one union leader put it, their reaction is, "Pay me more to do your stupid job."

Whether this view holds true for the public sector remains to be seen. But, certainly, classification, even using factor evaluation methodology, will be forced to cope with a new perspective if work redesign becomes a significant force.

CONCLUSION: FUTURE
DIRECTIONS FOR CLASSIFICATION

Classification theory and practice will surely face the job redesign challenge as it has the myriad criticisms that have always besieged classification—with understanding and concern for continuity and stability. Any change will come slowly and only after demonstration that organizational management wants such change incorporated into the organizational design. But certain trends seem likely:

First, classification methodology will be consolidated and updated through the widespread adoption of the factor evaluation ranking system.

Second, the increased use of job and position analysis (the pivotal data components for classification) should strengthen the relationships between classification and other personnel functions.

Third, classification will have to face and deal with (initially on an experimental basis) the work redesign movement and its corresponding impact on public sector work environments.

Classification, as the most independent of the personnel functions, has always undergone change in its own way at its own pace. While change is certain, one can be sure that classification will do it on its own terms.

REFERENCES

BARUCH, ISMAR. 1941. *Position Classification in the Public Service*. Chicago: Civil Service Assembly.

CAULKINS, DAVID. 1974. "Job Redesign: Pay Implications." *Personnel* 51 (May/June) 30.

CIVIL SERVICE COMMISSION. 1963. *Classification Principles and Policies*. Personnel Management Series #16. Washington, D.C.: G.P.O.

DAVIS, LOUIS E. and JAMES C. TAYLOR. 1979. *Design of Jobs*. Santa Monica, Calif.: Goodyear.

FINE, SIDNEY. 1955. "Functional Job Analysis." *Journal of Personnel Administration and Industrial Relations* 2: 1-16.

HACKMAN, RICHARD and GREG R. OLDHAM. 1980. *Work Redesign*. Reading, Mass.: Addison-Wesley.

HERZBERG, FREDERICK. 1974. "The Wise Old Turk." *Harvard Business Review* 52 (September-October): 72-75.

LAWLER, EDWARD E. 1972. "Worker Satisfaction, Job Design, and Job Performance. *Good Government* 89 Summer: 12-15.

MYERS, M. SCOTT. 1976. "Job Enrichment." In Robert Golembiewski and Michael Cohen, eds., *People in Public Service*. Itasca, Ill. F. E. Peacock.

PEARLMAN, KENNETH. 1980. "Job Families: A Review and Discussion of Their Implications for Personnel Selection." *Psychological Bulletin* 80 (January): 1-28.

PRIMOFF, EARNEST S. 1973. *How to Prepare and Conduct Job-Element Examinations*. Washington, D.C.: G.P.O.

REIF, WILLIAM and ROBERT M. MONCZKA. 1974. "Job Redesign: A Contingency Approach to Implementation." *Personnel* 51 (May/June): 18.

SHAFRITZ, JAY M. 1973. *Position Classification: A Behavioral Analysis for the Public Service*. New York: Praeger.

SHAFRITZ, JAY M., ALBERT C. HYDE, and DAVID H. ROSENBLOOM. 1981. *Personnel Management in Government*. New York: Marcel Dekker.

STAIIL, O. GLENN. 1976. *Public Personnel Administration*. New York: Harper & Row.

SUSKIN, HAROLD, ed. 1977. *Job Evaluation and Pay Administration in the Public Sector*. Chicago: International Personnel Management Association.

U.S. CONGRESS. Joint Commission on Reclassification of Salaries. 1920. *Report of the Congressional Joint Commission on Reclassification of Salaries*. H. D. 686, 66th Cong., Washington, D.C.: G.P.O.

U.S. DEPARTMENT OF LABOR. 1972a. *Handbook for Analyzing Jobs*. Washington, D.C.: G.P.O.

———. 1972b. *Dictionary of Occupational Titles*. Washington, D.C.: G.P.O.

———. 1976. *Analyzing Your Jobs*. Washington, D.C.: G.P.O.

U.S. Statute, 1949, 954, October 28.

YODER, DALE. 1970. *Personnel Management and Industrial Relations*. Englewood Cliffs, N.J.: Prentice-Hall.

Charlie B. Tyer
University of South Carolina

CHAPTER EIGHT
EMPLOYEE PERFORMANCE APPRAISAL: PROCESS IN SEARCH OF A TECHNIQUE

Evaluating and rating employee performance in both the public and private sectors is one of the most controversial and widely discussed topics in personnel management. The essence of performance appraisal is an evaluation of an employee's past and current performance, as well as future prospects, in an organization. The state of the art of performance appraisal, or evaluation, has been labeled "crude" by knowledgeable observers and the issue of appraising performance called the " 'issue of the next decade' " (Winstanley, 1980: 55).

To develop some feeling for those views expressed about performance appraisal, one merely has to browse through the voluminous literature on the subject and note the comments offered by both practitioners and academicians. For example, the following is a sampling of concerns gleaned from published articles and arranged in chronological order.

> Although formal worker-appraisal systems have been in vogue for some time, few enterprises seem satisfied that any system they use fulfills its intended purposes, let alone that it acts in a way which does not complicate other phases of their manpower development (Sokolik, 1967: 660).

> while survey results from a 1974 Bureau of National Affairs survey reveal that 93 percent of the firms polled have appraisal programs, only 10 percent of these firms' personnel executives felt that their appraisal programs were effective (Colby and Wallace, 1975: 37).

> most organizations are "flying blind"; they do not know what . . . appraisals are doing for—or to—the organization. Lacking that specific evidence, and in view of all the evidence reviewed, it is a safe generalization to state most performance appraisal ratings are of very low reliability (Winstanley, 1980: 58).

> performance appraisal systems do not and cannot possibly work. . . . (Thayer, 1981: 21).

These comments reflect some of the diverse opinions about performance appraisals. These opinions range from dissatisfaction with an appraisal system, to concern about reliability and validity of appraisals, to a feeling that appraisals cannot be carried out fairly and meaningfully. While most observers would probably not agree that performance appraisal is impossible, many would concur with Gardner (1961: 71) when he writes, "The sorting out of individuals according to ability is very nearly the most delicate and difficult process our society has to face."

The purpose of this chapter is to examine the issue of performance appraisal in terms of the obstacles and pressures on appraisal systems in the 1980s. We begin by reviewing briefly the purposes of performance evaluation, the major approaches to appraisal, and the evolution of performance evaluation. This is followed by an examination of the obstacles to effective appraisal and contemporary pressures on appraisal systems. We conclude with a brief discussion of trends in appraisals and recommendations for their improvement.

USES AND APPROACHES TO
PERFORMANCE APPRAISAL

Why do organizations engage in performance appraisals? Surveys tell us that appraisals are used in government to (1) aid in making annual salary recommendations, (2) assist in identifying employees capable of being promoted, and (3) justify adverse personnel actions, such as dismissals and demotions (Feild and Holley, 1975a; Lacho, Stearns, and Villere, 1979; Greiner et al., 1981).

Lopez (1968), an authority on performance evaluation, groups the primary uses, or purposes, of evaluation into three categories: information, motivation, and development. Of the informational uses of appraisal systems, chief among them are such purposes as improving communication between supervisors and subordinates concerning work expectations. Management may also use evaluations as sources of information about the work force to assess motivation, skills, training needs, and other factors. In addition, appraisals can provide useful information about the adequacy of various personnel management practices, such as selection procedures, examinations, placements and transfers, and training programs.

The second category of uses of appraisal systems—motivation—reflects the reason cited most frequently for performance appraisal. Salary determinations are the most common use of appraisal information, an area highlighted by the emphasis placed upon it in the Civil Service Reform Act of 1978. The assumption is that employees will be motivated to be more productive if they feel that their salaries will reflect their productivity. Other motivational uses include (1) the evaluation of employees on probationary appointments, either as new employees or as a result of promotion or transfer, prior to granting them permanent employee status in a position, and (2) promotional decisions that may be based in part upon evaluations.

Finally, performance appraisals can serve developmental purposes. This third category of uses is more recent than the other two and reflects the concern in administration and management with human relations. Developmental uses of appraisals emphasize management's responsibility to counsel and aid employees in realizing their potential to raise job satisfaction and encourage successful performance.

Hence, performance appraisals obviously can serve several purposes and have many uses. The uses generally found thus far in the public sector, however, have been focused rather narrowly upon salary decisions and specific personnel actions to serve the needs of the organization rather than the needs of the individual employee.

Just as several purposes and uses of performance evaluation exist, there are also varied approaches to appraising performance. These may be grouped around four key factors (Glueck, 1978): (1) the timing of appraisals, (2) the evaluator, (3) the factors selected for appraisal, and (4) the method, or technique, of appraisal.

Timing refers to the frequency of formal evaluations. Most federal agencies, state governments, and local governments appraise employees once a year. A few organizations appraise employee performance more often than once a year (usually twice). Usually an interview is held with the employee to discuss the appraisal.

The evaluator, or rater, in the appraisal process is typically an employee's immediate supervisor. Supervisory ratings may be reviewed in some organizations by higher-level administrators. In addition to supervisory evaluations, however, appraisals may be conducted using other evaluators. These include such approaches as

1. Using a committee of other supervisors.
2. Allowing one's peers, or fellow workers, to evaluate an employee.
3. Including subordinate evaluations of supervisory personnel.
4. Permitting self-evaluation by the employee.

Of these alternatives to simple supervisory evaluations, the use of self-evaluation by employees seems to be growing in popularity over the other approaches in the public sector (Lovrich et al., 1980). When used, however, it is usually coupled with supervisory evaluation and is regarded as a communication tool to enhance understanding between supervisors and their employees.

In terms of the factors that are evaluated during appraisals, two basic distinctions exist in practice. These are trait- or person-based evaluations and performance-based evaluations. Trait-based evaluations are the most common. These consist of an evaluation of general factors such as personality traits and general skills or duties that are not unique to a particular individual or job series based upon specific job requirements or performance standards. A typical example of such traits found in state government appraisals is provided in Table 1. Research on local government is

TABLE 1   Most Frequent Variables in Appraisal Forms of State Governments, 1975

VARIABLE	VARIABLES ON SUPERVISORY FORMS (%)	VARIABLES ON NONSUPERVISORY FORMS (%)
Quality of work	59%	67%
Quantity of work	49	56
Initiative	44	49
Human relations	41	33
Judgment	36	28
Job knowledge	33	39
Work habits	33	33
Dependability	31	41
Organizing and planning	31	N.I.
Supervisory ability	21	N.I.
Cooperation	N.I.	26
Attendance	N.I.	26
	(n = 39)	

N.I. – Not included.

SOURCE: H. S. Feild and W. H. Holley, "Performance Appraisal—An Analysis of State-Wide Practices, "*Public Personnel Management* 5 Vol. 4 (May-June), 148.

incomplete, but these examples appear to be typical of many public organizations in the early 1980s.

Performance-based factors refer to evaluations that focus upon work behavior and the results accomplished by an employee. Although no reliable data are available concerning the extent of appraisal systems using the approach, some public organizations and jurisdictions have adopted this approach entirely or in combination with a trait-based system. Performance-based systems are costly and time consuming to design and administer but, as we shall see, are being advocated increasingly for legal reasons as well as for being a better administrative practice.

Just as different evaluations and factors may be used in appraising performance, different methods or techniques of performance appraisal also exist. There is again a tendency for one or two approaches to be used predominately by organizations. Eight techniques of appraisal that have been used to varying degrees in the public or private sectors can be identified (Glueck, 1978; Stahl, 1976). These techniques differ widely in terms of the purpose they serve best and their administrative difficulty. They are[1]

1. Rating scales
2. Essay reports
3. Checklists
4. Critical incidents
5. Forced choice
6. Ranking or comparing
7. Forced distribution
8. Management by objectives

Rating Scales

Referred to as graphic rating scales or simply as rating scales, this technique is the most common method of appraising employee performance in the public sector. The instrument used in this technique contains a range of performance qualities and traits and is employed characteristically in trait-based appraisals. The rater appraises an employee "by checking a box, circling a number or letter, or placing a mark along a continuum line" (Locher and Teel, 1977) that describes employee performance as being "outstanding," "average," or some other descriptive phrase. The variables listed in Table 1 are commonly used for evaluation.

Rating scales are simple and inexpensive to devise and administer. This no doubt accounts for their widespread use. A major criticism of them, however, focuses upon the ambiguity and subjectivity of the traits used for evaluation. Such methods typically foster confusion among supervisors regarding what the traits mean and how to measure them. As a result, personnel experts have begun to shift away from the use of this technique; it still remains in wide use however.

Essay Reports

Essay reports may be either open-ended reports concerning an employee's performance, training needs, and potential, or structured instruments in which raters respond to specific questions about employees. This technique appears to be somewhat more prevalent in private companies than in public agencies (Locher and Teel, 1977; Bureau of National Affairs, 1975; Lacho, Stearns, and Villere, 1979; Feild and Holley, 1975a). While inexpensive to design, essay reports are not simple or easy to administer. A major criticism of this technique is that it depends heavily upon supervisors taking the time needed to write thoughtful evaluations (which many will not do) and upon good writing skills. On the positive side, this method may force raters to evaluate actual performance and results rather than employee characteristics and traits. Essay reports may be used in conjunction with other techniques, such as rating scales.

Checklists

The checklist method of appraisal uses a list of statements about employee performance. The evaluator checks those statements that he or she believes describe the employee. Weights are sometimes assigned to the statements. This technique tends to be person- or trait-based rather than performance-based. It also appears more often in private industry than in public organizations (Bureau of National Affairs, 1975).

Critical Incidents

In its formal application, the critical incident method of appraisal identifies the major job requirements of a position. Lists of good and poor performance indicators can then be prepared and given to supervisors. The supervisor is asked to keep a log in which to record systematically examples of an employee's good and poor performances as they occur. Periodic discussions are held with employees to review their performance. The advantage of this technique is that it is performance-based and relies upon facts and also highlights *both* good and poor performance. However, it is expensive to design and can be time consuming to administer. Moreover, it may overemphasize unusual behavior and overlook the typical or average performance of an employee. Informal record keeping of critical incidents is sometimes encouraged in conjunction with other appraisal techniques in an effort to emphasize specific job behavior.

Forced Choice

Found infrequently in the public sector, the forced choice method involves giving the supervisor a list of descriptive statements about employees that are both positive and negative. The supervisor rates the employee using these statements but is not told which statements refer to desirable employee behavior. The statements are usually prepared by personnel specialists and the results are tabulated by the personnel department. When used, this technique is more appropriate for job series that contain large numbers of employees. Although expensive to design, the technique is easy to administer but is difficult for supervisors and employees to understand and use for feedback purposes. As with the remaining techniques to be described, this method is used typically to overcome the tendency of other techniques to inflate employee ratings or otherwise sharply discriminate between employees' performance levels.

Ranking or Comparing

Ranking or comparing employees is relatively simple and easy. It may be either formal or informal. Indeed, when formal rankings or comparisons do not occur, they almost always are found informally due to the need for salary and promotion decisions. Ranking or comparing techniques may take different approaches, ranging from simple overall ranking, to alternative ranking, to paired comparisons. A simple ranking system refers to listing employees in rank order. Alternative ranking refers to ranking best and worst employee, the next best and worst, and so on until a complete list exists. Paired comparison refers to comparing each employee with every other employee and tabulating the results for an overall ranking.

Forced Distribution

Forced distribution is slightly different from the ranking technique. It relies upon the creation of categories, such as percentiles (top 10 percent, top 20 percent, middle 40 percent, low 20 percent, low 10 percent, for example), and the placement of employees in those categories. Ranking, comparison, and forced distribution systems are easy to design and administer but are usually limited to smaller organizational units in which a supervisor can gain familiarity with all the employees. The major problem with these techniques is that the standards or criteria used to evaluate employees are unclear. Thus, morale may suffer if employees feel that the system is unfair.

Management by Objectives (MBO)

Initially popular in the private sector, MBO and other coaching or collaborative appraisal techniques gained popularity in public agencies during the 1970s. Generally, MBO-style appraisal techniques refer to mutual objective setting by supervisors and subordinates in terms of results that are quantifiable and measurable. The supervisor plays a supportive role, like a coach, in assisting the employee to attain work objectives. Frequent evaluation or assessment discussions are held to monitor the employee's performance. MBO techniques may be expensive to design and administer. They require a great deal of time and sensitivity to human relations issues. Moreover, the emphasis on measurable objectives can be dysfunctional if short-range goals are emphasized at the expense of long-range goals. On the positive side, however, MBO techniques are performance-based and focus on results. They can also be used to varying degrees with other techniques either formally or informally.

Thus, the purposes, uses, and techniques for appraising employee performance are varied and numerous. Techniques of appraisal reflect the purpose and use of employee evaluations. Hence, if a variety of techniques exists, this reflects to some extent the different uses of appraisals. If the methods of appraisal seem confusing and poorly designed and administered, this too reflects confusion concerning why employees are appraised and the way in which evaluation information is used. Some of this confusion is a result of the evolving role of appraisals in management.

Although performance appraisals have been known in some form for hundreds of years, the first real interest in them in the United States began during and after World War I (Kelly, 1958). The emphasis of management in the early 1900s was upon control of employees and maximizing efficiency. At the national level, the Classification Act of 1923 overhauled the federal pay system and the efficiency ratings then in use. (The first uniform efficiency rating system was implemented during the administration of President Harrison.) In 1924 the graphic rating scale was introduced in the federal service. This system was revised in 1935, and ratings were used for such personnel actions as promotions, salary increases, reductions in force, and removal. The system was changed again with the Performance Rating Act of 1950, which left the number and format of appraisals up to individual agencies. Ratings remained the sole basis for within-grade salary increases and extra retention credits used during a reduction in force. The latest change occurred with the Civil Service Reform Act of 1978, discussed later in this chapter (GAO, 1978).

Prior to 1978, the use of appraisals in the federal service was oriented primarily toward making key personnel decisions with a focus upon efficiency and control. Private industry had exhibited similar emphases but had begun to reflect the effects of the human relations movement with its attention to psychology and motivation. After World War II, concern grew over the need to "develop" employees, not just to rate them as justification for specific personnel actions. This interest was transferred to the public sector during the 1960s and 1970s.

The result of the evolution of appraisals has been their adoption for a variety of purposes and uses as times have changed. These purposes have included emphases on salary administration, promotion and retention justification, productivity concerns, and interest in organizational development and team building. Such diversity in purposes and uses naturally led to confusion in the methodology and manner of approaches to employee appraisal. Thus, today, one finds a hodgepodge of appraisal systems in the public (and private) sectors. The experience of state and local governments seems to have followed closely developments in the federal government on this issue.

OBSTACLES TO EFFECTIVE
PERFORMANCE APPRAISAL

Why do appraisal systems fail? Some clues have been provided in the discussion thus far. To identify the reasons for failure more systematically, we can review the research available and group the reasons into four categories for discussion. These are problems related to the process of appraisal, instrumental errors, evaluator errors, and organizational climate.

Process Problems

Many general problems appear frequently to deter effective performance appraisals. Chief among these is a tendency for managers and organizations to have too many uses and conflicting objectives for appraisals. Some organizations attempt to use performance evaluations in multiple ways, such as for performance feedback to the employee, for salary decisions, for identifying potential among employees, for making promotional decisions, for assessing training needs, and so on (Lazar, 1980). Most experts agree that differing purposes of appraisal require differing approaches (Winstanley, 1980). Hence, multiple-purpose application based upon one approach increases the likelihood of the system's being ineffective.

Burke (1972) has identified additional process problems. These include viewing appraisal as a once-a-year activity, making it too formal, and viewing it as a zero-sum game. Often supervisors view appraisal as an activity that occurs only once or twice a year. They overlook the fact that they are actually continually appraising their employees but postpone feedback until the formal appraisal. This failure to use day-to-day opportunities effectively for feedback results in unnecessary employee apprehension and other problems during performance reviews.

Excessive formality can also be a problem. Too many supervisors view employee appraisal as a permanent indication of an employee's value to the organization and consider the appraisal results as a permanent part of the employee's personnel record. Too formal an approach can cause the appraisal process to resemble a legal case rather than an opportunity for feedback and employee development.

The appraisal process can also be distorted into a zero-sum game. At times, such as during salary determination, managers compare employees and inform them of their comparative standing with their peers. This is a zero-sum game, for, if one employee moves to the top, another will be displaced and moved down in rating. Yet organizations do not have to be zero sum. Employees may improve their performance without decreasing another employee's effectiveness and competence. Unfortunately, many appraisal systems do not communicate this to employees.

Stahl (1976) has identified additional process problems in performance evaluation. Among these are gauging employee potential, employee participation in the process, and administrative issues. Most appraisal systems focus on past performance for promotion or other assignments and not on an employee's potential, which may not be demonstrated on the existing job. Participation by employees in their appraisals has tended to be one way—receiving feedback rather than participating actively in the process through techniques of self-analysis and mutual goal setting, activities that many argue are essential for employee acceptance of appraisal systems. Finally, the administration of performance appraisal systems is frequently weak. Systems should be "simple, expeditious and not unduly burdensome on supervisors" (Stahl, 1976: 215). Continuous training of rating officials is needed concerning the objectives and process of appraisal used in an organization. And written reports should be reviewed by upper levels of management to assure that supervisors are conducting evaluations in an effective manner.

Instrumental Errors

Another source of obstacles to effective appraisals results from improperly designed appraisal forms or instruments. Often this is the result of the selection of irrelevant or ambiguous variables for evaluation. Instead of evaluating employees on the basis of their job performance and output, too frequently personality traits or other "proxies of performance" are selected for evaluation (Robbins, 1978: 216-243). Thus, appraisals will focus upon such factors as initiative, appearance, dependability, judgment, cooperation, and so on. While these traits may be important in relation to specific duties and assignments, by themselves they bear little relation to performance. Indeed, such factors are increasingly regarded as ambiguous and subjective. Supervisors frequently cannot agree among themselves concerning common definitions and measurements for such traits. The result is speculation by the evaluator, which renders the appraisal questionable in terms of its reliability and validity because such appraisals tend to lack consistency and may not reflect actual differences in employee performance (Burke, 1972; Feild and Holley, 1975b; Rogers, 1975).

A related instrumental error concerns the weighting of factors assessed during the appraisal process. Appraisal techniques that rely upon rating scales or checklists tend to assign equal values to each factor evaluated. Since all factors are not equally important in performing a job, the resulting evaluation may not be a valid assessment of an employee's performance.

Finally, Feild and Holley (1975a) provide some insight into common instrumental errors found in state government performance appraisal systems. In addition to the use of vague factors, they found three common problems among the states. First, rating scales tended to reflect more than one dimension within a single factor being evaluated, such as attitudes toward other employees *and* the public. Second, supervisors were required to evaluate employees on the basis of inference rather than observation. While factors such as learning ability or intelligence were being rated, these qualities are difficult to assess and require constant observation even to approximate a reliable judgment. Third, many instruments lacked internal consistency among factors rated. For example, supervisors may be evaluated on the same factors as nonsupervisory personnel, or clerical personnel may not be distinguished from manual laborers. Research has raised questions about the validity of using the same factors to evaluate employees in different job classifications and with widely different levels of responsibility (Landy and Farr, 1980).

Evaluator Errors

In addition to process problems and instrumental errors, another pitfall in the path of effective appraisals lies with the individual evaluator. Common problems include the high skill requirements of effective performance appraisal, the difference between day-to-day management skills and employee development skills, and the different frames of reference that evaluators bring to appraisal processes (Burke, 1972; Latham, Cummings, and Mitchell, 1981). As Burke (1972) notes, it is difficult to create conditions in which another person can improve, grow, and develop his or her potential. Thus, the very process of encouraging growth by employees in their jobs is difficult and requires skill. Unfortunately, such skills are frequently different from the day-to-day management skills needed by supervisors. In practice, supervisors tend to be results-oriented people who focus more on "traditional" activities associated with managing, such as delegation, monitoring, planning, budgeting, and so on (Whisler, 1958). The skills of being a helper or coach traditionally have not been rewarded by upper echelons of organizational management or by legislators. When the evaluator spends only one day a year trying to be a helper, the chance of success is slim. Special supervisory skills are also required to attribute properly employee performance to factors within or outside of the employee's control, skills that many supervisors lack.

Besides general evaluator obstacles to good appraisals, other specific pitfalls exist that may interfere with effective appraisals, but that may be alleviated in many cases by training. These include such pitfalls as halo, horns, and recency effects and leniency, central tendency, similar-to-me, and contrast effects (Glueck, 1978; Washington Local Government Personnel Institute, 1979; Conant, 1973). The halo effect refers to a tendency among supervisors to rate an employee high overall who scores well on one particular factor. Conversely, the horns effect is the reverse—a tendency to rate a person who is low or weak on one factor, or performance standard, low on others as well. Recency effects are similar to halo and horns and refer to a tendency to evaluate people primarily on the basis of recent behavior. These three evaluator errors are more likely to occur when certain techniques of appraisal are used, such as rating scales or checklists.

Leniency errors may be either positive or negative. Research has shown that some raters tend to give a disproportionate number of high or low ratings. Reasons may vary, ranging from the purpose or use of the appraisal affecting ratings (Gallagher, 1978) to the reluctance of supervisors to appraise performance. McGregor noted in 1957 that many managers feel uncomfortable "playing God" with employees' lives. This results from being asked to assess an individual's worth, make decisions about his or her career, award money, and so on. To avoid unpleasantness and hurting feelings, the manager tends to be generous. Depending upon the personality of the manager (obviously), the effects could be negative as opposed to positive leniency—for example, evaluating most everyone low. Moreover, one must note that a method or technique of appraisal that makes it difficult for the supervisor to justify his or her evaluation may foster leniency.

Related to leniency error is something called central tendency. This occurs when the evaluator does not group employees either too high or too low but, rather, groups them in the middle (Pizam, 1975). Central tendency has been attributed to a lack of ability on the part of some people to differentiate between stimuli and otherwise make fine distinctions.

Similar-to-me errors refer to a tendency of raters to give higher ratings to people who are similar to themselves in their attitudes, education, sex, race, and other factors.

Finally, the contrast effect refers to evaluating employees relative to each other rather than on the basis of their individual performance in assignments or duties. The pitfalls of leniency, central tendency, similar-to-me, and contrast effects may affect any appraisal technique. Thus, evaluator errors can be a major obstacle to effective performance appraisal.

Organizational Climate

The final group of obstacles to effective appraisals is generally classified as organizational climate. This concept refers to the interaction of such factors as leadership styles, organizational structure, work group norms, communication networks, and the nature of tasks being performed (Gibson, Ivancevich, and Donnelly, 1973: 313-339). Managers or other policymakers may adopt an unrealistic perception of the purposes and uses of appraisal systems. Should too many purposes be attached to one technique, successful appraisals are hampered. Moreover, poor communication between supervisors and subordinates can result in the failure of appraisal systems. Employees may not, for instance, be aware of what performances they are expected to exhibit or what equates with a job well done. And, as was noted earlier, managers frequently feel that "there is nothing in it for them" if they devote time and energy to performance appraisal. Most jurisdictions and agencies do not provide incentives to foster effective performance appraisals.

The attitudes conveyed by policymakers in government, be they department heads, chief executives, or legislators, affect management systems like the appraisals process. Many policymakers do not understand the management of large organizations and view public organizations as somehow unique or different from private organizations. For example, legislators may feel that public employees should work because of a "service" ethic and not require competitive wages or that public employees do not need "merit" raises since they should be performing at the highest level in any case. If a jurisdiction's appraisal system is oriented toward making salary decisions, attitudes such as those just described may affect the enthusiasm of supervisors and agency heads for conducting good performance appraisals.

In sum, there are numerous obstacles to effective employee performance appraisal. Any one or combination of them can result in an appraisal system's malfunctioning or failing altogether. These obstacles are not the only factors affecting performance appraisals, however. Other pressures can detract further from their effectiveness.

CONTEMPORARY PRESSURES
ON APPRAISAL SYSTEMS

Three developments during the past decade have impacted management's use of performance appraisal. These are the Equal Employment Opportunity Commission's (EEOC) *Uniform Guidelines on Employee Selection Procedures* and judicial interpretation of these guidelines, employee unions, and the Civil Service Reform Act of 1978.

The role of performance appraisals in personnel systems came under judicial scrutiny during the 1970s. Title VII of the Civil Rights Act of 1964 forebade employment discrimination against individuals on the basis of race, color, religion, sex, or national origin. The scope of employment practices encompassed by Title VII has been expanded by court cases and EEOC rulings so that, today, performance appraisal is considered an employment practice if used for such determinations as salary levels, promotions, or transfers. The 1978 *Guidelines* of the EEOC focus attention upon inequitable personnel practices and outline validation requirements for personnel procedures when a protected class of the citizenry is adversely affected by such procedures.

Court cases thus far have not challenged an employer's performance appraisal system directly. Rather, the courts have considered issues dealing with significant components of appraisal systems. Thus far, federal courts have found Title VII violations in several employment practices related to performance appraisal, including transfers, promotions, compensation, layoffs, and training. More specifically, in *Brito* v. *Zia Co.* (1973), a federal appeals court accepted performance appraisals as "tests" and thereby subject to EEOC *Guidelines* on selection procedures (Klasson, Thompson, and Luben, 1980).

The EEOC's *Guidelines* require validation of performance appraisal procedures, however, only if evidence exists of an adverse impact on an individual or group protected under Title VII. This evidence can be either statistical (disparate rejection rates, population comparisons, etc.) or prima facie. Once adverse impact is shown, the employer must then substantiate the questioned practice or procedure (Luben, Thompson, and Klasson, 1980). The result is that the federal government has become increasingly involved with personnel policies and practices in both the private and public sectors.

Federal court decisions indicate that appraisal systems are subject to challenge by protected classes in such instances as when (Holley and Feild, 1975; Schneier, 1978):

1. The rating method cannot be shown to be job related or valid.
2. The content of the rating method has not been developed through job analysis.
3. Raters have not consistently observed the performance of those rated.
4. Ratings are based on raters' evaluations of subjective or vague factors.
5. Racial, sexual, or other biases have influenced ratings.
6. Ratings have not been collected and scored under standardized conditions.

A high potential exists, therefore, for legal challenges by individuals or groups in the coming years, should employee appraisal systems continue to be used as a basis for certain types of personnel decisions. Methods of appraisal susceptible to bias or inaccuracies are not likely to withstand judicial scrutiny.

Another contemporary pressure on appraisal systems comes from employee unions. Unions have voiced concern about appraisal systems that give arbitrary power to supervisors and that are subjective. In some instances, collective bargaining has even included negotiations over appraisal procedures. In two states, unions have won contracts that call for step increases without regard to an employee's appraisal results (Greiner et al., 1981: 223). Thus, as public employees continue to organize, more pressure is likely to be exerted on employee appraisal systems—pressure that will surely affect the uses and methods of appraisal.

Finally, the Civil Service Reform Act of 1978 placed employee performance appraisal in the position of being a cornerstone of federal civil service reform (Sugar, 1979). The act requires each federal agency to develop one or more appraisal systems to be used periodically to rate employees and encourages employee participation in setting performance objectives. Federal actions, therefore, are encouraging more participative management and collaboration between supervisors and subordinates. Since reforms at the federal level are often emulated at the state and local levels of government, one can foresee the diffusion of the philosophy and techniques adopted by federal agencies to subnational governments.

THE FUTURE OF APPRAISALS:
PROCESS IN SEARCH OF TECHNIQUE

As we have seen, a great many factors influence the successful use of employee performance appraisals. Moreover, as a management tool for personnel decision making, appraisals are coming under judicial scrutiny. The amount of material written about appraisals is voluminous, indicating a great deal of interest in the topic among practitioners and researchers. Based upon what we know, then, what does the future hold for performance appraisal? To answer this question, let us recall the elements of appraisal—method or technique, timing, evaluator, and factors evaluated—and examine each briefly.

There seems to be some consensus among a variety of observers that the process of performance appraisal may be more important than the mechanics, or technique, used (Lawler, 1979; Olsen and Bennett, 1975; Sokolik, 1967; Burke and Wilcox, 1969; Ball, 1978; Yager, 1981; Lazer, 1980; Kindall and Gatza, 1963; Meyer, Kay, and French, 1965). In fact, Olsen and Bennett (1976: 27) even go so far as to write, "Performance appraisal as a management technique is dead." While this may not reflect widespread opinion, this statement does indicate a direction of thought increasingly being expressed. The appraisal process is being recognized as a critical facet of appraisal systems. Although techniques are not likely to be discarded by management, more emphasis is being given to process issues. Sokolik (1967: 662) expresses what seems to be a common thread among many writers: "we see the formal appraisal machinery as evolving–changing as its prior use leads to development of greater 'appraisal' competence among . . . managers." Thus, appraisals should be used more selectively in the future.

As managers become more knowledgeable and skilled at appraising employees, they should reduce their use of the traditional rating systems that are so error prone and rely more upon mutual goal setting and open communication processes between supervisors and their employees. When justification is needed for various personnel actions, it should be provided separately from the appraisal process. In essence, what occurs with this shift of philosophy is that performance appraisal becomes "an interpersonal process that occurs regularly and frequently between supervisor and worker" (Yager, 1981: 129). Annual reviews may be conducted, but they simply reflect a summary of preceding appraisals. The process is supreme.

While many observers argue for the triumph of process over technique, the technique issue will remain with us in the future. The reason, of course, is that everyone is not in agreement concerning the role or emphasis upon techniques in appraisals. In addition, there are over 80,000 units of government in the United States and even more individual agencies. Obviously, these agencies differ in terms of their mission, employee characteristics, structure, management style, and legal environment, not to mention levels of professional administration. If appraisal systems should or do evolve over time to maximize their effectiveness, then different units of government will constantly be undergoing change in their process and technique of appraisal reflecting different stages of evolution or development.

Whether the method of appraisal emphasizes process or technique, an effective system of appraisal should be both reliable and valid (Lazer, 1980). The reliability of appraisals refers to the consistency of evaluations by an individual rater as well as between different raters and the freedom of evaluations from various forms of bias. Validity refers to the extent to which an appraisal evaluates important job factors, is job related, and reflects actual differences in performance. These two criteria are being applied increasingly to appraisal systems by the courts. As one would expect, some techniques are more susceptible to validity and reliability problems than are others. Hence, for practical reasons, as well as for philosophical ones, we may see shifts toward appraisal techniques that are participative and results oriented.

The observations provided about the methods of appraisal in the future imply changes also in the timing, selection, and role of the evaluator and the factors evaluated. Research has shown that the increased frequency of evaluation feedback leads to more effective appraisals (Ford and Jennings, 1977). Indeed, the ongoing appraisal concept implies regular evaluative feedback rather than an annual or semiannual appraisal session.

Traditional appraisal systems have selected the supervisor as the evaluator, and the appraisal interview has consisted mostly of the supervisor's informing an employee of his or her rating and pointing out deficiencies needing correction. While the immediate supervisor is still the person usually recommended to act as evaluator, observers also suggest that (1) additional evaluators be used where appropriate to provide other perspectives and check against error, (2) evaluators be trained adequately in appraisal techniques and processes, and (3) employees be encouraged to participate in the appraisal process as much as possible (Luben, Thompson, and Klasson, 1980; Lovrich et al., 1980; Beer, 1981). In addition, many observers suggest allowing employees to appraise themselves as a method of gaining insight and perspective on their jobs and performance. Research has shown that appraisals are more effective when the evaluator allows a high level of employee participation in the appraisal process, has a helpful and constructive attitude, attempts to solve job problems hampering the employee's performance, and sets mutual goals with the employee for the near future (Burke and Wilcox, 1969). The role of the supervisor should change to include additional attributes, such as being supportive, coordinating the employees' work with that of other groups, and encouraging participative decision making.

Finally, the factors evaluated by supervisors should, most observers say, be job related. Factors such as personality traits that do not affect the results produced by the employee should not be included in appraisals. The issues of validity and reliability have generally raised serious questions about factors being evaluated that are not job specific, observable, and measurable (Lazer, 1980).[2] The use of performance standards based upon employee job descriptions is frequently advocated for use in appraisals (Sashkin, 1981).

As we see, there seems to be more specific agreement about performance appraisal when we discuss its timing, the evaluator, and the factors that should be appraised. When we turn to methods, however, we find less specificity about particular methods, although considerable agreement does exist here as well. Some techniques are obviously more error prone than others, but generally any technique can be improved if one devotes the necessary time and skill to it (such as job analysis). Hence, we come back to the title selected for this chapter—"Process in Search of a Technique." There simply is no best technique. The appropriate technique in a particular setting will depend upon many factors, such as time available for appraisals, supervisory attitudes, top management's attitudes, employees' attitudes, types of jobs involved, numbers of employees, and on and on. The search for *a* technique, therefore, is illusive. Many will continue to search for *it*, of course, whereas others will argue that process is all important and techniques are irrelevant. This seems to be the immediate future of appraisal systems. On this, perhaps, most observers can agree.

NOTES

1. The discussion of techniques and obstacles to performance appraisal is revised from an earlier article by Hays and Tyer (1980).
2. For a positive view of traits in appraisals, see Kavanagh (1971).

REFERENCES

BALL, R. R. 1978. "What's the Answer to Performance Appraisal?" *The Personnel Administrator* 23 (July): 43–46.

BEER, M. 1981. "Performance Appraisal: Dilemmas and Possibilities." *Organizational Dynamics* 9 (Winter): 24–36.

Brito v. *Zia Co.* 1973. 48 F.2d 1200.

BUREAU OF NATIONAL AFFAIRS. 1975. *Employee Performance: Evaluation and Control.* Personnel Policies Forum Survey No. 108. Washington, D.C.: BNA.

BURKE, R. J. 1972. "Why Performance Appraisal Systems Fail." *Personnel Administration* 35 (May–June): 32–40.

BURKE, R. J. and L. J. KEMBALL. 1971. "Performance Appraisal: Some Issues in the Process." *Canadian Personnel and Industrial Relations Journal* 18 (November): 25–34.

BURKE, R. J. and D. S. WILCOX. 1969. "Characteristics of Effective Employee Performance Review and Development Interviews." *Personnel Psychology* 22: 291–305.

COLBY, J. D. and R. L. WALLACE. 1975. "Performance Appraisal: Help or Hindrance to Employee Productivity?" *The Personnel Administrator* 20 (October): 37–39.

CONANT, J. C. 1973. "The Performance Appraisal: A Critique and an Alternative." *Business Horizons* 16 (June): 73–78.

FEILD, H. S. and W. H. HOLLEY. 1975a. "Performance Appraisal—An Analysis of State-Wide Practices." *Public Personnel Management* 4 (May–June): 145–150.

——. 1975b. "Traits in Performance Ratings—Their Importance in Public Employment." *Public Personnel Management* 4 (September–October): 327–330.

FORD, R. C. and K. M. JENNINGS. 1977. "How to Make Performance Appraisals More Effective." *Personnel* 54 (March–April): 51–56.

GALLAGHER, M. C. 1978. "More Bias in Performance Evaluation." *Personnel* 55 (July–August): 35–40.

GARDNER, J. W. 1961. *Excellence: Can We Be Equal and Excellent Too?* New York: Harper & Row.

GENERAL ACCOUNTING OFFICE. 1978. *Federal Employee Performance Rating Systems Need Fundamental Changes.* Washington, D.C.: G.P.O.

GIBSON, J. L., J. M. IVANCEVICH, and J. H. DONNELLY. 1973. *Organizations: Structure, Processes, Behavior.* Dallas, Tex.: Business Publications.

GLUECK, W. F. 1978. *Personnel: A Diagnostic Approach.* Dallas, Tex.: Business Publications.

GREINER, J. M., H. P. HATRY, M. P. KOSS, A. P. MILLER, and J. P. WOODWARD. 1981. *Productivity and Motivation: A Review of State and Local Government Initiatives.* Washington, D.C.: The Urban Institute.

HAYS, S. W. and C. B. TYER. 1980. "Human Resource Management: The Missing Link." *International Journal of Public Administration* 2: 297–330.

HOLLEY, W. H. and H. S. FEILD. 1975. "Performance Appraisal and the Law." *Labor Law Journal* 26 (July): 423–430.

KAVANAGH, M. J. 1971. "The Content Issue in Performance Appraisal: A Review." *Personnel Psychology* 24: 653–668.

KELLY, P. R. 1958. "Reappraisal of Appraisals." *Harvard Business Review* 36 (May–June): 59–68.

KINDALL, A. F. and J. GATZA. 1963. "Positive Program for Performance Appraisal." *Harvard Business Review* 41 (November–December): 153–167.

KLASSON, C. R., D. E. THOMPSON, and G. L. LUBEN. 1980. "How Defensible Is Your Performance Appraisal System?" *The Personnel Administrator* 25 (December): 77–83.

LACHO, K. J., G. K. STEARNS, and M. F. VILLERE. 1979. "A Study of Employee Appraisal Systems of Major Cities in the United States." *Public Personnel Management* 8 (March–April): 111–125.

LANDY, F. J. and J. L. FARR. 1980. "Performance Rating." *Psychological Bulletin* 87: 72–107.

LATHAM, G. P., L. L. CUMMINGS, and T. R. MITCHELL. 1981. "Behavioral Strategies to Improve Productivity." *Organizational Dynamics* 9 (Winter): 4–23.

LAWLER, E. E. 1979. "Performance Appraisal and Merit Pay." *Civil Service Journal* 19 (April–June): 13–18.

LAZER, R. I. 1980. "Performance Appraisal: What Does the Future Hold?" *The Personnel Administrator* 25 (July): 69–73.

LOCHER, A. H. and K. S. TEEL. 1977. "Performance Appraisal–A Survey of Current Practices." *Personnel Journal* 56 (May): 245–254.

LOPEZ, F. M. 1968. *Evaluating Employee Performance.* Chicago: Public Personnel Association.

LOVRICH, N. P., Jr., R. H. HOPKINS, P. L. SHAFFER, and D. A. YALE. 1980. "Quasi-Experimental Pilot Study of a Participative Performance Appraisal System in Six Washington State Agencies: Effects upon Job Satisfaction, Agency Climate, and Work Values." Paper prepared for the 1980 Conference of the International Personnel Management Association Assessment Council, Boston, July 6–10.

LUBEN, G. L., D. E. THOMPSON, and C. R. KLASSON. 1980. "Performance Appraisal: The Legal Implications of Title VII." *Personnel* 53 (May–June): 11–21.

MCGREGOR, D. 1957. "An Uneasy Look at Performance Appraisal." *Harvard Business Review* 35 (May–June): 89–94.

MEYER, H. H., E. KAY, and J. R. P. FRENCH, Jr. 1965. "Split Roles in Performance Appraisal." *Harvard Business Review* 43 (January–February): 123–129.

OLSEN, L. O. and A. C. BENNETT. 1975. "Performance Appraisal: Management Technique or Social Process? Part I. Management Technique." *Management Review* 64 (December): 18–23.

——. 1976. "Performance Appraisal: Management Technique or Social Process? Part II. Social Process." *Management Review* 65 (January): 22–28.

PIZAM, A. 1975. "Social Differentiation–A New Psychological Barrier to Performance Appraisal." *Public Personnel Management* 4 (July–August): 244–247.

ROBBINS, S. P. 1978. *Personnel: The Management of Human Resources.* Englewood Cliffs, N.J.: Prentice-Hall.

ROGERS, R. T. 1975. "Performance Appraisals: Why Don't They Work Better?" *The GAO Review* (Fall): 73–81.

SASHKIN, M. 1981. "Appraising Performance: Ten Lessons from Research for Practice." *Organizational Dynamics* 9 (Winter): 37–50.

SCHNEIER, D. B. 1978. "The Impact of EEO Legislation on Performance Appraisals." *Personnel* 55 (July–August): 24–34.

SOKOLIK, S. L. 1967. "Guidelines in the Search for Effective Appraisals." *Personnel Journal* 46 (November): 660–668.

STAHL, O. G. 1976. *Public Personnel Administration.* 7th ed. New York: Harper & Row.

SUGAR, M. M., P. L. LEVINSON, and C. H. ANDERSON. 1979. "Performance Appraisal—Cornerstone of Civil Service Reform." *Civil Service Journal* 19 (April–June); 19–20.

THAYER, F. C. 1981. "Civil Service Reform and Performance Appraisal: A Policy Disaster." *Public Personnel Management* 10: (Special Symposium Issue) 20–28.

WASHINGTON LOCAL GOVERNMENT PERSONNEL INSTITUTE. 1979. *Evaluating Employee Performance: A Manual for Local Governments.* Seattle, Wash. WLGPI.

WHISLER, T. L. 1958. "Performance Appraisal and the Organization Man." *Journal of Business* 31: 19–27.

WINSTANLEY, N. B. 1980. "How Accurate Are Performance Appraisals?" *The Personnel Administrator* 25 (August): 55–58.

YAGER, E. 1981. "A Critique of Performance Appraisal Systems." *Personnel Journal* 60 (February): 129–133.

Ronald D. Sylvia
University of Oklahoma

CHAPTER NINE
AN ORGANIZATIONAL PERSPECTIVE ON TRAINING AND DEVELOPMENT IN THE PUBLIC SERVICE

Training and development are key elements in modern personnel systems. A commitment to training at all levels of government is expressed in public policy pronouncements and resource allocations. Perhaps no other human resource activity, moreover, impacts as directly upon the career advancement of organization actors. The training seminars in which the developing manager participates and the advanced degree that is awarded are as important to career advancement as are the responsibilities that are undertaken in an employment position. Finally, systematic training efforts have become part and parcel of strategies for organizational change and adaption.

The discussion that follows treats training as a value in public personnel management. Training models are then discussed in the context of organization size and resource availability. Various training activities are then described in the context of the macro function of the organization. Finally, some of the problems surrounding current training strategies are considered, and an alternative approach in which training is tied directly to organization needs and is integrated with other organization activities is offered.

Training, in the generic sense, has come to be an important activity of government that is valued by program managers as well as by personnelists. For example, federal programs of assistance to state and local governments carry with them requirements that the programs be operated within clearly defined limits. Achieving program compliance requires a good deal of intergovernmental communication that includes program-specific training activities. State vocational rehabilitation programs, for example, are required to ensure that at least one-half of their clients are severely handicapped. Meeting this requirement necessitates a shifting of organization resources because placement success traditionally meant large numbers of persons with relatively *minor* handicaps were placed. A 50 percent severely handicapped rule therefore will consume far more than 50 percent of agency resources. To minimize the impacts of the 50 percent rule, the federal government sponsors training workshops in program productivity and effective resource allocation. These conferences are conducted by several universities under the provision of the Rehabilitation Act of 1973. The act also provides for programs in general management and supervisory skills.

Federal funding of various categorical programs carries with it the requirement that state governments operate merit personnel systems for persons employed in these programs. The merit provision stems from the belief that the public is served best by modern personnel management systems that operate free from political influence. These requirements include a commitment of federal funds to pay for training. Congressional authorization for funding of training for state and local officials is provided under the Intergovernmental Personnel Act of 1970 (IPA) and by various specific program mandates. At this writing, however, the proposed budget for fiscal 1982 has no provision for IPA training programs. An elimination or significant cutback in federal funding will seriously affect the training activities of state and local governments whose budgets are already strained.

At the federal level, the Office of Personnel Management (OPM) operates a variety of training programs through its regional offices, including seminars in supervisory-managerial training, statistical methods, equal employment opportunity, and computer programming, to name just a few. The federal government also operates management training centers at Kingspoint, New York; Berkeley, California; and Oak Ridge, Tennessee. Executive development is provided by the Federal Executive Institute at Charlottesville, Virginia.

As extensive as OPM training is, many agencies also operate training programs aimed at their specialized needs. The U.S. Postal Service, for example, operates technical centers to train employees in the operation of various mail-handling technologies and the State Department offers specialized training to its foreign service officers. Some estimates suggest that as much as 70 percent of the training in the federal government is conducted within the agencies themselves (Lee, 1979: 181).

State and local governments also are committed to the development of their personnel. In addition to the training provided at federal government impetus, many subgovernment entities maintain in-house units that offer a variety of training. Such training sometimes consists of general-interest seminars for senior managers. Training varies according to resource availability and managerial preferences. Some organizations, however, take a further step and engage in systematic data gathering to identify training needs and to develop programs targeted at specific organizational needs (Verheyen and Olivas, 1980).

Unfortunately, not all organizations possess sufficient financial resources or staff size to warrant training units. Several other options are available for these organizations. Some agencies dispatch their personnel to the training seminars operated by the regional offices of OPM (Crouch, 1976). Alternatively, organizations may choose to enter into training consortiums that can vary the training context according to the size of the government unit and the complexity of its operations (Mowitz, 1974). Some local managers of small municipalities engage in independent programmed instruction that is carried out on the job (Crouch, 1976).

TUITION REIMBURSEMENT

Training in some state and local governments is left to the individual employee who selects his or her own course of study at a local college, university, or technical school. Organization participation consists of complete or partial reimbursement of the employee's educational expenses. These courses of study may or may not be carried out on the organization's time. Frequently, the employer will specify that the reimbursement will occur only for training that is job related. The definition of what is job related, however, may be construed so loosely as to permit employees to obtain advanced degrees that are not related directly to their jobs.

Critics of tuition reimbursement argue that such programs may be counterproductive because the participants who achieve advanced training may do so with the expectation that they will achieve promotions as a result. If promotions or other forms of rewards are not forthcoming, they may leave the organization. A second criticism of the programs involves the consumption of organization resources through employees studying on organization time and/or the utilization of organization clerical services to produce term papers, theses, and the like (Kaimen and Robey, 1976). A recent case study of a tuition reimbursement program, however, found that program participants, their supervisors, and co-workers rejected the notion of misuse of city resources. Program participants, moreover, experienced a significantly faster rate of promotion than did nonparticipants (Daley and Sylvia, 1981).

CONTINUING EDUCATION
AND THE PUBLIC SERVICE

The public service emphasis on training generally, and managerial training specifically, has resulted in a nationwide proliferation of advanced-degree programs in public administration. At present, the National Association of Schools of Public Affairs and Administration (NASPAA) has over two hundred member institutions (NASPAA, 1980).

Persons engaged in continuing education for the public sector debate the relative emphasis that such programs should place upon ethics and values, managerial skills, and holistic efforts at developing the complete individual (White, 1979). Masters of public administration programs located in political science departments tend to place an emphasis upon the environment in which public programs operate and the necessity for instilling a sense of public accountability in public servants. Programs located in schools of management or administration tend to place a greater emphasis upon management as a technology that is equally applicable in public and private organizations alike (McCurly, 1978). Some observers (Fisher, 1973; Denhart, 1979) argue that continuing education should shift away from the academic emphasis upon learning that is to be applied after graduation toward an emphasis upon student-centered learning that the practitioner student can apply immediately. Other observers (Wolf, 1979) argue that the on-the-job needs of the student and the preservation of a theoretical emphasis are not mutually exclusive and that an accommodation can be achieved between the two without sacrificing program content.

A recognition of the special needs of students pursuing a public service career has resulted in innovative program delivery systems that depart from the traditional semester. Both the University of Oklahoma and the University of Southern California operate programs on the intensive semester basis. The intensive semester format requires the student to engage in advanced preparation for seminars and utilizes lengthy contact hours in a condensed period and study by correspondence. These innovative delivery systems have made advanced study possible for persons who lack access to traditional university facilities.

THE PROFESSIONALIZATION
OF THE PUBLIC SERVICE

Government has traditionally been the principal employer of teachers and social workers. In recent decades, moreover, government at all levels also utilizes the services of doctors, lawyers, engineers, planners, and other professionals (Mosher, 1968). Unfortunately, the curricula of most professional schools place no emphasis upon the acquisition of supervisory and/or managerial skills, and they lack a public service orientation. As a result, government has found it necessary to supplement the training of many professionals to equip them with managerial skills and to resocialize them away from their professional frames of reference toward a broader organizational perspective (Bayton and Chapman, 1972).

Advanced training in public administration constitutes the newest form of professionalization in the public service. The problems associated with other professions in the public service, however, should be reduced greatly among public administration professionals because the curricula of public administration programs is specifically managerial. The National Association of Public Affairs and Administration guidelines, moreover, prescribe an emphasis upon the public sector context of decisions and stress ethics and accountability—an emphasis that is coterminous with agency values.

AN ORGANIZATIONAL
PERSPECTIVE ON
TYPES OF TRAINING

The reader by now may have the impression that training in the public sector, by and large, is concerned with the development of management skills. The rubric "training," however, currently encompasses a range of activities including training that is related directly to the delivery of services, training aimed at planned change in the organization, training that seeks to socialize employees to organization values, and training designed to manage conflict. Some of this training is as traditional as on-the-job interactions between the employee and the supervisor. A good deal of what is thought of as training involves innovations that are intended to impact upon the entire operation of the organization. Rather than listing and describing types of training, the discussion that follows organizes various training activities according to how they relate to the functioning of the organization.

All organizations from the nuclear family unit to the largest government agency can be analyzed using a functional framework. The following utilizes four macro or critical functions of the organization that were adapted from the work of Katz and Kahn (1966). The four functions are production, adaption, socialization, and coordination.

The *production* function refers to the principal activity of the organization.

In the case of General Motors, the production function might refer to the actual work of the assembly plant. In the case of the Social Security Administration, the production function is the delivery of social security, Medicaid, and Survivors Insurance benefits to eligible clientele. In the case of General Motors, production involves high technology and large capital investments in machinery and equipment. In the case of the Social Security Administration, the principal technology involves interaction among individuals, various work units, and agency clientele. In both organizations, new employees must learn the content of their positions through training. Such training involves the acquisition of specific job skills and an orientation to the rules and procedures of the organization.

The delivery system of skills and orientation training frequently involves the line supervisor and/or peers in the work group. Many organizations, unfortunately, do not recognize that this one-on-one format constitutes the principal training activity of the organization. As a consequence, the organization assumes that the supervisor possesses the interpersonal and communication skills necessary to impart the required knowledge. Organizations should evaluate their commitment to the training of the trainers in whom the organization entrusts its most critical training activity. Only through systematic training of supervisors can the organization be certain that proper operation of organization technology will be taught to new employees and that organization rules and regulations will be internalized.

Skills training for managers and supervisors receives a greater emphasis in government agencies than does the training of rank-and-file employees. Skills training for supervisors involves working through and with others rather than doing it oneself. Skills training for managers may also involve budgeting, planning, quantitative data-based decision making, and other activities. Frequently, however, organizations partake of such training irregularly in response to announcements from external training sources such as the OPM regional offices or private vendors. Determining the impact of such training is difficult, although managers intuitively believe it to be beneficial.

Training relevant to the production function in government, by and large, is conducted on the job by supervisors of members of the work group. An emphasis, therefore, should be given to developing the training skills of supervisors. Training aimed at developing the job skills of current and potential managers has been the focus of many government training programs. Unfortunately, the systematic utilization of such programs by individual agencies has been limited by a scarcity of resources.

Adaption refers to organization effort to deal effectively with changing demands from the organizational environment. Adaption is particularly important for public organizations that have accountability to external forces mandated in their legislative authorization. For example, at the federal level, an agency is accountable to the Congress, the president, and the congressional and presidential auditing agencies—which are, respectively, the General Accounting Office and the Office of Management and Budget. In addition, agencies must deal with other agencies engaged in related activities, private competitors, and organized groups that consume the services of the agency (Nigro and Nigro, 1976). Legislative changes in social policy and/or the organization of auxiliary agencies that provide services to line agencies may also require systematic adaption efforts. A case in point is the 1978 Civil Service Reform Act, which divided the functions of the old Civil Service Commission among new and existing agencies and caused agencies to make several adaptions.

The personnel functions of the old commission are now performed by the Office of Personnel Management. The merit protection function was assumed by a newly created Merit Systems Protection Board. Equal employment opportunity enforcement was moved from the managerial-oriented commission to the advocacy-oriented Equal Employment Opportunity Commission. The act also created a Federal Labor Relations Authority for the administration of collective bargaining between federal agencies and public employee unions. Collective bargaining formerly existed by executive order. Each of these administrative entities generates rules and regulations with which line agencies must comply. Preparing line managers and staff units for dealing with these external actors required a good deal of activity to formulate agency policies and to orient personnel as to policy. Normally, much of this activity is organized and implemented by training units.

Two additional provisions of the act impact directly upon the internal operation of the agencies. First, the act calls for the creation of a Senior Executive Service (SES) comprised of those positions that were formerly General Service (GS) grades 16-18. These executives are to be responsible for the development and implementation of public policy. Their rewards will depend on their performance relative to their peers. Agencies that do not already have such training activities should initiate systematic programs for the development of superior employees in anticipation of their advancement into the executive ranks.

The second impact upon internal operations of agencies is the provision that requires the salary increments of GS 13-15 supervisors to be based upon objective performance appraisal systems. Developing such systems constitutes major organizational adaptions involving training supervisors and subordinates in the effective use of a new reward system. Again, most likely, the responsibility for coordinating the development of the new system and conducting the orientation sessions will fall to the training units of the agencies. However, if the new systems are developed arbitrarily at the top and imposed upon the organization, they may be disruptive of management styles or "systems" that are currently operating in a satisfactory manner, such as management by objectives. Interfacing the old and the new systems may involve considerable orientation and training aimed at conflict resolution (Sylvia, 1980).

Organization adaptions do not occur solely in reaction to mandates from the environment. The fact is that a growing number of organizations in the public and private sectors engage in systematic assessments of themselves and their environments to achieve organizational goals more effectively. These self-assessments produce strategies for planned changes in the organization that can be categorized broadly under the heading of "organizational development" (OD). OD can be defined as change that is "1. planned, 2. organization-wide, and 3. managed from the top to 4. increase organization effectiveness and health through 5. planned interventions in the organizations 'process' using behavioral science knowledge" (Beckhard, 1969: 9).

Traditionally, OD is conducted with the assistance of an external change agent drawn from the ranks of university faculties or private consulting companies. Recently, public agencies have developed their own organizational development units that act as change agents. Persons assigned to these units generally act only as consultants to line managers and as trainers in team-building and conflict resolution programs. They do not perform line management duties. Perhaps the most ambitious OD effort in government is operated by the U.S. Army. The Army has trained a number of career officers who assist line managers in the latters' efforts to upgrade and improve unit effectiveness (Schaum, 1978). Smaller units of government continue to rely upon external consultants because organizational resources are inadequate to sustain permanent units (Bell and Rosenweig, 1978).

A number of approaches are associated with the term "OD." These include the managerial grid (Blake and Mouton, 1964), which is used as an analytical technique for defining organizational climate as a prelude to systematic change efforts. Bennis (1969) is associated with the notion of planned change in organizations by means of systematic assessments of the organization's resources and actors in the environment. This assessment process is a prelude to specific strategies for change. Finally, team-building exercises aimed at building a consensus among organization actors are frequently a part of OD strategies (McGregor, 1976).

Planning exercises, grid analysis of the organization, and line managers place a great deal of emphasis upon defining where they are and where they wish to go to the neglect of how they will go about getting there. The transition phase in which new operating procedures are put in place requires carefully planned task assignments and a clear delineation of the supports that various units are to contribute to the effort (Beckhard and Harris, 1977). Neglecting the management of the change process can doom the best laid plan to failure.

Organization adaptions also may involve the development of new technologies for program delivery that require skills training and other adaptions. Suppose, for example, that a state welfare agency decided that payments to families with dependent children would no longer be made by county offices because payments could be made more efficiently and with a reduction in fraud if they were distributed by one centrally located computer. Efficiency would result because the computerized process would require fewer employees. Fraud could be reduced by programming the computer to cross-check the addresses and social security numbers of recipients. Changing from the decentralized manual system to the centralized computer-based system would require significant adaptions in agency operating procedures, interfaces between the central office and county offices, and the teaching of new skills that were not available previously in the organization.

Training associated with adaption may be imposed upon the organization by actions in the environment. With growing frequency, however, training is necessary to support planned change efforts generated from within the organization with or without the assistance of external change agents. Finally, training is frequently necessary to facilitate the transition to the use of new technologies. In all cases, however, as much emphasis should be placed upon managing the transition process as is currently placed upon the design of changes.

Organizations also engage in training aimed at shaping the attitudes and perceptions of organization members. New members may enter the organization with no preconceived notions about the proper functions of government bureaucracies. New members also may enter with a set of reference points acquired in their professional training. Alternatively, persons may enter the organization with attitudes and reference points developed in other organizations. Internally, persons may be promoted into positions of supervision or management that require a different set of reference points than are required of professionals engaged in program delivery.

Organizations may engage in extensive orientation programs designed to impart organization rules and the value perspectives of the organization to the new employee before he or she assumes regular duties and responsibilities. The most intensive form of this type of socialization training is mixed with basic skills training by the military service that operates induction facilities for recruits. In the case of commissioned officers, each branch of the services operates an academy in which an academic curriculum is combined with a military life-style designed to perform the socialization function (Donnbush, 1955). The academies are supplemented by Reserve Officer Training Corps programs (ROTC), which provide military training within the context of the general university.

Civilian organizations that utilize professionally trained employees (social workers, teachers, rehabilitation counselors, masters of public administration, etc.) would do well to borrow a leaf from the military's ROTC book. All too frequently, professionally trained recruits enter the bureaucracy with unrealistic expectations regarding work loads and resource availability. Public managers at all levels of government can ease this cultural shock by becoming involved with university faculties in the design of curricula and by providing the opportunity for students to gain practical experience as part of their training. The latter occurs, to some degree, in internship programs and student teaching assignments. Unfortunately, this real-world experience, where it exists, occurs rather late in the educational experience, after professional expectations are well formed in the minds of students.

Frequently, socialization of new employees occurs on the job concurrently with job skills training. The socialization agents are supervisors and peers. More systematic socialization training is necessary to ensure that new employees are exposed to organization values. Some mix of on-the-job skills training and systematic socialization training, moreover, is within the resource availability of most organizations.

Systematic socialization is particularly important for persons whose previous experience was in private industry. Private organizations emphasize productivity, market share, and profit margins. Government agencies frequently engage in continuing service activities, the productivity of which is difficult to quantify. Market position is generally irrelevant as an agency reference point. Finally, profit also is irrelevant in government, where the emphasis is more likely to be upon efficiency and effectiveness. Socialization in government, therefore, should emphasize a client service orientation and the necessity of maintaining the highest personal and professional standards in one's work. Finally, the socialization of government employees should focus upon accountability to elected officials and an overall public service orientation.

Socialization of employees who are promoted is important as well because, along with the necessity for new skills, a new supervisor or manager must undergo a change of perspective. Many managerial development programs seek to supplement decision-making and problem-solving training with socialization aimed at inculcating the trainee with a human relations perspective on the role of the manager.

A human relations perspective postulates that individuals can and will accept responsibilities, are capable of and seek to engage in independent thought, and, as employees, can and will internalize organization goals as their own (McGregor, 1960). In organizations that are human relations oriented, supervisors and managers must be willing to delegate authority as well as responsibility, be willing to share decision making, and be committed to the nurturing and development of their subordinates.

Obviously, many people are not innately capable of accepting the uncertainty that accompanies delegation and shared decision making. Supervisors and managers, engaged in the press of day-to-day activities, may not see the intrinsic value in nurturing and developing subordinates or close cooperation with other work units. Ideally, management development programs in government would place a coequal emphasis upon the human relations perspective and decision making.

The upper-level development programs of the federal government seek to blend attitudinal socialization with managerial skills training. This is particularly true of the Federal Executive Institute, where the emphasis of the curriculum is upon the development of the complete individual based upon his or her self-assessment.

Unfortunately, at other echelons of the federal government and at the state and local levels, resource limitations and the diversity of agencies make the systematic development of managers difficult, if not impossible.

Some training, on the other hand, specifically focuses upon the development of the manager as a person in the belief that, if he or she can be made a healthier personality, then there will be a direct benefit to the organization. The T group (T stands for training) is an example of such training (Golembiewski, 1967). The T group usually involves sending the manager to a site away from the organization where he or she interacts with persons from other organizations about their own behavior and about the nature of group processes. Ideally, the participants learn to interact in an open, straightforward fashion without depending upon symbols of power or the manipulation of others.

Critics of T group training point out that, when such training occurs detached from the organization, only the participants acquire the ability to respond openly and spontaneously. The organization continues to operate in its traditional fashion. The returning participant (unless in a position of power to impose the new perspective on the organization) will suffer culture shock and/or find it necessary to reconstruct his or her own defenses to survive. T group training is more effective when integrated into a long-term effort at systematic interventions using the OD planned change model (Beckhard, 1965).

The macro function of socialization accounts for a significant portion of both planned and de facto government training activities, even though it may not be so recognized. The initiation of new members and the resocialization of supervisors and managers are critically important to the efficiency and general health of the organization. Consequently, top management should decide upon the managerial perspective and value positions that the organization will endorse. The organization should then engage in systematic programs that socialize members to the organization's perspective.

Socialization training may involve inculcating new employees with the values and norms of the organization, converting managers to a human relations perspective in their management styles, or training aimed at making managers healthier personalities. Whether formal and systematic or informal, socialization occurs in all organizations. With the exception of the military services, however, few agencies engage in unabashed efforts at a wholesale reshaping of employees' values and attitudes to the perspective preferred by the organization. The need for socialization training, however, should be recognized and dealt with systematically at least insofar as efficiency, accountability, and a public service orientation are concerned.

Coordination is generally thought of as a principal activity of management. Most modern bureaucracies are complex organizations characterized by a high degree of task differentiation and subunit loyalty (Weber, 1974). Because mission complexity dictates a division of labor, there is a high probability that the goals of subunits will displace the macro goals of the organization in the minds of subunit members, which may result in conflicts among task groups.

Interunit conflict frequently occurs when staff units, such as personnel or accounting, impose time demands on line managers. Personnel, for example, may demand significant amounts of the line manager's time to assure compliance with equal employment opportunity requirements. The personnelist may perceive these requirements as legitimate and necessary to meet external requirements. The line managers may perceive these demands as unwarranted consumptions of time and energy that should be channeled into the achievement of the agency's mission.

A common solution to such problems is to bring in an outside consultant to analyze the problem and suggest solutions. The solutions that the consultant might prescribe involve activities aimed at reasserting the macro goals of the organization and achieving a commitment to them among the various subunits of the organization. The specific interventions involve conflict management, which is designed to improve intergroup processes by making the various units aware of the mission and time perspectives of the other interdependent units (Lawrence and Lorsch, 1967).

The importance of work unit coordination also is reflected in the skills training that is emphasized in various government training programs. Such programs emphasize shared decision-making models, technologies such as matrix management, operations research, and planning—all of which emphasize the necessity of coordination among work units.

MAKING TRAINING WORK

Training is expensive. The cost of training can be computed by summing the actual costs of training programs in direct outlays with the lost time to the organization that results from participant absences. The benefits of training are more difficult to calculate, particularly when one is attempting to assess the aggregate value of all the available training. Proponents of training intuitively believe that the Intergovernmental Personnel Act has been beneficial, and they can point to examples of individual program successes. Direct and consistent improvements in state and local government that have resulted from the expenditure of training funds, however, are virtually impossible to demonstrate.

Critics also have questioned the benefits of various types of training at the organization level. Some advocates of change in government programs, for instance, argue in part that educational training has little impact upon agencies because of the individual focus of such programs, the delivery of such programs outside the organizational context, and the fact that these programs reinforce existing structures (Greg and Van Maaner, 1973). At the federal level, critics decry the lack of career development programs that would initiate the development of promising individuals early in their careers. The critics also argue that federal training programs should place a greater emphasis upon presenting a diversity of opinion rather than only presenting noncontroversial views (Wynia, 1972).

The bureaucratic structure of organizations also is seen as an impediment to training effectiveness. Critics cite rigid classification systems, the fact that reward systems are not tied to the acquisition of skills or to the development of subordinates, an overemphasis upon technical rather than managerial qualifications for advancement, and pension systems that discourage the movement of uniformed personnel into general management positions (Heisel, 1980).

The charge that training efforts have not lived up to their advanced billing applies equally to organizational development efforts aimed at self-analysis and modifications in organization culture. Unfortunately, funding limitations and/or a lack of executive commitment have often precluded the creation of ongoing training programs to implement the desired changes. Other organizations that dispatch "available" personnel to training seminars that may or may not be related directly to the needs of the organization may also experience limited organizational benefits.

Many of the foregoing problems can be dealt with if the leadership of the organization is willing to fund training programs that are based upon careful self-analysis of the organization's goals and are integrated with other management systems. The first step is for management to decide where the organization is and where the organization is likely to be in the foreseeable future. The organization should then decide upon the appropriate mix of technical, clerical, and managerial skills necessary to achieve the desired ends. Only then should the organization turn its attention to the design of training programs. Resource limitations, of course, may necessitate ordering the priorities of training plans.

Training and development programs should also be integrated into the operating procedures of the organization. One promising integrated approach involves the utilization of on-the-job training (OJT) for managers and executives (Wolf and Sherwood, 1981). Traditionally, OJT has been associated with trainees at lower levels of the organization. OJT, however, can be an effective tool for the development of newly appointed or promoted managers and executives. Such a program could utilize senior-level managers and/or retired executives in a program of coaching new managers and executives. Such an OJT program could be particularly effective in easing the transition of the manager and/or executive into his or her new role. The coach would also help the trainee to identify skill deficiencies and assist the trainees with the development of problem-solving skills.

An integrated program of manager-executive development has several advantages. First, the focus is upon the training needs of the individual—as they relate to the organization. Second, trainer-trainee contact can be ongoing and as intense as necessary. Third, there is no requirement for outright expenditures of resources. Such a program of OJT, however, could provide the framework for a rational determination of training needs.

Whether or not the organization utilizes the OJT model, an integrated approach requires that the organization somehow identify the ideal skill mix necessary for successful performance in a given position. The incumbent in the position is then assessed with regard to the skills that he or she actually possesses. An individualized training program can then be designed to develop and prepare the incumbent for advancement to higher echelons (Mealiea and Duffy, 1980).

Training and development programs should also be integrated with other managerial systems, such as making subordinate development a criterion in the performance appraisals of managers. In addition, organizations should develop career paths for these lower-echelon employees who are willing to acquire skills needed by the organization. Career paths allow employees to plan their professional careers rationally without developing unrealistic expectations of the organization. Concommitantly, organizations should make the acquisition of specified training a prerequisite to advancement to upper levels of the organization.

CONCLUSION

Training and development are integral parts of modern personnel systems. The decade of the 1970s saw a proliferation of alternative training programs competing actively for public sector dollars. The proliferation was due partially to management recognition of the benefits of training and partially to the availability of federal funding to pay for the training. The 1970s also witnessed a nationwide growth of graduate programs in public administration.

The types of training models found currently in the public sector include comprehensive in-house operations, programs in which small entities pool their resources in training consortiums to meet their common needs, and organizations that send representatives to external training programs on an ad hoc basis. Finally, training in some organizations consists of tuition assistance programs.

The term "training" has come to symbolize a variety of activities that include the acquisition of technical and managerial problem-solving skills. Other activities that fall under the heading of training include organization adaptions to demands from the environment, activities that are systematic efforts at long-range change, and activities aimed at problem solving, team building, or conflict management.

Although training has become a value internalized in the minds of many managers, some observers have begun to question the efficacy of some types of training for meeting the needs of individual organizations. Recently, however, a number of alternative training models have been proposed involving systematic planning, a utilization of on-the-job training, and an integration of the training function with other organizational systems.

The benefits of training per se are generally accepted; however, as is true for all organizational activities, training can succeed best when approached in a systematic fashion. The ad hoc dispatching of "available" personnel to external training programs as funding is available will generally result in a consumption of the available funding. Benefits to the organization under such an approach, at best, will be accidental. The current era of cutback management, moreover, demands that all organization activities, including training, be retained on the basis of their essentiality and relative effectiveness vis-à-vis other programs (Lewis and Logalbo, 1980). Only systematically planned and implemented training programs can hope to survive the scrutiny of cutback management.

REFERENCES

BAYTON, J. A. and R. L. CHAPMAN. 1972. *Transformation of Scientists and Engineers into Managers*. Sp. 291. Washington, D.C.: NASA.

BECKHARD, R. 1965. "The Appropriate Use of T Groups in Organization." In B. Blackwell, ed., *ATN Occasional Papers*. #2. *T-Group Training: Group Dynamics in Management Education*. New York: Oxford University Press.

——. 1969. *Organization Development: Strategies and Models*. Reading, Mass.: Addison-Wesley.

BECKHARD, R. and R. J. HARRIS. 1977. *Organizational Transition: Managing Complex Change*. Reading, Mass.: Addison-Wesley.

BELL, C. H. and J. E. ROSENZWEIG. 1978. "O.D. in the City: A Potpourri of Pluses and Minuses." *Southern Review of Public Administration* 2 (March): 439–448.

BENNIS, W. G. 1969. *Organization Development: Its Nature, Origins and Prospects*. Reading, Mass.: Addison-Wesley.

BLAKE, R. R. and J. S. MOUTON. 1964. *The Managerial Grid.* Houston: Gulf.

CROUCH, W. 1976. *Local Government Personnel Administration.* Washington, D.C.: International City Management Association.

DALEY, H. and R. SYLVIA. 1981. "A Quasi-Experimental Evaluation of Tuition Reimbursement." *Review of Public Personnel Administration* 1 (Spring): 13–22.

DENHARDT, R. B. 1979. "On the Management of Public Service Education." *Southern Review of Public Administration* 3 (December): 273–283.

DONNBUSH, S. 1955. "The Military Academy as an Assimilation Institution." *Social Forces* 33: 316–321.

FISCHER, F. 1973. "Give a Damn About Continuing Adult Education in Public Administration." *Public Administration Review* 33 (Sept/Oct): 488–498.

GOLEMBIEWSKI, R. 1967. "The Laboratory Approach to Organizational Development." *Public Administration Review* 27 (May/June): 215–217.

GREGG, R. and J. VAN MAANER. 1973. "The Realities of Education as a Prescription for Organizational Change." *Public Administration Review* 33 (Nov/Dec): 522–533.

HEISEL, W. D. 1980. "A Non-Bureaucratic View of Management Development." *Public Personnel Management* 9 (March/April): 95–98.

HOWARD, L. L. 1973. "Executive Development: An Intergovernmental Perspective." *Public Administration Review* 33 (Jan/Feb): 101–110.

KAIMEN, R. and D. ROBEY. 1976. "Tuition Refund Asset or Liability." *Personnel Journal* 55 (August): 389–399.

KATZ, D. and R. KAHN. 1966. *The Social Psychology of Organizations.* New York: John Wiley.

LAWRENCE, P. R. and J. W. LORSCH. 1967. *New Direction for Organizations.* Boston: Graduate School of Business Administration, Harvard University.

LEE, R. 1979. *Public Personnel Systems.* Baltimore: University Park Press.

LEWIS, C. and A. LOGALBO. 1980. "Cutback Principles and Practices: A Checklist for Managers." *Public Administration Review* 40 (March/April): 184–188.

MC CURLEY, H. E. 1978. "Selecting and Training Public Managers: Business Skills vs. Public Administration." *Public Administration Review* 38 (Nov/Dec): 571–578.

MC GREGOR, D. 1960. *The Human Side of Enterprise.* New York: McGraw-Hill.

——. 1976. *The Professional Manager.* New York: McGraw-Hill.

MEALIEA, L. W. and J. F. DUFFY. 1980. "An Integrated Model for Training and Development: How to Build on What You Have Already." *Public Personnel Management* 9 (4): 336–343.

MOSHER, F. 1968. *Democracy and the Public Service.* New York: Oxford University Press.

MOWITZ, R. 1974. "Training Model for State and Local Governmental Personnel." *Public Personnel Management* 3 (Nov/Dec): 451–453.

NATIONAL ASSOCIATION OF SCHOOLS OF PUBLIC AFFAIRS AND ADMINISTRATION. 1980. *Directory of Programs in Public Affairs and Administration.* Washington, D.C.: NASPAA.

NIGRO, F. and L. NIGRO. 1976. *The New Public Personnel Administration.* Itasca, Ill.: F. E. Peacock.

SCHAUM, F. L. 1978. "The Strategy and Practical Realities of O.D. in the U.S. Army." *Southern Review of Public Administration* 1 (March): 449–462.

SYLVIA, R. 1980. "Some Potential Impacts of the Actor Reforms upon Agencies with MBO Systems." *The Bureaucrat* 9 (Summer): 48–52.

VERHEYEN, L. and L. OLIVAS. 1980. "Attitude Survey Supports Training Needs." *Public Personnel Management* 9: 31–35.

WEBER, M. 1974. *The Theory of Social and Economic Organizations.* New York: Oxford University Press.

WHITE, O., ed. 1979. "Symposium: Towards a Grounded Approval to Public Administration Education." *Southern Review of Public Administration* 3 (Dec): 244–308.

WOLF, J. F. and F. SHERWOOD. 1981. "Coaching: Supporting Public Executives on the Job." *Public Administration Review* 41 (Jan/Feb): 73–76.

WOLF, L. A. 1979. "In Defense of the Ivory Tower." *Southern Review of Public Administration* 3 (Dec): 264–272.

WYNIA, B. 1972. "Executive Development in the Federal Government." *Public Administration Review* 32 (May/June): 316.

Michael S. March

University of Colorado at Denver

CHAPTER TEN
RETIREMENT BENEFITS FOR PUBLIC EMPLOYEES

Retirement benefits are an important instrument of personnel policy in public agencies and constitute an increasingly large and expensive portion of public personnel costs. Retirement plans cover age or service retirement benefits and, in more and more systems, disability retirement and survivorship payments in the event that the employee dies in service or after retirement. Pensions are important for government purposes and for the welfare of public servants. However, because of their deferred or contingent nature, complex provisions, and the necessity for funding retirement and related benefits for many decades ahead according to complex actuarial methods using uncertain assumptions, many public employee pension systems in the United States have been fraught with financial, structural, and administrative problems (March, 1980b).[1]

DEVELOPMENT AND PURPOSES

History of Public Employee Retirement Systems in the United States

It is not commonly realized, but pensions for public personnel in the United States were first enacted for disabled veterans of the Revolutionary War. Indeed, payments from the general funds of the Treasury have been enacted for the veterans and dependents of veterans of every American war—and still continue to be a multibillion-dollar expenditure in the U.S. budget. Veterans' "pensions" for those not disabled in the service, and disability and death "compensation" for those disabled or deceased from service causes, have been provided largely to meet the claims of "citizen soldiers." They are not commonly discussed under the topic of "retirement," although they are an alternative to military retirement pay.

"Staff retirement" benefits for "regular" military personnel were the first true "retirement" provisions to be provided in the United States. Congress in 1855 enacted retirement benefits for unfit or overage Naval officers and extended such benefits to regular Army officers in 1861. Municipal disability pensions for police, another "dangerous" occupation, were enacted first in 1857, and retirement benefits were provided first in 1878. The early civil retirement plans were special plans for police, firefighters, and teachers. Gradually public pension systems spread and covered more occupations, but until the 1920s they were undercut by funding insufficiencies. In 1920 a major step toward adequate funding was taken with the enactment of the *contributory* Civil Service Retirement Act for federal civilian employees, who then totaled 691,000 (Reticker, 1941).

By 1950 there were nearly 9.3 million workers and retirees under private plans and 4.7 million civilian government personnel covered by pension arrangements, including nearly 2.9 million state and local employees. In 1966 about 29.5 million workers and retirees were in private plans; 10 million were in public sector plans, including 6.9 million state and local government workers and retirees (Institute of Life Insurance, 1969). Comparisons with employment data indicate that from 1930 to 1966 the proportion of active federal civilian employees covered by staff retirement systems rose from about 75 percent of the work force in 1930 to approximately 90 percent in 1966. The ratio of state and local active employees rose from around 30 percent to over 70 percent (*Economic Report of the President*, 1981; Munnell and Connolly, 1979).[2]

Once underway, both the military and civilian federal retirement systems were liberalized through numerous amendments and occasional substantial revisions. By the mid-1930s the military system had become by far the most liberal retirement plan in the country for a large group of personnel. It provided retirement after thirty years of service at any age with compensation equal to 75 percent of active-duty pay. Following World War II, retirement on half pay was provided at any age after only twenty years of service (U.S. Department of Defense, 1976).

Survivors' benefits for the uniformed services were also enacted in 1953, revised in 1961, and improved greatly in 1972. (Substantial survivors benefits also have long been provided under separate veterans' laws.) Moreover, military service, which had been credited on a partial basis under social security during World War II and subsequent war periods, was covered fully after 1956—thereby giving military personnel two sets of retirement benefits without any offsets.[3] In 1965 cost-of-living adjustments were enacted for military retirees.

The Civil Service Retirement Act program for civilian federal personnel was also improved. Election of a reduced annuity to provide a joint survivorship annuity was authorized in 1939. In 1942 the act was extended to virtually all officers and employees not otherwise covered. Compulsory retirement was required at age 70 after fifteen years of service; voluntary retirement permitted at age 60 after thirty years of service, or at age 62 with fifteen years; and at age 55 optional retirement on a reduced annuity was allowed after thirty years of service. The reduction was eliminated in 1966 (P.L. 89–504), thereby permitting optional retirement at age 55 after thirty years of service and adding a provision for full retirement at age 60 with twenty years' service.

In 1956 the computation formula was liberalized. Also, immediate reduced annuities were authorized for involuntary separation after age 50 with twenty years of service. In 1973 this was permitted at any age after fifteen years of service.

In 1962 a permanent arrangement for adjusting annuities in keeping with cost-of-living index increases was authorized—the first for any retirement program. The wage base computation formula for annuities was revised in 1969 from a high-five-year to a high-three-year average. However, unlike military personnel, federal civilian workers were not covered under social security, except to the extent that they acquired such coverage through part-time employment or during breaks in their federal careers.

State and local governments also continued to adopt new plans and to improve existing employee retirement systems. For 1966-67 the *1967 Census of Governments* reported 2,165 plans covering 6.5 million contributors and possessing

$39.3 billion in assets—up from $1.9 billion in 1942. The *1977 Census of Government* for 1976-77 found 3,075 state and local government retirement systems with 9.7 million active members and owning $12.3 billion in assets.[4]

During the years 1942 to 1976-77 the proportion of employees covered by general-coverage state and local staff retirement systems (as opposed to special-purpose plans for teachers, police, firefighters) increased from 38 percent to 62 percent, reflecting greater uniformity in benefits within jurisdictions. The Census reports also showed that about 50 percent of the employees in the state and local systems in 1957 were covered by social security for all or part of their members. By 1976-77 the proportion had risen to 62 percent.[5]

Growth of Benefit Outlays

On the benefit payments front, public employee pension systems developed slowly, but in the last decade they have become real budget-busters for federal, state, and local governments.

The growth in expenditures escalates as retirement groups mature, beneficiaries accumulate on the rolls, benefit rates and retirement standards are liberalized, and inflation boosts benefits in plans in which annuities are geared to final pay (or averages of the three or five highest years) and/or include benefit escalators for retirees based on the cost-of-living index. A rule of thumb for approximating the "doubling time" for a benefit roll is to divide 70 by the annual rate of increase (e.g., a 10 percent rate of increase means that the level of expenditures will *double* in approximately seven years).

By fiscal 1950 expenditures for federal retirement systems totaled $508 million, of which $325 million was for military retirement. In 1965-66 the federal total had increased to $3.2 billion, including $1.6 billion for military retirement. State and local retirement payments rose from $300 million in fiscal 1949-50 to an estimated $1.87 billion in 1966-67 (U.S. Department of Health, Education and Welfare, 1968).[6]

The federal civil service retirement system in fiscal 1970 paid approximately $2.5 billion to 962,000 annuitants. By 1980 the outlays had reached $14.5 billion to 1.73 million annuitants. The system had 2.72 million active employees in that year. There were a number of small, special retirement systems not included in these large totals. Likewise, U.S. Department of Labor workmen's compensation benefits for on-job disabilities and social security payments are not included.

Data from the decennial *Census of Governments* show that state and local systems paid annuities of $2.1 billion for 1.03 million beneficiaries in 1966-67. These increased to $8.5 billion for 2.27 million beneficiaries in 1976-77. In addition, there were refunds of contributions of $1.1 billion and "other" payments of $208 million, including lump-sum payments to survivors.

In all, by 1980 the federal military and civilian staff retirement systems and the state and local systems together were paying about $39 billion in annuities to 6 million retirees and survivors.[7]

Rationales for Pensions and Survivorship Benefits

It is clear from the history of retirement systems in the United States that the "hazardous" occupations—military service, policing, firefighting—were the first to achieve pensions. And disability pensions were the first to be provided. In these occupations, provision of retirement was a means of eliminating superannuated employees to help maintain an able and efficient work force. This philosophic justification was also used for both military and U.S. civil service retirement benefits. Conversely, the holding out of attractive deferred retirement benefits was used as a tool for retention of experienced, able personnel whom the employer wanted and needed to keep for effective operations. These personnel policy objectives have long been a core rationale for pension systems.

A related theme found in the early literature on pensions is that pensions are warranted as rewards for long and faithful service. This concept recognizes the moral obligation of the employer to provide support in old age to the worker who served long and conscientiously (Harbrecht and Harbrecht, 1959; McGill, 1965).

The *deferred wage theory* emerged in the 1940s and 1950s, largely as a practical way to sidestep wage controls by providing deferred compensation in the form of pensions. In the 1970s and 1980s, the deferral of compensation through pensions to be paid after retirement reduces pay and marginal tax rates, thereby finding favor as a means of tax deferral and avoidance. With the emergence of "supply-side" economics and adoption of this economic theory by the Reagan administration, additional emphasis has been placed on tax and other incentives to stimulate savings for retirement and, it is hoped, to increase investment.[8]

After the broad social insurance program under the Social Security Act of 1935 began to demonstrate its central importance in the U.S. economic security system (and the public began to see the advantages of systematic social insurance for retirement, disability, and survivorship), the *economic security* rationale was increasingly adopted by many staff pension systems. Plans that began with a heavy or sole focus on age retirement increasingly added provisions covering disability among younger workers and benefits for the surviving widows and minor children of deceased workers. This was especially essential for groups that were excluded from social security protection. Such staff plans added basic welfare benefits to protect the disabled, the survivors, and even the shorter-service or low-wage employees.

Other rationales include (1) the early concept of *human depreciation* (a counterpart of depreciation of productive physical assets) and (2) the *wage replacement* concept, which appears to be embodied in the calculations of benefit adequacy adopted by the recent President's Commission on Pension Policy (Melone and Allen, 1966; Carlson, 1962; President's Committee on Corporate Pension Funds, 1965).[9]

RECENT STATUS OF PUBLIC EMPLOYEE PLANS

Overview

Retirement plans for public personnel have a potential universe of 18 percent of the U.S. labor force, although they cover only about 15 percent, because more than one-fifth of state-local employees are still without staff retirement plan coverage. The beneficiary rolls in the large federal civil service retirement and military plans in 1980 already exceeded 60 percent of the active members in the plans. In the less mature state and local plans, they were probably less than half this ratio, based on extrapolation of past trends to 1980.

Viewed broadly, the retirement, disability, and survivorship benefit plans for public personnel present a troubled arena. There is an amazing lack of uniformity in the levels of benefits provided. The uniformed services retirement system, as compared with the civilian plans, is extremely lenient in its provisions and very costly, largely because it allows retirement after twenty years of service regardless of age. Most police and firefighter plans also provide very early retirement and are expensive. Some state and local plans are well below the average. Others provide more than 100 percent replacement of prior take-home pay if dual coverage under social security is considered.

Whether or not an employee group makes out extremely well or poorly depends to a large extent on whether dual social security coverage is provided. Dual coverage is available for the uniformed services personnel and for an estimated 70 percent of state and local employees. The remaining 30 percent of civil servants do not have social security, unless they acquire it in side jobs or by breaking the continuity of their government employment.

Variations in contribution rates, vesting, benefit computation formulas, and benefit eligibility provisions are also substantial among public plans.

Lack of adequate funding and the specter of continuing high inflation are two major dangers confronting many public personnel retirement systems. The military retirement system is totally unfunded. The civil service retirement system has unfunded liabilities that are about five times its assets. The funding status of state and local systems is highly variable. However, pension systems in several large cities, including that in New York City, are in trouble as are many smaller systems, especially for police and firefighters.

Double-digit inflation rapidly devalues the purchasing power of annuities, unless they are adjusted for cost-of-living increases. Federal adjustment provisions for civil service and military retirement payments are being questioned. On the other hand, two-thirds of state and local employees are under plans that have no regular provision for cost-of-living adjustment. In the recent climate of public negativism toward government, public employees who are members of inadequately financed retirement plans and/or plans that do not adjust for inflation on a regular and objective basis run a considerable risk of having their promised retirement benefits challenged and even cut back or allowed to depreciate under the impact of inflation. In large measure, this present situation results from the lack of accepted standards for the adequacy, financing, coordination, and administration of public pension plans in a volatile economy. Various magazines have published provocative articles about the reliability of pensions and the sensibility of the financial commitments that were made but not carried out (Boyd, 1978; *Newsweek*, four features in June 1, 1981 issue).

Much new information has been assembled and developed on pensions for public personnel in the last several years at the initiative of Pension Task Force of the House Committee on Education and Labor; the General Accounting Office in a series of probing reports; and the President's Commission on Pension Policy, assisted by a grant-financed study by The Urban Institute. These have added to earlier data compiled by the Bureau of the Census. A substantial part of the preceding generalizations and much of what follows is based on information from these studies.

Membership and Vesting Provisions

Membership refers to eligibility to participate in a retirement system. Not all employees in a government or agency with a pension system may be "members." For example, temporary federal employees may be excluded from the civil service retirement system and instead covered by social security. Such service may not be credited toward computing staff retirement benefits, even if the employee becomes a member.

The Pension Task Force (U.S. House, 1978: 85) identified various types of bars to membership in both federal and state and local systems, such as length of service requirements, minimum or maximum age, and minimum hours of work per year. On these criteria, except for the 1,000-hour-per-year requirement, the federal plans are less restrictive than are state and local plans.

Vesting relates to continued ownership of some or all of the employer-financed pension (or at least contributions) if the member leaves the employment covered by the plan. The vested rights may be to cash or to a deferred pro rata pension.

The Pension Task Force (1978: 88) found that state and local plans have more stringent requirements for vesting than do federal civilian plans. Approximately 60 percent of the members under the federal civil service retirement system had met its five-year vesting standard. The more common requirements of six to ten years had been met by only 32 percent of locally run plans and 39 percent of state-administered systems. In contrast, the federal military retirement plan has no vesting provision, short of qualifying for twenty-year retirement or going out on disability retirement.[10]

The requirement for continuous service to achieve vesting was another feature analyzed by the Pension Task Force. Its report pointed out that 90 percent of state plans, like the federal civil service retirement system, count all service, even with breaks. However, about 46 percent of local plans and 17 percent of federal plans require continuous service to meet their vesting requirements.

Portability Provisions

Portability refers to the right to transfer service credits from one retirement system to another when changing jobs within the public sector. There are various forms and degrees or conditions for portability (e.g., payment of all or part of the actuarial cost, existence of reciprocity agreements, in-state only, etc.).

Pension Task Force data show that credit for military service is the most common portability provision in civilian plans. Larger state and local systems tend to have more provisions for portability than do smaller ones. Teachers' plans rank high, as do state plans. Over 70 percent of all state and local employees have one or more portability features on the basis of reciprocity provisions among plans in their states.

Turnover and Qualification for Pensions

The combined effect of membership, antivesting, nonportability, unemployment, job switching, sickness, and mortality factors tends to make the earning of retirement benefits from a given staff pension system a highly uncertain proposition.

In our highly mobile society, actuarial decrements for employee turnover tend to be high. A sample of actuarial assumptions for state and local plans shows that typically only one out of twelve entrants would stay for thirty years. The federal civil service retirement actuaries assume that one out of twenty-five entrants stays to complete thirty years (U.S. Department of Health, Education and Welfare, 1980). The social security insurance system offers by far the most effective portability in the United States for benefit rights, covering approximately nine out of ten jobs in the economy. The reason that typical "staff" pension plans can promise seemingly good benefits to their new entrants is that, in the end, so few workers stick with the organization sufficiently long to qualify for retirement benefits.

Employee and Employer Contributions

For 1978–79 state and local pension systems received contributions of $6.1 billion from employees and $15.3 billion from employers (U.S. Department of Commerce, 1980). For fiscal 1980 federal appropriations to pay military retirement benefits—financed on a nonfunded, pay-as-you-go basis—totaled nearly $12.0 billion (Executive Office of the President, 1981: I-G8). Appropriations to the civil service retirement system, which is financed on a partially funded basis, totaled $14.8 billion and employee contributions ran $3.7 billion (Executive Office of the President, 1981: I–V118). Thus the governmental retirement systems probably received a total of about $57 billion of contributions in 1980, of which employees paid about $10 billion and governments appropriated around $47 billion. These amounts do not include social security contributions and contributions to lesser federal systems, nor do they include Veterans Administration costs for military personnel or workmen's compensation for workers.

The relatively low present share of employee contributions in the aggregate (18 percent) is attributable to the noncontributory federal military system, the failure in the past to fund past service costs adequately for the civil service retirement system, and the typically modest required rates of payroll contributions by members of state and local pension systems.

Contributions by employees to a pension system both help to finance it and to give the workers a moral claim to the promised benefits when they come due— even though the typical employee share is but a fraction of ultimate total costs. However, military personnel have never contributed, so the military retirement system is little different, except for the rhetoric, from the Veterans Administration pensions, which have long been recognized to be gratuities. Federal civilian personnel have always been required to contribute to the civil service retirement system, initially 2.5 percent and recently 7 percent of pay for general employees. Members of state and local plans most commonly contribute 5 or 6 percent, although a few rates exceed 10 percent. About 25 percent of the state and local plans (with 15 percent of the members) are noncontributory.

Governmental contributions to their pension systems tend to be inadequate to meet actuarial standards, but thus far only a few systems are in serious trouble. Benefits of military retirement systems depend entirely on an annual general fund appropriation. Federal civil service retirement benefits are paid from a trust fund, which is appropriated permanently. It is fed by (1) current employee contributions; (2) roughly matching contributions by employing agencies; (3) a permanent appropriation by the Treasury, authorized in 1969, to cover interest on the unfunded liability and the costs of military service credits; and (4) earnings on investments.

State and local retirement plans depend on a mixture of arrangements for governmental funding. The Pension Task Force (U.S. House, 1978) noted that, whereas state plans are not subject to arbitrary limitations on taxes, pension appropriations are normally subject to the regular appropriations processes.

Local plans are more circumscribed. About 25 percent of locally run and 40 percent of state-administered plans covering local employees receive state subsidies. Both state and local plans rely on federal funds. The report (1978: 142) stated that "The financing of many pension plans covering local government employees lacks stability and predictability due to state imposed taxing restrictions as well as to the indeterminate amount of funds available from federal revenue sharing, state insurance taxes, etc."

Employee Benefits

The amount and total lifetime value of a retirement benefit that an employee receives from a plan is governed typically by four factors: (1) the age at which retirement is permitted, (2) the years of service required for retirement or permitted to be included in the benefit computation, (3) the percentage factor per year of service by which the final pay or average pay is multiplied to compute the annuity, and (4) the method by which the wage base is averaged or used in making the annuity computation. Tax treatment of benefits is also a factor.

For example, in the U.S. civil service retirement system an employee may retire optionally at age 62 with five or more years of service; at age 60 with twenty years; or at age 55 with thirty years. The benefit computation factor per year of service is 1.5 percent for the first five years, 1.75 percent for the second five years, and 2.0 percent thereafter, subject to a maximum of 80 percent of pay (Greenough and King, 1976: 129). Thus an employee with thirty years of service would receive 56.25 percent or 1.87 percent per year. The wage base used is an average of the three highest (usually last) years. The same formula is used in computing total disability benefits, which are available after five years of service, except that a floor of 40 percent of high-three-year average pay is guaranteed. Survivors benefits for minor children are also provided. Benefits are taxable as income after the employee's own contributions have been repaid—including the disability benefits.

A "massive exodus of top government officials" has been reported by the Commission on Executive, Legislative and Judicial Salaries. Retirements of senior federal executives rose from 19.3 percent in 1977 to 51.8 percent in 1980 of those eliglble to retire. This unprecedented "brain drain" reflected employees' reactions to the $50,112 yearly pay ceiling, low morale in a government beset by program cuts, and availability of generous pension provisions (*U.S. News & World Report*, 1981: 22-24).

The federal military retirement system allows regular officers and enlisted personnel to retire at any age after twenty years of service. The computation factor is 2.5 percent per year of final pay, subject to a maximum of 75 percent of pay. However, basic pay is used in the computation, leaving out the allowances that are tax free during service. (Thus in this system preretirement promotions may be a factor, but service after thirty years does not add to the retirement benefit, except as active-duty pay increases enter.) Disability retirement pay is computed by the same method, except that the serviceman may elect Veterans Administration disability compensation if it is higher. Both the military and VA disability benefits are tax-free income.

Unlike civil service retirees, military personnel have dual coverage under social security. Thus, ex-servicemen are eligible at age 62 for reduced Old Age insurance benefits and for full payments at age 65 without any offset in their retirement pay. The military system has provisions, improved in 1980, for survivorship benefits, which are government subsidized, in addition to social security survivorship protection (with some offsets) and Veterans Administration rights.

Military personnel in great numbers take advantage of their early-retirement rights, which permit them to retire even before age 40 on 50 percent of basic pay and receive lifetime cost-of-living escalated benefits. An American Enterprise Institute (1980: 19) analysis has reported that

> Data compiled by the President's Commission on Military Compensation are cited to show that 33.8 percent of the officers and 52.1 percent of enlisted personnel in fact retire at twenty years of service and that at twenty-three years of service 64 percent of the officers and nearly 84 percent of enlisted personnel have retired.

The early-retirement provisions have been justified traditionally on the grounds that military personnel were required to discharge physically demanding duties and to be young, vigorous, and alert. However, there are counterarguments that only a fraction of military personnel serve as combat troops (Rushford, 1977: 26–30).

The lesser federal retirement systems have varying provisions. It should be noted that special provisions have been enacted for members of Congress and congressional staffs requiring somewhat higher contributions and providing much higher benefits (e.g., 2–5 percent per year) than for regular civil servants. Likewise, "safety" occupations in the federal service receive more generous treatment (e.g., retirement at age 50 with twenty years of service for air controllers and Congress members and at age 55 with twenty years for law enforcement officers and firefighters) (U.S. *Code*, 1978, Title 5).

Benefit provisions of state and local pension systems are quite variable. About 82 percent are "defined-benefit" plans, which contain specific benefit formulas similar to the U.S. civil service and military systems instead of using a "money purchase" approach.

The Department of Health, Education and Welfare (1980: 156) described the prevailing practice in state and local employee plans as follows. General plans permit retirement at age 60 or 65, usually with a minimum of five or ten years of service. Some large plans have normal retirement at age 55; teacher plans at age 60 with ten years, sometimes at 65 with five years; police and firefighter plans at ages 50 or 55 with twenty years—or after twenty years at any age. In addition, state and local general plans often provide early retirement with reduced benefits (e.g., at ages 50 to 55 with five or ten years of service or at any age with twenty-five years of service). Teacher plans may do so at age 55 with twenty years of service, or just twenty-five years.

Pension Wage Replacement Rates

Data compiled by the Pension Task Force (U.S. House, 1978: 117) on staff pension systems for public employees showed that, for an average worker with thirty years of service, the average wage replacement rates of gross wages for staff pensions in 1976 for all public systems were as follows: 51 percent for all employees, 58 percent for employees not covered by social security, 56 percent for employees covered by social security in which the plan was integrated with it, and 46 percent where the plan was not integrated.

The federal civil service retirement plan had a wage-replacement rate of 54 percent; the military retirement plan had 75 percent (plus social security, which is provided on a nonintegrated basis). Federal judges had a 100 percent replacement rate and Congress members 71 percent.

State government plans overall had wage-replacement rates of 73 percent for employees not covered by social security, 48 percent for those covered by social security and integrated with it, 48 percent for those covered by social security and not integrated with it, and 58 percent overall.

Local government plans had wage replacement rates of 62 percent for employees not under social security, 57 percent for those covered by social security and integrated with it, 46 percent for those under social security and not integrated, and 53 percent overall. Teachers in lower education had similar rates, professors lower rates, and police and firefighters somewhat higher rates, except where their plans were integrated with social security.

State and local pensions are exceedingly generous in the substantial proportion of cases where social security coverage is also provided. It should, of course, be remembered that only a small proportion of people who enter the public service qualify for thirty-year pensions; but those who do and also have social security coverage receive benefits that are difficult to justify where effective integration is not provided.

Pension Costs in Relation to Payroll

Perspective on the overall generosity of a pension plan can be gained by analyzing the ratio of actuarial costs on a standardized funding basis to the current wage payroll.

The President's Commission on Pension Policy (1981: Appendix) provides data on federal pension system costs as a percentage of payroll. For the civil service retirement system, the total cost was 79.8 percent of payroll, including 29.8 percent for normal cost and 50.0 percent for amortization of unfunded past service liabilities. For the military retirement system, the level total cost was 100.3 percent of payroll, divided 30.0 percent for normal costs and 70.3 percent for amortization. Total costs for other smaller federal systems ranged from 2.9 percent to 107.1 percent of payroll, the latter being for the foreign service retirement plan that has comparatively early retirement.

In contrast, computations published by the Department of Health, Education and Welfare (1980: 184) for a sample of twenty-five state and local government plans on the same basis as that cited above showed total actuarial costs ranging from 11.3 percent to 52.1 percent of payroll and averaging around 28 percent.

Funding of Public Employee
Pension Plans

Public employee retirement systems as a group are on shaky ground because of disregard of prudent actuarial funding principles and practices. A retirement system is "fully funded" actuarially when the value of assets is sufficient to cover the present value of future pension benefits to the members who are already retired plus the earned benefits based on past service for active employees (U.S. House, 1978: 163). However, very few plans meet this standard, and actuaries have invented many different approaches that skirt financial soundness.

Notwithstanding the confusion created by the diversity of actuarial methods used, the logical principle is that employee pension costs should be accrued and fully funded year by year as the services by the particular employees are being rendered to the public. This principle would allocate the full cost of public services to taxpayers when the public receives them. As a corollary, unfunded liabilities should be amortized over a reasonable period. Disregard of these standards in most federal staff retirement plans and many state and local plans encourages the making of rash pension benefits commitments and pushes off to future generations financial obligations that should be borne more properly by present taxpayers. It also creates financial "time bombs" that can blow up pension systems for personnel who spent their lives thinking they were earning security for themselves and their dependent survivors.

The major federal retirement systems have huge and rapidly growing unfunded actuarial liabilities. The General Accounting Office (GAO) has called attention to the underfunding of the federal retirement systems and to the understating of agency costs of operations. In 1976 the GAO (1976: 6) reported that the unfunded actuarial liability of the civil service retirement system was $53 billion. The appendix to the 1980 report by the President's Commission on Pension Policy shows that this fund has unfunded liabilities of $403 billion and only $64 billion in the fund. These reports also show that the unfunded liabilities of the military retirement system rose from $103 billion in 1970 to $356 billion recently. This system has no cash fund whatever. The President's Commission on Pension Policy reported that in 1980 the government's contribution to the civil service retirement fund was only 39 percent of computed actuarial cost; military retirement appropriations on a pay-as-you-go basis were 62 percent.

The Pension Task Force report (1978: 164) found a less than comforting financial situation among the 70 percent of the large state and local plans that it analyzed. Forty-seven percent of these plans had less than 50 percent of assets to accrued liabilities, including about 14 percent with less than 20 percent of liabilities covered. Another 33 percent had between 50 and 70 percent of liabilities covered. Only 2.3 percent had over 90 percent.

Moreover, this congressional study found that actuarial practices with respect to public pension plans were lax and in many cases undermined the accuracy of the figures. For instance, the assumptions used in valuating New York City plans had been subject to "gimmickry" that led to understatement of costs. Many of the actuarial studies were based on a static methodology and neglected the effect of inflation (U.S. House, 1978: 158-162).

The significance of using proper assumptions is indicated by a recent comparison of data on the U.S. civil service retirement fund for which "static" (no-inflation) methods showed a "normal cost" of 13.73 percent of payroll, whereas "dynamic" calculations assuming 6.5 percent wage and 6.0 percent cost-of-living increases produced a cost figure of 36.46 percent of payroll (President's Commission on Pension Policy, 1981b). This suggests that many of the existing "static" actuarial valuations of public retirement systems are misleading the policymakers and the public.

As of 1975 the unfunded pension liabilities of state and local plans were estimated at $270 billion (Munnell and Connolly, 1979: 47). Since then, benefit outlays have increased at least 50 percent—and if unfunded liabilities have kept pace, the figure by 1980 could be on the order of $400 billion. Plan assets at the end of 1978-79 were about $162 billion.

Long-range projections for 100 state and local plans in a grant-funded study prepared by The Urban Institute and associated organizations for the President's Commission on Pension Policy and other federal agencies suggest that benefits as a percentage of payroll will rise but that the fund status of these pension plans will improve by 27 percent by the year 2024 (President's Commission on Pension Policy, 1981a: 57). This hopeful finding, however, is subject to the uncertainties of uncontrolled inflation and the growing negativism toward public spending.

Cost-of-Living Adjustments

The high rate of inflation in the last fifteen years has made it the largest threat that retirement systems face. High inflation cuts the purchasing power of fixed annuities unconscionably. For example, 10 percent inflation will cut the real value of an annuity by nearly half in seven years and by nearly three-fourths in fourteen years. It also hurts the investment returns of fixed-obligation portfolios of pension funds. It also makes static actuarial calculations mislead plans into making lower contributions than they need.

If cost-of-living adjustments (COLA) are provided, the retirees are spared impoverishment by inflation. But the unfunded liabilities of the plans skyrocket. The result is that many pension plans are converted from a funded basis to an unsound pay-as-you-go basis (The Urban Institute, 1981: 10-11).

The Pension Task Force report (U.S. House, 1978: 108-109) shows that 98 percent of federal employees were covered by automatic, full COLA provisions. The civil service retirement system moved in this direction in 1962, and the military system followed in 1965. Only about 5 percent of state and local government employees had this full protection. However, over 90 percent of the state and local personnel had some form of adjustment—45 percent automatically with a limit (commonly 3 to 5 percent) and most of the rest on an ad hoc basis.

Administration of Pension Plans

The public pension arena is characterized by an absence of sound, accepted standards for designing, financing, and running pension plans. The congressional Pension Task Force (U.S. House, 1978: 2-5, 61-82) reported that many public employee pension plans are not well managed. State laws do not provide adequate standards. Disclosure deficiencies exist. There is a lack of adequate actuarial standards and valuations. Uniform accounting is absent and audits are not performed. Fiduciary responsibilities are neglected, and politics and favoritism figure into benefit determinations and financial management. In Colorado, the Public Employees' Retirement Association, which administers a system with $3 billion of liabilities, was found to be sending its members a financial statement showing the liabilities of the plan to equal assets, thereby not disclosing $1 billion of unfunded liabilities to its membership (Price, 1981: 729-731).

The General Accounting Office (1976, 1980) has forcefully identified problems with respect to the federal plans. It has pointed out that there is a policy and leadership void with respect to the whole set of income security programs and has urged creation of a National Income Security Commission. The President's Commission on Pension Policy (1980, 1981) sought to create an additional layer of pensions in the private economy and neglected the difficult task of rationalizing the hodgepodge system that exists in both the private and public areas. However, a tough, independent, standard-setting, investigative, and evaluative body is necessary on a continuing basis in the pension area to develop proposals and policies for restructuring the public pension nonsystem. The proposed "Public Employee Income Security Act of 1980" could be a move in the direction of federal standards, but it might also begin the road to federal "bailouts" of state and local pension systems that enacted unwise benefit commitments and then refused to fund them (U.S. House, 1980).

KEY PUBLIC EMPLOYEE PENSION ISSUES

The description and analysis in the foregoing sections shows that employee retirement programs for public employees are spiked with numerous large and thorny issues. These public policy and management problems are so severe in some instances that they pose a threat to the ability and/or willingness of governmental jurisdictions and legislative bodies to pay the promised benefits in future years. This section describes briefly some of the larger issues.

Many of these problems are long standing. Development of solutions for them will require determined and innovative action and understanding by the federal government and the states, as well as local jurisdictions, because pension design and management is a complex undertaking, requires a high degree of financial responsibility, and will have to surmount the barriers posed by existing divided authority between the federal, state, and local levels of government.

Lack of Coordination. Whether there are 3,075 state and local retirement plans for public employees as the Census Bureau reports, or 6,630 as the House Education Committee found, one thing is clear: pension plans for public employees are a nonsystem permeated with structural inconsistencies, financial weaknesses, ill-advised provisions, and poor management.

The most glaring of the structural defects is the failure to cover around 8 million federal, state, and local civilian employees under the social security insurance system (President's Commission, 1981: 772). A second problem is the absence of an effective mechanism for the portability of staff pension rights from plan to plan within and among the three levels of our "marble cake" federal governmental system. Pension plans for public employees operate much like a lottery.

The failure of policymakers to take these two steps undercuts and diminishes protection for millions of public sector workers and their families. It also inhibits desirable mobility of the public labor force. In addition, these structural flaws lead to a great deal of financial waste.

Multiple Benefits and Gaps. The existing structure of employee retirement, disability, and survivorship programs has grown up piecemeal through a hodgepodge process. In this unplanned nonsystem, large groups of retirees receive two or three sets of benefits; but it is likely that millions of former governmental employees who have shifted careers are lucky if they can qualify for one benefit—that being social security in most cases.

Widespread receipt of excessive benefits entails obvious waste and misuse of public resources. It undercuts support by taxpayers for pension systems when they must pay taxes for benefits that far outrun what they can themselves ever hope to draw.

On the other hand, when large numbers of public workers drop between systems or acquire disproportionately low benefits, injustice and harm is done to the people who were "led on" by pension promises that became for them a mirage. There is cause for concern about these outcomes, which are pointlessly costly in some cases and needlessly inhumane in others. Better social engineering is necessary, and the social welfare can be enlarged by judicious realignment of the existing nonsystem.

Early Retirement. Early retirement provisions are one of the main causes for exceptionally high costs in retirement systems. Retirement at any age after twenty years of service in the large military system is a major reason for the high cost of the plan. Police and firefighter plans and various other "safety" or "high-stress" occupations also have early retirement. Finally, the federal civil service retirement system and some large state and local plans permit retirement at age 55 after thirty years of service or even at earlier ages. Early retirement is often used in involuntary separations—and is a very costly method of getting rid of people.

Growing life spans, diminished birth rates, and a sharply growing proportion of the elderly in the population—all bring into serious question the practice of retiring workers before age 65. Present early-retirement provisions, coupled with considerable wage-replacement rates in public pension plans, encourage people to stop being productive. Moreover, such plans place unnecessary burdens on taxpayers. Even for the military system, serious proposals have been made that early retirement should be restricted (GAO, 1978). Likewise, proposals have been made for reevaluating policies for federal pensions for law enforcement and firefighter personnel (GAO, 1977). This is even a more serious problem at state and local levels where police and firefighter pensions are typically costly and underfunded.

Lax Disability Standards. In federal as well as state and local retirement systems, the common practice is to use occupational disability standards to retire people when they are unfit for their particular job instead of using a more rigorous disability standard. Inadequate policing of recovery from disability and lax earning standards contribute to excessive growth of disability rolls (GAO, 1976).

Absence of Adequate Policies and Standards. The development and liberalization of many pension systems has been marked by pressure politics and poor financing on the basis of static actuarial assumptions and estimates that understate true costs. Failure to take account of inflation on a realistic basis, even when cost-of-living escalators were being adopted, has resulted in many unpleasant surprises— and more to come (Jorgensen, 1980: 143). Profit-making pension consultants and actuaries, eager to keep lucrative contracts, have not been able to prevail against politicians who want to promise big benefits but do not want to support the contributions or the taxes necessary to fund them on an adequate actuarial basis.

The accomplishments of the congressional Pension Task Force, the President's Commission on Pension Policies, and The Urban Institute in pulling together relevant data and facts on public pensions show the need for a continuing professionally staffed organization to investigate and evaluate public pensions. Such an organization, ideally at the federal level and with adequate authority, should also develop and promote adoption of adequate and more uniform standards for the design, funding, investment, and administration of pension systems and monies. An independent policy-monitoring body with review authority over all federal, state, and local pension plans and related income security programs might well be set up along the lines of the proposal made in 1980 by the General Accounting Office for the creation of a National Income Security Commission.

Funding of Public Employee Pension Systems. Because staff pensions for particular groups involve multidecade or even intergenerational commitments, they must be financed adequately as they are earned ("accrued"). Actuarial methods are used for this purpose, but they have not been fully adequate in technique to cope with inflation in many plans and they have frequently been disregarded. Many actuaries have been too quick to come up with clever plans or modified figures that postpone the necessity for raising contributions. Economists have not helped much in predicting the persistence and high level of inflation.

By 1980 unfunded actuarial liabilities in federal, state, and local employee retirement plans probably exceeded $1 *trillion* by an unhealthy margin. Proper actuarial funding is the essence of sound pension plans. Adequate funding standards and methods using dynamic assumptions need to be developed and implemented under federal legislation.

NOTES

1. The 1980 paper by March presents a summary of an extensive review of the recent literature on the problems and issues raised by public employee pension systems. The basic research for that article was done in preparing a consultant report for the President's Commission on Pension Policy entitled *An Analysis of the Development and Rationales of the United States Income Security System, 1776-1980*. The monograph is being printed by the Select Committee on Aging, U.S. House of Representatives. The facts developed and documented in those two earlier works are drawn on for this current perspective piece.

2. Employment data in the *Economic Report of the President*, 1981, p. 273, were compared with the coverage figures cited in the preceding paragraph after the latter were reduced by the number of beneficiaries cited by Munnell and Connolly (1979: 33). Beneficiaries for 1930 were estimated roughly from HEW expenditures.

3. These developments are documented in author's research monograph cited in note 1, pp. 61-62.

4. See citations under U.S. Department of Commerce for 1967 and 1977 *Census of Governments*.

5. See 1967 and 1977 *Census of Governments* reports previously cited, pp. 1-3, respectively. These ratios somewhat overstate social security coverage, because part of the employees may not be covered. See Pension Task Force data in a later section that give a higher ratio for 1975.

6. For expenditure data from 1929-30 to 1965-66, see U.S. Department of Health, Education and Welfare (1968: 200-201).

7. For military retirement data, see 1972 and 1982 appendixes to *Budget of the United States Government* (Executive Office of the President 1971: 288; 1981: I-G8).

8. One important by-product of the proposal for a "minimum universal pension system" recommended in 1981 by the President's Commission on Pension Policy would be the creation of a substantial pool of investment funds through a 3 percent payroll contribution (1981: 42-43, 57).

9. See, for instance, the commission's computation of a standard of living geared to prior earnings up to $50,000 (1981: 42).

10. See the Pension Task Force figures (U.S. House, 1978, 55-59) and the succinct summary in Munnell and Connolly (1979: 3).

REFERENCES

AMERICAN ENTERPRISE INSTITUTE. 1980. *Military Retirement: The Administration's Plan and Related Proposals*. Washington, D.C.: American Enterprise Institute for Public Policy Research.
BOYD, M. 1978. "Pensions: The Five-Trillion-Dollar Scandal." *The Washington Monthly* 9 (February): 37-41.
BRONSON, D. C. 1957. *Concepts of Actuarial Soundness*. Homewood, Ill.: Irwin.
CARLSON, V. 1962. *Economic Security in the United States*. New York: McGraw-Hill, pp. 140-141.

ECONOMIC REPORT OF THE PRESIDENT. 1981. Washington, D.C.: G.P.O., p. 273.

EHRBAR, A. F. 1977. "Those Pension Plans Are Even Weaker than You Think." *Fortune* 96 (November): 104–108.

EXECUTIVE OFFICE OF THE PRESIDENT. Office of Management and Budget. 1971. *The Budget of the United States Government 1972*. Washington, D.C.: G.P.O., Appendix 288.

———. 1981. *Budget of the United States Government Fiscal Year 1982*. Washington, D.C.: G.P.O., Appendix I-G1, I-G8.

GENERAL ACCOUNTING OFFICE. 1976a. *Civil Service Disability Retirement: Needed Improvements*. FPCD-76-61. Washington, D.C.: G.P.O., November 10.

———. 1976b. *Special Retirement Policy for Federal Law Enforcement and Firefighter Personnel Needs Reevaluation*. FPCD-76-97. Washington, D.C.: G.P.O., February 24.

———. 1977a. *The 20-Year Military Retirement System Needs Reform*. FPCD-77-81. Washington, D.C.: G.P.O., March 13.

———. 1977b. *Federal Retirement Systems: Unrecognized Costs, Inadequate Funding, Inconsistent Benefits*. FPCD-77-48. Washington, D.C.: G.P.O., August 3, p. 6.

———. 1978. *Inconsistencies in Retirement Age: Issues and Implications*. PAD-78-24. Washington, D.C.: G.P.O., April 17.

———. 1980. *U.S. Income Security System Needs Leadership, Policy, and Effective Management*. HRD-80-33. Washington, D.C.: G.P.O.

GREENOUGH, W. C. and F. P. KING. 1976. *Pension Plans and Public Policy*. New York: Columbia University Press.

HARBRECHT, P. P. and S. J. HARBRECHT. 1959. *Pension Funds and Economic Power*. New York: Twentieth Century Fund, pp. 5–16.

INSTITUTE OF LIFE INSURANCE. 1969. *Life Insurance Fact Book 1969*. New York: ILI, p. 40.

JORGENSEN, J. 1980. *The Graying of America*. New York: Dial.

MCGILL, D. M. 1965. *Fundamentals of Private Pensions*. Homewood, Ill.: Irwin, pp. 1–31.

MARCH, M. S. 1980a. "Pensions for Public Employees Present Nationwide Problems." *Public Administration Review* 40 (July–August): 382–389.

———. 1980b. *An Analysis of the Development and Rationales of the United States Income Security System, 1776–1980*. (Monograph in publication process.)

MELONE, J. T. and E. ALLEN, JR. 1966. *Pension Planning*. Homewood, Ill.: Dow Jones-Irwin, pp. 1–17.

MUNNELL, A. H. and A. M. CONNOLLY. 1979. *Pensions for Public Employees*. Washington, D.C.: National Planning Association, p. 33.

NEWSWEEK. 1981. "Can You Afford to Retire" 97 (June 1): 24, 25–27, 28–34, 37.

PRESIDENT'S COMMISSION ON PENSION POLICY. 1981a. *Coming of Age: Toward a National Retirement Income Policy*. Washington, D.C.: Office of Management and Budget, pp. 42–43, 57.

———. 1981b. *Coming of Age: Toward a National Retirement Income Policy*. Appendix. Washington, D.C.: Office of Management and Budget (approx. 1,500 pp. processed).

PRESIDENT'S COMMITTEE ON CORPORATE PENSION FUNDS AND OTHER RETIREMENT AND WELFARE PROGRAMS. 1965. *Public Policy and Private Pension Programs*. Washington, D.C.: G.P.O., pp. 1–5, 11–19.

PRICE, C. R. 1981. *The Colorado Personnel System: Systems Analysis and Recommendations*. Denver: University of Colorado at Denver, Graduate School of Public Affairs. Doctoral dissertation reviewing the entire Colorado system under an IPA OPM grant.

RETICKER, R. 1941. "Benefits and Beneficiaries Under the Civil Service Retirement Act." *Social Security Bulletin* 4 (April): 29.

RIFKIN, J. and R. BARBER. 1978. *The North Will Rise Again: Pensions, Politics and Power in the 1980s.* Boston: Beacon Press.

RUSHFORD, G. G. 1977. "How the Defense Department Can Save Billions Without Worrying About National Security." *The Washington Monthly* 9 March: 26–30.

U.S. *CODE.* 1978. Chapter 83, Title 5, Subchapter III. *Civil Service Retirement.* Federal Personnel Manual Supplement 831-1. Washington, D.C.: G.P.O., May 15.

U.S. DEPARTMENT OF COMMERCE. BUREAU OF THE CENSUS. 1968. *1967 Census of Governments: Employee-Retirement Systems of State and Local Governments.* Washington, D.C.: G.P.O., Sec. 6-2:1.

——. 1978. *1977 Census of Governments: Employee-Retirement Systems of State and Local Governments.* Washington, D.C.: G.P.O., Sec. 6-1:1.

——. 1980. *Finances of Employee-Retirement Systems of State and Local Governments in 1978-79.* Government Finances GF79 No. 2. Washington, D.C.: G.P.O., May, p. 1.

U.S. DEPARTMENT OF DEFENSE. THIRD QUADRENNIAL REVIEW OF MILITARY COMPENSATION. 1976. *Military Compensation Background Papers: Compensation Elements and Related Manpower Cost Items, Their Purpose and Legislative Background.* Washington, D.C.: G.P.O., pp. 147-164, 245.

U.S. DEPARTMENT OF HEALTH, EDUCATION AND WELFARE. SOCIAL SECURITY ADMINISTRATION. 1968. *Social Welfare Expenditures Under Public Programs in the United States 1929-1966.* Research Report No. 25. Washington, D.C.: G.P.O., pp. 195, 200.

——. UNIVERSAL SOCIAL SECURITY COVERAGE STUDY GROUP. 1980. *The Desirability and Feasibility of Social Security Coverage for Employees of Federal, State, and Local Governments and Private, Nonprofit Organizations.* Washington, D.C.: G.P.O., March.

U.S. HOUSE OF REPRESENTATIVES. COMMITTEE ON EDUCATION AND LABOR. 1978. *Pension Task Force Report on Public Employee Retirement Systems.* 95th Cong., 2d sess., Committee Print, March 15, 935 pp.

——. COMMITTEE ON EDUCATION AND LABOR. 1980. *Hearings on the Public Employee Retirement Income Security Act of 1980.* H.R. 6525, 96th Cong., 2d sess. Washington, D.C.: G.P.O.

U.S. NEWS AND WORLD REPORT. 1981. "Is the Federal Service Dying of Pensionitis" 91 (September 7): 22–24.

WINKLEVOSS, H. E. et al. 1979. *Public Pension Plans, Standards of Design, Funding, and Reporting.* Homewood, Ill.; Dow Jones-Irwin.

PART THREE
PERSONNEL POLICIES AND ISSUES

New personnel policies are emerging constantly even as issues of longer standing undergo metamorphosis. The traditional, technical concerns of the personnel manager remain important, but an increasing proportion of his or her time must be spent on new policy concerns such as reduction in force, productivity improvements, and affirmative action.

The single development that is expected to dominate public personnel policy-making during the 1980s is economic decline and work force retrenchment throughout most of the American public sector. While growth management and an expanding work force may continue to concern some personnel managers (especially in the Sunbelt and energy-rich states), organizational decline and cutback management strategies will suffuse the thoughts and policies of administrators throughout the great majority of public jurisdictions.

Levine and Wolohojian describe and analyze the organizational uncertainty, drift, and disinvestment that have accompanied the decline of public organizations and suggest management strategies for coping with such trying conditions. Kearney explores the implications of economic decline and cutback management on public employment and public employee unions, concluding that the promise of increasing citizen-public employee confrontation over scarce resources is fairly strong, especially in jurisdictions that are affected by taxation and expenditure limitations.

With government retrenchment and increasing resource scarcity has risen a heightened interest in productivity improvements—doing the same (or better) with less. But, as DeMarco points out, measurement problems, civil service systems, and political factors sometimes hinder productivity gains and preclude the facile application of business management techniques to government. Nonetheless, with the immediate alternatives being service reductions or tax increases, public personnel managers will feel considerable pressure to develop and implement productivity improvements.

Perhaps the personnel issue that has drawn the most distinctive battle lines is *affirmative action*; it seems that one is either for it or against it, often depending upon one's own racial and sexual characteristics. Three chapters on affirmative action are presented: one praising it (Lepper), one criticizing it (Kelso), and one that examines levels of support for affirmative action among a sample of local government officials (Davis and West). The sexual aspects of affirmative action receive special treatment by Neugarten and Miller-Spellman in their chapter on sexual harassment, which outlines an issue that has only recently been brought to the attention of public management.

Finally, the abiding issue of ethics in the public service is raised and discussed within the context of the 1980s. Plant suggests that personnel managers especially should become more cognizant of the ethical dimensions of public employment and offers some guidelines for confronting them. His chapter deserves careful consideration by personnel managers who often discover that even their most mundane decisions are fraught with ethical concerns.

Charles H. Levine
University of Kansas
and
George G. Wolohojian
U. S. Department of Commerce

CHAPTER ELEVEN
RETRENCHMENT AND HUMAN RESOURCES MANAGEMENT: COMBATTING THE DISCOUNT EFFECTS OF UNCERTAINTY

Organizations are structures of opportunity and risk. People join and contribute to organizations for all kinds of reasons—money, prestige, the need to belong to something, and a host of other explanations. As Barnard pointed out many years ago, it is the balance between the organization's inducements for its members (employees) and the members' contributions in exchange for those inducements that holds organizations together (1938: 140-143). But what happens to an organization when it is no longer able to provide inducements to its employees at the same level it used to? What happens to the human resource pool of an organization when its opportunity structure turns lean and the prospects for future career growth and security in that organization become more risky? And, finally, what management strategies can offset the debilitating effects of austerity on the organization's human resource pool?

RETRENCHMENT AND UNCERTAINTY

The answers to these questions are not as straightforward as one might think. Not all organizations slide into a long-run terminal decline when their budgets are cut, and not all employees leave for another set of opportunities. In fact, there are at least four different kinds of cutback situations that condition the resilience of organizations and the attachment of employees to them. Two variables underlie these differences: the extent of decline the organization is experiencing and the amount of uncertainty about the organization's long-term prospects. These relationships are presented as a typology in Table 1.

The labels in the four cells of the typology indicate, first, the form of organizational response to decline and uncertainty and, second, the forms of employee response to both the environmental situation and the organization's response. In cell I, where small cutbacks are called for, an organization will stretch its resources by small productivity improvements, absorbing attrition, deferring maintenance, and rationing travel. Employees will respond with a moderate degree of unease and some will search for another job, but, if there is clear evidence that the cutback will last only one or two budget cycles, attrition will be moderate.

A more uncomfortable situation is depicted in cell II. Here cutbacks will be severe, say, in excess of 10 percent in one year or 25 percent over three years. In this case the organization will have to prioritize services by indicating which programs, projects, and services it will offer, which ones it will scale down, and which ones it will terminate. In this more severe case, one can anticipate employees taking a protective posture. Those who have seniority will fight to structure layoffs to protect themselves (Levine, 1978: 325). Those employees with the strongest unions will campaign to protect their agency. At the same time, low-seniority employees and employees in low-priority programs will leave quietly to protect their recall and rehirement rights once openings reappear.

Under conditions of greater uncertainty, the behavior of both organizations and employees becomes more turbulent. In cell III, the organization cannot predict

TABLE 1 Four Types of Retrenchment Situations

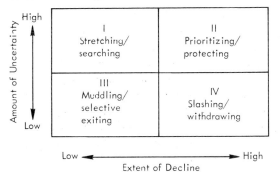

what long-term effects that stretching decisions will have. For example, if a police patrol car is stretched into use for a fourth year rather than replaced after three years, will it have to be stretched into a fifth or even sixth year, or will money be budgeted to replace it before the fifth year? Planning and a ranked agenda of needs are called for. However, ordering priorities under conditions of uncertainty is also difficult, because cuts have to be severe enough to force policymakers to confront the politically difficult problem of making trade-offs among agencies, programs, projects, clients, and employees. Therefore, under conditions of mild cutbacks (decline) and uncertainty, organizations will most likely muddle through by adopting some initial productivity improvement measures, stretching here and there, and perhaps cutting some low-priority programs where it is politically feasible to do so. Above all, the organization confronted with cutbacks and uncertainty will attempt to buy time in hopes that its budgetary future will be clarified, stabilized, and perhaps even improved. Employees will respond to this uncertainty with selective exiting.[1] That is, those employees who can find as good a job in a more promising opportunity structure (organization) will do so; those who cannot leave will stay with the organization, often hedging on their emotional commitment to it by continuing their search for another job.

Finally, cell IV portrays the most dire of circumstances—when the organization will have to take large cuts without knowing what its future will be or even if it will have a long-term future at all. Under these conditions, budgets are balanced on a year-to-year basis by slashing those programs with little political support to fund programs that might attract and retain powerful political allies so that the organization's resource base can be stabilized and its survival assured. In this situation, employees hang onto the organization by their fingernails, on the one hand, anxious to find a more stable and secure job while, on the other hand, needing to collect a paycheck. Employee attachment and commitment to the organization and its goals is minimal. Caution, withdrawal, anxiety, and tentativeness dominate employee behavior. People become unwilling to try new things, fearing that, if they try and fail, they will lose their jobs.

In the aggregate, the four types of situations impact differentially on the human capital base of affected organizations. In the first instance, damage will be minimal. A few high-quality employees may leave, but they can be replaced once the decline is stabilized. In the second case, damage will be somewhat more severe. While some programs will be slashed, the higher-priority programs will be left protected. Over time, retirements will allow new employees to be added to the reduced work force.

The third case is even more severe because it could set in motion a self-fulfilling prophecy that could eventually debilitate or destroy the organization. With the most marketable employees exiting, highly valuable skills and expertise exit also. The overall quality of the employee pool will decline and the quality of middle managers will decline as those who are more aggressive find better opportunities elsewhere.[2] It should be noted that the availability of other opportunities may be affected by external economic conditions such as a widespread general recession or by lean market conditions in a specific job sector. Exiting and turnover would be averted temporarily under such conditions. However, as soon as it is possible, employees who have options can be expected to exit. Without being able to replace people with critical and/or exotic skills, the organization could slip very quickly into becoming an "old boys club" (or, under a veteran preference system, an "old vets club"), unable to attempt anything new and innovative. The stage would therefore be set for the fourth type of organization—one without special expertise or a clearly defined mission—waiting and needing to be exploited by whatever special interest might come along to salvage it.

THE DISCOUNT EFFECTS
OF A BLEAK FUTURE

At the core of the problem of coping with decline is the fact that nothing will work if employees believe that no matter what they do the organization will die and they will be unemployed.[3] If uncertainty, risk, and the fruitlessness of staying on are severe enough, employees will reason that there is no sense investing time, energy, and emotional attachment to an organization that will not be around to reward them or whose opportunity structure is so lean that it cannot make promotions or provide opportunities for those who demonstrate talent. A declining organization loses prestige, its employees become physically and emotionally stressed, interpersonal relations become strained, and the best people leave. From the perspective of the inducements-contributions bargain, the organization's inducements become discounted because of their limited time value and because of the organization's lowered prestige. In response, employees attempt to cut their losses; they disinvest from the organization by reducing their contributions relative to the organization's inducements. The effect is that the organization's store of rewards buys less—becomes inflated—because the long-term payout from its investment is reduced drastically by the riskiness of the future.

Within this context it may be useful to consider the concept of human resource accounting proposed by Rensis Likert. Discussing the social and organizational impact of budgetary cutbacks, Likert argues that traditional methods of cost reduction result in

> many unfavorable and costly changes in the human organization that often are not recognized as stemming from this action. It produces less favorable and less cooperative attitudes, greater fear and distrust, more "yessing" of the boss, poorer communication, lowered performance goals, and greater restriction of production. It also results in increased turnover. This turnover occurs most often among the more able and valuable employees since they are the employees who, when disaffection occurs, most readily obtain outside employment offers. Labor relations worsen, grievances increase, and work stoppages become more of a problem after a year or two. These and related developments occur when the usual approach to cost reduction is used. *All of them reflect a decrease in the value of the human organization.* [Emphasis added.]
> To produce, say a five to ten percent decrement in the value of a firm's human organization and its productive capability does not take much loss of confidence and trust; poorer communication; worsened motivation; less concern for quality and scrap loss; greater restriction of production; increased turnover among the better engineers, managers, scientists, and trained workers, and worsened labor relations.[4]

The preceding scenario presents a disturbing profile of an organization experiencing retrenchment and decline. Is the organization helpless in this situation? Is there anything that management can do to combat uncertainty, drift, and disinvestment?

MANAGEMENT STRATEGIES

Combatting Uncertainty

The existence of uncertainty within an organization's environment contributes very heavily toward negative attitudes and dampened morale for the employees. They may (justly or unjustly) perceive that a current condition of decline will lead to their own inevitable downfall. However, a number of strategies are potentially available to the manager seeking to reduce the costs of uncertainty. These include long-term forecasting, performance appraisal, open communication between management and employees, and bumping and rehiring rights.

The first management strategy of *long-term forecasting* is really a process of information gathering. Three forecasting methods come to mind here: the application of subjective probabilities, the PRINCE (Probe, Interact, Calculate, Execute) method, and the Delphi technique. Utilizing the first method requires the manager to determine how much information is necessary to deal with uncertainty by first identifying how much uncertainty exists in the environment. If many possible events can occur, and they all seem equally likely, then a high degree of uncertainty exists. Conversely, if only a few events are possible, or if one or two events stand out in a group as being much more likely than the others, then less uncertainty exists. Given any situation involving uncertainty, the decision maker(s) will have some beliefs about the relative likelihood of a particular event's occurrence. Such beliefs may be operationalized by attempting to assign subjective probabilities to events. According to MacCrimmon and Taylor (1976: 1406),

> Any set of consistent beliefs can be assigned substantive probabilities; however, to be assigned subjective probabilities, an event need not have an extensive record of frequencies, as in mortality tables. *The very process of attempting to satisfy the consistency requirements of subjective probabilities can pinpoint inconsistent beliefs*, and hence allow a decision maker an opportunity to make changes. [Emphasis added.]

Therefore, as the highlights of MacCrimmon and Taylor's remarks indicate, the process of seeking a consistent and systematic understanding of alternative possible futures will in and of itself improve the ability of decision makers to handle their problems with better information and somewhat more control.

One forecasting method that is particularly useful for gaining a better understanding of political problems is the PRINCE method (Coplin and O'Leary, 1976). Following this method, the manager develops a scenario of his or her political environment by collecting information about the relevant actors. Their relative power, position, and salience on a particular policy and its related issues are assigned values that are placed in a matrix. A straightforward multiplicative process indicates the likelihood of the particilar policy's succeeding as well as providing a "snapshot" of the relevant actors who might have an impact on its outcome. This approach can aid a decision maker in systematically accounting for the political variables that impose themselves on the feasibility of particular decisions or events taking place. During times of retrenchment, this is particularly useful as decision making becomes politically more intense.

A final and well-known method of information collection and long-term forecasting was introduced by Dalkey and Holmes (1963)—the Delphi technique. In this procedure, the participants (experts in the particular area under consideration) are isolated from one another and are presented with a series of questionnaires in which their opinions and bases for those opinions are solicited. After each round of questionnaires is completed, information from the participants is consolidated and circulated anonymously to each member of the group. Several interactions take place to see if the group moves toward a consensus opinion that could be used to indicate future alternatives and increase the certainty of information about them. For managers whose organizations are plagued with uncertain futures, this method can be adapted to include members from the organization as well as outside experts within the interactive groups. This can be valuable for cross-fertilizing ideas as well as for gaining a sense of employee mood.

A second strategy that can be used to reduce uncertainty for employees is the clear use of *performance appraisal*. During times of uncertainty and decline, employees may begin to feel that they are being evaluated with criteria of which they are unaware or had no part in developing. Even worse they may believe that such criteria are not "performance" but "personality" related. Such a situation can appear to leave too much discretion to the manager. McGregor suggests that formal performance appraisal plans are designed to meet three needs, two of which take into account the fears for the future that might exist. According to McGregor the advantages of such plans are that (1957: 89–94):

> (1) They provide systematic judgments to back up salary increases, promotions, transfers, and sometimes demotions or terminations.
> (2) They are a means of telling a subordinate how he is doing, and suggesting needed changes in his behavior, attitudes, skills, or job knowledge; they let him know "where he stands" with the boss.
> (3) They also are being increasingly used as a basis for the coaching and counseling of the individual by the superior.

Effective employee development does not necessarily include coercing people into accepting the goals of the enterprise, nor does it mean manipulating their behavior to suit the organization's needs. What it does require is the creation of a relationship where the person can take responsibility for developing his or her own potential. As McGregor concludes (1957: 93),

> There is little chance that a man who is involved in a process like this will be in the dark about where he stands, or that he will forget he is the principal participant in his own development and responsible for it.

Furthermore, it should be noted that performance appraisal activities are most useful when they are implemented in concert with clearly established bumping and rehiring rights. This avoids the initial fears that the appraisal process might be used as an arbitrary "hatchet" mechanism to get rid of unwanted personnel.

A third uncertainty reducing strategy requires increased *open communication between top management and employees*. Such an increase in communication is important regardless of how great or how little previous communication has occurred between management (middle or top level) and labor. The need and expectation of employees for such an increase results from their perception of a change in the environment. As such changes tend to cloud their view of what the future holds, employees will demand verification of their status from higher and higher levels of management as they seek legitimate sources of information that they are willing to trust. Managers sensitive to these needs can neutralize the negative effects of these perceptions of uncertainty by opening up the communication links. One real-world example of how this process can work is illustrated by the case of Cincinnati, Ohio. In 1978, the city manager, William V. Donaldson, began a process of rotating two middle-management workers into and out of his office (with desks adjacent to his own) every two months. Department heads who have been responsible for management breakthroughs relate their experiences and methods to colleagues at regularly scheduled seminars. To break down barriers, Donaldson looked to the establishment of interdepartmental project teams and used third-level management personnel in leadership roles (Peirce, 1978: 11).

Techniques of open communication such as those used in Cincinnati have two other advantages for the manager seeking to reduce uncertainty. First, the more open the communication, the less likely the employees are to be affected by the rumors that can develop as personnel tension heightens. The trust developed through open communication lines can go a long way toward diffusing such rumors. Second, the vehicle of increased communication can offer top management the opportunity to seek statements of commitment for the employees from high-ranking elected officials. Such political backing will further bolster the employees' beliefs in their long-term value for the organization.

A fourth strategy to combat uncertainty calls for the *formalization of bumping and rehiring rights*. In an era of organizational decline, reductions in force (RIFs) are not uncommon, and the fears resulting from employee uncertainty about RIF procedures can be detrimental to productivity and morale. The decision rule that tends to be followed most by managers needing to cut back their personnel is seniority. Of course, seniority guarantees have little to do with either equity or efficiency per se. Instead, they are directed at another value of public administration; that is, the need to provide secure career-long employment to neutrally competent civil servants. Seniority criteria also have roots in the widespread belief that organizations ought to recognize people who invest heavily in them by protecting long-time employees when layoffs become necessary (Levine, 1978: 325). However, since seniority usually dictates a "last-in, first-out" retention system, personnel cuts following this decision rule tend to inflict the greatest harm to minorities and women who have been the most recent entrants to public agencies (Levine, 1978: 321). This raises a problem of another kind. According to Rosenbloom (1979: 298),

> Here, again there is a conflict between the values of neutral competence and representation. Despite their harsh racial and gender impacts, bona fide seniority systems are likely to be upheld in court unless they perpetuate illegal discrimination, that is, discrimination occurring after and in contravention to the 1972 EEO Act.

Yet, despite its problems, the method of seniority is most likely to be the procedure followed to set forth the bumping and rehiring rights for employees in organizations facing decline. For those who get "bumped," there may be some hope that time will work to their advantage. Since more senior personnel are often older as well, retention based upon seniority may reduce the overall problem of the future employability (and reemployability) for dismissed personnel (Rosenbloom, 1979: 298).

Combatting Drift

Organizations facing risky and unclear futures experience a phenomenon that can be described as "drift." Under conditions of drift, units within the organization fearing loss of turf or domain will move off the mark of their major objectives and begin to suboptimize (March and Simon, 1958: 38). Individuals within the system also fearful of the uncertainty will increase their focus and efforts on protective and turf maintenance actions resulting in further goal displacement for the organization (Thompson, 1967: 127).

For example, employees who believe that their particular positions are in jeopardy or that the functional responsibility and authority of their work unit is to be cut back might attempt to thwart such occurrences by withholding information, initiating union grievance procedures, slowing down the work process, publicizing the potential action, and/or seeking public and political support against the changes. However, all these drift activities are counterproductive for the organization as a whole as well as for the development of the individual employees. Two management strategies come to mind as methods to combat this drift: management by objectives and total performance management.

The first strategy of *management by objectives* (MBO) was initially presented in 1954 by Drucker. The MBO approach involves the establishment and communication of agency goals, the setting of individual objectives pursuant to the organizational goals, and the systematic review of performance as it relates to those goals. This approach was also advocated by McGregor (1957) in his concern about performance appraisal as a way to increase employee involvement and open up communication.[5] Thus the utilization of MBO strategies can reduce personnel tension and focus employee activity away from counterproductive actions onto more purposeful activity. In their review of MBO applications, Carroll and Rosi suggest (1973: 18) that

> MBO seems to be associated with positive attitudes toward the work situation. Managers tend to feel that their abilities are better utilized and that the scope of their authority has broadened. They also have greater feelings of security about their jobs. However, the latter may occur because of increased certainty about the nature of the job, which results from increased superior-subordinate interaction.

A second management strategy that can help to combat drift is *total performance management* (TPM). TPM, a new tool that draws upon previously developed techniques, was developed by the General Accounting Office in conjunction with the National Center for Productivity and Quality of Working Life.[6] TPM is both a measurement tool and a productivity analysis technique. Measurement indicators include data on both output per unit of input and consumer perceptions of service quality (National Center for Productivity and Quality of Working Life, 1978: 1).

> When an agency uses the TPM method, it not only measures its own productivity in traditional quantitative terms, but also finds out what employees think

of their jobs, and how satisfied citizens are with the services the agency provides. The agency then goes on to show its workers the information it has gathered and to involve every employee in a bottom-up effort to solve problems and eliminate shortcomings that have been identified.

What really distinguishes TPM from other productivity improvement techniques is its process. In particular, the system provides for the meaningful participation of employees, making them, rather than management, the clients of the process. This involvement helps to allay the fears of personnel who might potentially believe that the system had been designed only as a "weeding out" mechanism. Their interaction and involvement with management in the process cuts down considerably the problems of goal displacement and organizational drift.

The usefulness of the TPM method is exemplified best by considering its application in a particular case. Again, we focus on the city of Cincinnati, Ohio where the city's Highway Maintenance Division implemented TPM as part of a nationwide experiment. The innovative superintendent of that division felt that management-employee relations could be improved if a labor management committee were created to be a forum for issues of mutual concern. This committee became the focal point for the TPM experiment. The following suggest some of the beneficial outcomes for Cincinnati (Management Information Services, 1978):

- The opening up of communication channels throughout the Division. TPM allowed both management and labor personnel to freely express their opinions, suggestions, interests, frustrations and desires with the full assurance of anonymity and confidentiality.
- The Labor Management Committee's credibility and status were improved and a further endorsement was given to the Highway Maintenance Division Superintendent's effort at participative management.
- Improved communications led to improved understanding of the respective roles of labor and management in the Division.
- Greater mutual trust and respect among employees of the Division was fostered.
- Management learned that many of its stereotypes of nonmanagement personnel were false. The program revealed that nonmanagement employees in the Division not only enjoyed their jobs, but had a real desire to improve the level of service provided.
- Management also benefitted from realizing the untapped resources it possessed in the form of employee suggestions and recommendations to improve performance.
- Management was made aware that crucial long-term problems had been overlooked in the rush of day-to-day activities.
- Labor was given a voice in the TPM program and was able to see some of its suggestions implemented.

Combatting Disinvestment

As uncertainty grows and drift continues, employees will value less and less their stake in the organization. If nothing is done to combat disinvestment, employees will see no sense in giving their time, energy, or emotional attachment to the organization. A number of strategies exist that can help the manager faced with personnel who are cutting their losses through disinvestment. These strategies include assuring employees of the long-term value of their investment in the organization, carving out special rewards for employees, and refocusing capital investment to current capital maintenance.

The first strategy of *assuring employees of the long-term value of their investment in the organization* is crucial not only to maintaining good labor-management relations but also to boosting overall morale levels. In organizations facing decline, management can help to maintain employees' hope for the future by being open and honest about the variables affecting the long run. Employees need to know that retrenchment strategies do not necessarily imply that the organization will disappear totally. One way in which to indicate the likelihood of future existence is to involve employees in long-term planning functions for the organization. Employee involvement in planning would help them to understand better the constraints on the organization as well as allow them to participate in establishing the procedures for RIFs and other retrenchment steps. While none of these subjects can be expected to be greeted by employees with wild enthusiasm, at least if they are privy to the details, some of their uncertainty can be reduced. Earlier discussion of the advantages of TPM and open management-labor communication also bear out the values of involving employees in functions related to the long-term survival of the organization.

A second approach to combatting disinvestment involves *carving out special rewards for employees.* Such rewards may take a number of different forms, including management development programs, rapid promotions, and performance bonuses. Management training and development is seen as a major component of both the MBO and TPM systems discussed earlier. Such programs indicate to personnel that the institution believes enough in its future to invest time and resources in them. A promotion can also indicate to an employee that the organization is investing in him or her. Promotions may be a function of merit and service, or they may follow the completion of the previously mentioned management training programs. Finally one-time awards of performance bonuses may be used to reinforce the commitment between an individual and an organization. A prime example of this approach can be seen in the newly reorganized Senior Executive Service and new Merit Pay System in the federal government. In both cases, "Federal employees can work with greater intensity and dedication, knowing that superior performances soon will be recognized with monetary, as well as intrinsic, rewards" (Campbell, 1980: 10).

Finally, an organization can indicate its willingness to invest in the future if it reevaluates its procedures for capital funds outlays. Given the nature of politics and tenure in office, elected officials often defer maintenance of equipment, buildings, and roads to delay the present cost to a time when they may no longer be in office to pay the political price. However, a *refocusing of capital budgets away from long-term projects to the maintenance of existing assets* would indicate a belief in the long-run viability of the unit (Peirce, 1978: 11). Furthermore, such an investment of capital funds would provide continued employment for current personnel.

THE FUTURE

As was illustrated in Table 1, uncertainty about the future is a key variable in managerial approaches to retrenchment. The length of time that conditions of fiscal constraint and cutback will continue become paramount in the minds of employees as well as top managers. The strategies outlined here assume that such conditions will exist for at least most of the 1980s. Most commentators and public officials predict that tight budgets are likely to characterize governments until such time as there is a major turnaround in our economy, and inflation is brought under steady control. Among the most pessimistic forecasters, Boulding (1975) has predicted that retrenchment conditions are likely to be around for the next fifty years as the United States moves into a long-term era of slowdown. While the concept of an overall slowdown is not contemplated by the new administration in Washington, the 1982 federal budget-cutting decisions seem only a precursor of further cuts to be applied in the future. More and more managers and employees have begun to take the "era of decline" very seriously.

CONCLUSION

The topic of retrenchment and decline in organizations has been more the subject for doomsday prognosticators than for those interested in management development and employee relations. However, just as we have outlined what we see as the discount effects of a seemingly bleak future, we also believe that managers need not be helpless in the face of uncertainty, drift, and disinvestment on the part of their employees.

The strategies we have outlined as methods to combat these problems are not to be taken as foolproof or accepted as necessarily discrete in their application. In fact many of the strategies, including performance appraisal, MBO, TPM, increased labor-management communication, and clearly delineated bumping and rehiring rights, can be part of an overall management program. Together, they aim at reducing employees' fears about their future, to involve them more directly in the retrenchment process, and to assure the long-term health of their organizations in the difficult times that lay ahead.

NOTES

1. This phenomenon has been identified as the "free exiter problem" in Levine (1979: 182).
2. Hirschman has discussed at length the problem of the exiting of organizational members leading to a deterioration of output. However, Hirschman's view of the problem of decline is

based on the optimistic (but probably not realistic) assumption that slack and decline are cyclical phenomena for which, if nothing else works, the passage of time may bring about some equilibrium (Hirschman, 1970).

3. For a discussion of the topic of organizational death, see Kaufman (1976).

4. An interview with Likert is quoted in National Academy of Public Administration (1973).

5. For a further discussion of the advantages of cooperative interaction and problem solving, see Likert and Bowers (1969).

6. Some early TPM test sites, including Cincinnati, referred to the process as total performance "measurement." As TPM progressed, however, some participants in the various projects felt that total performance "management" was a more descriptive title. Most later references to the TPM process have used this title rather than the earlier one.

REFERENCES

BARNARD, Chester. 1938. *The Functions of the Executive.* Cambridge, Mass.: Harvard University Press.

BOULDING, KENNETH. 1975. "The Management of Deline" *Change* 9 (June): 8–9

CAMPBELL, ALAN. 1980. *Civil Service Reform: A Report of the First Year.* Washington, D.C.: Office of Personnel Management.

CARROLL, STEPHEN and HENRY TOSI. 1973. *MBO: Applications and Research.* Riverside, N.J.: MacMillan.

COPLIN, WILLIAM and MICHAEL O'LEARY. 1976. *Everyman's Prince.* North Scituate, Mass.: Duxbury.

DALKEY, N. and O. HOLMES. 1963. "An Experimental Application of the Delphi Method to the Use of Experts". *Management Science* 9: 458–467.

DRUKER, PETER. 1954. *The Practice of Management.* New York: Harper & Row.

HIRSCHMAN, ALBERT. 1970. *Exit, Voice and Loyalty.* Cambridge, Mass.: Harvard University Press.

KAUFMAN, HERBERT. 1976. *Are Government Organizations Immortal?* Washington, D.C.: Brookings Institution.

LEVINE, CHARLES. 1978. "Organizational Decline and Cutback Management." *Public Administration Review* 38 (July–August): 316–325.

———. 1979. "More on Cutback Management: Hard Questions for Hard Times." *Public Administration Review* 39 (March–April): 179–189.

LIKERT, RENSIS and DAVID BOWERS. 1969. "Organizational Theory and Human Resource Accounting." *American Psychologist* 24 (June): 585–592.

MacCRIMMON, KENNETH and RONALD TAYLOR. 1976. "Decision Making and Problem Solving." In Marvin Dunnette, ed., *The Handbook of Organizational and Industrial Psychology.* Chicago: Rand McNally: 1397–1453.

McGREGOR, DOUGLAS. 1957. "An Uneasy Look at Performance Appraisal." *Harvard Business Review* 35 (May–June): 88–94.

MANAGEMENT INFORMATION SERVICE. 1978. *Total Performance Management in Cincinnati, Ohio.* Washington, D.C.: International City Management Association.

MARCH, JAMES and HERBERT SIMON. 1958. *Organizations.* New York: John Wiley.

NATIONAL ACADEMY OF PUBLIC ADMINISTRATION. 1973. *The Report of the Ad Hoc Panel on Attracting New Staff and Retaining Capacity During a Period of Declining Manpower Ceiling.* Washington, D.C.: NAPA Foundation.

NATIONAL CENTER FOR PRODUCTIVITY AND QUALITY OF WORKING LIFE. 1978. *Total Performance Management: Some Pointers for Action.* Washington, D.C.: G.P.O.

PEIRCE, NEAL. 1978. "City Finds Cost-Cutting Formula." *Public Administrator Times* 4 (June 1): 2–5.

ROSENBLOOM, DAVID. 1979. "City Personnel: Issues for the 1980's." In John Blair and David Nachmias, eds., *Fiscal Retrenchment and Urban Policy.* Beverly Hills, Calif.: Sage, pp. 285–305.

THOMPSON, JAMES. 1967. *Organizations in Action.* New York: McGraw-Hill.

Richard C. Kearney
University of South Carolina

CHAPTER TWELVE
PUBLIC EMPLOYMENT AND PUBLIC EMPLOYEE UNIONS IN A TIME OF TAXPAYER REVOLT

Examined from the perspective of today, the decade of the 1980s does not bode well for public employees. Economic and political forces adverse to public workers seem to be mounting on all sides. On the economic front, a lingering period of stagflation combined with periodic shortages of petroleum have presented the greatest threat to the U.S. economy and way of life since the Great Depression. For the first time in the American experience, broad assumptions of an abundant economy buoyed by continuous growth and increased productivity have been challenged seriously. Indeed, "It is a symptom of resource scarcity at a societal, even global, level that is creating the necessity for governments to terminate some programs, lower the activity level of others, and confront tradeoffs between new demands and old programs rather than expand whenever a new public problem arises" (Levine, 1968: 316).

As the American standard of living has declined, increasing public attention has been directed toward the functions and costs of government at all levels. Government, to many people, presents a choice scapegoat for their personal monetary problems. Taxes, after all, are highly visible and almost universally deplored in the United States. Furthermore, taxes seem to be rising relentlessly, even though government services appear to remain constant at best or deteriorate at worst. Politically, such circumstances have led to a declining trust by the people of their federal, state, and local governments.

The erosion of trust in government is not a phenomenon of the past several years. Indeed, it has been documented steadily since 1958 by the University of Michigan election studies (Miller, 1979). In 1978, 70 percent of those responding to the national survey agreed that "Government cannot be regularly trusted to do what is right"; 56 percent felt that "Government is run by people who don't know what they are doing"; and an almost overwhelming 79 percent proclaimed that "Government wastes a lot of tax dollars." It is this last sentiment that has been expressed most strongly during the past several years. When asked to be specific about which tax dollars were wasted, 51 percent of a national sample in July 1979 responded that state income taxes were "excessively" or "somewhat" high, 53 percent believed the same about social security taxes, whereas 63 percent claimed that property and real estate taxes were "excessively" or "somewhat" high. In sum, according to Ladd (1979), "It is apparent that large numbers of Americans are profoundly unhappy with the amount of taxes they have to pay and with aspects of the way government uses their tax dollars."[1]

A direct political consequence of public unhappiness with government and the way in which it spends the peoples' money is the so-called "taxpayers' revolt." "Down with big government" has become the rallying cry of financially struggling Americans. An easy target of taxpayer frustration is the public employee, who many perceive to be underworked and overpaid. An overt, legislative expression of dissatisfaction with government in general and public employees in particular was made in 1981 in the federal government through congressional approval of the Reagan administration's tax program, consisting of the largest income tax reductions in the history of the United States. In state and local government, the voters and their elected representatives have spoken through a series of taxation and expenditure limitations (TELs). By restricting the levels of taxation and/or government expenditures, the public reasons, government and its workers can be forced to be more efficient and less wasteful.

Although the TELs movement began in New Jersey in 1976, when the state legislature imposed a ceiling on spending tied to increases in per capita personal income, the most widely heralded event was the passage of Proposition 13 in California, also known as the Jarvis-Gann Amendment. Proposition 13 focused attack on the tax bailiwick of local government by rolling back property taxes by $7 billion and restricting future increases in assessed property values to 2 percent a year. Other states followed with TELs of their own. By the end of 1980, at least seventeen states had adopted some form of TELs: Arizona, Arkansas, California, Colorado, Florida, Hawaii, Idaho, Massachusetts, Michigan, Missouri, Montana, New Jersey, Ohio, Tennessee, Texas, Washington, and Wyoming. Additional TELs are likely to be legislated in other states during the next few years.

It is the thesis of this chapter that TELs, compounded by a recession and inflation-prone economy and decreasing federal aid to state and local governments (including the possibility of termination of federal revenue-sharing monies and countercyclical aid), portend dramatic and far-reaching changes in the nature of public employment and the lot of public workers and public employee unions. Each of these subjects will be treated at length in the sections that follow.

PUBLIC EMPLOYMENT, COMPENSATION, AND THE TAXPAYER REVOLT

Depending upon the level of government and the service function under consideration, personnel expenditures can range from 40 to 90 percent of the operating budget. When TELs or other economic factors force government decision makers to reduce expenditures, they are certain to examine labor costs closely. Two basic strategies are available: (1) reduce the level of employment and (2) limit the wages and fringe benefits awarded to public employees.

The experience to date indicates that government will move first to limit employment levels through attrition or hiring freezes, thereby avoiding the unpalatable task of dismissing workers. Often, these strategies are implemented in tandem, with no new employees hired to replace those who resign, retire, die, are dismissed, or otherwise leave the organizations. Attrition and hiring freeze policies are convenient and relatively painless in the short term. However, as noted by Levine (1978: 321–322),

> In the long run . . . hiring freezes are hardly the most equitable or efficient way to scale down organizational size. First, even though natural and self-selection relieves the stress on managers, it also takes control over the decision of whom and where to cut away from management and thereby reduces the possibility of intelligent long range cutback planning. Second, hiring freezes are more

likely to harm minorities and women who are more likely to be the next hired rather than the next retired. Third, attrition will occur at different rates among an organizations' professional and technical specialties.

When hiring freeze and attrition policies do not go far enough in reducing the personnel budget, layoffs are the next logical step. Although there has been some disagreement over the exact number of employees laid off in California as a result of Proposition 13, there is no doubt that the taxpayer revolt has cost many government workers their jobs. According to one state survey, Proposition 13 fallout has contributed to 17,000-18,000 dismissals, 2,000 early retirements, and 92,000 job vacancies left unfilled as a result of hiring freezes (*GERR*, 2/19/79: 10-11). From March 1978 to March 1979, state and local employment in California dropped by 114,000, or 8 percent of the total work force (*GERR*, 8/13/79: 47).[2] In Massachusetts, "Proposition 2½" may result in layoffs of as many as 20,000 local government workers (Peirce, 1981).

During 1979 and 1980, the industrial Northeast and Midwest were especially hard hit by employee layoffs: Newark dismissed 355 workers; Toledo, 135; Philadelphia, 135; Detroit, almost 2,000; Wayne County, almost the entire county work force. In New York City, which serves as a useful prototype of the impact of fiscal crisis on government employment, over 45,000 workers—15 percent of the city labor force—were laid off in 1975. As of late 1981, the tax revolt and a sluggish national economy were forcing consideration of substantial public employee layoffs in a majority of the fifty states.

As in the case of hiring freezes, layoffs can be imposed either selectively or across the board. The latter "are expedient because they transfer decisionmaking costs lower in the organization, but they tend to be insensitive to the needs, production function, and contributions of different units. The same percentage cut may call for hardly more than some mild belt tightening in some large unspecialized units" or virtual immobilization of smaller, specialized functions (Levine, 1978: 322). Selective layoffs do not apply to all functions but, rather, are aimed at particular services. In California, libraries, parks and recreation, schools, and health and welfare programs have been particularly hard hit. Summer school programs have been eliminated in many areas throughout the state, and in San Francisco alone, 1,157 professional staff were fired, administrative staff were cut by one-half, and thirty schools were closed in mid-1979 (*GERR*, 6/18/79: 21). In the City of New York, the largest personnel reductions from fiscal years 1975 to 1977 were in higher education, health and hospitals, and education. Layoffs also may be instituted through curtailment of certain services, as elimination of summer school programs illustrates. In New York City, San Francisco, and elsewhere, hospitals, fire stations, and police precincts also have been shut down. Other local governments have begun seriously to consider consolidating government services (such as police and fire functions into a Department of Public Safety) and contracting out services (either to another government or to a firm in the private sector) to reduce the payroll (Straussman, 1981). Whether selective layoffs are imposed in particular departments or through service cutbacks, decisions should be made on the grounds of productivity improvement rather than politics. Levine (1978: 322) recommends the use of zero-base budgeting as an aid in making resource allocation decisions.

It was mentioned that hiring freezes can exert an adverse influence on the employment of minorities and women. It also should be noted that layoff decisions almost always are based on the criterion of seniority. When the last hired is the first fired, women and minorities tend to suffer disproportionately. Thus, layoffs inspired by the taxpayer revolt often undermine the affirmative action efforts of government. In Detroit, for example, of the more than 1,600 dismissals during 1980, 45 percent were black males and 30 percent black females. Furthermore, seniority-based layoffs may produce a substantial shift upward in the age of the average worker. For instance, Behn (1978: 336) reports that the New York City fiscal crisis "resulted not only in the closings of public schools, the laying off of 16.5 percent, or 13,000, of the city's teachers, and an increase in the pupil-teacher ratio from 20–25, it also resulted in an increase in the average age of teachers from 28 to 41."

Clearly, the taxpayer revolt has had a serious and harmful impact on employment levels in some local governments. A second important effect of deteriorating economic conditions and the taxpayer revolt is on government employee compensation levels. There is no doubt that mandated limitations in expenditures will translate ultimately into fewer dollars available for wages and benefits. As long as the size of the government labor force can be reduced somewhat through hiring freezes and attrition, public workers will continue to seek, and often gain, the pay increases to which they have become accustomed. But when the situation dictates a trade-off between layoffs among the present work force and reductions in pay and benefits, the latter option usually is perceived to be more palatable by both public workers and management.

Wage reductions can be achieved by denying merit increases or cost-of-living adjustments, by restricting normal provisions for "step" increases, by imposing a wage freeze, or through a restructuring of fringe benefits. These strategies for coping with budgetary shortfalls are being implemented more and more frequently. Public employees in New York City, for example, agreed (1) to defer previously won wage increases for 1975–1976 in return for a management pledge not to lay off any further workers unless faced with conditions of "extreme necessity," (2) to forego a cost-of-living increase unless productivity gains were made, (3) to increase their share of pension contributions, (4) to limit overtime work and pay, and (5) to freeze promotions (Anderson, 1976). In 1978 a coalition of thirty-one municipal unions in that city consented to a small 7.2 percent wage increase over the next two years. Similar policies of financial retrenchment have been implemented in Philadelphia, Cleveland, Detroit, Wayne County, the states of Michigan, Massachusetts and Connecticut, and many other jurisdictions.

It is somewhat ironic that smaller compensation increases should become obligatory in the public sector at a time when government workers in most areas have achieved only recently a measure of parity with their counterparts in private employment. For many years public employment was valued more for the job security and fringe benefits it offered rather than the pay, which lagged considerably behind that available for similar work in the private sector. Then with the tremendous increase in public employment in the late 1960s, public workers, aided by their unions, played an effective game of "catch-up." By the early to mid-1970s, the earnings of many federal, state, and local government employees had attained parity with, and in some cases even exceeded, private sector wages (Perloff, 1971; Smith, 1976). By 1978 the situation had been reversed in many places, as public employees were forced to limit themselves to wage increases considerably below those being awarded in private employment.[3] Even the heretofore sacrosanct fringe benefits began to decline relative to those in the private sector.[4]

What impacts have layoffs, hiring freezes, decreasing relative wages and benefits, and the politics of TELs had on public employees? These developments certainly have not been salutary from the perspective of the public worker. With the decline in relative compensation and the loss of job security has come a loss of morale, which is almost certain to spread as long as employment conditions are unsettled. According to Bott (1979), the taxpayer revolt and government economic crises have led to increasing worker anxiety and insecurity, "more bitching, greater cynicism, and other undercurrents of discontent."

Employees may respond to their situation in a number of specific ways. First, those workers who stay on the job may have a propensity to react to an expanding work load with minimal job effort. Under conditions of austerity, productivity and the quality of service provision are likely to decline under the best of circumstances. For instance, Behn (1978: 336) reports that, as a result of New York City's fiscal crisis, firefighters "who formerly had continued to work during a fire, despite minor injuries or mild exhaustion, were much more prone to stop work and seek medical assistance." With workers suffering a loss of morale and incentive (after all, one cannot hope for a substantive wage increase, and the possibility of a layoff may be iminent), service provision is likely to deteriorate further. The specter of a vicious cycle of continually deteriorating government services and steadily increasing taxpayer hostility toward public employees is not a pleasant one to evoke, but it is a definite possibility during the decade of the 1980s.

Second, turnover among public employees is likely to surge, especially among the better workers. A report in the *Tax Revolt Digest* (*GERR*, 11/5/79: 16-18) asserts that Proposition 13 produced the "resignation of key middle-executive personnel, loss of ambitious, talented young people, and a declining ability to recruit trained specialists." Young workers are especially likely to view public employment more negatively because of the relatively low wages and the poor likelihood of progressing in the organization through promotions. When an organization is unable to recruit talented young workers, its output and productivity have a tendency to decline considerably. The problem of turnover could be eased somewhat by stepping up training programs for existing workers. Unfortunately, during times of fiscal crisis, one of the first candidates for government budget cuts is training and employee development.

Finally, workers may respond to layoffs, hiring and wage freezes, and the other accompaniments of a troubled economy and the taxpayer revolt through their employee organizations. This is the subject that will be addressed in the remainder of this chapter.

UNIONS AND THE TAXPAYER REVOLT

With some exceptions, mainly in the South and Southwest, the public employee union movement has been quite successful throughout the United States. With the issuance of President John F. Kennedy's Executive Order 10988 in 1962, unionization spread rapidly in the industrialized states of the Midwest and Northeast and quickly gained footholds in large and medium-sized cities around the United States. By 1974, over one-half of all public employees claimed membership in an organization that represented them in negotiations with their employers. Some type of labor relations policy exists today in forty-two states and in more than 11,500 local governments. The largest public employee union—the American Federation of State, County, and Municipal Employees (AFSCME)—reached a membership figure of more than 1 million during 1978, making it, at the time, the largest organization in the AFL-CIO. The organizing success of public unions during the decades of the 1960s and 1970s is in marked contrast to the fortunes of unions in private employment. Whereas public union membership rose approximately 400 percent from 1968 to 1978, private sector unions were losing membership steadily.

But what of the future? The forecast for private unions is beyond the scope of this chapter. For public employee organizations, the outlook is mixed. Generally, union membership should be expected to continue growing, especially in the Sunbelt states. Public workers will persist in organizing for a collective voice in pursuit of their own political and economic interests. The decade of the 1980s is one of impending government fiscal strain, a factor that should aid rather than hinder organizing efforts. Government workers during a time of government retrenchment and taxpayer revolt will turn increasingly to their unions for the exercise of political and economic power to achieve wage and benefit gains and, in some localities, simply to hold onto what they already have won.

However, public workers and their organizations are likely to confront an increasingly hostile citizenry, especially where they are blamed for high taxes, poor service delivery, and the financial problems of government. The gargantuan fiscal difficulties of New York City may offer a lesson for other hard-pressed cities. According to Anderson (1976: 512),

> Clearly the fiscal crisis in New York has chilled the public's attitude there and in other large cities toward public employee unions and collective bargaining, and it has prompted a reexamination of the collective bargaining process as opposed to the traditional political role of the legislature and executive in determining conditions of employment for public employees.

Nationwide, there is a trend toward a negative perception of public employees and their unions. The favorable image of public workers held by Americans from 1970 to 1977, the polls show, was reversed from 1977 to 1978 (*GERR*, 1/15/79: 12-14). The Gallup poll of May 1979 found that public approval of labor unions has declined from 76 percent in 1957 to 55 percent in 1979, a forty-three-year low (*GERR*, 9/10/79: 24-25). In some instances, employees have only themselves to blame. The aggressiveness and recalcitrance of New York City unions have been well documented (Horton, 1973), as have the extraordinarily high salaries and fringe benefits of laborers in San Francisco (Raskin, 1976). Specific acts of some workers also have bred public hostility. In Hartford, Connecticut, for example, a "stall-in" deliberately created a traffic jam near the Civic Center where the 1976 World Cup Tennis Match was being held. In Knoxville, Tennessee, striking teachers alienated many citizens by boycotting local merchants and withdrawing from the United Fund. More serious accusations were leveled against unions in Memphis where, during a firefighter and police strike in the summer of 1978, 166 homes burned within a twenty-four-hour period (6 to 7 house fires was the norm).

The public has responded with an array of antiunion measures. In California, San Francisco voters have approved a number of referenda in recent years, including the alteration of wage parity formulas and authorization for firing any police or fire-fighter participating in a strike; voters in San Rafael and San Diego approved the dismissal of striking police and firefighters; in Santa Barbara, automatic cost-of-living raises for employees were eliminated. Perhaps in response to the increasing public disapproval of government workers, the courts also have tightened the screws on unions in recent years. In Kansas City, Missouri, firefighters were ordered to pay over $150,000 in damages to the city for expenses incurred in calling out the Na-tional Guard during a 1975 strike; a Massachusetts superior court judge in 1979 levied a $260,000 strike fine against the Fall River Education Association; in late 1977, a California state district court ruling supported the right of California cities to sue a public union for damages arising from a strike; during the air traffic con-troller strike of 1981, one federal judge fined the union (PATCO) $100,000 *per hour* of the walkout; and, in many areas of the United States, strong new efforts at "union busting" have been observed (*GERR*, 3/19/79: 10-12). To union leaders, such activities reflect an attempt to make public employees scapegoats for urban problems not of their doing. Some unions, particularly AFSCME, have responded with substantial advertising campaigns intended to improve the image of public employees.

The antagonistic atmosphere that has begun to envelope the public and their "servants" has a tendency to encourage the workers to "circle their wagons" to protect themselves from citizen attacks. In areas where the level of public employ-ment is stable or still growing, union membership gains should ensue. However, where labor force cutbacks have been made through layoffs or other means, union membership is almost certain to decline. This is doubly troublesome to unions that suffer both a loss of political influence and a forfeiture of income as a result of decreasing membership rolls (Horton, 1976).

If, as it seems likely, a crisis atmosphere continues to pervade public sector labor relations, unions can be expected to become increasingly aggressive in their relations with management. At the bargaining table, there will be strong union attempts to expand the scope of bargaining beyond the traditional concerns of wages and fringe benefits and into the more nebulous area of "working conditions." Facing a smaller pool of dollars from which to extract compensation gains for their membership, the unions will turn increasingly to nonmonetary issues such as personnel policy, work rules, and job security issues.

Job security will become a particularly pertinent issue during a decade of declining demand for labor (Hollis, 1979). "Contracting out" provisions will be fought by the unions as they seek to protect jobs. Union leaders will call for attrition clauses in collective bargaining contracts to restrict management options in cutting back the number of employees; early-retirement incentives such as lowering the retirement age or offering bonuses for early retirement will be promoted by unions as will employment and wage security provisions, so that laid-off workers will receive priority for possible recalls after reductions in force; RIF provisions will become a topic for bargaining,[5] with seniority favored by unions as the dominant or sole criterion for determining the order in which to dismiss workers; finally, severance pay for laid-off workers will become a subject for bargaining.

Unions may be expected to become increasingly militant over all bargaining issues, invoking the strike weapon with greater frequency. As Abe Zwerding, general counsel for AFSCME has stated (*GERR*, 1/22/79), "If the union can't produce, the members will begin to think about different leadership, and the way for aspiring leadership to get support is to be more militant." During 1981 state employees walked off the job in Massachusetts, New Hampshire, and Minnesota. At the beginning of the school year in 1979, which began with 190 strikes, more than 10 000 teachers walked off their jobs in California, Ohio, Michigan, Pennsylvania, Indiana, and New Jersey. In San Francisco, 3,600 teachers struck for six weeks over the demand that 1,200 laid-off teachers be rehired and a substantial pay increase be granted. In that city and other places where citizen hostility toward the unions has grown, elected officials find themselves in a somewhat untenable situation, being placed "in the position of choosing between labor peace and irate citizenry, or service disruption and, of course, irate citizenry. Perhaps it will be a matter of choosing between degrees of 'irateness'" (Mulcahy, *GERR*, 5/7/79: 20). In any event, the number, duration, and intensity of public sector strikes is likely to increase for at least the next few years.

As the unions and public employers square off in a battle over the allocation of government resources during an era of scarcity, many issues will have to be resolved in the courts. As indicated, some courts have ruled against unions with regard to strike damages. In other cases, the unions have carried issues to the courts with some success, from retaining job security during municipal expenditure reductions (*Board of Education, Yonkers City School District* v. *Yonkers Federation of Teachers*, July 1976) to striking down a statewide ban on wage increases imposed as a result of Proposition 13 in California (*Public Employees Association of Riverside County, Inc.* v. *County of Riverside*, July 1978).

Other changes in labor-management relations that may ensue as a result of the taxpayer revolt and an economy on the downswing are related to the participants in the collective bargaining process. Two trends appear to be discernible. First, there will be efforts to shift financial burdens one level of government higher. This situation already has developed in California, where the state has transferred surplus funds to local governments to maintain or at least slow down the decline in the level of education, recreation, and library services. As similar situations evolve elsewhere, we are likely to observe a gradual shift in decisionmaking authority in the same direction as financial responsibility. In other words, the states will steadily assume more power over local government affairs, and the federal government may increasingly be forced to intervene in the traditional spheres of both state and local governments (Lovell, 1981).

New York again provides a helpful case study of alterations in intergovernmental relations resulting from fiscal crisis. As the crisis in New York City worsened, the state applied leverage through various legislation intended to help the city cope with its staggering debts, including creation of the Municipal Assistance Corporation ("Big Mac") and the Emergency Financial Control Board. Both organizations have "given state officials and private businessmen increased political influence at the expense of city officials" (Weitzman, 1979). Additionally, the federal government was asked to intervene on several occasions during the crisis by both the City and State of New York, primarily to make federal loans. A predictable consequence has been "growing involvement of state and federal government in city affairs, particularly labor relations" (Weitzman, 1979: 342) with "substantial limitations on the city's financial and legal ability to negotiate" (Anderson, 1976: 515). Although municipal unions and management both opposed these developments, the severity of the city's financial condition made local opinion almost irrelevant.

A second change in labor relations occurring as an outcome of fiscal strain and taxpayer resistance is related to the shift in financial and decision-making responsibility upward, namely, an increase in "coalition" or "coordinated" bargaining by the unions. Coalition bargaining refers to further collectivization of union interests into multiemployee bargaining units. The intent, of course, is to enhance political power through speaking in a single voice to the government employer. Although public employee unions have imitated their private sector counterparts in constantly squabbling among themselves (labor solidarity is somewhat of a joke in the United States), there have been some meaningful efforts at coordination. Coalition bargaining has taken place in Michigan, Illinois, California, and Oregon through coordination of teacher bargaining units into statewide coalitions by the National Education Association (NEA). McDonnel and Pascal (1979) predict that state and federally mandated education programs, school finance reform, and TELs will result in further centralization of decision making at the state level, which eventually may result in a two-tiered bargaining system with economic items negotiated with the state and nonmonetary matters decided at the school district level. Statewide union bargaining units would be a necessary outcome of this development. On the national level, CAPE (Coalition of American Public Employees) recently has stepped up its activities in issuing prounion propaganda, making public policy statements (especially on tax reform) and lobbying Congress and the president (CAPE is composed of AFSCME, NEA, American Nurses Association, National Association of Social Workers, National Treasury Employees Union, and Physicians National House Staff Association). Federal employees have also acted in concert recently. On June 14, 1979, a mass demonstration by a ten-union coalition of federal workers posted 3,500 pickets in front of the White House to protest an unsatisfactory wage and benefit proposal of the president, mandatory pay controls for federal employees, and proposed changes in the federal compensation system.

CONCLUSION

There is no doubt that mandated limitations in taxation and expenditures combined with a declining national economy will translate ultimately into fewer dollars for public employee wages and benefits. Governments in the United States have begun reducing employment levels through attrition policies and hiring freezes—convenient and relatively painless short-term solutions that nonetheless pose serious problems for the long-term quality of the public labor force. Harder-pressed governments have taken the more onerous step of laying off workers—more than 45,000 during one year in New York City alone. Ideally, layoffs should be implemented in accordance with productivity criteria for individual workers and government agencies. Unfortunately, however, seniority often determines the order of employee dismissals. With minorities and women generally found in the ranks of the last hired, government affirmative action policies can suffer dramatically.

Clearly, the fortunes of public employees and the quality of the public work force are, as Horton (1976) suggests, "highly dependent on changing economic conditions." Significant wage and benefit gains won by workers and their unions during the late 1960s and early 1970s are likely to fade away in the decade of the 1980s. One serious consequence is that government employment will lose its attractiveness for bright, well-educated young people searching for a career. After all, who needs inadequate wages, inferior fringe benefits, and increasingly intensive public hostility toward "bureaucrats"? Tragically, a vicious cycle could develop with citizen animosity toward public employees spurring more and more layoffs and compensation reductions, leading to poor service delivery and further hostility toward public workers. One blanches at the thought of predicting the final outcome of such an unsavory situation.

The almost astonishing growth spurt in public employee unionism during the 1960s and early 1970s developed within a prolonged period of expansion and growth in public employment and in the national, state, and local economies. While it remains to be seen what the effects of a troubled economy and TELs will be on the unions, logic and past experience indicate that union recruitment efforts should not suffer and might be enhanced. However, where labor force reductions occur, unions will sustain membership losses and some economic hardships. Clouding the organizing situation somewhat is the matter of an increasing taxpayer disaffection for public unions.

In some cities, such as San Francisco, Memphis, Atlanta, and Chicago, a siege mentality has developed, pitting unions against government officials with the citizens' interests sometimes abandoned by the wayside. Under such circumstances the unions tend to become increasingly aggressive in their collective bargaining demands and in their tactics. The siege mentality may be an offspring of the taxpayer revolt that will spread across the nation to other troubled jurisdictions. If so, there will be more strikes, of longer duration, and involving a greater number of public employees. As the 1981 air traffic controller strike demonstrated, even the federal government is not immune. As that strike also showed, union busting may take on an air of increased respectability.

Clearly, many issues and confrontations will be resolved ultimately in the courts. This is a trend that has come to pervade all the functions of public personnel administration in the United States, from hiring to promotions to dismissals. Just as clearly, a trend is emerging in which financial and decision-making responsibilities are being shifted upward in the governmental hierarchy, with the federal and state governments increasingly assuming responsibilities for local government services. Labor relations will follow the tendency toward centralization as coalition bargaining becomes more widespread and as state and federal officials assume a more direct role in the labor affairs of troubled local governments.

If there is a respectable way in which to escape the assorted conundrums outlined, the answer would probably be related to two requisites. First, a genuine and meaningful role must be assumed by the "public" in public sector labor relations—the citizens themselves. Experiments with sunshine bargaining offer some degree of hope for the future. The second requisite is perhaps stated best by Weitzman (1979: 346):

> Labor and management in New York and in other areas beset with deficits must stop blaming each other for the crisis and start reforming their relationships along mutually beneficial lines. Union and city leaders have the most to gain if their efforts are successful, and the most to lose if the current economic malaise persists. Failure to deal effectively with labor-management problems during this critical period will not only destroy collective bargaining in the public sector, but will have serious consequences for the continued survival of our cities.

NOTES

1. Of course, the American people have never been known for their ability to tie together the theoretical with the practical. After passage of California's Proposition 13, a CBS/*New York Times* poll of Californians found that only 3 percent favored cutting back heavily on police services, 5 percent advocated reducing expenditures on trash collection, 9 percent wanted spending reduction in public transportation, and 6 percent desired cutbacks in the schools. Only welfare and social services received substantial support as candidates for heavy spending reductions (43 percent) (Ladd, 1979: 130).

2. Layoffs in California would have been much more widespread had the state not used a budget surplus in excess of $4 billion to ease the effects of Proposition 13.

3. See, for example, Stelluto (1979).

4. According to a recent Friend (1978) survey, the dollar value of fringe benefits for municipal employees during the 1975-1977 period grew from 7.2 to 9.0 percent, whereas the benefits of workers in private industry increased from 8.4 to 9.3 percent.

5. In education, RIF provisions increased strikingly in labor contracts from 1970 to 1975, rising from 13 percent to 44 percent in teacher contracts studied by McDonnel and Pascal (1979).

REFERENCES

ANDERSON, ARVID. 1976. "Local Government Bargaining and the Fiscal Crisis: Money, Unions, Politics, and the Public Interest." *Labor Law Journal* 27 (August): 512-520.

BEHN, ROBERT D. 1978. "Closing a Government Facility." *Public Administration Review* 38 (July–August): 332-338.

BOTT, DONALD E. 1979. "Scarcity and Sanity: Can They Coexist?" *Public Personnel Management* 8 (September–October): 305-308.

FRIEND, EDWARD H. 1978. *Third National Survey of Employee Benefits for Full-Time Personnel of U.S. Municipalities.* Washington, D.C.: Labor-Management Relations Service.

GOVERNMENT EMPLOYEE RELATIONS REPORTER. 1978-1979. Various issues.

HOLLIS, JAMES. 1979. "Educational Labor Organizations and Declining Labor Demand: Analogies from the Private Sector." *Journal of Collective Negotiations* 8: 223-233.

HORTON, RAYMOND D. 1973. *Municipal Labor Relations in New York City: Lessons of the Lindsay-Wagner Years.* New York: Praeger.

——. 1976. "Economics, Politics, and Collective Bargaining: The Case of New York City." In A. Lawrence Chickering, ed., *Public Employee Unions.* San Francisco: Institute for Contemporary Studies, pp. 183-201.

LADD, EVERETT CARLL, JR. 1979. "The Polls: Taxing and Spending." *Public Opinion Quarterly* 43 (Spring): 126-135.

LEVINE, CHARLES H. 1978. "Organizational Decline and Cutback Management." *Public Administration Review* 38 (July–August): 316-325.

LOVELL, CATHERINE H. 1981. "Evolving Local Government Dependency." *Public Administration Review* 41 (January): 189-202.

McDONNEL, LORRAINE M. and ANTHONY H. PASCAL. 1979. "National Trends in Teacher Collective Bargaining." *Education and Urban Society* 11 (February): 129-151.

MILLER, WARREN E. 1979. "Crisis of Confidence. II. Misreading the Public Pulse." *Public Opinion* 1 (October–November): 9-15, 60.

PEIRCE, NEAL. 1981. "States Preview a Tax Revolt Doomsday." *Public Administration Times* 4 (June 1): 2, 5.

PERLOFF, STEPHEN. 1971. "Comparing Municipal, Industry, and Federal Pay." *Monthly Labor Review* 94 (October): 46-50.

RASKIN, A. H. 1976. "Conclusion: The Current Political Contest." In A. Lawrence Chickering, ed., *Public Employee Unions: A Study of the Crisis in Public Sector Labor Relations.* San Francisco: Institute for Contemporary Studies. 203-224.

SMITH, SHARON P. 1976. "Pay Differences Between Federal Government and

Private Sector Workers." *Industrial and Labor Relations Review* 29 (January): 179–197.

STELLUTO, GEORGE L. 1979. "Federal Pay Comparability: Facts to Temper the Debate." *Monthly Labor Review* (June): 18–28.

STRAUSSMAN, JEFFREY D. 1981. "More Bang for Fewer Bucks? Or How Local Governments Can Rediscover the Potentials (and Pitfalls) of the Market." *Public Administration Review* 41 (January): 105–157.

WEITZMAN, JOAN P. 1979. "The Effect of Economic Restraints on Public-Sector Collective Bargaining: The Lessons of New York City." In Hugh D. Jascourt, ed., *Government Labor Relations: Trends and Information for the Future*. Oak Park, Ill.: Moore, pp. 334–346.

John J. DeMarco
University of Georgia

CHAPTER THIRTEEN
PRODUCTIVITY AND PERSONNEL MANAGEMENT IN GOVERNMENT ORGANIZATIONS

Effective personnel management contributes greatly to the productivity of any organization. Personnel systems help to make organizational performance possible by, among other things, attracting and developing talented people, by contributing to their motivation to perform, and by matching structured jobs and individuals. Efforts to improve the productivity of government must, if they are to be successful, focus on the efficient use of human resources since so much of what government does centers on people who produce services.

However, public personnel systems, as with governments in general, are designed to achieve multiple goals, and they have many unintended as well as intended consequences for public management. In addition to organizational effectiveness and efficiency, civil service regulations and procedures also seek to foster equity, merit, due process, the well-being of individual employees, and a responsive human resources policy. Thus, public personnel systems can be impediments to organizational productivity and detract from productivity improvement. Hamilton's review of productivity improvement efforts in New York City (1972: 785) noted that "parts of state civil service laws sometimes appear to have been written precisely to frustrate a productivity effort."

The relationship between public personnel management and productivity is a complex one. Public personnel systems have been observed to both contribute to and detract from the efforts of public managers to improve the productivity of government. This relationship is examined with four objectives in mind: (1) to note the actual or potential contributions that public personnel management makes toward productivity, (2) to examine public personnel management as an impediment to productivity improvement, (3) to review the problems associated with productivity improvement in general, and (4) to discuss some of the prospects for productivity improvement as they relate to personnel management. The chapter proceeds in the order of the foregoing objectives. But first, a definition of productivity is needed. We must consider what productivity is and what it is not.

DEFINING PRODUCTIVITY

Bahl and Burkhead (1977), building on previous work by Bradford, Malt, and Oates (1969), present a conceptual framework for viewing the production of public goods that provides a clear definition of productivity. The system includes five components:

1. Environment
2. Inputs
3. Activities
4. Outputs
5. Consequences

The *environments* of public organizations have needs and make demands for public goods. They also provide resources in the form of funds, personnel, materials, and technologies as well as constraints in the form of laws, regulations, or political pressure. *Inputs* are the labor, capital equipment, and technologies purchased by government. Most government functions, because they consist of the provision of services, are labor intensive; that is, labor is the most costly input. *Activities* are the actual behaviors of government workers and may range from garbage collection to researching the effects of industrial pollution. *Outputs* are the tangible results of activities such as tons of garbage collected or a five-hundred-page report with twenty-five recommendations. *Consequences* are not the direct result of outputs, since they manifest themselves in the environment that is affected by many forces besides government. For example, a local government may effect a significant increase in the tonnage of garbage collected, but the consequences—the cleanliness of streets—may change in an undesirable direction because the environment produces more and more waste.

Productivity is the ratio of outputs to inputs and is often termed efficiency or technical efficiency. However, citizens are usually more concerned about the effectiveness of government, which is the relationship between consequences and the needs and demands provided by the environment. The public also tends to be concerned about the quantity of inputs acquired by the public sector from the environment, in other words, the economy of government. To most of us, this means the amount of taxes we must pay. The Proposition 13 movement in California was more a public statement about the quantity of resources consumed by government than the efficiency or effectiveness of government operations. We should keep in mind that the productivity or efficiency of a government organization may be independent from its effectiveness and economy. A local government, for example, may tax its citizens heavily and may meet their demands quite effectively, but be very inefficient compared with another jurisdiction.

PUBLIC PERSONNEL MANAGEMENT AS A CONTRIBUTION TO PRODUCTIVITY

Nigro and Nigro (1981: chs. 2-3) examine the way in which public personnel systems contribute to organizational survival and effectiveness. Their discussion is relevant to organizational productivity as well. They note that public organizations must extract resources successfully from their environments and also harness their internal resources. Public personnel systems are critical to both processes.

External Resource Extraction— Personnel Planning, Recruitment, and Selection

For public personnel systems, the difficulty lies not in finding people to fill government jobs, but in finding the right people and convincing them to work for government instead of the competition. The process begins with personnel planning—

estimating the future personnel needs of the organization and designing a strategy to ensure that those needs will be met. To know what kinds of people the organization needs to recruit and select, one needs to know the present composition of the work force and how it will change in the near future due to turnover, retirement, and so on. Personnel planners must also estimate the future personnel needs of the organization as a result of new programs and technologies and the ability of the labor market, as the ultimate supplier, to provide those personnel.

Once information is acquired about future personnel needs and opportunities, recruitment specialists must design effective and efficient systems for reaching the kinds of people that will be needed. The nature of the labor market is important here. If it has been determined that a public organization will need fifty computer operators over the next five years, for example, then recruitment efforts will vary in intensity depending on the available supply of computer specialists in the labor market. If competition for computer specialists is high or if the supply is limited, extensive recruitment efforts will be called for. Organizational productivity is enhanced when an appropriate number of people with the right kinds of skills are assembled to meet the needs of the organization.

Over the last twenty years or so, the major problem facing government recruitment specialists has been attracting people with specialized skills that are in high demand. Getting people to apply for entry-level jobs is not the problem. In fact, recently the Office of Personnel Management has begun closing down its job information centers that were an important part of the federal recruitment system. These centers tended to attract many more applicants for entry-level positions than there were jobs available. It was decided that processing some 1 million applicants per year for whom there were no jobs was wasteful and contributing to ill will due to the unmet expectations of job seekers.

The fact that many more people apply for jobs than there are jobs available, together with minimum qualifications for most positions, guarantees the importance of the selection process. In effect, selection specialists must estimate how well an applicant is matched to a particular job. They must do this with incomplete information since the only way to know for sure is to actually hire the applicant. It is impractical to give all applicants a chance to perform in a job, and, because governments spend considerable resources on orientation and training, an incorrect selection decision can be very wasteful.

Thus, a personnel system maximizes its contribution to organizational productivity by identifying accurately personnel needs, by attracting needed personnel and only needed personnel to apply, and by selecting individuals who remain with the organization as productive employees.

Internal Resource Extraction

There are three major ways in which public personnel systems contribute to productivity by extracting human resources from the internal environment of an organization: motivating employees to perform; matching individuals' skills, desires, and aptitudes with job positions; and dealing with public employee unions (Newland, 1972).

Organizations seek "contributions" from individual employees in the form of certain kinds of behavior such as regular attendance, good performance, and innovative problem solving by offering certain "inducements" (Nigro and Nigro, 1981: ch. 3). These inducements may be tangible, such as salary and benefits, or intangible, such as job satisfaction or challenge. This is the essence of employee motivation and worker productivity, and it is clearly associated with several basic personnel functions. Compensation management, employee benefits, job enrichment efforts, and a concern for the overall satisfaction of employees are functions normally assigned to personnel departments. The degree to which a personnel system is effective in rewarding employee performance and in structuring a productive work climate determines to a large extent how well an organization can keep productive employees, correct poor performance, and promote employee initiative.

Second, personnel systems seek to match individuals' skills and ambitions to structured organizational roles or positions. Personnel professionals can modify both the individual and the job in attempting to structure a productive match. Training and career development programs are conducted to identify employee interests and increase their skills, knowledge, and abilities. Position management involves the structuring of jobs—determining the scope of work, the appropriate level of effort, and the rank and compensation levels commensurate to a job. To the extent that personnel systems provide the right combination of employee development and position structuring, productivity can be enhanced greatly.

Finally, the emergence of public employee unions and collective bargaining has opened up a new era of opportunities and problems to be overcome in the utilization of human resources (Stanley, 1972). Effective labor relations includes both the negotiation of labor agreements and the day-to-day administration of them. In the last several years, the practice of productivity bargaining has been identified as an important potential source of productivity improvement. Productivity bargaining is a process whereby "management, in exchange for increased economic benefits, obtains the union's agreement to contract clauses providing greater efficiency" (Nigro and Nigro, 1981: 184). The City of Detroit engaged in such productivity bargaining with its sanitation workers' union and agreed to give bonuses to workers from a savings pool resulting from negotiated changes in the way refuse was to be collected (National Commission on Productivity, 1978). In effect, both sides can benefit from increased efficiency. However, even without productivity bargaining, effective labor relations can impact greatly on organizational productivity by providing labor peace, a clear understanding of management expectations and employee rights, and more employee participation in shaping the work environment.

This brief review has pointed to a number of ways in which effective personnel management can contribute to overall productivity. It is not surprising that personnel has such potential since government is, for the most part, a service provider. However, for years observers in and out of government have noted that personnel systems make demands on other parts of organizations and can detract from the efforts of public managers to improve productivity. This side of personnel management is considered in the next section.

PUBLIC PERSONNEL SYSTEMS
AS IMPEDIMENTS TO
PRODUCTIVITY IMPROVEMENT

Government organizations exist in environments that constantly present them with paradoxes—multiple demands that are inherently conflictual. These environmental paradoxes are partially the result of American society's basic view of public bureaucracy (Whorton and Worthley, 1981: 357):

> American society gives its public bureaucracy enormous powers and expects public managers to energetically provide desired services. On the other hand, there is distrust and disdain evident in the public's view of the governmental bureaucracy. Public managers are given considerable resources and broad discretion for administering programs, but are subjected to an array of laws, procedures, and norms intended to closely control their behavior.

In general, public managers find themselves facing more multiple objectives (many of which are conflicting), greater public scrutiny, more constraints on their activities, and a higher set of expectations than are their private sector counterparts (Rainey, Backoff, and Levine, 1976). Examples of the strains conflicting objectives place on public personnel systems are noted by Levine and Nigro (1975). Government organizations are expected to provide their mandated services effectively and efficiently, but, at the same time, a national personnel policy dictates affirmative action requirements and government as an employer of last resort.

By drawing on another example, we can see how concerns for equity combined with a rigid and slow to change personnel system can detract from productivity. In recent years the offices of private and public organizations have enjoyed significant productivity improvement as a result of the use of new technology in the form of word processors as replacements for standard typewriters. The problem that has been developing is that word processor operators can command much higher salaries than can clerk-typists in the private sector, but the federal personnel system has yet to respond to this. There is no unique classification and commensurate pay schedule for word processor operators in the federal system. The result is that the federal government invests considerable resources (it can take six months to a year to develop a skilled operator) in training only to lose the employee to the private sector. Not only is the federal investment in training lost, but also the productivity benefits one would expect to obtain from the use of relatively expensive word processors are not realized because operator staffs are perpetually inexperienced and in a learning phase. Part of the reason that the position management system has not effected needed changes is due to equity considerations. It must be shown with little room for doubt that word processor operation is qualitatively different from a clerk-typist's job because of a federal personnel policy that is geared strictly toward equal pay for equal work with little regard for the labor market. Part of the problem is simply that the federal personnel system is so large and cumbersome that changes are difficult to effect quickly. In this one area alone, the loss of potential productivity improvement is immense.

These environmental paradoxes have been observed for quite some time. The recent interest in public productivity has only made them more obvious. Sayre (1979) writing in 1948 noted that merit system regulations, concerns for equity, the logic of scientific management, and the emphasis on a career public service, while stemming from legitimate goals, carry with them "costs" in terms of the ability of public managers to manage and forge a productive work environment. He argued, in effect, that the use of "correct" personnel techniques had become more important than the ultimate purpose of personnel management—organizational effectiveness and efficiency. Fourteen years later Golembiewski (1962) made similar observations. He argued that civil service procedures produce a number of unintended consequences that have the effect of increasing the burdens of managing work. In more recent times, the debates surrounding the passage of the Civil Service Reform Act of 1978 repeat this theme, as Nigro (1979: 196) notes:

> The predominant objective of reform had become to make merit a reality rather than a meaningless label for a personnel system which was widely viewed as so enmeshed in red tape, so inflexible, and so inefficient that it was largely responsible for the failure of government to "work."

While few would argue with these general observations, a number of observers have cautioned against heaping all the blame for low government productivity on personnel systems. Whorton and Worthley (1981) argue that the tendency to automatically cite civil service requirements as impediments to productivity improvement may be a psychological "out" for frustrated managers and foster the notion that government performance will always be less than it could be. Peirce (1975: 1675) conducted extensive interviews with public managers about civil service obstacles to efficient management and concluded his study as follows:

> We found in over 600 interviews that in many cases the blame for the inability to make any progress programmatically was placed by management on the civil service system, when in fact the management did not know where it wanted to go, what it wanted to do, and as a result what kind of people it wanted. So it tended to make the system the scapegoat.

In essence, public personnel systems are designed to achieve a number of goals and objectives besides productivity. Many of these objectives are inherently at odds with a single-minded concern for productivity improvement. Through improvements in personnel and general management, some of these conflicts may be eliminated so that the pursuit of other goals will not detract automatically from efficiency. In the case of other conflicts, changes in the ways in which human resources are managed can reduce impediments to productivity. In some cases, however, nonproductivity-related objectives simply have costs attached to them in the form of reduced efficiency. These cases call for a clearer understanding of the trade-offs involved so that policymakers will be in a better position to evaluate the costs and benefits of a particular personnel policy.

As noted, public personnel systems sometimes become the scapegoat for unsuccessful productivity improvement efforts. Part of the reason for the lack of success many public managers encounter in their efforts to improve efficiency stem from the difficulty of measuring and enhancing productivity in government organizations. The next section examines some of the problems associated with government productivity improvement.

PRODUCTIVITY IMPROVEMENT— THE PROBLEMS

A major problem associated with government productivity is that it is usually not what citizens are most concerned about when they express their demands to government. Effectiveness and, in some cases, economy are far more visible and important to the public (Ross and Burkhead, 1974). If a public manager, with the limitations on his or her knowledge and ability to act, must decide between (1) risking a temporary lessening in effectiveness or economy by making changes designed to improve efficiency and (2) maintaining a relatively unproductive system that at least meets citizens' immediate demands, the latter course of action is more likely to be chosen. Effectiveness and economy are highly visible to the public, efficiency usually is not.

Conceptually, we know what government productivity is—the ratio of outputs to inputs. But, for most government functions, we cannot measure outputs directly, and the surrogate measures often employed are badly flawed (Bahl and Burkhead, 1977). Only for a few common functions such as sanitation have reasonable measures of outputs been developed. For most functions, measures of activity are used as surrogates for measures of outputs (Mundel, 1975). When measures of inputs and activities are compared, we measure unit cost, but it is not productivity. There is no way to know if the activities being carried out contribute to the production of outputs. Consider a local police department. We can measure inputs by looking at the department's budget, and we can measure activities such as the number of arrests. With this information we can compute unit cost—the average cost of one arrest. Yet this does not tell us much about the productivity of that police department. Police in one city could concentrate on arresting easily caught minor offenders to maximize their arrest statistics. We would not conclude on the basis of this information that they are more productive than another city police force that concentrates on difficult and time-consuming cases involving homicides or drugs. It is a fairly accurate generalization to say that people will try to increase that which is being measured at the expense of that which is not measured.

Even in those cases where reasonably good measures of productivity are available, public managers do not always know as much as they need to about how to improve productivity (Newland, 1972). Campbell (1972) states this rather well. He notes that most productivity advances in the private sector were not the result of increased employee motivation or improved organizational structures, but were due to new equipment and production systems. What has been done in the area of manufacturing may not be feasible for the production of public services. Downs (1967: 137) notes that for public bureaucracies "the detection of true waste is a matter of judgment and opinion rather than logic or empirical measurement."

Even if productivity can be measured adequately and ways of improving it are generally known, public managers still face what Levine (1979: 181) calls the productivity paradox: "it takes money to save money . . . productivity improvement requires up front costs incurred by training and equipment expenses." Resource scarcity is the most common impetus for productivity improvement efforts, but these efforts require investments that may not be available in a scarce environment. This is related to another difficulty associated with productivity improvement. The process of increasing organizational productivity is a relatively long-term one. The payoffs may not be realized for several years. However, public managers exist in a political environment that stresses the short term.

Public employee unions have been cited as often detracting from the efforts of public managers to improve productivity. The process of productivity bargaining as a method for making labor relations a positive force for productivity was discussed. However, Horton's (1976) review of productivity bargaining experiences suggests that they add little to productivity improvement and may even decrease efficiency. He argues that bonuses promised to employees are likely to exceed the savings realized. He also notes that the quality of services may suffer to increase the quantities upon which bonuses are based. The track record of productivity bargaining tends to support this view. It has seldom been used successfully, and in cases where it was attempted, overall increases in efficiency were not realized (National Commission on Productivity, 1978).

A final difficulty to be discussed here concerns the reasons that public officials attempt productivity improvement. Borut and Carter (1974: 9) note that "productivity improvement seems to be . . . a concept which can generate good will and public support." There is no way of knowing how many, but some productivity improvement efforts are undertaken to convince the public that efficiency is considered important and is being improved. Officials will announce with great fanfare that government productivity is being increased while at the same time providing insufficient resources and support for the efforts to succeed or pursuing other goals such as budget cutting.

This review of the difficulties associated with public sector productivity improvement should not be interpreted as an argument that it cannot be done or that present conditions cannot be improved. It would also be incorrect to conclude that personnel management can make no substantial contributions to increased government efficiency. In the next section, some prospects will be examined.

PRODUCTIVITY IMPROVEMENT—
SOME PROSPECTS FOR
PERSONNEL MANAGEMENT

The surge of interest and activity in government productivity improvement during the 1970s was largely a result of resource scarcity (Westmeyer and Westmeyer, 1977; Suess, 1976; Quinn, 1978; Hamilton, 1972; Campbell, 1972; Borut and Carter, 1974; Balloun and Maloney, 1972; Balk, 1976). As Hayes (1978: 17) points out, "local departments and agencies do not spontaneously develop or undertake major productivity improvements." They are not expected to do so, and they rarely have the necessary resources and flexibility to undertake significant efforts. It was the pressure of scarce resources that prompted central authorities to turn to productivity efforts to cope with resource decline. The objective of most public productivity projects is to achieve productivity improvement by reducing expenditure growth while holding important service levels constant. This emphasis on productivity improvement to promote economy is likely to result in personnel cuts by attrition, employee reassignments, and even reductions in force becoming priorities for many government personnel offices. The degree to which personnel managers deal effectively with these changing priorities will have a significant effect on the degree of disruption and turmoil that cutback management tends to promote.

One significant aspect of this move toward greater government economy is likely to bypass personnel. Historically, personnel allocation decisions in government organizations have been centered in budget departments. At the federal level, for example, it is the Office of Management and Budget, not the Office of Personnel Management, that determines agency personnel ceilings.

Personnel units themselves will not be immune from the trend toward cutting back. The federal Office of Personnel Management is currently in the process of shifting its emphasis to "bedrock" personnel management (Andronicos, 1981). This constitutes a move away from a total human resource management concept toward the more traditional, familiar, and administrative functions associated with personnel. Shifts of this type may indeed increase the productivity of personnel units since they will attempt to do less and concentrate their efforts on the more familiar. However, we cannot predict at this point what the ultimate impact will be on personnel's contribution to overall organizational effectiveness and efficiency. Nevertheless, the new direction for personnel management, at the federal level at least, is to do less.

One area of personnel management is enjoying a renewed emphasis at the state, local, and federal levels. Performance appraisal is an announced priority of the Reagan administration. The Civil Service Reform Act of 1978 requires that all federal agencies have a developed performance appraisal process in place by October 1, 1981. Personnel managers at all levels of government will be involved closely in attempts to improve the evaluation of employee performance and ultimately employee productivity. It would seem, at this point, that performance appraisal is "where the action is" in terms of personnel's contribution to productivity.

Another technique designed to enhance organizational productivity is the use of quality circles. Although they were developed first in the U.S., only recently have public organizations in this country begun to experiment with them. A quality circle is a group of employees who meet regularly under the direction of a facilitator, usually a supervisor, for the purpose of identifying new, more effective, and more efficient ways of doing work. The circle is also charged with implementing and evaluating improvements. The idea behind quality circles is that the employees who actually perform the work are in the best position to suggest and implement successfully productivity improvements. The Office of Personnel Management and several Defense Department agencies have had some experience in their use, but the verdict is not yet in on their value.

The attempts of public managers to develop productivity measures are likely to continue. As was discussed these measures are difficult to design and the surrogate measures that tend to be used are badly flawed. Nevertheless, they have the potential, if used properly, to aid managers, including personnel managers, in improving productivity. Even activity-based measures can be used as scanning devices by management to help point out problem areas in government service delivery. For example, if a public manager notices that unit cost figures are increasing at an unusual rate, the manager can scrutinize the departments in question more closely to find out why and then take whatever actions are appropriate. Even if productivity cannot be measured directly, this does not mean that attempts to design better measures of performance should be abandoned. Public personnel managers can play an important role in developing and refining useful measures of individual performance.

CONCLUSION

Public personnel management both contributes to and detracts from the efforts of government managers to improve productivity. This mixed role will continue so long as personnel systems must respond to a number of legitimate needs in addition to organizational efficiency. The task facing public personnel professionals is to improve and refine the management of human resources and to reduce impediments to productivity improvement so that personnel can make a maximum contribution to the efficiency of government without sacrificing the other goals that must be addressed. The need is to strike a balance between productivity as a desirable characteristic of public organizations and the other demands we place on our public institutions.

REFERENCES

ANDRONICOS, W. 1981. "Devine-Ordered Shakeup at OPM Set for August 3," *Federal Times*, (August 3): 4–14.
BAHL, R. and J. BURKHEAD. 1977. "Productivity and the Measurement of Public Outputs." In C. Levine (ed.), *Managing Human Resources: A Challenge to Urban Governments*. Beverly Hills: Sage Publications: 253–269.

BALK, W. 1976. "Decision Constructs and the Politics of Productivity," In M. Holzer (ed.), *Productivity in Public Organizations.* Port Washington, New York: Kennikat Press: 173-195.

BALLOUN, J. and J. MALONEY. 1972. "Beating the Cost Service Squeeze: The Project Team Approach," *Public Administration Review,* 32 (September-October): 531-538.

BORUT, D. and S. CARTER. 1974. "Local Productivity Programs: An Overview," *Public Management,* 56, (June): 9-11.

BRADFORD, D., R. MALT, and W. OATES. 1969. "The Rising Cost of Local Public Services: Some Evidence and Reflection," *National Tax Journal,* (June): 185-202.

BURKHEAD, J. and P. HENNIGAN. 1978. "Productivity Analysis: A Search for Definition and Order, "*Public Administration Review,* 38, (January-February): 34-40.

CAMPBELL, A. 1972. "Old and New Public Administration in the 1970's," *Public Administration Review,* 32, (May-June): 343-347.

DOWNS, A. 1967. *Inside Bureaucracy.* Boston: Little, Brown.

GOLEMBIEWSKI, R. 1962. "Civil Service and Managing Work: Some Unintended Consequences," *American Political Science Review,* 56, (December): 961-973.

HAMILTON, E. 1972. "Productivity: The New York City Approach," *Public Administration Review,* 32, (November-December): 784-795.

HATRY, H. 1978. "The Status of Productivity Measurement in the Public Sector," *Public Administration Review,* 38. (January-February): 28-33.

HAYES, F. 1978. "City and County Productivity Programs," *Public Administration Review,* 38, (January-February): 15-18.

HAYWARD, N. 1980. "Productivity Improvement in the Public Sector," In J. Peterson and C. Spain (eds.), *Essays in Public Finance and Financial Management.* Chatham, New Jersey: Chatham House: 165-176.

HORTON, R. 1976. "Productivity and Productivity Bargaining in Government: A Critical Analysis," *Public Administration Review,* 36 (July-August): 407-414.

LEVINE, C. 1979. "More on Cutback Management: Hard Qustions for Hard Times," *Public Administration Review,* 39, (March-April): 179-183.

LEVINE, C. and L. NIGRO. 1975. "The Public Personnel System: Can Juridicial Administration and Manpower Management Coexist?," *Public Administration Review,* 35, (January-February): 98-107.

MUNDEL, M. 1975. *Measuring and Enhancing the Productivity of Service and Government Organizations.* Hong Kong: Nordica International Limited.

NATIONAL COMMISSION ON PRODUCTIVITY. 1978. "Improving Municipal Productivity: The Detroit Refuse Collection Incentive Plan," In J. Uveges (ed.), *Cases in Public Administration.* Boston: Holbrook: 131-151.

NEWLAND, C. 1972. "Personnel Concerns in Government Productivity Improvement," *Public Administration Review,* 32, (November-December): 807-815.

NIGRO, F. 1979. "The Politics of Civil Service Reform," *Southern Review of Public Administration,* 3, (September): 196-239.

NIGRO, F. and L. NIGRO. 1981. *The New Public Personnel Administration* (2nd ed.). Itasca, Illinois: Peacock.

PEIRCE, N. 1975 "State-Local Report: Proposed Reforms Spark Civil Service Debate," *National Journal,* 7, (December 6): 1673-1678.

QUINN, R. 1978. "Productivity and the Process of Organizational Improvement: Why We Cannot Talk to Each Other," *Public Administration Review,* 38, (January-February): 41-45.

RAINEY, H., R. BACKOFF, and C. LEVINE. 1976. "Comparing Public and Private Organization," *Public Administration Review*, 36, (March–April): 233–244.

ROSS, J. and J. BURKHEAD. 1974. *Productivity in the Local Government Sector*. Lexington, Massachusetts: Lexington.

SAYRE, W. 1979. "The Triumph of Technique Over Purpose," in F. Thompson (ed.), *Classics of Public Personnel Policy*. Oak Park, Illinois: Moore Publishers: 30–35.

STANLEY, D. 1972. *Managing Local Government Under Union Pressure*. Washington, D.C.: Brookings Institution.

SUESS, T. 1976. "Productivity Immeasurable Despite Current Research," *National Civic Review*, 65, (November): 511–512.

THOMPSON, F. 1975. *Personnel Policy in the City: The Politics of Jobs in Oakland*. Berkeley: University of California Press.

WESTMEYER, T. and W. WESTMEYER. 1977. "Public Worker Productivity Found to be Elusive," *National Civic Review*, 66, (July): 370–371.

WHORTON, J. and J. WORTHLEY. 1981. "A Perspective on the Challenge of Public Management: Environmental Paradox and Organizational Culture," *Academy of Management Review*, 6, (July) 357–361.

Mary M. Lepper

Syracuse University

CHAPTER FOURTEEN
AFFIRMATIVE ACTION: A TOOL FOR EFFECTIVE PERSONNEL MANAGEMENT

The field of public personnel management has become a growth industry over the past ten years. Whereas new personnel approaches, techniques, and skills are enjoying widespread institutional support and popularity, the one that is expected to produce a broad range of talented people for service in the public sector—*affirmative action*—is also the most controversial. No other single personnel issue is debated as hotly.

Convictions run high among proponents and opponents alike of affirmative action programs, although the supporters and detractors themselves are not necessarily divided along lines of sex or ethnicity. Individual women and minorities oppose the application of affirmative action in both admissions to educational institutions and employment whether public or private.

Furthermore, some supporters of equal employment opportunity (EEO)[1] in the abstract object to specific applications such as affirmative action. This phenomenon of support for a general policy, but opposition to specific applications, occurs in many social and political contexts. Prothro and Griggs (1960: 276-294) found that there was no consensus in the polity on a number of statements that related principles of majority rule to specific applications of minority rights. A number of political science researchers have documented the lack of ideological consensus on the basic principles of democracy.[2] In the mid-1960s at the height of the civil rights movement, McClosky (1964: 361-382) found that the American citizen supports the idea of liberty in the abstract but is less likely to support specific applications of civil rights.

The demands of government—as with the society it both serves and mirrors—are changing and growing in complexity and at an accelerated rate. It is no longer sufficient just to carry out current missions and meet crises as they arise; rather, the challenge is to anticipate problems and develop solutions before serious situations arise. The past two decades have been ones of social and political turmoil, raising questions regarding the efficacy of basic values and established institutions. Institutions need constant reexamination not only in the context of what is happening at a given time, but also in terms of what is in the offing. The immediate need is to devise new methods and techniques to foresee and manage changes that are occurring in American society.

Affirmative action is one approach devised to meet the economic and social needs of women and minorities.[3] However, the rhetoric is fierce, by both supporters and those opposed, passions run deep, and objective analysis becomes increasingly difficult. Adding to the difficulty with this policy are the many connotative meanings surrounding affirmative action. Lack of a definitional consensus precludes even a language for arguing the issues surrounding this policy.

Diffusing the rhetoric and examining the viability of affirmative action programs raise a number of important questions: What is the societal objective of affirmative action? Is the objective a legitimate one for political pursuit? Are the current affirmative action procedures the appropriate mechanisms for reaching the societal goals identified at the outset? These questions are linked inextricably, but for purposes of discussion, the policy issues will be addressed separately from the implementation procedures. The sections that follow will examine (1) a working definition of affirmative action and some of its pros and cons as a public policy, (2) a philosophic argument in support of affirmative action as public policy, (3) economic and social issues that support the need for affirmative action, (4) a brief legal history of affirmative action, and (5) specific implementation strategies for affirmative action personnel procedures (recruiting, testing, selection, promotion, and termination).

WHAT IS AFFIRMATIVE ACTION?

Some of the confusion surrounding affirmative action results from the erroneous use of three terms interchangeably: equal employment opportunity, nondiscrimination, and affirmative action. These terms have quite different meanings, implications, and applications.

   Equal employment opportunity is the most inclusive term. It exists when all employees and applicants are judged on individual abilities, without regard to race, sex, or ethnic background. Notice its resemblance to the concept of merit.[4] Nondiscrimination and affirmative action are subsets of equal employment opportunity that operate independently but are mutually complementary. *Nondiscrimination* means that no employee or applicant for employment or admission to educational and professional schools can be subjected to different treatment based on race, color, religion, sex, or national origin. Recently, physical and mental handicaps and age have been added to this list. *Affirmative action* requires that special actions be taken to ensure that groups previously excluded from employment or admission be included in those activities to overcome past discrimination.

   Of these two equal employment opportunity concepts, *nondiscrimination* is essentially passive and negative: "Thou shall not." In contrast, *affirmative action* is dynamic and positive: "Thou shall 'remove all barriers however formal and subtle' that prevent minorities and women from having equal access to all levels of the nation's educational, industrial, and governmental institutions" (Benokraitis, 1978: iii). The two concepts are consistent, but each requires different compliance procedures.

   Nowhere was the inability of equal employment opportunity to yield equal results illustrated better than by the testimony in a suit alleging gender discrimination against A.T. & T.'s New York Telephone Company brought under Title VII of the Civil Rights Act of 1964. The executives and their attorneys were sophisticated in their knowledge of the requirements of nondiscrimination in employment. They understood that persons are often able to establish employment discrimination based on bias in tests used in the selection process. The company personnel director explained that New York Telephone's hiring and promotion decisions were not based on tests alone but on a "total person concept." How this concept was determined was left vague, but the white males conducting the interviews consistently chose other white males for jobs and promotions. Asked about these results, the director explained that women and minorities were rejected at the interview stage because they failed to meet the "total person" standard; when asked in what way, the reply was, "They are different" (Ginsberg, 1977: 8-14).

Rein (1976: 94) explains this phenomenon, saying that people often hold and act upon a set of beliefs of which they are not aware, thus making the beliefs difficult to detect and change. Other students of social phenomena point out that discrimination is composed of a lot of unacknowledged attitudes that afflict "unprejudiced" white males. Thalberg (1972: 45-48) terms this protective camouflage "visceral racism." Visceral racism, thus, allows those in the dominant group to misperceive the society as progressing with all deliberate speed toward equality. In these circumstances they see no need for special actions such as affirmative action requires, for society is a nondiscriminator. Indeed, affirmative action strikes them as unfair.

To sort out the components of equal opportunity policy, imagine a continuum. One end represents *discrimination*, the conscious or unconscious efforts to exclude groups of individuals on the basis of their race, sex, national origin, or religion. The other end represents *affirmative action*, a corrective effort to include the previous targets of discrimination. In the middle is *nondiscrimination*, a passive policy that regards traditional mechanisms for hiring and standards of employment as acceptable insofar as there is no intentional discrimination. Some would argue that discrimination and nondiscrimination are equivalent to the extent that a policy of nondiscrimination may tolerate and perpetuate unintentional biases and do nothing to rectify conditions caused by earlier discriminatory practices or entrenched cultural mores.

The difficulty lies in determining whether the impact of a certain policy is in fact equal and, if it is, whether the equality is also equitable or just. An assumption often made is that equal treatment produces equity[5] or at least substantive equality. There is a widely accepted myth in the United States that equal opportunity produces equity. It does not. The failure of the Fourteenth Amendment to the Constitution to achieve equal access to the goods and rewards of society is compelling evidence of the fallacy of this reasoning. It was one hundred years before the passage of the Civil Rights Act of 1964, which contained sanctions for discrimination, that a beginning of meaningful access to at least economic and political if not social equality began for blacks (Dorn, 1979).

Proponents of affirmative action believe that adherence to affirmative action, philosophically and procedurally, can promote social equity and, in the public sector, lead to a more representative bureaucracy.[6] Social equity and representative bureaucracy are very much in the forefront of current interests and concerns of public administration theorists and practitioners.[7]

Opponents of affirmative action are equally convinced that not only will affirmative action destroy merit as a basis of employment but also that it threatens (Glazer, 1975: 197)

the abandonment of our concern for individual claims to consideration on the

> basis of justice and equity, now to be replaced by a concern for rights for
> *publicly* [emphasis added] determined and delimited racial and ethnic
> groups.

Critics such as Glazer raise legitimate concerns. Yet, from the perspective of political science or public administration, is there a better means to make this determination on distribution of rewards in a democracy than publicly?

Those resisting the principles of affirmative action often fail to appreciate the magnitude of unintentional and intentional discrimination or their systemic qualities. They denounce affirmative action's potential for infringing upon an individual's rights in the currently highly competitive labor market; in so doing they ignore the broader problem affirmative action is meant to correct—systemic discrimination that has as its basis a multitude of ethical, moral, social, economic and political values.

THE PHILOSOPHIC ISSUES

The capacity of public policy to alter social behavior is a complex problem (Sabatier and Mazmanian, 1979: 481). Any chance of societal changes occurring requires policy to be grounded on clear conceptual grounds to build support for the implementation process in the body politic. During the congressional debate on the Civil Rights Act of 1964, a comment often heard was "You cannot legislate attitudes." But following the passage of the act, customs and practices did change, whether attitudes did or not, resulting in a better quality of life for many people. Perhaps the educative process embodied in the law is not valued enough, for once the law is operative and effective it proves wrong the myth of "It can't work."

Affirmative action is a redistributive policy. It has worked only minimally to improve the social and economic status of minorities and women, as will be shown in the next section. The failure of supporters of affirmative action to demonstrate clear philosophic and legal bases is one reason that the approach does not work well. Confusion reigns among both supporters and opponents.

The questions affirmative action raises are difficult ones. Does previous discrimination justify a policy of preference at the present time? Are minorities and women entitled to compensation if the discrimination was not illegal at the time it occurred? Does retribution for past wrongs require the government to tell employers, private and public, how they must change their personnel procedures? Must retribution be made to a class, some of whom may not have been harmed? How far can preference go before it becomes reverse discrimination?[8]

The establishment of a process to recruit more women and minorities into educational and employment institutions, and the establishment of numerical goals and timetables as affirmative action requires, have split the ranks of individuals and groups who formerly fought discrimination. As one critic (female) notes (Black, 1974: 93),

> The specific conceptual and moral conflict . . . is the displacement in law of individual justice, wherein a designated person is held responsible for wrongs which can be laid to him, by the introduction of its opposite: collective edicts wherein an entire group is held corporately and legally responsible for past wrongs (or for current unwanted social effects) impossible to lay to any determinate individuals.

Others who oppose affirmative action principles generally and specifically reject numerical goals and timetables, calling them "quotas,"[9] include Daniel Bell, Sidney Hook, and Daniel Boorstin.[10]

While recognizing the claims by minorities and women of discrimination against them, philosophers, jurists, politicians, and citizens believe that current affirmative action programs challenge traditional thought on guaranteed constitutional rights and raise ethical questions as to the rights of individuals as defined by the liberal ethos (Schaar, 1978: 14). The critics argue that, even if compensation is due for discrimination, it can only apply to individuals, not to groups. Their position is that only individuals have been harmed—not all those comprising the group. Supporters of affirmative action argue that this is a "straw man" argument, since all members of those groups identified by the terms "minority" and "female" have been so disadvantaged educationally, economically, and most important psychosocially that they require restitution to overcome past institutionalized inequities (Lepper, 1976: 368).

Equality has long been a source of political controversy. Aristotle noted that it is in their striving for what is fair and equal that men become divided. Plato expressed the wisdom of the established order with the claim that nature produces a hierarchy of superiority in which rulers and philosophers emerge at the top. Through the ages, in societies where power and privilege are not distributed equally, it is assumed that nature has caused the disparity. When man creates unequal opportunity, he can be obliged or even forced to change the system (Frankena, 1962: 13).

The participants in both the American and French revolutions believed that they had put in place a radical egalitarism: in principle, if not always in practice, *men* become equal before the law, and the idea of the worth of the individual establishes a principle of moral equality. The most basic moral and political principle of this egalitarism is equality of opportunity for individuals. Equality of opportunity is seldom questioned as being other than in the best interest of all. However, Blackstone (1977: 64) argues persuasively, "But distribution on the basis of merit is fair only if those who compete on that basis have an equal opportunity to acquire meritorious characteristics or abilities." To reject or adopt this principle has wide-ranging implications for public policy: "what is at stake fundamentally is a redefinition of equality and much of the future shape of social policy rests on the outcome of the debate" (Schaar, 1978: 16).

The reasons for continuing inequality are numerous and complex. As is true for many social phenomena, it is difficult to identify precise causal links when the interaction of the variables is uncertain. To blame lack of ability (blaming the victim) or racism and sexism (blaming those in power) is too simplistic. Inequality is not only a matter of individual abilities and aptitudes; it is also a social fact. The opportunities of an individual are in part governed by her or his position in society (Beteille, 1969: 15). All talents are not desired equally by any given society. Some will be admired or rewarded more than others. According to Schaar (1967: 229), "Every society has a set of values and they are arranged in a more or less tidy hierarchy . . .. Commitment to the formula implies prior acceptance of an already established social-moral order."

Boulding (1973: 1051) suggests the following explanation of the continuing inequality in economic rewards given to women and minorities:

> It is less well recognized that discrimination among members of the labor force is only a case of a much larger process of role learning and role acceptance, which begins almost from the moment of birth. It is not merely that differences in skills are learned, as in Adam Smith's famous passage about the porter and philosopher, but images of possible roles on the part of both the role occupants and the role demanders are likewise learned in the long process of socialization.

The model of choice in the American system is based on the characteristics that the white male evinces. Minorities' and women's talents are considered to have minimum value.

To ignore the already developed hierarchy of characteristics as well as role socialization and claim that inequalities are not systemic biases but based on lack of personal ability is a cruel doctrine. This suggests that equal opportunity is itself a discriminator in that it promotes and supports the present inequitable system. Overcoming all the present barriers to equity may require a redefinition of equality and justice.

Rawls's *A Theory of Justice* (1971) offers such a definition: "A conception of social justice, then, is to be regarded as providing in the first instance, a standard whereby the distributive aspects of society are to be assessed" (1971: 9). For Rawls, justice is fairness and the foundation of fairness rests initially on two principles (1971: 14–15):

> First, each person is to have an equal right to the most extensive basic liberty compatible with similar liberty for others.
> Second, social and economic inequalities are to be arranged so that both (a) [are] reasonably expected to be to everyone's advantage, and (b) attached positions and office [are] open to all.

Rawls points out that institutions that favor certain starting places over others are especially deep inequalities. "Not only are they pervasive, but they affect men's initial chances in life" (1971: 7). He points out that if one has a *just* society, then it is only necessary to "police" it, but if one starts with an unjust society, then there is an obligation to eliminate the institutional causes of injustice.

Rawls's first principle applies to the political system and the second to the economic and social system. He argues that individuals can hold different conceptions of justice and "still agree that institutions are just when no arbitrary distinctions are made between persons in the assigning of basic rights and duties and when the rules determine proper balance between competing claims to the advantages of social life" (1971: 5). He considers those inequalities based on "natural chance or the contingency of social circumstances" to be particularly onerous (1971: 367). They require retribution. He says that rational men will agree to principles that regulate their claims against each other and decide what is just and unjust since, in the first instance, they will not know what is to their own advantage. "Somehow we must nullify the effects of specific contingencies which put men at odds and tempt them to exploit social and natural circumstances to their own advantage" (1971: 137).

The Voting Rights Act of 1965 overcomes the inequalities that conscious choice had established in the political system. However, present conditions do not meet Rawls's second premise of what constitutes justice, and thus we have an unjust society. One could only accept the inequalities if those who are perpetuating the inequalities could be presumed to be "behind a veil of ignorance" not knowing which provisions are to their own benefit (1971: 136-142). The egalitarian principle of equal consideration of interests is not the same as Rawls's account of justice as fairness (Benn, 1967: 72).

Boulding's acknowledgment of the difficulty of overcoming role socialization and Rawls's call for distributive shares of the goods and rewards that overcome inequalities based on chances of birth to achieve the just society provide a strong philosophic base for a policy requiring not just *nondiscrimination* but *affirmative action*.

Rawls's argument is complex, but any definition of equality that requires a redistribution of the goods and rewards of society is difficult to achieve. Before people will agree to a redistribution of the goods and rewards, they have to be convinced that there is a true inequality based not on individual action but an inequality that has been chosen consciously by some in the society to the detriment of others. Therefore, it is instructive to examine some of the inequalities that are present in society today.

SOCIAL AND ECONOMIC
INDICATORS OF INEQUALITY

The social and economic inequalities are different for women than are those for minorities. In this section, those differences will be highlighted wherever possible. There are different types of information available for study of each group. Out of a variety of indicators, the following will be examined: unemployment statistics, income, type of job, and educational levels. Two areas that will not be addressed but that are of concern are access to quality housing and access to medical care. Both these areas of discrimination are related to a complex of interacting variables: a job with sufficient income to allow the person to pay for goods and services; stereotypes and myths regarding minorities and women's work force behavior and income potential as perceived by banks and financial institutions; and availability of transportation to job, housing, and medical facilities. At present, it is difficult to weight these variables in a way to reflect reality since they may act on one another differently, based on other cultural mores.

While some of people's behavior is based on a set of values that is so internalized that a person is often unaware of it, public opinion polls demonstrate that there is a clear difference in how whites and blacks perceive the quality of life for blacks. Whites are much more optimistic about the improved conditions for blacks, with 80 percent feeling the quality of life of blacks in the United States has gotten better over the past ten years, whereas only 55 percent of blacks believe that their life is better than it was ten years ago. A poll taken in December 1980 by the Gallup opinion organization (*Gallup Opinion Index*, 1981, 35–36) illustrates this difference and that blacks are themselves becoming more pessimistic about their treatment since as recently as May 1980. The question was as follows:

> Looking back over the past 10 years do you think the quality of life of blacks in the U.S. has gotten better, stayed the same or gotten worse?

Responses from all participants are in Table 1.

Table 2 presents the findings based on a variety of demographic characteristics. The pattern of answers is very close in all variables. There are some slight differences in region, with 80 percent believing that life had improved for blacks in the South. Republicans were 10 percent more likely than Democrats to believe that treatment for blacks and whites is comparable. More generally, older people and those with more education believe the quality of life for blacks has gotten better. The answers are too close to generalize, but a limited case can be made that those who are further away from the problems are more sanguine.

At the time of the December poll, a question was asked on attitude toward affirmative action. It tends to support the hypothesis made earlier in this chapter

TABLE 1   Quality of Life of Blacks, May–December 1980 versus 1970

	IMPROVED	STAYED SAME	WORSENED	NO OPINION
December	77%	13%	6%	4%
May	71	17	8	4

SOURCE: *Gallup Opinion Index*, February 1981, pp. 35–36.

TABLE 2 Quality of Life of Blacks in Last Ten Years, December 1980 versus 1970

Looking back over the last 10 years, do you think the quality of life of blacks in the U.S. has gotten better, stayed the same or gotten worse?

	IMPROVED	STAYED SAME	WORSENED	NO OPINION
National	77%	13%	6%	4%
Sex				
Male	76	13	6	5
Female	77	12	7	4
Race				
White	80	11	5	4
Nonwhite	55	22	18	5
Education				
College	78	14	5	3
High school	78	11	7	4
Grade school	71	13	7	9
Region				
East	69	18	7	6
Midwest	74	15	6	5
South	83	7	6	4
West	80	11	6	3
Age				
Under 30, total	72	16	9	3
18–24 years	74	13	9	4
25–29 years	69	20	9	2
30–49 years	77	13	6	4
50 and older	79	10	5	6
Income				
$25,000 and over	79	13	4	4
$20,000–24,999	81	9	5	5
$15,000–19,999	76	15	5	4
$10,000–14,999	76	9	12	3
$5,000–9,000	76	16	4	4
Under $5,000	70	15	10	5
Politics				
Republican	80	10	6	4
Democrat	75	13	7	5
Independent	78	13	5	4
Religion				
Protestant	77	13	6	4
Catholic	79	10	5	6

TABLE 2   Quality of Life of Blacks in Last Ten Years, December 1980 versus 1970 (Continued)

	IMPROVED	STAYED SAME	WORSENED	NO OPINION
Occupation				
Professional and business	78	11	6	5
Clerical and sales	86	7	6	2
Manual workers	75	15	7	3
Nonlabor force	80	11	4	5
City Size				
1,000,000 and over	69	14	10	7
500,000–999,999	72	17	8	3
50,000–499,999	80	10	7	3
2,500–49,999	78	12	5	5
Under 2,500, rural	80	12	4	4
LABOR UNION				
Labor union families	77	12	6	5
Nonlabor union families	76	13	7	4

SOURCE: *Gallup Opinion Index*, February 1981, p. 36.

in regard to the issue being clouded by rhetoric and confused understanding about what affirmative action is. The question was worded,

> Some people say that to make up for past discrimination, women and members of minority groups should be given preferential treatment in getting jobs and places in college. Others say that ability as determined by test scores, should be the main consideration. Which point of view comes closest to how you feel on this matter?

It is impossible not to wonder if the wording of the question did not bias the answers. But even allowing for this, it is obvious that there is not much support for

TABLE 3   Preferential Treatment, 1977–1979

	GIVE PREFERENCE	ABILITY MAIN CONSIDERATION	NO OPINION
Latest	10%	83%	7%
1979[a]	14	80	6
1977			
October	11	81	8
May	10	83	7

[a]Asked of full-time college students representing sixty campuses.

SOURCE: *Gallup Opinion Index*, February 1981, p. 37.

affirmative action at present. The only discernible difference of more than 1 or 2 percent is that between Democrats and Republicans, with the Democrats being eight percentage points more favorable toward "Preference."

The attitudes expressed in the Gallup poll may help to explain why from 1948 until 1980 unemployment has increased for everyone, but to a greater degree among minorities (see Table 4). Some of the differences may be due to the passage of the Civil Rights Act of 1964 causing increased numbers of minorities to actively seek employment. Unemployment for women is also higher, but, again, much of the increase may be a function of more women moving into the labor market in greater numbers than was true historically. Table 5 indicates the duration of employment by race and Hispanic origin, with that for minorities being higher.

The type of occupation is another indicator of status and rewards. As the level of skill and professionalism rises, the participation by minorities and women declines. The problem that minorities experience in moving into professional categories is particularly acute. They are faced with two decision points at which discrimination may be present: getting into higher education and professional schools and, then, being able to score well on the credentialing tests. Participation in professional schools remains low (see Table 6).

Blacks represent 11 percent of the population yet constitute 2.2 percent of all physicians or roughly 1 black doctor for every 3,500 black citizens. There is 1 white physician for every 750 white persons in the general population. There appear to be only 250 Hispanic and Native American physicians in the entire United States. According to 1970 census figures, the ratio of lawyers is 1 to 720 white, 1 to 4,195 blacks, 1 to 6,677 Native Americans, and 1 to 35,000 Mexican Americans.

A 1973 survey of the seventeen largest law firms in Chicago reveals that of 1,364 attorneys there are only 1 black partner, 13 black associates, and 8 Spanish-surnamed persons, 7 of whom work for the same firm (O'Neill, 1975: 94). What makes this particularly troublesome is that in many ways Chicago has been a better place for blacks economically and socially for a longer period of time than have most other large U.S. cities (Myrdal, 1944).

TABLE 4   Unemployment Rates by Sex and
Race, 1948 versus 1980

SEX/RACE	1948	1980
White males	3.4%	5.2%
Black and other males[1]	5.8	11.4
White females	3.8	5.6
Black and other females[1]	6.1	11.1

[1] Black and other: American Indians, Asian Americans, and Eskimos.

SOURCE: U.S. Department of Labor, *Monthly Labor Review*, May 1981, p. 74.

TABLE 5 Unemployed Persons by Duration of Unemployment, Race, and Hispanic Origin, 1978–1979

WEEKS OF UNEMPLOYMENT	TOTAL		WHITE		BLACK AND OTHER		HISPANIC ORIGIN	
	1978	1979	1978	1979	1978	1979	1978	1979
	Duration							
Total, 16 years and over	6,047	5,965	4,620	4,577	1,427	1,386	435	415
Less than 5 weeks	2,973	2,869	2,212	2,263	581	606	218	210
5 to 14 weeks	1,875	1,892	1,413	1,438	462	454	127	133
15 weeks and over	1,379	1,202	995	876	384	326	90	71
15 to 26 weeks	746	684	553	518	193	166	53	48
27 weeks and over	633	518	442	359	191	159	38	23
Average (mean) duration, in weeks	11.9	10.8	11.3	10.3	14.0	12.7	10.9	9.3
Median duration, in weeks	5.9	5.4	5.5	5.1	7.2	6.4	5.0	4.9
	Percentage Distribution							
Total unemployed	100.0%	100.0%	100.0%	100.0%	100.0%	100.0%	100.0%	100.0%
Less than 5 weeks	46.2	48.1	47.9	49.4	40.7	43.8	50.0	50.7
5 to 14 weeks	31.0	31.7	30.6	31.4	32.4	32.8	29.1	32.1
15 weeks and over	22.8	20.2	21.5	19.1	26.9	23.5	20.9	17.1
15 to 26 weeks	12.3	11.5	12.0	11.3	13.5	12.0	12.2	11.6
27 weeks and over	10.5	8.7	9.6	7.8	13.4	11.5	8.7	5.6

SOURCE: U.S. Department of Labor, *Monthly Labor Review*, April 1981, 40.

TABLE 6 Minority Participation in Professional Schools, 1980–1981

Medical School	
Black	5.7%
Native American	0.3
Hispanic, Mexican-American	1.5
Hispanic, Puerto Rican	0.5
Total Minority	8.0
Law school	
Black	4.0
Native American	0.3
Hispanic, Mexican-American	1.0
Hispanic, Puerto Rican	0.4
Total Minority	5.7

SOURCE: Unpublished information from U.S. Department of Education, Center for Educational Statistics.

Income is another important indicator of economic and social equity, as life-style is often tied very closely to income. However, to generalize about income, it is necessary to relate it to education attainment and work experience. The earnings differential by race is smallest for college-educated men who have been out of school fewer than six years and largest for men with some high school education and fewer than six years of work experience (Taylor, 1981: 29). Nearly two out of five black and Hispanic men but only one out of five white men earned under $200 weekly in 1979. Black and Hispanic men are about half as likely as white men to average $400 or more a week. These figures demonstrate a pattern, but at the same time they conceal many earnings differences between racial and ethnic groups. Among the factors accounting for some of the differentials are relative youthfulness of blacks and Hispanics compared with whites and the industries and occupations in which they are employed.

Interestingly, the earnings patterns among black and white women employed full time are more similar than are those of black and white males. Black and Hispanic women are somewhat more likely than white women to be earning less than $150 weekly. However, there is little difference in the proportions of black and white women at the higher earnings levels—$400 or more weekly. A number of general social and economic indicators suggest that black women managers are approaching parity with white women managers.

The difference in income levels is linked closely to occupations. White males, white females and black females are clustered in white-collar positions; black males cluster in blue-collar work. However, a comparison of men's and women's earnings in the same job categories presents a clear pattern of divergence. Absent any other difference, this gap appears to be discrimination based on gender. Table 7 demonstrates this gap. This gap becomes even more significant considering that 80 percent

TABLE 7 Male versus Female Earnings in Same Job Category

OCCUPATION	WOMEN	MEN
Sales	$0.45	$1.00
Clerical	0.64	1.00
Service	0.65	1.00
Manufacturing	0.59	1.00

SOURCE: U.S. Commission on Working Women. (1981). "News Release." (Jan.): 1.

of the women in the work force are in clerical, sales, service, factory, or plant jobs. This helps explain the gap in annual earnings of men and women. It also suggests one reason why so many female heads of household do better economically on some form of public assistance than they do in paid employment.

Another way of describing the inequities faced by women and minorities is to examine the poverty rate. The poverty rate among blacks is three times that of whites, and Hispanics are two and one-half times more likely to live below the poverty level than are whites. Families headed by white females are much more likely to live below the poverty status than are those headed by white males (U.S. Department of Commerce, 1978).

LEGAL AND HISTORICAL DEVELOPMENT OF EQUAL EMPLOYMENT OPPORTUNITY AND AFFIRMATIVE ACTION

Economic and social indicators offer convincing proof that women and minorities are not sharing equally with white males in the goods and rewards of society. President John F. Kennedy, recognizing that nondiscrimination was not yielding very much progress, took his lead from the so-called "Philadelphia plan,"[11] which required numerical goals and timetables for bringing minorities into construction unions and called for affirmative action by federal contractors.[12] President Lyndon Johnson broadened Executive Order 11246 by giving specific instructions as to how affirmative action plans were to be developed and by adding sex as one of the protected categories in 1967.

Under a refinement in the order, known colloquially as "Revised Order 4"[13] calling for written affirmative action plans, and including white-collar positions as well as blue-collar ones, the stage was set for controversy because those who previously were not threatened by nondiscrimination would be under the revised order.

Affirmative action has the potential for overcoming the existing psychosocial, educational, and economic obstacles facing women and minorities. The objective of affirmative action is not to deprive those now holding the positions; rather, affirmative action requires the white male to compete—to be better, if you will— with those with whom he would have been competing all along except for *his preferred position*. Affirmative action does not require the taking of incompetent people, whether for admissions to higher education or employment. It only requires that, where the employer identifies job categories in which the representation of minorities and women is lower than chance would indicate based on their presence in the labor pool, and two people of equal skills and abilities apply, the preference be given to the minority or woman.

Equal employment opportunity and its subset affirmative action are derived from a collection of executive orders, legislation, and court decisions. Fair employment law and civil rights law both provide for EEO policies. The two types of law have different legislative and judicial histories. This is often overlooked in commentaries on judicial decisions in the area of affirmative action. The Court's finding may differ substantially depending on the legal basis for the suit. This will be illustrated in a later comment on *Washington* v. *Davis* (1976).

Beginning with the Civil War constitutional amendments, a wide range of governmental action has been taken to provide equal opportunity. There has been progress, but the end is not yet achieved, as evidenced by the flurry of charges of "reverse discrimination" as well as the failure to ratify the Equal Rights Amendment.

The Fourteenth Amendment to the Constitution requires that "No state shall deprive any person of life, liberty, or property, without due process of law; nor deny to any person within its jurisdiction the equal protection of the laws." For the next eighty years the focus was on ensuring that there was no discrimination by the state. However the existence of "Jim Crow laws" made a mockery of the concept of equality. To some, the Supreme Court's allowing states to mandate "separate but equal" was a travesty of justice.[14]

It was not until 1941 that the federal government began to enforce equal employment opportunity in private industries that held government contracts.[15] And not until 1954 did the Supreme Court declare "separate" as fundamentally unequal in education.[16]

Franklin Roosevelt issued Executive Order 8802 on June 25, 1941 requiring nondiscrimination by contractors. It is likely that it was only because of the wartime coalition that Congress let stand what many were to call an abridgment of an individual's right to do what he wanted with his personal property (e.g., a business) (Sovern, 1966). The requirement to develop affirmative action plans for federal agencies was not implemented until 1969.

The civil rights movement of the 1950s and 1960s called for equal treatment for all minorities in all areas of life—education, economic, transportation, public accommodations, and suffrage. During the height of the movement, the question of whether discrimination on the basis of race and ethnicity was against the policy of the United States was an open issue. Specifically, the question posed, "Should the government stop private parties from discriminating against ethnic and racial minorities?" (Winter, 1975: 1). The answer was the passage of the Civil Rights

Act of 1964. This represented a major shift in public policy. The act required nondiscrimination by both private and public parties in education if they were receiving public aid, housing, and employment. In 1965 suffrage was guaranteed by the Voting Rights Act. Buttressed by additional legislation, momentous court decisions, and executive orders, the questions now revolve around whether the government should require employers, private and public, to bring about not only nondiscrimination but equity as well. Must employers change the criteria by which they make employment decisions to provide for a public policy that seeks to prevent discrimination currently and to require retribution for previous discrimination through changing even neutral procedures that allow systemic bias to continue?

The judiciary at both state and federal levels are enormously influential in setting the boundaries of policy but ultimately the political process, not the courts, must work out a reconciliation of conflicting claims, interests, and values. A critical question is whether the government can implement a policy lacking substantial consensus when such a policy raises fundamental questions of guaranteed rights. This section will not provide a definitive answer to that question but will provide a framework regarding what legal parameters are in place. A limited discussion of specific court cases will be given since additional material that applies to EEO and affirmative action is discussed in Chapter 3, "What Every Public Personnel Manager Should Know."

The experience gained through administering EEO laws over the past quarter-century highlights the difficulty in changing institutions that are linked tightly to the nation's political, ethical, and social mores. The initial effort to guarantee EEO was part of state fair employment laws. The basis of the movement toward greater equity is found in the executive orders begun by Franklin D. Roosevelt in 1941 and broadened and strengthened by each subsequent president.

The early efforts stemmed from the belief that simple prohibition of discrimination would ensure equality of opportunity. However, the executive orders, legislation, and court decisions of the 1960s and 1970s reflect a recognition that removing discriminatory practices will take "affirmative action." The pressures have been strong on both sides of the issue. The evidence suggests that the failure of equal employment programs to yield equity is more from lack of implementation than from lack of legal grounds for taking affirmative action. An examination of the legal bases is instructive in this regard.

MAJOR STATUTES AND ORDERS REQUIRING EQUAL EMPLOYMENT OPPORTUNITY AND/OR AFFIRMATIVE ACTION

1. *Executive Order 11246 as amended by Executive Order 11375* prohibits discrimination in employment by all employers who hold federal contracts and requires affirmative action programs by all federal contractors and subcontractors. Firms with contracts worth more than $50,000 and involving fifty or more em-

ployees must develop and implement written programs of affirmative action. This order is enforced by the Department of Labor's Office of Contract Compliance Programs.

— *2. Executive Order 11478* (34 F.R., August 10, 1969) *as amended by Executive Order 12106* (44 F.R. 1053, December 30, 1978) requires federal agencies to develop equal employment opportunity programs including affirmative action plans. Administered originally by the Civil Service Commission but transferred to the Equal Employment Opportunity Commission under the Reorganization Plan No. 1 of 1978, EEOC has issued guidelines for development and implementation of the affirmative action plans for minorities and women, nondiscriminatory policy as part of Section 501 of the Rehabilitation Act of 1973, and Section 403 of the Vietnam Veterans' Readjustment Assistance Act of 1974.

EEOC's guidelines for governmental affirmative action plans cover the same aspects of the personnel process as are called for by OFCCP's affirmative action regulations, which are spelled out in Section 41 CRF 60-2 of the Executive Order 11246 (often referred to as Revised Order 4), a series of results-oriented procedures to which an employer makes a commitment to apply "good faith efforts." A minimum development of a plan requires the following:

1. Developing a data base for all job classifications.
2. Identifying all areas of underutilization.[17]
3. Analyzing all employment practices for possible practices that are having an adverse impact on women and minorities.
4. Identifying problems and developing a program of change that affirms commitment to affirmative action.
5. Appointing an individual to be responsible for the implementation of the program.
6. Developing numerical goals and timetables to overcome any underutilization identified.

The sections of the executive orders that have been the most controversial are numerically based remedies. The use of numbers as goals, or in some instances as remedies for established discrimination, has been required by federal agencies and upheld by the courts.[18]

The goals arrived at are generally expressed in a flexible range rather than by a fixed number. Goals are not semantic ploys to avoid the negative connotations of a quota since determinations of compliance are not made solely on the question of whether the goals are actually reached but on the organization's "good faith effort" to implement and fulfill the total affirmative action plan.

The employer is not compelled to hire unqualified persons or to compromise genuinely valid standards of employment to meet the established goals. Goals can provide a valuable standard for determining whether the process is providing the relief envisaged in the same manner as the setting of objectives by management for all the organization's activities. Although goal and timetable provisions, as is true for all other legal requirements, are subject to misinterpretation and abuse in individual cases, there is very little evidence that such abuse has occurred despite the many claims of "reverse discrimination." For example, a number of Jewish groups filed a large number of "reverse discrimination" allegations involving higher education employment. As a consequence, a person was appointed to review all these allegations for a period of two years. What was found was that many white males were receiving rejection letters indicating that the reason they were not hired was due to "affirmative action requirements"; the investigations revealed that in less than one-tenth of 1 percent was a woman or minority hired.[19]

3. *Title VII of the Civil Rights Act of 1964, as amended by the Equal Employment Opportunity Act of 1972,* forbids discrimination on the basis of race, color, national origin, religion, or sex in any term, condition, or privilege of employment by unions and by employers. Title VII covers all private employers of fifteen or more persons; it was amended on March 24, 1972 to cover all public and private educational institutions, state and local governments, and all public or private employers, whether or not they receive any federal funds. It is enforced by the Equal Employment Opportunity Commission. Employers are not required to develop affirmative action plans unless there is a finding of discrimination. The basic body of legal principles applying to employment discrimination has been developed in Title VII litigation and in cases involving the Fifth and Fourteenth Amendments to the Constitution.

4. *The Equal Pay Act of 1963* was the first sex discrimination legislation enacted, requiring equal pay for equal work regardless of sex. The law is enforced by the Wage and Hour Division of the Department of Labor, and reviews can be conducted without prior complaint.

If a violation is found following a review, the employer is asked to settle by raising wages and awarding back pay to underpaid workers. Should the employer refuse, the Department of Labor is authorized to go to court. No affirmative action is required other than back pay. Differentials in pay based on seniority, merit, or any factor other than sex are permissable.

5. *Age Discrimination in Employment Act of 1963* and amended in 1974 covers state and local government, bans discrimination for persons at least 40 but less than 65 years of age, and applies to any organization with twenty or more employees. It is enforced through the Wage and Hour Division of the Department of Labor.

6. *The State and Local Government Assistance Action of 1972* amended in 1976 and 1980, Public Law 93-112 (commonly known as Revenue Sharing), requires nondiscrimination by state and local governments on the basis of race, ethnic origin, religion, and sex. It is enforced by the Office of Civil Rights of the Department of Treasury. With a finding of discrimination the governmental unit receiving

revenue-sharing funds can be required to set goals and timetables or risk losing funds.

7. Section 503 of the Rehabilitation Act of 1973 prohibits discrimination against the handicapped if an agency has a federal contract of $2,500 or more and requires nondiscrimination against physically or mentally handicapped employees or applicants in any job for which the persons are qualified. There must be affirmative action to hire, promote, and otherwise treat handicapped individuals without discrimination in all employment policies. Goals and timetables are not required. The Office of Federal Contracts Programs of the Department of Labor is responsible for enforcement.

The main arbiters of policy questions regarding equal employment practices are the courts. Since 1964 a substantial body of employment law has developed as a result of enforcing the orders and legislative acts cited.

Many of the cases involve private employers, but the decisions are used to establish the permissable and nonpermissable procedures in the public sector as well. A number of personnel practices, such as recruitment, testing, selection, and seniority, are addressed in the court findings. The courts have ordered public sector employers to develop affirmative action plans containing goals and timetables if a finding of discrimination is made. These findings allow some generalization toward standard procedures as well as substance, although some decisions are narrow and are restricted to the cases under review.

A private case of great importance to the agencies charged with enforcement of equal opportunity statutes is *U.S.* v. *Hayes International Corporation* (1969). In making a finding the Court relied almost exclusively on statistics to support the charge of discrimination under Title VII. The decision indicated that having a highly disproportionate numerical representation of minorities or females in any job classification in relation to their presence in the work force constitutes strong evidence of discriminatory practices. The burden of proof is on the employer to show that this underrepresentation is not due to overt or institutional discrimination. Allowing the use of numbers to establish a prima facie case strengthens the ability to establish discrimination.

If *Brown* v. *The Board of Education* (1953 and 1954) is the landmark case in school desegregation, then the landmark case for nondiscrimination in employment is *Griggs* v. *Duke Power* (1971). The Court ruled that, while some employment practices or procedures may be neutral on the surface or in intent, they cannot be maintained if they operate to freeze the status quo of prior discriminatory practices. The Court maintains that Congress, in passing Title VII, was concerned with the consequences of employment practices and not merely intent and that the Court recognizes "inadequacy of broad and general testing devices as well as the infirmity of using diplomas or degrees as fixed measures of capability" (*Griggs*, 1971: 65). The use of testing continues to be a major issue as it applies to discrimination. The Court said in *Griggs* and *Albermarle Paper Co.* v. *Moody* (1975) that the test must be job related. In a more recent case, *Washington* v. *Davis* (1976), the Court made clear that the *Griggs* standard cannot be applied unless the case is brought on Title VII grounds. Thus, even though the tests are having an adverse impact, they are not necessarily illegal. Under the constitutional due process rights of the Fifth Amendment, the use of the written personnel tests by the police department can be sustained despite the fact that four times as many blacks as whites fail the tests.

In *U.S.* v. *City of Chicago* (1978), the Court ruled that the Chicago police department had violated Title VII because the test that was used excluded a disproportionate percentage of minority applicants for invalid reasons. In a similar case, *U.S.* v. *City of Syracuse* (1980), a consent decree was agreed to that requires the police and fire departments to recruit and set goals affirmatively for five years to overcome the past effect of civil service tests. Both cases stemmed from violations of the nondiscrimination clause of the State and Local Assistance Act of 1976.

The concept of providing equal pay for equal work without regard for race, ethnic group, or sex has been difficult to implement. Minority males earn less than white males, but this is generally due to their being clustered in low-paying occupations and industries. The problem is different for women regardless of race. A typical practice is to require the same work but to give the job a different title and a lower pay rate when it is performed by a woman. The issues are complicated by the notion of comparable worth. Are some jobs held traditionally by females of "comparable worth" to the organization as other jobs performed traditionally by males? The Equal Pay Act does not address this latter issue. The Court, in *Peltier* v. *City of Fargo* (1976), told a police department that it could not change the name of the duty just because it is now performed by women. In this case, the police department had hired women as "car markers" and paid them less than they had previously paid patrolmen for doing the same work. All that was different was the name of the activity. The police department justified the difference in pay because the patrolmen could do other duties if needed. As the economy constricts, women and minorities may face increasing resistance to the requirement of equal pay.

In the area of allowing preference, the one most often given in the public sector is veterans preference. The courts have upheld the legality of this practice despite the disparate impact on minorities and women. Most recently, in the case of *Massachusetts* v. *Feeny* (1979), involving a challenge to the state in allowing veterans preference, the Court said it was allowable under the Equal Employment Opportunity Act of 1972, which specifies that nothing in the act was to modify veterans preference. The Court has held that Congress has had the opportunity to change this practice. The issue was raised specifically during the debate on the Civil Service Reform Act of 1978, and Congress was not willing to disallow veterans preference.

The importance of public employment as a source of jobs and economic betterment cannot be overlooked. The quantity, quality, and impact of jobs with federal, state, and local governments have given them prime importance in the nation's social and economic life. By late 1975, nearly one out of every five Americans was a public employee (not counting public educational institutions). These public employees worked in the largest "industry" in the nation, one that has grown phenomenally during the twentieth century, particularly since the end of World War II. It is an industry less affected by recessions or depressions than others: public employment almost doubled during the Great Depression, and in the 1974–1975 recession it increased by nearly a million employees. It is projected to continue to be the fastest-growing employment field despite current desires for reducing the size of the public sector.

Fueled by huge increases in federal aid to states and local governments, the sharpest increases in government employment for the past decade have occurred at the nonfederal level. Paid more than $150 billion annually in direct compensation, public employees at all levels perform the full range of jobs in the nation's economy with increasing emphasis on white-collar and service work. Because of the great quantity and variety of jobs available in the public sector and because of the quantity and pay of those positions, public employment is of great importance to the nation and the economy, particularly for minority groups and women. Employment in the public sector provides status and prestige that allow minorities and female heads-of-households sufficient income to have the capability to borrow money and to secure better housing, medical care, and education for the young.

Data on the employment and utilization of minorities and women in federal, state, and local governments are not easy to obtain or interpret, but some patterns do emerge despite the limitations of such data collection.[20] Despite the widely accepted myth that women and minorities are beginning to dominate public sector employment, they are found to be underrepresented in virtually every governmental jurisdiction compared with their proportions in the population. It is this last phrase—"to their proportions in the population"—that causes employers the most trouble. What population does one use as the base for determining availability of women and minorities? There is no clear-cut answer. Different agencies use different bases. Those who claim this problem prevents them from establishing goals and timetables are probably not very interested in doing so. Great flexibility is allowed to the organization for goal and timetable setting. Meeting the goal is not required in an absolute sense; rather, measurement is based on "good faith effort."

DEVELOPING
THE AFFIRMATIVE
ACTION PROGRAM

It is not easy for the average manager or personnel specialist to understand fully and implement an affirmative action program. As was discussed earlier in this chapter, there is a whole maze of rules and regulations that often appear to be in conflict, both with the merit system and with the commitment to integrate minorities and women into the labor force. Often there is a misperception of the numbers of women and minorities available with the requisite job skills. There is even confusion in knowing how to establish the criteria upon which selection will be made due to the difficulty in validating bona fide occupation qualifications (BFOQ).

The only way for the public sector to meet the challenge is for management to assume an affirmative duty to make specific results-oriented commitments. The first requisite for a successful affirmative action program is strong leadership by those responsible for the personnel system. They must be sure the first-line supervisors and middle management know what affirmative action is and how to implement it. They must stress that a real merit system is compatible with affirmative action—people are selected and promoted for their job-related abilities. Affirmative action and the merit system provide both objectivity and due process in the personnel system.

Upon completion of the utilization analyses, the next step is establishment of goals and timetables based on the analyses and the identification of problem areas. The responsible persons must design specific action-oriented programs to correct the problem areas (deficiencies) and achieve the goals. Such action-oriented programs must as a minimum include

1. Specific procedures to assure that persons of each underutilized racial, ethnic, and sex group apply for employment in the organization at least in proportion to their presence in the appropriate labor market for position vacancies in each job group or organizational unit in which they are underutilized; a goal is required.
2. For any criterion determined through the analysis of the personnel process to be the cause of a problem area and that is a test or "other selection technique," a program for further analysis to determine whether it is causing an "adverse effect." If this analysis indicates an adverse effect, a program to validate the criterion should be undertaken.
3. Specific programs to change or overcome the effect of policies and practices that produce the problem areas in a manner as to prevent a future adverse effect.

What all this suggests is that taking affirmative action can lead to good personnel management. It is important to realize that common sense and good faith efforts will go a long way toward a successful marriage of merit and affirmative action. Each organization will have problems unique to its situation; for this reason, it is advisable not to look for "the model plan" but to develop one based on the needs that the audit of the organization has shown to be needed and possible (Kerner Commission, 1968).

Merit and equal employment opportunity have the same objective: to ensure that selection is based on individual abilities and skills. The tensions that have arisen between them are due to the unskilled application of both "merit system" and "affirmative action" procedures. Affirmative action does not deny opportunities to those who are presently holders of the positions, but allows each person to achieve his or her full potential. Discrediting affirmative action will not cause the problem of lack of social and economic equity to vanish. The objectives that one sets and the methods that one uses depend on how critical the situation is perceived and an analysis of what forces must be overcome (Edel et al., 1977: 123).

In summary, affirmative action programs are steps that employers take to change their future employment profiles. This is the core of affirmative action's meaning. An effective affirmative action program is one way of providing that the organization is capable of continuous renewal by developing to the fullest its human resources, removing obstacles to individual fulfillment, respecting individual dignity, and developing the most efficient and productive staff possible.

How you view affirmative action will depend upon your concept of justice and equity. It is unlikely that consensus on the meaning of justice, equity, and equality is possible. The questions are real. Is it enough to give opportunity to compete or should there be a policy that will cause the present employment pattern for women and minorities to change? Critics of affirmative action have focused on procedures to the exclusion of considering whether the social objective is one that the government should pursue. Do we have a just society that needs policing, or do we have an unjust society that requires basic institutional change before there will be fairness?

Whatever one's view as to the meaning of "just," the absolute minimum criterion for evaluating the justness of the activity is that it cannot be such as to result in the sheer continuation of the injustice to the outsiders. This is the minimal requirement. The maximum requirement is the actual achievement of an order that will bring the outsiders into full participation in the society and its goods. The task of affirmative action is to guarantee the minimum and move toward the maximum (Edel et al., 1977: 122).

NOTES

1. Equal employment opportunity refers to the body of statutes, executive orders, and case law aimed at preventing and overcoming individual and systemic discrimination based on racial, ethnic, and sex categories.

2. Some of the political scientists who have examined this phenomenon are Philip E. Converse, Robert E. Lane, Herbert McClosky, and V. O. Key, Jr. A discussion of political attitudes and behavior is found in Irish and Prothro (1971: chs. 2 and 5).

3. For purposes of this chapter, the definition of minority will be that used by the Commission on Civil Rights (1977: 3): "A minority group is a group of persons distinguished by race or ethnic origin, who share common ancestry, physical characteristics, cultural background, and experience, and who, because of overt discrimination and institutional barriers are denied equal access to social, economic and political opportunities, and/or who continue to suffer the effects of past discrimination."

4. Merit means the selection of individuals based on their competence and achievement. See Bell (1972: 29-68). A distinction is drawn between this concept of the merit principle and the term "merit system." The merit system refers to a network of civil service laws, rules, and regulations that jointly embrace the merit principle and is used interchangeably with "civil service system." For a discussion of the relationship between EEO and merit, see Stewart, "EEO, Merit and the Political Environment of Public Sector Employment," *Policy Studies Journal*, forthcoming.

5. In this chapter the definition to be used for "equity" is that of *Black's Law Dictionary*: "In its broadest and most general signification . . . [equity] denotes the spirit and the habit of fairness, justness, and right dealing which would regulate the intercourse of men with men,— the rule of doing to all others as we desire them to do to us; or, as it is expressed by Justinian 'to live honestly, to harm nobody, to render to every man his due.' It is therefore the synonym of natural right or justice. But in this sense its obligation is ethical rather than jural, and its discussion belongs to the sphere of morals. It is grounded in the precepts of the conscience, not in any sanction of positive law" (Black, 1957: 63).

6. The concept of representative bureaucracy is developed by Harry Krantz in *The Participatory Democracy* (Lexington, Mass.: Lexington Books, 1976).

7. See Frederickson (1974, 1980). Frederickson is both a scholar and, as president of East Washington State University, a practitioner.

8. "Reverse Discrimination" is a term that has been adopted to signal the problem of a white male who does not get some reward or honor due to the belief that giving it to a minority or a woman discriminates against him. Some students of affirmative action believe it to be much overused and probably not reflective of reality. However, as has been noted in the body of the paper, if people believe a phenomenon to be true, the consequences are the same whether or not it reflects reality.

9. Quotas are the number or proportion that is allowed or admitted. Critics of affirmative action insist that a numerical goal and timetable operates as a quota. Supporters of affirmative action do not agree in that goals are process-oriented rather than absolute.

10. Bell (1972: 29–68) presents a lucid argument that is representative of Boorstin, Hook, and others' opposition to affirmative action.

11. Executive Order 10925, 3 CFR 442 (1961). These plans applied only to blue-collar workers in the construction industry and called for "Plans for Progress' requiring numerical goals for minority membership in the unions. They are known as "Philadelphia plans" as this was the first city to be required to meet the standard. These plans provided the basis for later affirmative action plans and surprisingly those who were later to oppose numerical goals were supportive of this requirement.

12. Executive Order 11375, 3 CFR 320 (1967).

13. 41 CFR 60-2 (1973).

14. See, for example, *Black Law Journal* 3 (1922); *Howard University Law Review* 15 (1968–69); *University of Chicago Law Review* 36 (1968–69).

15. Executive Order 8802, 3 CFR 957, 1941. Issued by President Franklin D. Roosevelt.

16. *Brown* v. *Topeka School Board* (1954) 347 U.S. 483. There are five suits in this group but they are all known as "Brown."

17. Underutilization is a term that is used for the purposes of setting numerical goals and timetables under the executive orders. It is established from reviewing all job categories and determining which of them have fewer women and minorities than proportionally are available in the relevant labor pool.

18. The courts have required numerical goals and timetables in a number of cases involving private employers as well as some public ones. Examples are *Carter* v. *Gallagher* (1972) 452 F.2d 315; *Franks* v. *Bowman Transportation* (1976) 424 U.S. 747; *U.S.* v. *City of Chicago* (1978), 573 F.2d 416. Consent Decree: *U.S.* v. *City of Syracuse* (1980) 80-Cv-53.

19. As director of the Higher Education Division, Department of Health, Education and Welfare, the author was responsible for making the determination whether or not there has been discrimination against white men as the complaints alleged.

20. It is difficult to compare the participation rates of women and minorities in all the public sectors. State and local governments are required to file a form EEO-1 with the Equal Opportunity Commission, but making comparisons is difficult because there are so many different job classifications and pay rates involving many small jurisdictions. The International City Management Association collected some material on women in local government in 1979, but, not having more recent comparable data, it was decided to not generalize in this area.

REFERENCES

"Affirmative Action Outranks Seniority." 1981. *Public Administration Times* 4 (June 1): 11.

BARRY, BRIAN. 1973. *The Liberal Theory of Justice: A Critical Examination of* the Principal Doctrines in *A Theory of Justice by John Rawls.* New York: Oxford University Press.

BEAUCHAMP, TOM L. 1977. "The Justification of Reverse Discrimination." In William T. Blackstone and Robert D. Heslep, eds., *Social Justice and Preferential Treatment.* Athens: University of Georgia Press.

BELL, DANIEL. 1972. "On Meritocracy and Equality." *The Public Interest 29.* (Fall): 29–68.

BENN, STANLEY I. 1967. "Egalitarianism and the Equal Consideration of Interest." In T. Roland Pennock and John W. Chapman, eds., *Nomos IX–Equality.* New York: Atherton, 72–74, 104–126.

BENOKRAITIS, NIJOLE V. 1978. *Affirmative Action and Equal Opportunity: Action, Inaction, Reaction.* Boulder, Colo.: Westview Press.

BETEILLE, ANDRE. 1969. *Social Inequality.* Baltimore: Penguin Books.

———. 1977. *Inequality Among Men.* Oxford: Basil Blackwell.

BLACK, HENRY CAMPBELL. 1957. *Black's Law Dictionary.* St. Paul, Minn.: West.

BLACK, VIRGINIA. 1974. "The Erosion of Legal Principles in the Creation of Legal Policies." *Ethics* 84 (No. 2): 90–96.

BLACKSTONE, WILLIAM T. 1977. "Reverse Discrimination and Compensatory Justice." In William T. Blackstone and Robert D. Heslep, eds., *Social Justice and Preferential Treatment.* Athens: University of Georgia Press, 52–83.

BORGATTA, EDGAR F. 1976. "The Concept of Reverse Discrimination and Equality of Opportunity." *American Sociologist 11* (May): 62–72.

BOULDING, KENNETH and BARBARA REAGAN. 1973. *The American Economic Review* 63 (No. 5): 1049–1061.

BOWERS, NORMAL. 1981. "Youth Labor Force Activity: Alternative Surveys Compared." U.S. Department of Labor, Bureau of Labor Statistics, *Monthly Labor Review,* 102 (March): 3–16.

BOYLES, WILEY R. 1978. "Court-Ordered Affirmative Action." *Public Personnel Management* 7 (November–December): 394–398.

BRANDT, RICHARD B. ed. 1962. *Social Justice.* Englewood Cliffs, N.J.: Prentice–Hall.

Califano v. *Webster.* 1977. 430 U.S. 313.

Carter v. *Gallagher.* 1972. 452 P.2d 315.

CARTER, ROBERT L. et al. 1965. *Equality.* New York: Pantheon.

CASSEL, ROBERT. 1978. "Are Present Laws Effectively Ending Employment Discrimination Against Women and Minorities?" *Commonwealth Club of California Transactions 72* (November): 3–27.

Castro v. *Beecher.* 1972. 469 R.2d 725.

CATLIN, JAMIE BETH, JOHN A. SEELEY, and MARGARET TALBURTT. 1974. *Affirmative Action: Its Legal Mandate and Organizational Implications.* Ann Arbor, Mich.: Center for the Study of Higher Education.

CHAPMAN, WILLIAM. 1977. "White Males and 'Reverse Discrimination'." *Washington Post* (March 20): 7

COMMISSION ON CIVIL RIGHTS. 1977. *To Eliminate Employment Discrimination.* Washington, D.C.: G.P.O.

———. Maryland Area Council. 1981. *A Civil Rights Agenda for the 1980's.* Washington, D.C.: G.P.O.

CONVERSE, PHILIP E. 1964. "The Nature of Belief Systems in Mass Publics." In David E. Apter, ed., *Ideology and Discontent.* New York: Free Press, pp. 206–261.

COUNTRYMAN, VERN. 1965. *Discrimination and the Law.* Chicago: University of Chicago Press.

DAHRENDORF, RALF. 1962. "On the Origins of Social Inequality." In Peter Laslett and W. G. Runciman, eds., *Philosophy, Politics and Society.* New York: Barnes & Noble.
DORN, EDWIN. 1979. *Rules and Racial Equality.* New Haven, Conn.: Yale University Press.
EDEL, ABRAHAM. 1977. "Preferential Consideration and Justice" in William Blackstone and Robert Heslep, eds., *Social Justice and Preferential Treatment.* Athens, Georgia: University of Georgia Press, pp. 112–140.
EQUAL EMPLOYMENT OPPORTUNITY COMMISSION. 1979. *Federal Affirmative Action Instructions Pursuant to Section 717 of the Civil Rights Act of 1964.* EEO-MD 702. Washington, D.C.: G.P.O.
——. 1979b. *Instructions for Affirmative Action Program Plans for Hiring, Placement, and Advancement of Handicapped Individuals Including Disabled Veterans for Fiscal Year 1980.* EEO-MD 703. Washington, D.C.: G.P.O.
FREDERICKSON, H. GEORGE, ed. 1974. "Symposium on Social Equity and Public Administration." *Public Administration Review* 34 (January–February). 1–51.
——. 1980. *New Public Administration.* University: University of Alabama Press.
FRANKENA, WILLIAM. 1962. "The Concept of Social Justice." In Richard B. Brandt, ed., *Social Justice.* Englewood Cliffs, N.J.: Prentice-Hall.
"Female Workers 'Worth Less' Than Men." 1980. *Public Administration Times* 3 (January): 7.
GALLUP POLL INDEX, 1981. Princeton, N.J.: American Institute of Public Opinion (February).
GINSBURG, RUTH BADER. 1977. "Women, Equality and the Bakke Case." *Civil Liberties Review* 4 (November–December): 8–15.
GLAZER, NATHAN. 1975. *Affirmative Discrimination: Ethnic Inequality and Public Policy.* New York: Basic Books.
——. 1978. *Affirmative Discrimination: Ethnic Inequality and Public Policy.* New York: Basic Books.
GLENCHUR, PAUL. 1979. "Women Still Work for the Lowest Pay." *Syracuse Post Standard* (October 22): 7.
GOLDMAN, ALAN H. 1979. *Justice and Reverse Discrimination.* Princeton, N.J.: Princeton University Press.
GOODMAN, CARL F. 1977. "Equal Employment Opportunity: Preferential Quotas and Unrepresented Third Parties." *Public Personnel Management* 6 (November–December): 371–397.
HARMON, MICHAEL M. 1974. "Social Equity and Organizational Man: Motivation and Organizational Democracy." *Public Administration Review* 34 (January–February): 11–17.
HART, DAVID K. 1974. "Social Equity, Justice, and the Equitable Administrator." *Public Administration Review* 34 (January–February): 3–10.
HAWORTH, J. G. 1975. "Earnings, Productivity and Changes in Employment Discrimination." *American Economic Review* (March) 65: 158–168.
IRISH, MARIAN D. and JAMES W. PROTHRO. 1971. *The Politics of American Democracy.* Englewood Cliffs, N.J.: Prentice-Hall.
KENYON, D. 1965. In Tobert Carter et al., eds., *Equality.* New York: Pantheon, Section IV.
KERNER COMMISSION. 1968. *Supplemental Reports, National Advisory Commission on Civil Disorder.* Washington, D.C.: G.P.O.
KEY, V. O., JR. 1961. *Public Opinion and American Democracy.* New York: Knopf.

KLINEFELTER, JOHN and JAMES THOMPKINS. 1976. "Adverse Impact in Employment Selection." *Public Personnel Management* 5 (May–June): 199–204.

KLUGER, RICHARD. 1975. *Simple Justice: The History of Brown v. Board of Education and Black America's Struggle for Equality*. New York: Random House.

KOVARSKY, IRVING. 1968–1969. "Testing the Civil Rights Act." *Howard Law Journal* 15: 227–248.

LANE, ROBERT E. 1965. "The Politics of Consensus in an Age of Affluence." *American Political Science Review* 59 (December): 874–895.

LEON, CAROL BOYD. 1981. "The Employment-Population Ratio: Its Value in Labor Force Analysis." *Monthly Labor Review* 10 (February): 36–45.

LEPPER, MARY M. 1975. "The Continuing Struggle for Equal Opportunity," *Phi Delta Kappan*. (Fall): 14.

——. 1976. "The Status of Women in the United States, 1976: Still Looking for Justice and Equity." *Public Administration Review* 36 (September–October).

LEPPER, MARY M. and DEBRA W. STEWART. 1977. "Equal Employment Opportunity in the Public Sector: An Affirmative Action Focus." Englewood Cliffs, N.J.: Prentice-Hall. (Public Personnel Administration Looseleaf Series.)

LIPSET, SEYMOUR MARTIN and WILHAM SCHNEIDER. 1978. "The Bakke Case: How Would It Be Decided at the Bar of Public Opinion." *Public Opinion* 1 (March–April): 38–44.

MCCLOSKY, HERBERT. 1964. "Consensus and Ideology in American Politics." *American Political Science Review* 58: (June) 361–382.

MCGREGOR, EUGENE B., JR. 1974. "Social Equity and the Public Service." *Public Administration Review* 34 (January–February): 18–28.

MARIMONT, ROSALIND B., KENNEDY P. MAIZE, and ERNEST HARLEY. 1976. "Using FAIR to Set Numerical EEO Goals." *Public Personnel Management* 5 (May–June): 191–197.

MILLER, LOREN. 1965. In Robert Carter, et al., eds., *Equality*. New York: Pantheon, Section III.

MOUNTS, GREGORY. 1981. "Labor and the Supreme Court: Significant Decisions of 1979–80." *Monthly Labor Review* (April).

MYRDAL, GUNNAR. 1944. *An American Dilemma*. New York: Harper Bros.

NAGEL, T. 1973. "Rawls on Justice." *Philosophical Review* 82 (Fall): 220–34.

OFFICE OF PERSONNEL MANAGEMENT. 1979a. "Standards for a Merit System of Personnel Administration." Washington, D.C.: G.P.O.

——. 1979b. *Equal Opportunity in Employment*. Washington, D.C.: G.P.O.

——. 1979c. *Equal Employment Opportunity Statistics*. Washington, D.C.: G.P.O.

——. 1979d. *Equal Employment Opportunity Court Cases*. Washington, D.C.: G.P.O.

O'NEIL, ROBERT M. 1971. "Preferential Admissions: Equalizing the Access of Minority Groups to Higher Education." *Yale Law Journal* 80 (March): 88–112.

——. 1975. *Discriminating Against Discrimination: Preferential Admissions and the DeFunis Case*. Bloomington: Indiana University Press.

PROTHRO, JAMES W. and CHARLES M. GRIGGS. 1960. "Fundamental Principles of Democracy: Bases of Agreement and Disagreement." *Journal of Politics* 22 (May): 276–294.

RAWLS, JOHN. 1962. "Justice as Fairness." In Peter Laslett and W. G. Runci-

man, eds., *Philosophy, Politics and Society*. New York: Barnes & Noble.
——. 1971. *A Theory of Justice*. Cambridge, Mass.: Harvard University Press.
REIN, MARTIN. 1976. *Social Science and Public Policy*. New York: Penguin.
SABATIER, PAUL and DANIEL MAZMANIAN. 1979. "The Conditions of Effective Implementation: A Guide to Accomplishing Policy Objectives." *Policy Analysis* 5 (Fall): 481–504.
SCHAAR, JOHN H. 1967. "Equality of Opportunity and Beyond." In T. Roland Pennock and John W. Chapman, eds., *Nomos IX—Equality*. New York: Liebers Atherton.
——. 1978. *Equality: It's Bearing on Justice and Liberty*. Washington, D.C.: American Political Science Association.
SOVERN, MICHAEL. 1966. *Legal Restraints on Racial Discrimination in Employment*. Millwood, Colorado: Kraus.
STEWART, DEBRA W. (forthcoming). "EEO, Merit and the Political Environment of Public Sector Employment." Submitted for publication in symposium issue, *Policy Studies Journal*.
STUART, REGINALD. 1981. "Black Business Still Facing an Uphill Battle." *The New York Times* (July 26).
STRUM, PHILLIPPA. 1980. "Pink Collar Blues: For Women Who Work, It Still Doesn't Add Up." *Civil Rights Perspectives*: 33–37.
TAYLOR, DANIEL E. 1981. "Education, On-the-Job Training and the Black-White Earnings Gap." *Monthly Labor Review* 104 (No. 4): 28–34.
THALBERG, IRVING. 1972. "Visceral Racism," *The Monist* 56: 42–63.
THOMPSON, FRANK and BONNEL BROWNE. 1978. "Commitment to the Disadvantaged Among Urban Administrators: The Case of Minority Living" *Urban Affairs Quarterly* 13 (March): 355–378.
U.S. CIVIL RIGHTS COMMISSION. 1977. *Statement on Affirmative Action*. Washington, D.C.: G.P.O.
——. 1980. *The State of Civil Rights: 1979*. Washington, D.C.: G.P.O.
U.S. CIVIL SERVICE COMMISSION. Bureau of Intergovernmental Personnel Programs. 1976. *Goals and Timetables for Effective Affirmative Action*. Washington, D.C.: G.P.O.
U.S. CIVIL SERVICE COMMISSION. 1978. *Equal Opportunity in Employment*. Personnel Bibliography Series Number 95. Washington, D.C.: G.P.O.
U.S. COMMISSION ON WORKING WOMEN. 1981. *News Release* (January).
U.S. DEPARTMENT OF COMMERCE. Census Bureau. 1978. *Social Indicators of Equality for Minorities and Women*. Washington, D.C.: G.P.O.
——. 1981. *Census of Population Supplementary Reports, 1980*. Washington, D.C.: G.P.O.
U.S. DEPARTMENT OF HEALTH, EDUCATION AND WELFARE. 1977. "Nondiscrimination on Basis of Handicap." *Federal Register* 42 (May):
U.S. DEPARTMENT OF LABOR. Bureau of Labor Statistics. 1981a. "Current Labor Statistics: Household Data." *Monthly Labor Review* (May). 102: 71–75.
——. 1981b. "Employment and Unemployment Developments in 1979." *Montnly Labor Review* 102 (May): 69.
WEALE, ALBERT. 1978. *Equality and Social Policy*. London: Routledge and Kegan Paul.
WESTCOTT and BEDNARZIK. 1981. "Employment and Unemployment: A Report on 1980." *Monthly Labor Review* 104 (February): 4–14.
WHITE, ORION, JR. and BRUCE L. GATERS. 1974. "Statistical Theory and Equity in the Delivery of Social Services." *Public Administration Review* 34 (January–February): 43–51.

WINTER, RALPH K. Moderator. 1975. *Affirmative Action: The Answer to Discrimination?* Washington, D.C.: American Enterprise Institute for Public Policy Research.

ZASHIN, ELLIOT M. 1978. "Affirmative Action, Preferential Selection, and Federal Employment." *Public Personnel Management* 7 (November–December): 378–393.

William Kelso

University of Florida

CHAPTER FIFTEEN
SEARCH FOR A JUSTIFIABLE DEFENSE OF AFFIRMATIVE ACTION

In the last three decades the struggle to eliminate discrimination in employment and to guarantee all individuals their basic civil rights has undergone tremendous changes. Beginning in the 1950s the civil rights movement sought to expand job opportunities for minorities by striking down employment barriers that penalized people arbitrarily because of their race, religion, or sex. The goal was to create a society that was essentially colorblind in its evaluation and assessment of prospective employees.

Proponents of the civil rights movement saw correctly that the denial of work to people because of their race or sex was an unconscionable act that violated people's right to be judged on the merits of their work. Furthermore, they argued that the widespread use of discriminatory practices undermined society's efforts to expand its economy and improve the public welfare. When employers automatically refused to consider minorities and women for job openings, they were failing to utilize the full talents of the available labor market. The ability of the economy to thus benefit fully from the skills of numerous individuals was severely restricted. In this sense, society as well as the immediate victims of discrimination suffered from the consequences of widespread job discrimination.

To overcome the effects of racial prejudice, the civil rights movement forged a coalition that pressured Congress to strike down all odious distinctions based on racial or ethnic considerations. The successful culmination of these efforts occurred when the legislature passed the Civil Rights Act of 1964. In a phrase that was repeated constantly, Congress declared that it was legally unacceptable to make any distinctions concerning a person's right to employment on the grounds of "race, color, religion, or national origins."

Ironically, at the very point in time at which the civil rights movement succeeded in declaring that discrimination based on racial considerations was illegal, counterpressure developed to use race as one of the principal mechanisms of hiring and firing employees. Instead of using racial distinctions to penalize minorities, a segment of the civil rights movement now began to argue that racial factors should be used to assist minorities in finding work. In pursuit of that goal, they insisted that the government take "affirmative action" to guarantee that ethnic or racial groups find gainful employment in the public and private sectors.

In the process of altering the goals of the early civil rights movement, the new activists also managed to change the original meaning of the term affirmative action. The Kennedy administration used that term first when it discovered that many government contractors were selecting their employees from an all-white labor force. President Kennedy thus issued an executive order requiring all government contractors to act affirmatively to select employees on a nondiscriminatory basis. The objective of this order was to ensure that special efforts would be made to contact previously excluded ethnic or racial groups so that they would apply for all government openings and thus be in the pool of available applicants. But the final decision as to who would be hired was to be one that ignored racial or ethnic considerations.

However, more recently it has been argued that affirmative action should mean not just enlarging the labor pool but actually hiring prospective employees on the basis of racial or sexual characteristics. Instead of exclusively filling job slots on the colorblind standards of achievement or ability, it is now maintained that ascriptive criteria should be used in determining who is hired and fired.

While the existing statutes and presidential orders governing affirmative action and hiring practices prohibit racial quotas, of either a malicious or benign nature, they have been interpreted in a manner that allows preferential hiring programs based on race. As we shall soon see, the Equal Employment Opportunity Commission (EEOC), the agency that is responsible for the employment section of the 1964 Civil Rights Act, has transformed affirmative action successfully from a "doctrine of prospective equal opportunity to a doctrine of retrospective statistical representation or quotas" (Sowell, 1980: 250).

In this chapter, we assess the desirability of government-required quotas for minorities or women. In debating this controversial issue, we need to keep separate two very different issues. First, we need to ask if there are any situations or conditions that would warrant government-imposed quotas? Second, we need to inquire if the present efforts of the EEOC and other government regulatory bodies requiring the use of race or sex as a factor in hiring people are desirable? While it is possible to argue that certain kinds of benign quotas are acceptable, that does not necessarily mean that present government efforts in the employment field are justifiable and should be continued.[1]

THE JUSTIFICATION
OF EMPLOYMENT QUOTAS

If we try to analyze why the goals of the civil rights movement began to diverge in the late 1960s and early 1970s, we see that two sorts of arguments were advanced to support the idea of employment targets or outright quotas. The first, which focuses on the past, holds that preferential treatment for minorities and women is justified and in fact required for past acts of discrimination (Nagel, 1973: 2). The second, which focuses on the future, insists that hiring practices must take into account racial or sexual characteristics to promote some desired social end such as public happiness, equal opportunity, or a more equitable society.

Affirmative Action
and the Idea of Compensation

Those who want to institute employment quotas for minorities because of past discrimination often want to draw an analogy between the treatment of veterans and the treatment of blacks. Since existing civil service requirements give preferential treatment to people who served in the armed services, it is suggested that we should make comparable allowances to minorities in their efforts to secure public employment. Unfortunately, the analogy is not totally accurate. The reason for veterans receiving special consideration when seeking public employment is that the country is rewarding them for their prior service. In contrast, the argument for instituting preference programs or quotas for minorities who have suffered from acts of prejudice is based on the idea of redressing past grievances. Whenever the evidence indicates that minority members have been denied equal opportunities because of an arbitrary characteristic such as race, it seems only fair that they be entitled to compensation. Were it not for past incidences of discrimination, such individuals would have been able to achieve as much upward mobility as their talents warranted.

While this argument seems inherently attractive, two objections can be lodged against it. First, if the government chooses to pursue a policy of compensating victims of unjustified discrimination, there could be large costs to society. People who have been denied meaningful jobs in the past are not likely to be highly trained or to possess skills that are in great demand. Once they are hired, there is likely to be a transition period during which the efficiency and productivity of affirmative action employees may fail to live up to industry norms. However, it is possible to argue that this is a minor cost to pay to ensure that people who have been harmed unfairly in the past are compensated for their troubles.

The second and more serious objection to affirmative action programs based on compensation concerns the implementation of these programs. In many cases, if a public agency or private firm is under orders to fill a specific quota, the agency, to reduce its administrative costs, will pursue a policy of compensating groups rather than individuals. If applications from minority members have been rejected arbitrarily in the past, an employer will often try to make amends by filling a certain percentage of all new openings from the members of the aggrieved minority. The problem with this type of policy is that it fails to make proper restitution. One does not necessarily compensate individuals who have suffered past acts of discrimination by hiring any member of the same minority group. To do so is in effect to perpetuate yet another injustice to the individual whom the preferential program was designed to compensate.

The problem is compounded when competitive forces from the marketplace also influence the operation of affirmative action programs (Goldman, 1979: 90-93). To satisfy both federal regulatory bodies and the pressures of the market, which demand that businesses be efficient and productive, firms will hire the most talented members of the appropriate group. Unfortunately, these women and minorities are likely to be the individuals who have suffered the least from discrimination. Rather than compensating past victims of racism or sexism, affirmative action programs may be inverting the relationship between harm and benefit. Those individuals who have been the most wronged often receive the fewest benefits; those who have suffered the least discrimination may receive the most benefits. For these reasons, affirmative action programs that indiscriminately hire minority members to satisfy a goal or quota cannot be defended on grounds of fairness alone.

In a similar vein, affirmative action programs often seem flawed in that they place the burden of compensating victims on innocent third parties. To be fair, an affirmative action program should require the perpetrators of discriminatory hiring practices to make restitution to those individuals they have wronged. Unfortunately, in most preferential hiring programs, it is young white males who are asked to forego some desired job opportunity. Because established firms and government agencies do not like to let go of experienced workers or because union work rules create seniority systems, most organizations are reluctant to fire senior employees. As a consequence, in most preferential hiring programs, it is young white males who are penalized to make way for minorities. Since these individuals bear little responsibility for the past actions of others, they often become the innocent victims of well-meaning government programs. In making young white males bear the main costs of preferential hiring programs, the government is once again inverting the relationship between guilt and costs. Those individuals who are least responsible for past acts of discrimination end up paying the highest costs; older white males who directly limited opportunities for minorities and women incur few additional costs.

Proponents of affirmative action programs have often tried to counter this argument by insisting that young white males are responsible indirectly, if not directly, for retarding black economic progress. If white males, for instance, sat by passively, while other people actually discriminated against minorities, they must bear some degree of accountability for their inaction. After all, one can be responsible for a deplorable situation through an act of omission as well as an act of commission.

While this argument sounds plausible, it raises a number of issues. For instance, at what point does a person's indirect responsibility for an action become so tenuous that it no longer makes sense to hold him or her accountable at all? It is probably very true that many younger people said or did nothing when the larger society discriminated against blacks. In a similar vein, many blacks probably passively sat back when the U.S. government discriminated against Japanese-Americans during World War II. Are we to penalize them for their act of omission? In a real sense both parties are equally guilty of not protesting major acts of discrimination. However, both young people and blacks may have lacked the opportunities or resources to have effectively challenged or altered the conditions affecting other minority groups. If that is the case, can we still hold them indirectly accountable for not doing anything? To insist that the answer is "yes" requires that we ask what is the appropriate punishment for such indirect forms of responsibility. Advocates of affirmative action fail to see that proving that an indirect sense of responsibility exists is not the same as proving that the denial of job opportunities is the appropriate corrective action to take. It seems only reasonable that indirect forms of responsibility should warrant compensation of a nature different from loss of employment.

The difficulties inherent in the idea of indirect responsibility have led some advocates of affirmative action to make the additional argument that the government is justified in penalizing young whites because these individuals benefited from discrimination against minorities. Were it not for the past history of discrimination in this country, many of the positions for which young whites are applying would have already been filled by minority members. Any positions denied to Caucasians are thus positions they should never have been entitled to in the first place. Filling a quota system with minority members is merely a way of restoring people to their rightful position.

The problem with this argument is that it is very difficult to implement in a way that is fair and just to all parties involved. If a position does come open in a particular firm, how do we know that the minority member who receives the position because of a quota system would have actually beaten out the particular white individual who is denied a job? Because it is extremely difficult to answer this question, firms and government agencies are likely to fall back on penalizing and rewarding groups rather than individuals. But, in so doing, there is no guarantee that the individual being penalized actually did benefit from previous acts of discrimination. It is very possible that the applicant could have been better qualified than all candidates who would have applied, even if discrimination had been eradicated completely.

From this discussion we see that proponents of affirmative action programs based on fairness would have to insist on a flexible rather than a rigid quota system. In developing a labor policy, the government should only favor preferential hiring programs when the victims of past discrimination and the agents responsible for such actions can be identified clearly. In pursuit of rectifying inequities in the employment field, we must be careful that we do not perpetuate yet other injustices to innocent third parties or to the legitimate interests of the victims themselves.

The Egalitarian View
of Affirmative Action

Because of the problems noted, many have argued that, even if not required by fairness or compensatory justice, affirmative action programs should be implemented to achieve some desirable social end. They maintain that, if justifications focus on the future rather than the past, we can avoid the sticky problem of identifying different degrees of guilt and harm in society (Nagel, 1973: 348-363). We can thus decide to rectify an undesirable situation regardless of how that situation came about in the first place. Those who focus on social goals offer three different kinds of arguments. The first, which is basically egalitarian, insists that affirmative action programs should be implemented to equalize the opportunities for individuals to gain access to important positions in society. Egalitarians justify their position by attacking the idea that income or prestige should be allocated on the basis of native talent or merit. They insist that the rewards of society should not be handed out in an ethically arbitrary or capricious way. However, if positions are allocated on the basis of ability, people will be rewarded for traits that they inherited and that they have therefore done little to earn. Individuals who have ability have merely received those talents by the luck of the genetic shuffle. In no sense can we say that they deserve their skills and thus morally ought to enjoy the benefits that accompany the exercise of ability.

Interestingly, egalitarians who offer this view are not arguing for an egalitarian society in which all differences between individuals are leveled out. On the contrary, they are still defending a stratified society; they merely want to equalize access to the positions that are ranked hierarchically in society. In fact, many egalitarians seem willing to allocate most positions in society on a random rather than a meritorious basis. They would thus be more than willing to support rigid across-the-board quotas in most fields of endeavor. Whether or not a particular person was a victim of discrimination would be an irrelevant consideration. To broaden chances of access to all fields of employment, all public and private firms would have to develop quotas that reflected the distribution of various ethnic groups in society.

Unfortunately, the arguments for adoption of such a quota system seem based on faulty theoretical and empirical grounds. First, it is not clear that one is only entitled to something when it is fully earned (Goldman, 1979: 41-47). Individuals may receive gifts from relatives or friends that they have not earned but that they are certainly entitled to keep and enjoy. Similarly, while people may not have earned their native abilities, they certainly seem entitled to the benefits created through their use and exercise of those abilities. If any right seems basic, it is the right of the individual to have control over his or her own faculties and actions.

Second, egalitarians who insist that people have not earned their native ability seem to think that the less talented have earned a right to share in the benefits of the more talented. But this is an assumption that does not follow logically from, and in fact seems to contradict, the egalitarian argument that one is entitled only to those things one has earned. If one has not earned one's abilities, it is even more difficult to see how one can claim to have earned the consequences of someone else's labor.

Third, if we ever did randomly assign people to various jobs to fulfill employment quotas, the economy could be severely affected. If factors other than merit are to determine who occupies what position, we cannot expect the economy to operate in the most productive fashion. Increasingly, individuals would have to spend more time trying to determine if their lawyer, doctor, or social worker were competent enough to take care of their basic needs. An affirmative action program that downplays the notion of competence in filling positions may adversely affect the services presently enjoyed by all citizens, including minority members.

Affirmative Action and the Utilitarian Position

Because the egalitarian argument departs so radically from traditional ideas that hiring and promotion should be based on merit, it has won few adherents. Most advocates of affirmative action are willing to set aside a certain percentage of positions for the disadvantaged, but they insist that the vast majority of positions should be awarded to those who are most capable. Thus, the second and more widely accepted justification for affirmative action based on social ends is a utilitarian argument that focuses on equal opportunity and social harmony. Utilitarians insist that the widespread unemployment and underemployment of minorities and women is a tremendous drain on the country's welfare. If millions of Americans are not employed productively, the overall utility or happiness of society is lowered correspondingly.

Utilitarians consequently support affirmative action because they believe that quotas are necessary to improve the job prospects for minorities and women. They argue that government efforts to eliminate discrimination and promote the adoption of colorblind standards have been proven to be less than successful in promoting upward mobility for minority members. The only chance for blacks to achieve full racial equality and economic parity is for private and public employees to adopt a system of employment quotas.

Utilitarians further argue that, once minorities or women are placed in prominent positions, they in turn can become much needed role models for others. Without affirmative action, underprivileged children may have very few successful individuals of their own race after whom to model their lives. Moreover, to have incentives to work hard, minorities and women must have some tangible proof that they can get ahead and secure desirable job opportunities. As a consequence, the goal of affirmative action programs is not to give preferential treatment to those who have suffered the most discrimination in the past. On the contrary, the objective is to give the edge to minority members who will prove to be successful business or government officials and whom other blacks will then seek to emulate. In a similar vein, utilitarians see affirmative action not as a permanent part of the employment process as egalitarians suggest, but as a temporary measure by which to bring minorities into the competitive marketplace. Once blacks and other racial groups have acquired a larger stake in the economic system, affirmative action programs can then be phased out.

While the utilitarian position is the most compelling of the arguments for affirmative action we have yet examined, it is based on factual assumptions that are open to doubt. The defenders of quotas assume that racial groups such as blacks have made very little progress in securing worthwhile and lucrative positions in the past two decades. But it is possible to argue that the colorblind legislation promoted by the early civil rights movement has been much more effective in improving the financial situation of minorities than critics are willing to admit. To prove this point, we need to look at the record of black accomplishments from the early 1960s until the start of quotas in 1972. We find, for example, that in 1969 black husband-wife families under the age of 35 in the North and West were earning 91 percent of the median income of white families with the same characteristics. In 1971 those figures had climbed to 93 percent (Glazer, 1975: 4). When both the husband and wife worked, an increasingly common phenomenon among both black and white families, the figures for the two years were 99 percent and 101 percent, respectively. Among all black husband-wife families, a similar pattern of improvement was evident as the median black family income rose steadily from 62 percent to 85 percent of median white income in the years 1959 to 1972 (Glazer, 1975: 4). While the income of all blacks was rising, younger members of the black population were doing especially well. From this data we can surmise that, as racial barriers came tumbling down in the late 1960s, younger blacks in particular were enjoying the full benefits of racial equality.

Concurrent with their improving financial situation, blacks and other races were also moving into occupations of greater security and higher status. As Table 1 shows, only 21.2 percent of blacks and other races were in white-collar jobs in 1963 whereas ten years later over 41 percent occupied comparable positions (Glazer, 1975: 42). During this same period whites only increased their percentage of white-collar positions from 60.8 percent to 63.3 percent. By a variety of economic indicators, blacks, in recent years, have improved their economic situation at a much faster clip than whites.

To clarify the improving situation of blacks further, we can quote from two sophisticated econometric studies that tried to determine what role discrimination played in affecting the income level of black and white employees. Freeman (1974: 18), the author of one of these studies, found that

> The income and occupation position of black workers improved significantly relative to those of whites in the sixties . . . women, young men, young male college graduates . . . experienced especially large economic gains. By the 1970s black women had earnings as high or higher than comparable white women in the country as a whole; young black male college graduates earned as much as their white counterparts. As a result of increased incomes for highly educated and skilled black workers, the historic pattern of declining black white income ratios with ascending skill no longer prevails . . . these advances suggest that traditional discriminatory differences in the labor market are abating rapidly.

In yet another study Hall and Kasten (1973: 785) compared the salaries of blacks and whites who were from similar family backgrounds and had comparable levels of education. They found that

> Holding these [factors] constant, we find that young black men entering the labor market were just as likely as whites to find high paying jobs and just as

TABLE 1   Black and White Workers' Job Distribution, 1963 versus 1973

	1963		1973	
	NEGRO AND OTHER RACES	WHITE	NEGRO AND OTHER RACES	WHITE
White-collar workers	21.2	60.8	41.5	63.3
Professional and technical	7.8	13.5	12.0	14.9
Clerical workers	10.2	33.8	24.4	35.7
Private-household workers	34.3	4.9	12.4	2.9

SOURCE: N. Glazer. 1975. *Affirmative Discrimination.* New York: Basic Books, 11.

likely to escape from bad jobs. The sixties saw the nearly complete elimination of racial bias in the way that the labor market assigned individuals to occupations.

Besides blacks, other racial groups have made significant gains in income in recent decades. Perhaps the classic case of upward mobility in this country involves Japanese-Americans. During World War II they encountered tremendous racial discrimination. All the Japanese on the West Coast not only had their property confiscated but they were forced to spend the duration of the war in special detention camps. In the short space of thirty-five years Japanese-Americans, who were near the bottom of the socioeconomic ladder in 1945, have pulled themselves up to where they now have the second highest per capita income of all ethnic groups in the nation. Contrary to the claims of affirmative action proponents that the early civil rights movement was a failure in its efforts to strike down racial discrimination and bring minorities into the mainstream of the economy, the evidence seems to indicate the opposite. The improving situation of ethnic groups suggests that there is little need for the government to impose quotas on either public or private agencies.

In addition to being unnecessary to improving the lot of minorities, there may be some cases in which employment quotas could be downright harmful to racial groups. As mentioned earlier, many proponents of quotas believe that they are necessary to create attractive role models for black or Hispanic children. However, if business or government agencies fill their quotas or goals with individuals who are less than qualified, they may tarnish the image of minority role models. Minority children are only likely to look up to members of their own race who are considered competent in their occupations. If there are considerable discrepancies between the skills of regular and quota-hired employees, the stereotype that minorities "cannot make it" will be reinforced rather than attenuated. Minorities may grow up thinking that they owe their position more to the paternalism of the larger white society than to their own innate abilities. The data that Sindler compiled recently on the success rates of minority and nonminority students taking the bar exam in the State of New York is instructive in this regard. He found that, from 1969 to 1975, 72 percent of all applicants passed the bar exam and became practicing attorneys. Among black students only 18 percent who took the bar exam achieved a passing score (Sindler, 1978: 120). In their desire to increase minority enrollment, many law schools apparently accepted numerous students who were not qualified to become full-fledged attorneys. The costs of such a quota system on the students who flunked the bar exam and on other minority students looking for promising role models will undoubtedly be immense. If college, businesses, or government for that matter are not very selective in filling quota programs, their well-meaning efforts to help minorities may end up stigmatizing them permanently.

In addition, quota programs may be damaging psychologically to blacks who have worked hard to improve their situation without any outside government assistance. A widespread affirmative action program will inevitably raise unnecessary doubts about the ability of successful black members. Minority members who achieved professional positions on their own merits will always have to prove to others that they are not affirmative action employees who achieved their present position merely because of their racial characteristics. While in the short run minority members may benefit from a quota system, in the long run it may create identity problems for blacks that will be more difficult to eliminate. One well-known black economist who has criticized affirmative action programs for this very reason writes (Sowell, 1972: 292),

> What the arguments and campaigns for quotas are really saying, loud and clear, is that black people just don't have it, and that they will have to be given something in order to have something. The devastating impact of this message on black people—particularly black young people—will outweigh any few extra jobs that may result from this strategy.

The fear that quota programs may somehow permanently label blacks as being inherently incapable of making it on their own may explain the Gallup poll data we cited earlier that indicates that blacks reject preferential treatment by a 2-to-1 margin.

Besides the damage to black self-respect, there is the additional danger that so-called "temporary quota" programs could become permanent fixtures of our political and economic life. There is a tendency among most social programs to expand with time. Once certain elements start to receive benefits, the expectation is created that those benefits will continue indefinitely. Some members of minority groups may thus feel that affirmative action benefits are entitlements that are due as a matter of right. If this attitude develops, yet other groups such as poor whites or ethnic groups such as Poles and Italians may start demanding their own quotas as well. Rather than being a temporary measure for the creation of an integrated, colorblind society, affirmative action schemes may become permanent entitlement programs that will allocate society's resources according to race, ethnic background, or religion. Whereas utilitarian advocates of affirmative action will argue that such an ossified pluralistic system is not their goal, it is possible that the programs they champion will acquire a life of their own and become impossible to terminate. The unfortunate irony in this situation is that, in the desire to build a colorblind society free of invidious racial distinctions, we may create a community that permanently emphasizes racial characteristics by institutionalizing hiring practices based on ascriptive criteria.

Affirmative Action
and the Populist Position

Finally, the last defense of affirmative action based on social ends is the populist position that argues that quotas are acceptable when the representatives of a majority of citizens approve of them (Ely, 1977). Essentially, the populist view combines a belief in the public's right to enact whatever policy it sees fit with a utilitarian notion that all programs of preferential treatment should maximize overall happiness. But it recognizes, as the utilitarian argument often does not, that the utilities to be realized from establishing quotas have to be weighed against the disutilities resulting from the denial of job opportunities to whites. Unfortunately, the traditional utilitarian position on affirmative action provides no institutional mechanism for weighing and balancing the various benefits and costs of quota programs. To correct that oversight, the populist insists that preferential treatment should be instituted only when the appropriate legislative body has formally approved a quota program. The procedures used to enact quotas are as important as the alleged consequences of quotas in deciding on the merits of affirmative action.

In formulating this rule, populists make two key points. First, the right of the majority to maximize its utility does not give it a right to establish a quota system that benefits itself exclusively at the expense of minority groups. Populists do not believe that the majority has any right to trample unfairly on the rights of minority groups. However, a populist maintains that, if proper safeguards are undertaken, the majority has the right to institute a preferential hiring program to benefit a minority at its own expense. The electoral process guarantees the citizenry the power to check or rein in their legislative representatives if they go too far in allocating scarce job opportunities on the basis of ascriptive criteria. When legislative bodies impose a quota on the majority, the legislative body will not abuse its power for fear of retaliation at the next election. However, when the same legislative body imposes a quota on a minority, it is less likely to be restrained since elected representatives have less reason to fear the electoral clout of a minority.

Second, populists insist that only the legislature—rather than courts or government agencies—should have the ability to establish preferential hiring treatment. Whenever institutions are insulated from popular pressures, as are the judiciary and executive agencies, they may become insensitive to the hardships imposed on innocent third parties. To compare the utility gained from helping minorities at the expense of the majority is a difficult and trying experience. Any time that quotas are established, the potential for abuse exists. In the attempt to correct one injustice, there is always the danger that the legitimate rights of other individuals seeking gainful employment will be ignored. Because legislators are constantly accountable to the electorate, they are likely to act quickly to minimize any such abuses. For these reasons, only elected representatives should have the final say as to when government-mandated employment programs are acceptable as public policy.

Of the various positions on affirmative action we have examined, the populist argument has much to recommend it. It provides maximum flexibility to society in designing, implementing, and terminating affirmative action programs. Since it focuses on the consequences of programs, it does not need to determine complex questions of guilt or harm. Because it vests responsibility for quotas in Congress, it provides some built-in checks and balances on the operations of preferential hiring programs. However, one of the most serious problems with the populist position is that it may be too optimistic about the ability of the average citizen to control the actions of his or her own representative. From innumerable studies of congressional elections, we now know that the public often has trouble in identifying how his or her representative voted on various issues. The ability of the average citizen to hold a Congress member accountable for his or her vote on a specific issue may not be as great as advocates of the populist position believe. Nevertheless, the question of accountability may be a relative one. It certainly seems that the legislature, in spite of its faults, is much more responsive to public sentiment than are either agencies or the courts. If that is the case, legislatively imposed affirmative action programs are likely to be more palatable to the public at large than are those mandated by non-elected bodies. While the public, according to Gallup poll data, is opposed to most preferential treatment programs, it is likely to accept and support quotas if such quotas have been drafted by elected officials.

GOVERNMENT POLICY IN THE AFFIRMATIVE ACTION FIELD

As noted earlier, any discussion of government quotas involves two different issues. First, it is crucial that we ask if there are any situations in which government supported quotas are justifiable. Second, we need to determine if the present policy of the government in the employment field satisfies these conditions and is thus defensible philosophically. Having just examined a variety of reasons for preferential treatment, it is now necessary to analyze existing government policy to see if it is acceptable from a compensatory, egalitarian, utilitarian, or populist point of view.

However, in discussing existing policy on affirmative action, we need to keep in mind that government statutes explicitly forbid racial quotas. The 1964 Civil Rights Act states specifically that no one's right to a job shall be affected by "race, color, religion or national origins." In steering this legislation through the Senate, Senator Hubert Humphrey stressed that the Civil Rights Act "does not provide that any preferential treatment in employment shall be given to Negroes or to any other person or group. In fact, the title would prohibit preferential treatment for any particular group" (110 *Congressional Record*: 11848).

Government agencies that have wished to pursue a policy of quotas have thus had to proceed in an indirect fashion. What they usually do is force employers to admit that they are underutilizing minorities in their work forces. By underutilization, the Labor Department and EEOC mean that the percentage of minorities in an employer's work force is below the percentage of minorities found in the population as a whole. The groups that the EEOC defines as minorities for legal purposes include blacks, Indians, Orientals, and Hispanics. Once the appropriate government agency identifies an employer who is underutilizing minorities, the employer is asked to design a specific affirmative action plan, if he or she wishes to remain eligible for federal contracts. In most cases, the government agency does not tell an employer exactly how many people from each designated ethnic group should be chosen. Rather, it retains the right to disapprove of the goals until an acceptable percentage of minorities is finally hired (Sowell, 1980: 252).

This whole process of pressuring firms indirectly to hire on the basis of ascriptive criteria is extremely cumbersome because a variety of government agencies including EEOC, the Justice Department, Health and Human Resources, and the Labor Department are involved in reviewing employment goals. Often an affirmative action plan that is acceptable to one agency may be vetoed by another agency. Employers who thus wish to comply with government demands for more minority hiring have difficulty in determining in advance what they are required to do. Part of this confusion is a result of various government agencies surreptitiously pursuing a policy that the existing civil rights statutes explicitly forbid them from implementing in the first place (Sowell, 1980: 253).

The key question we need to ask is whether affirmative action programs based on utilization studies are the ideal type of quota system to adopt. Of the four positions we looked at, only egalitarians would find present policy as worthy of support. In accordance with egalitarian principles, the EEOC's policy seems more concerned with achieving statistical parity than with maximizing public happiness or redressing past acts of injustice.

Its insistence that all employment slots have the same number of minorities as found in the population seems like a first step toward a rigid egalitarian society in which racial factors largely determine employment policy. Existing government regulation makes no provision for the fact that different segments of society may be attracted to different types of work. Nor do they allow employers to make special provisions only for individuals who might be attractive role models or for victims of past acts of discrimination.

The government's insensitivity to individuals victimized by discrimination explains why proponents of affirmative action based on compensation would have reservations about current federal policy. Existing employment requirements are clearly designed to reward groups rather than individuals. Merely because an employer hires the same percentage of blacks as that found in the population is no guarantee that those people who have suffered the most from past acts of discrimination will be employed. Achieving a desirable racial balance among one's employees is not the same thing as achieving racial justice.

The government's insistence on fixed quotas also creates problems for utilitarians. By using simple statistical figures to determine the appropriate quota, the government would make it extremely difficult for organizations to effect a proper identification of individuals who might become viable role models. Any quota system based on population figures also ignores the fact that tremendous disparities in age distribution exist among various ethnic groups. For example, "half of all Hispanics in this country are either infants, children or teenagers. Their median age is about a decade younger than the Irish or Italians and about a quarter of a century younger than the Jews" (Sowell, 1980: 251). Unfortunately, the EEOC fails to take these age differences into consideration in its demands that minorities not be underrepresented in all employment positions. Most mid- and top-level management positions are usually filled by people with considerable years of experience. If business or government agencies actually complied with the EEOC's utilization studies, they would have to hire numerous individuals who would undoubtedly be too young for the available slots. While the efforts of the EEOC to help minorities are laudable, the commission has failed to see that automatically filling a quota with a member of a particular racial group is not the same thing as recruiting minority role models whose success will prompt other individuals to work hard and become productive citizens.

Finally, the manner in which the government has formulated its affirmative action programs would force a populist to have serious reservations about current quota programs. Without explicit legislative sanction, government agencies such as the EEOC are implementing programs that clearly violate both the letter and the spirit of the 1964 Civil Rights Act. Undoubtedly, the officials responsible for implementing affirmative action programs feel that they are pursuing a worthwhile course of action. In advancing the rights of minorities, they are violating the important principle of legislative control of government agencies by ignoring the legitimate right of Congress to set public policy. In deciding on a policy as important as employment quotas, elected officials, rather than insulated civil servants, should have the final say.

CONCLUSION

As we have seen, the goals of the civil rights movement have dramatically changed in the last decade or two. Unfortunately, recent critics have failed to appreciate the accomplishments of the original movement that sought to eradicate racial prejudice by evaluating people on the basis of their attitudes and inclination for hard work. For a variety of reasons, many of which are contradictory, proponents now insist that the government adopt a policy of benign discrimination. However, what kind of quota system and how long the quota system should be in operation are issues that provoke heated debate. Moreover, the existing policy of the government is one that very few proponents of affirmative action can wholeheartedly endorse. Regardless of how preferential hiring programs are justified, current affirmative action programs raise issues of individual justice, long-term social welfare, and government responsibility that must be considered. Even though it is possible to develop attractive arguments for quotas based on populist or even compensatory grounds, a persuasive case exists for limiting or even totally rescinding the current practices of EEOC and the Labor Department.

NOTES

1. In analyzing the arguments for and against affirmative action, it is important to realize that the recent changes in the civil rights movement are extremely controversial. In Gallup polls there is evidence of a dramatic shift in the public's attitude toward minorities. By large majorities, most people now feel that any form of discrimination against ethnic or racial groups is indefensible and should be eliminated. However, the same majority rejects government pro-

grams that provide preferential treatment for ethnic groups or women. Interestingly, that sentiment is shared by many people who would ostensibly be the beneficiaries of such quota programs. For instance, Gallup finds that blacks reject preferential treatment almost 2 to 1, whereas women oppose it by a 4-to-1 margin (*Gallup Opinion Index*, 1977: 23). The existing survey data indicate that the early civil rights movement has been so successful that its beliefs are now the prevailing orthodoxy in this country. The defenders of employment quotas thus appear to be advocating proposals that even most minority members do not necessarily approve.

REFERENCES

CONGRESSIONAL RECORD. 1964. 110: 11848.

ELY, JOHN. 1977. "The Constitutionality of Reverse Discrimination." In B. Gross, ed., *Reverse Discrimination*. Buffalo, N.Y.: Prometheus Books, 208–216.

FREEMAN, RICHARD B. 1974. "Changes in the Labor Market for Black Americans." In *Brookings Papers on Economic Activity*. Washington, D.C.: Brookings Institution.

GALLUP OPINION INDEX. 1977. (June) Report: 143.

GLAZER, NATHAN. 1975. *Affirmative Discrimination*. New York: Basic Books.

GOLDMAN, ALAN. 1979. *Justice and Reverse Discrimination*. Princeton, N.J.: Princeton University Press.

HALL, ROBERT and RICHARD KASTEN. 1973. "The Relative Occupational Success of Blacks and Whites." In *Brookings Papers on Economic Activity*. Washington, D.C.: Brookings Institution.

NAGEL, THOMAS. 1973. "Equal Treatment and Compensatory Discrimination." *Philosophy and Public Affairs* 2 (Summer): 1–14.

SINDLER, ALLAN P. 1978. *Bakke, DeFunis, and Minority Admissions*. New York: Longman.

SOWELL, THOMAS. 1972. *Black Education: Myths and Tragedies*. New York: McKay.

——. 1980. *Knowledge and Decisions*. New York: Basic Books.

Charles E. Davis
Suffolk University

and

Jonathan P. West
University of Miami

CHAPTER SIXTEEN
SUPPORT FOR AFFIRMATIVE ACTION IN A METROPOLITAN BUREAUCRACY: AN ANALYSIS OF NONMINORITY ADMINISTRATORS

The goal of a more representative public service received considerable impetus from the passage of the Equal Employment Opportunity Act of 1972. Public employers are required by law to prepare and implement affirmative action plans as a demonstration of good faith in their efforts to increase employment opportunities for women and minorities. Charges of employment discrimination may be investigated by the Equal Employment Opportunity Commission, and, if no conciliation is achieved, the Department of Justice may file suit against the agency in question. The approval of affirmative action goals and timetables as a means of assessing the performance of public agencies lends additional credibility to the policy intentions of governmental decision makers.

Despite the noble sentiments expressed within this legislation and associated executive actions designed to promote minority hiring, several recent studies have directed attention to a number of problems associated with the implementation of affirmative action programs in local governmental bureaucracies. Lack of progress has been attributed to a variety of political, economic, and administrative-labor pool constraints not subject to manipulation by local administrators. As Meier (1979) suggests, the cumulative effect of these factors is to reduce the degree of flexibility available to administrators in the design of programs to recruit and promote minorities. Less evident is the extent to which program implementation is affected by the attitudes of agency administrators and supervisory personnel. The policy concerns of these individuals are of considerable importance since they often possess sufficient discretionary authority to affect the hiring, promotion, or dismissal of subordinates. The central issue addressed in this article involves the compatibility of affirmative action goals with the interests and/or biases of local administrators and supervisors.

In this chapter, we consider the possibility that attitudinal barriers to the realization of equal employment opportunities for minorities are, in part, a consequence of the work-related concerns of nonminority (i.e., white) employees. Unfortunately, there are few empirical studies to guide our analysis. Moreover, existing studies do not satisfactorily encompass the perceptual dimensions of affirmative action programs. To many, support for affirmative action implies the desirability of greater minority representation in governmental bureaucracies. Others insist that such a program must not compromise merit principles; thus, the maintenance of educational or experience requirements for a position is held to be sacrosanct. Another interpretation of affirmative action emphasizes the obligation of government to give preferential treatment to women and minority job candidates as compensation for past inequities in hiring and promotional practices.

While this list could be easily expanded, it is clear that the distribution of varying interpretations has important policy implications. Unlike the majority of public policy issues, affirmative action may be viewed by supervisory personnel in terms of opportunity costs. In a "worst case" scenario, competition for a dwindling number of administrative positions in local government may conceivably lead to resentment among unsuccessful nonminority candidates, particularly if the criterion of a more representative public bureaucracy is perceived to be of greater importance in the process of awarding promotions than "merit" or "seniority."

The purpose of this chapter is to examine the relationships between various job-related characteristics of supervisory personnel in a southwestern metropolitan bureaucracy and their attitudes toward equal employment opportunity (EEO) issues ranging from the desirability of greater numerical representation of minorities in the public service to the utilization of "quotas" as a recruitment and promotional strategy. Relevant job characteristics include respondent perceptions of pay satisfaction, departmental autonomy, and career opportunities based on merit as well as such objective measures as occupational status, job tenure, and the within-agency percentage of minorities. Although our central concern in this study is the impact of work-related factors on employee acceptance of affirmative action, we cannot discount the possibility that these attitudes may have been affected by preexisting values, experiences, and/or group affiliations. Significant relationships will be tested by controlling for age, gender, political party identification, and education.

This research partially replicates a pair of studies by Thompson (1977, 1978) dealing with the attitudes of public personnel administrators toward hiring minority employees. However, our research builds on Thompson's work in three respects. First, our survey includes county departmental supervisors from a single metropolitan area. We thus have a much wider assortment of occupational groups in addition to personnelists that are involved, either directly or indirectly, in making personnel-related decisions.

Second, our survey (which is described in the following section) includes items pertaining to promotions as well as to hiring decisions. This underscores an important conceptual distinction. Attitudes toward hiring programs and on-the-job policies may differ, in part, because of perceived differences in opportunity costs. For many, the general principle of a representative bureaucracy that is open and accessible to all groups is easily accepted. A smaller percentage of individuals would probably agree that proportional representation requires the implementation of such compensatory measures as minority training programs, preferential promotions, or the relaxation of educational standards. Obviously, such measures can be expected to be more threatening to organizational incumbents than are hiring decisions, which do not ordinarily influence their career paths (the distribution of organizational benefits—such as training and promotions—is generally a zero-sum game).

Self-interest as a motivating force becomes more apparent when the distribution of minorities in the managerial and professional categories of employment is considered. A glance at the sociological literature on reference group theory and relative reward (Merton, 1968: 294–295) suggests that support for affirmative action programs by nonminority administrators may be affected by a subjective comparison of personal costs (or opportunities) resulting from equal employment opportunity and affirmative action with the benefits accruing to minorities and women. In other words, the perception of "reverse discrimination" is likely to stem from the belief that opportunities for advancement in the agency will be based on criteria other than merit or seniority. While these propositions seem plausible, they have been largely ignored by current scholars. A recent study by Bellone and Darling (1980) reports results from a county employee survey on affirmative action that gives some attention to career development issues. However, the authors do not directly relate promotional prospects of nonminority administrators to support for affirmative action.

Third, we examine the effects that the presence of minority co-workers have on the attitudes of Anglo employees toward affirmative action. Data summarizing the distribution of minority employees in various governmental agencies were obtained from the county personnel department and were merged with the survey information.

DATA AND METHODS

The setting for this study is Pima County (Tucson), Arizona, a rapidly growing metropolitan community with a sizable percentage of Chicano residents (approximately 24 percent). Mexican-Americans comprise a fifth of the county work force, although occupational representation ranges from 10 percent among administrators and professional employees to a high of 47 percent among skilled craft workers. Our data were obtained from a survey of county supervisory personnel in Pima County, conducted in the spring of 1977. Questionnaires were completed by approximately 53 percent (n = 320) of all county supervisors. Our sample was generally representative of the population of county supervisors, although women, minorities, and younger supervisors were slightly overrepresented. Our analysis is restricted to the attitudes and background characteristics of white supervisors (n = 235). There are both analytic and practical reasons for doing so. Results from an earlier study by the authors (Davis and West, 1978) indicate that Mexican-Americans are considerably more supportive of affirmative action than are their Anglo counterparts. To repeat those findings here would be unduly repetitious. In addition, we believe it is important to place emphasis not only on the policy-relevant dimensions of the job but on the appropriate target group(s) as well. To the extent that recommendations for improvement and/or corrective actions will be deemed necessary by public officials, it is evident that the successful implementation of such actions on a day-to-day basis will require the cooperation of white supervisors whose numerical superiority is overwhelming.

Our sample includes first-line supervisors above the rank-and-file employees but below the level of middle management. In drawing the line between rank-and-file workers and supervisors, we considered the work that each performed. We operated on the assumption that a true supervisor would have the authority to "effectively recommend" personnel actions and, unlike subordinates, would spend the most time planning, laying out work, controlling, deciding, and ordering supplies and equipment. An examination of job titles and descriptions as well as pay levels helped to identify these supervisors. In differentiating these supervisors from "middle management," we relied heavily on the judgments of department heads and staff of the county personnel department.

We decided to analyze support for affirmative action, the dependent variable in this study, by examining individual responses to the following statements:

1. Greater representation of women, blacks, and Mexican-Americans in local government is a useful idea.
2. Greater use of quota systems to promote the hiring of minorities is unfair and discriminatory.
3. Minorities should not be hired unless they can fulfill the educational or experience requirements of the job.

To facilitate measurement of support, a Guttman scale was constructed.[1] Individuals expressing agreement with the first item and disagreement with the remaining statements received the maximum support score (high). Those who responded favorably to affirmative action on two of the three statements were classified as moderate (medium) supporters, and those indicating a pro-affirmative action sentiment on only one or none of the items were categorized as least supportive (low). For any scale item, respondents in the "undecided" or "don't know" categories were classified as nonsupporters. As a result, the scale underestimates the number of potential supporters but is probably a more realistic indicator of firm or actual support. The results of subsequent tests, the coefficient of reproducibility (C. R. = 0.96) and the coefficient of scalability (S = 0.65), indicated that the minimal criteria for an acceptable scale were easily met.

FINDINGS

The general pattern of support for EEO is reported in Table 1. A surprisingly large proportion of supervisors can be classified as "low" in support for affirmative action on the basis of their responses to our scale items, whereas half indicated agreement with the general idea of greater representation for women or minorities in the public service. Few respondents indicated a willingness to either increase the percentage of minority and/or female co-workers through the imposition of "quotas" or to reconsider the educational and experience requirements for public sector jobs. In short, the general outlook for employee support of EEO policy is not an optimistic one. The implications of these attitudinal patterns are explored more fully in the following sections.

TABLE 1   Distribution of Support for Affirmative Action

	SUPPORT FOR AFFIRMATIVE ACTION	
	%	(*n*)
Low	37%	(87)
Medium	49	(114)
High	15	(34)
Total[1]	101%	(235)

[1] Figures do not add to 100 percent due to rounding.

EFFECTS OF JOB-RELATED ATTITUDES

In looking for job-related correlates of support for affirmative action, we examined attitudes toward pay satisfaction, department autonomy, and opportunities for advancement. Our decision to include financial rewards was based on the assumption that dissatisfaction with working conditions in general, including pay, would result in a lesser tendency for supervisors to accept new policy decisions (Beyer and Trice, 1978: 84-85). We also expected to find that supervisory preferences for greater departmental autonomy in the hiring and firing of personnel would be related inversely to support for affirmative action. According to Stewart and Cantor (1974: 26-28), supervisors prefer to control as many of the circumstances surrounding job performance as possible. As a result, they would view the implementation of a policy imposed from outside their sphere of power with a measure of skepticism. And, finally, we hypothesized that support for affirmative action would be affected by perceptions of career opportunities within the county. Employees with a pessimistic evaluation of their own chances for promotion would not be inclined favorably toward a policy that is perceived to be unduly advantageous to others.

In analyzing the relationship between job-related attitudes and support for affirmative action, Pearson's r was used as our measure of association.[2] The data presented in Table 2 suggest that attitudes toward affirmative action were affected less by individual concern for financial rewards than by the perception of opportunities for advancement or a preference for departmental autonomy in hiring decisions. Whether pay was based on merit rather than seniority, or whether it was relatively low as compared with the salaries of rival agency employees, did not affect support. However, respondents expressing pessimism about their chances for promotion were significantly less supportive of affirmative action. A like tendency was found among individuals who disagreed that departmental hiring practices were fair and impartial. Similarly, those in our sample who thought departmental promotions were based on personal contacts rather than merit were significantly less receptive to affirmative action as were those who thought that "each department should have sole responsibility for hiring and firing."

TABLE 2 Relationships Between Job-Related Attitudes and Support for Affirmative Action (Pearson's r)

JOB-RELATED ATTITUDES	SUPPORT FOR AFFIRMATIVE ACTION			
	LOW % (n)	MEDIUM % (n)	HIGH % (n)	TOTAL % (n)
Satisfaction with pay "I am satisfied with my present salary level"				
Agree	33% (21)	47% (30)	20% (13)	100% (64)
Disagree	37 (51)	52 (72)	12 (16)	101[a] (139)

$r = -0.07$

267

JOB-RELATED ATTITUDES	SUPPORT FOR AFFIRMATIVE ACTION							
	LOW % (n)		MEDIUM % (n)		HIGH % (n)		TOTAL % (n)	
"Compared with other agency employees, I am well paid"								
Agree	36	(47)	45	(29)	19	(12)	100	(64)
Disagree	35	(39)	51	(57)	14	(15)	100	(111)
				$r = -0.02$				
"Pay raises in my department are based on merit rather than on seniority"								
Agree	37	(47)	46	(59)	17	(22)	100	(128)
Disagree	38	(27)	49	(35)	14	(10)	101	(72)
				$r = -0.03$				
Opportunity for advancement "Promotions in my department are based on who you know rather than competence"								
Agree	52	(17)	49	(16)	—	—	101	(33)
Disagree	33	(52)	50	(79)	18	(28)	101	(159)
				$r = 0.18*$				
"I feel that my opportunities for advancement in the agency are good"								
Agree	28	(29)	51	(52)	21	(21)	100	(102)
Disagree	44	(34)	47	(37)	9	(7)	100	(78)
				$r = -0.18*$				
Departmental autonomy "Each department should have sole responsibility for hiring and firing"								
Agree	45	(41)	45	(41)	10	(9)	100	(91)
Disagree	31	(36)	49	(58)	20	(24)	100	(118)
				$r = -0.17*$				
"The procedures used for hiring personnel in my department are fair and impartial"								
Agree	33	(53)	49	(78)	18	(29)	100	(160)
Disagree	47	(18)	42	(16)	11	(4)	101	(38)
				$r = -0.15*$				

[a]Row does not add to 100 percent due to rounding.

*Significant at the 0.01 level.

OBJECTIVE MEASURES
AND SUPPORT FOR
AFFIRMATIVE ACTION

In explaining employee concerns about EEO, it is useful to consider objective indicators of an individual's work and immediate task environment as well as job-related attitudes. Two measures of job involvement used commonly in organizational research are occupational status and job tenure. These variables, in part, represent the organizational stakes of employee participation; however, the direction of the relationship between occupational status and EEO is not easily specified. For example, one might argue, on the one hand, that employees in high-status positions would have reservations about affirmative action because of (1) personnel selection procedures that tend to place greater emphasis on validation than discretionary (or professional) judgment and (2) a perceived conflict between the goal of increased numeric representation of minorities and women in public sector employment and professional standards of education and training. On the other hand, a recent study by Thompson (1978: 337) indicated that several indices of professionalism were somewhat related to favorable attitudes toward minority hiring.

With respect to job tenure, there is little empirical evidence to guide our analysis. If we accept Downs's assumption (1967: 81-83) that public officials are "utility maximizers" acting at least partially from self-interest, it seems likely that nonminority employees with low job tenure would evince greater apprehension about affirmative action than colleagues with more seniority.

It appears, however, that these variables are not particularly useful in providing an explanation for employee attitudes. As Table 3 indicates, neither positional status nor job tenure was significantly related to support for EEO.

TABLE 3   Relationships Among Employee Characteristics, Within-Agency
Percentage of Minority Co-workers, and Support for Affirmative
Action (Pearson's r)

	SUPPORT FOR AFFIRMATIVE ACTION	
EMPLOYEE CHARACTERISTICS	r	(n)
Job tenure (number of years employed by county)	0.05	(231)
Positional status[1]	−0.01	(222)
Within-agency percentage of minority co-workers	0.06	(212)

[1] Our measure is based on status rankings of job titles. Employees surveyed ranged from high-status positions such as engineers or personnel analysts to front-line supervisors in lesser-status occupations (service workers, maintenance, etc.).

It is also conceivable that EEO-related attitudes may be shaped by daily contact with minority co-workers. However, surveys of the organizational literature on interethnic attitudes and behavior by Taylor (1974) and Amir (1969) give little indication of whether proximity per se would have a positive or negative effect on the attitudes of whites toward members of ethnic minorities (or, by extension, social policies designed to benefit minority employees). Our data indicate that supervisors working in agencies with a higher percentage of minority colleagues are slightly more inclined to support affirmative action, though not to a statistically significant degree.[3]

EFFECTS OF DEMOGRAPHIC CONTROLS

At this point it is necessary to examine the impact of extraorganizational variables on the relationships between job-related attitudes and EEO support. As Table 4 indicates, the cumulative impact of age, education, political party identification, and gender (as measured by fourth-order partial correlation coefficients) is virtually nil. This does not imply that these variables are necessarily unimportant in accounting for attitudes toward affirmative action. It does suggest that within the context of an individual's work environment (our primary research concern) that job-related indicators of EEO support are relatively independent of the effects stemming from our respondents' background attributes.

TABLE 4   Relationships Among Perceived Opportunity for Advancement, Departmental Autonomy, and Affirmative Action by Age, Sex, Education, and Political Party Identification

	SUPPORT FOR AFFIRMATIVE ACTION	
	r (ZERO ORDER)	PARTIAL r (FOURTH ORDER)[1]
Opportunity for advancement		
Promotions based on personal connections, not merit	0.18	0.19
Opportunities for advancement viewed as good	–0.18	–0.16
Departmental autonomy		
Hiring and firing decisions left to department	–0.16	–0.15
Departmental hiring procedures viewed as fair and impartial	–0.14	–0.16
	(n = 225)	

[1] Controlling for age, gender, education, and political party identification.

SUMMARY AND DISCUSSION

Our analysis of the relationships among employee characteristics, job-related attitudes, and support for affirmative action produced mixed results. Somewhat unexpectedly, job tenure, occupational status, and the within-agency percentage of minority colleagues were not found to be useful indicators of support. Attitudes toward pay satisfaction were also of little consequence. We did find that support for affirmative action was affected by perceptions of opportunity for advancement as well as attitudes pertaining to the autonomy and fairness of departmental hiring practices. It thus appears that the only aspects of the work environment that affect a nonminority supervisor's evaluation of EEO-related policies are those perceived to have direct personal impact on personal career prospects or a relative degree of influence over departmental hiring practices.

In our sample, white officials who were pessimistic concerning their own advancement opportunities and the extent to which merit criteria were used in promotions were significantly less supportive of the goals and means of affirmative action. Further, those who questioned the fairness of departmental hiring practices and who preferred to lodge hiring and firing responsibilities solely in the department were significantly less likely to be affirmative action advocates. Probably the most interesting of these findings is the lesser receptivity to affirmative action by those who perceive their personal prospects for advancement to be bleak. This is likely explained by the unwillingness of nonminority supervisors to grant a competitive edge to minorities in the job market. These first-line supervisors have not yet "made it" to middle and higher management positions, unlike Thompson's (1977, 1978) high-level personnel administrators, and the former appear to be more concerned about the impact of minority recruitment on their job fortunes than administrators in the higher ranks would be. Additional research might profitably explore in greater detail officials' perceptions of the relationship between specific programs, such as affirmative action, and their own individual career aspirations.

One policy implication of these findings is that implementation of affirmative action plans cannot be considered independently from career advancement issues. We speculate that these supervisors might have been more supportive of the county's affirmative action policies if they had received some assurance from middle and upper management that their career advancement needs were being considered and that their promotional prospects would not be jeopardized by implementation of the affirmative action plan. When promotional opportunities to middle and upper management are perceived to be limited, or to be based on criteria other than merit, the likelihood of establishing and maintaining the necessary support for an effective affirmative action program is diminished. We concur with Bellone and Darling (1980: 191) concerning the importance of communicating accurate information about affirmative action and personal career advancement opportunities to first-line supervisors and the utility of training activities to reduce the anxieties of nonminority employees regarding the criteria for promotion and the impact of affirmative action on their own advancement prospects. The chances of gaining the support necessary for a successful affirmative action program are enhanced when these types of well-devised career development programs and training activities are available within the organization.

Because of the relatively low magnitude of the correlation coefficients and the absence of comparable survey data from other metropolitan areas, our findings must be regarded as tentative. However, our data do suggest that greater attention might be directed to the organizational consequences of employee attitudes. Failure to consider the perception of opportunity costs by nonminority employees in the development or restructuring of personnel policies within public agencies may lead to a decline in morale and/or efficiency. Following Thompson (1977: 95), we may speculate that a work-related concern for many Anglo employees is the suspicion that merit-related criteria are being unduly sacrificed. It may be useful for local policymakers to consider strategies designed to increase employee awareness of the purpose and justification for affirmative action programs but with the additional reminder that promotional decisions are based on a variety of criteria—including job performance indicators.

NOTES

1. A Guttman scale provides a unidimensional measure of an attitude by looking at each scale item response in relation to every other response; that is, items are arrayed in a cumulative fashion so that an endorsement of one implies endorsement of all previous items. See, for example, Garson (1971).

2. Pearson's r is a statistic that provides a quantitative assessment of the strength of the relationship between two variables. A useful description of this technique is found in Blalock (1972).

3. Our data must be interpreted cautiously on this point since we were unable to ascertain the proportion of minority employees in supervisory versus nonsupervisory positions or the frequency of daily contact.

REFERENCES

AMIR, Y. 1969. "Contact Hypothesis in Ethnic Relations." *Psychological Bulletin* 71 (May): 319–342.

BELLONE, J. and D. H. DARLING. 1980. "Implementing Affirmative Action Programs: Problems and Strategies." *Public Personnel Management* 9 (March): 184–191.

BEYER, J. M. and H. M. TRICE. 1978. *Implementing Change.* New York: Free Press.

BLALOCK, H. 1972. *Social Statistics.* New York: McGraw-Hill.

DAVIS, C. E. and J. P. WEST. 1978. "Analyzing Perceptions of Affirmative Action: A Study of Mexican-American Supervisors in a Metropolitan Bureaucracy." *Midwest Review of Public Administration* 12 (December): 246–256.

DOWNS, A. 1967. *Inside Bureaucracy.* Boston: Little, Brown.

GARSON, G. D. 1971. *Handbook of Political Science Methods.* Boston: Holbrook, pp. 120–126.

MEIER, K. 1979. "Constraints of Affirmative Action." *Policy Studies Journal* 7 (Winter): 208–212.

MERTON, R. K. 1968. *Social Theory and Social Structure*. New York: Free Press.

STEWART, D. and M. CANTOR. 1974. *Varieties of Work Experience*. New York: John Wiley.

TAYLOR, D. 1974. "Should We Integrate Organizations?" In Howard L. Fromkin and John J. Sherwood, eds., *Integrating the Organization: A Social Psychological Analysis*. New York: Free Press, pp. 340–361.

THOMPSON, F. J. 1977. "Institutional Barriers to Equity in Local Government Employment: Implications for Federal Policy Derived from Attitudinal Data." In C. H. Levine, ed., *Managing Human Resources: A Challenge to Urban Governments*. Beverly Hills, Calif.: Sage, pp. 83–108.

——. 1978. "Civil Servants and the Deprived: Socio-Political and Occupational Explanations of Attitudes Toward Minority Hiring." *American Journal of Political Science* 22 (May): 325–345.

Dail Ann Neugarten
University of Colorado at Denver
and
Monica Miller-Spellman
Colorado State Department of Personnel

CHAPTER SEVENTEEN
SEXUAL HARASSMENT IN PUBLIC EMPLOYMENT

"Physiological drives are not left in the parking lot or the train station. People bring their sexuality to work and many have difficulty managing that sexuality. This has proven to be a considerable difficulty, especially for those who are victimized in some manner" (Quinn, 1980).

Both romantic and coercive relationships develop between men and women in work environments. Romantic relationships can be pleasurable and rewarding for the individuals involved and may have a positive effect on motivation and productivity. Coercive relationships, on the other hand, are painful for at least one of the persons involved; they inhibit organizational harmony and effectiveness, hamper productivity, and pose potentially serious legal problems.

Sexual harassment at work is a topic of growing concern to managers and personnel specialists as well as to Equal Employment Opportunity (EEO) officers and attorneys. What began as an issue for women's groups and individual victims has become a serious management problem. Despite increasing awareness, uncertainty surrounds the issue. There is debate about what constitutes sexual harassment, how widespread it is, how serious the consequences are for employee well-being and productivity, where the responsibility lies for preventing and/or eliminating sexual harassment, and how best to curb its effects.

In spite—or perhaps because—of these questions, the issue of sexuality in organizations is rapidly gaining the attention of researchers, managers, the legal profession and government agencies. A clearer picture of the problems that exist, as well as prospects for the future, is beginning to emerge.

WHY IS SEXUAL HARASSMENT
A MANAGEMENT CONCERN?

In 1980, Department of Labor statistics showed a total work force of about 105 million individuals. Females over the age of 20 accounted for 37.5 million of these workers; men over 20 accounted for 51 million. Since 1975 women have joined the work force at a faster rate than have men: the percentage of females entering the job force has increased by 20 percent whereas men have shown only a 7 percent increase.

Many of the social and economic factors that have contributed to the increase of women workers have indirect, but important, implications for the changing relationships between men and women in the work setting. All types of women are now working—single women, married women, women with children, young women, older women, more educated women, less educated women. And they are working for a variety of reasons: because they need the income, because they find intellectual and social stimulation in the workplace, and because they view work as intrinsically interesting. Although men, too, work for a variety of reasons, the changing demographics of organizations have disrupted many traditional behaviors.

The roles and positions of women in the work force have led to changing behaviors and expectations for men and women alike. As increasing numbers of women

strive for career mobility and professional development, men's goals and work behaviors change as a result. But despite these changes, female participation in the
work force remains characterized by relative segregation, discrimination, and sexual
stereotyping. Clerical positions—secretaries, typists, bank tellers and telephone operators—the largest job category for women, are still filled by six of every ten women
in the work force. And, although women are more likely than men to be in white-
collar jobs, those jobs are usually less skilled and lower paid. While it is true that increased numbers of women are moving into management positions, these too tend to
be low and middle levels.

Change, of course, is inevitable. Whereas the overall pattern has not yet been
altered, the impact of recent and dramatic educational gains for women and the emphasis on equal opportunity will surely result in rising numbers of women in top-
level technical and management positions. Laws mandating equal opportunity, equal
protection, and equal treatment of women in the workplace have been passed and
are being defined by organizations and the courts. As the weight of protective legislation increases, the relationships of men and women at work will continue—of
necessity—to change. As they move into positions of authority, women will become
more vehement about their rights and about the responsibility of their employers to
protect these rights. As this happens, the view that sexual harassment is an expression of personal attraction beyond the responsibility of management will no longer
be in vogue. Abolishing sexual harassment will become a predominant concern, not
only of social scientists and researchers interested in the broad issues of human behavior, but of managers anxious to achieve increased productivity and organizational
harmony—and to avoid lawsuits.

WHAT IS SEXUAL HARASSMENT?

A major difficulty in understanding and dealing with sexual harassment from both
the employee and management perspectives involves defining the term. What exactly
is sexual harassment? Clearly, the manager who makes sexual favors a requirement
for hiring, promotion, or retention is harassing employees. But what about an "off-
color" remark? A pinch on the rear end? The flippant invitation to bed? Nude pin-
ups?

The Equal Employment Opportunity Commission (EEOC) took a major step
toward eliminating some of the confusion when, on November 10, 1980, it issued
its guidelines on sexual harassment. These guidelines, which define sexual harassment as a form of sex discrimination and therefore a violation of Title VII of the
1964 Civil Rights Act (45 *Fed. Reg.* 74676, 1980), state

> Unwelcome sexual advances, requests for sexual favors, and other verbal or
> physical conduct of a sexual nature constitute sexual harassment when (1)
> submission to such conduct is made either explicitly or implicitly a term or
> condition of an individual's employment, (2) submission to or rejection of

such conduct by an individual is used as the basis for employment decisions affecting such individual, or (3) such conduct has the purpose or effect of unreasonably interfering with an individual's work performance or creating an intimidating, hostile, or offensive working environment.

Sexual harassment is defined more broadly by other federal agencies.

The Office of Personnel Management's definition expands sexual harassment to include unacceptable behavior that, although not necessarily sex discrimination, may be a prohibited personnel practice or violation of the standards of conduct in the federal workplace (OPM, 1979: 3):

Sexual harassment is a form of employee misconduct which undermines the integrity of the employment relationship. All employees must be allowed to work in an environment free from unsolicited and unwelcome sexual overtures. Sexual harassment debilitates morale and interferes in the work productivity of its victims and co-workers. . . . Sexual harassment is a prohibited practice when it results in discrimination for or against an employee on the basis of conduct not related to performance, such as the taking or refusal to take a personnel action, including promotion of employees who submit to sexual advances or refusal to promote employees who resist or protest sexual overtures. . . . Specifically, sexual harassment is deliberate or repeated unsolicited verbal comments, gestures or physical contact of a sexual nature which are unwelcome.

The difficulty with both these definitions is that what one person defines as sexual harassment another may define as flattery. Indeed, while many women argue that unwelcome sexual advances or overtures of any kind, by themselves, constitute harassment, courts have determined that it is *not necessarily the advances* that violate Title VII but rather the *retaliatory* measures taken, once the advances are refused, that violate the law.

HOW EXTENSIVE IS SEXUAL HARASSMENT?

Recent studies indicate that the incidence of sexual harassment is common in both the private and public sectors. Representative James M. Hanley, chairman of the Subcommittee on Investigations of the House Committee on Post Office and Civil Service, in recent Hearings on Sexual Harassment in the federal government, said that "several surveys done by private groups indicated that sexual harassment is widespread. Unfortunately, our preliminary investigation has shown that the problem is not only epidemic, it is pandemic, an everyday, everywhere occurrence" (U.S. House, 1980: 1).

Hanley's committee mandated a survey of sexual harassment in the federal government that has become a landmark study with wide implications. The Merit Systems Protection Board's (MSPB) Office of Merit Systems Review and Studies conducted a survey of 23,000 randomly selected male and female federal civilian employees. The rate of return was 85 percent—considerably higher than required for statistical validity. The study, the first scientifically controlled survey of this depth and breadth, is also the first to be conducted with the full cooperation of the employer—in this case, the federal government—and is clearly the most complete survey of sexual harassment in public employment.

To explore the extent of sexual harassment, the MSPB study asked federal workers whether they had received, during the twenty-four-month period from May 1978 to May 1980 "any of several forms of uninvited and unwanted sexual attention" from a person or persons with whom they worked (Merit Systems, 1981: 26-37).

The forms of behavior identified were

1. Actual or attempted rape or sexual assault.
2. Pressure for sexual behaviors.
3. Deliberate touching, leaning over, cornering, or pinching.
4. Sexually suggestive looks or gestures.
5. Letters, phone calls, or materials of a sexual nature.
6. Pressure for dates.
7. Sexual teasing, jokes, remarks, or questions.

Approximately 42 percent of the women and 15 percent of the men reported being sexually harassed during this period. These victims—one of every four federal employees—reported many forms of sexual harassment, and, with the exception of "actual or attempted rape or sexual assault," harassment was reported by a sizable percentage of both men and women. The most severe form of harassment was reported by only 1 percent, but given the total number of federal employees, this means that about 12,000 people may have had to deal with actual or attempted rape or sexual assault. The survey also concluded that sexual harassment, especially for women, is not a one-time occurrence. Many victims were repeatedly subjected to harassment, lasting for periods of one week to over six months. "Severe sexual harassment" (letters, phone calls, pressure for favors, touching, etc.) was reported by 16 percent, which would equal 300,000 workers, with 8 percent or the equivalent of 150,000 workers reported being harassed by sexual teasing, jokes, and suggestive gestures.

Although the methodological approaches used in many of the other sexual harassment surveys conducted recently leave much to be desired, they are valuable for illustrating the dimensions of the problem. In 1976, *Redbook* magazine solicited its readers' views about sexual harassment. An unprecedented 9,000 women returned the questionnaire. The majority were married, in their 20s and 30s, working in white-collar jobs and earning between $5,000 and $10,000 per year. Nearly 90 percent reported that they had been sexually harassed on their jobs and over 90 percent considered the problem to be a serious one. Further, most victims found the harassment embarrassing, intimidating, and demeaning, while only a small minority said they felt "flattered." (These findings may not be truly representative since it is likely that women who had experienced harassment were more apt to respond to *Redbook*'s questionnaire.) (Safran, 1976).

As a follow-up to its 1976 survey, and in an attempt to learn what management-oriented people felt about the subject, in the spring of 1980 *Redbook* asked the *Harvard Business Review* to conduct a joint survey on the issue of sexual harassment in the workplace. More than 7,000 *Harvard Business Review* subscribers were surveyed, with a 25 percent return rate. Survey results indicated that most people agreed on what sexual harassment is, but that men and women disagreed strongly on how frequently it occurs. While fewer than one-third of the women surveyed felt that sexual harassment was greatly exaggerated, 67 percent of the men agreed with that statement (Collins and Blodgett, 1981).

Women surveyed by *Harvard Business Review* indicated further that they "despaired" of having traditionally male-dominated management understand how much harassment humiliates and frustrates them and also despaired of having management support any efforts to resist it.

Many other studies have been conducted on the subject by groups as diverse as the Working Women's Institute (Crull, 1979) and the United Nations (United Nations, 1977). These surveys ultimately support the same findings:

1. Sexual harassment is widespread and occurs regardless of a woman's age, marital status, appearance, ethnicity, occupation, or salary level.
2. If sexual harassment is as pervasive as these studies indicate, the inequitable treatment of women, the discriminatory effects, and the potential for abuse are enormous.

The surveys and current literature on the subject reveal three major views about sexual harassment (Merit Systems, 1981: 21–22):

1. That it is an abuse of power exercised by those with power, usually male supervisors, over low-status employees, usually women.
2. That individuals with certain low-status, low-power characteristics (such as youth and low organizational rank who are tied economically to jobs) are more vulnerable to sexual harassment than are others.
3. That sexual harassment is an expression of personal attraction between men and women that cannot and should not be stopped.

The last view is most likely articulated by those who feel that the attention placed on the subject and the broad nature of the definitions of sexual harassment issued by both EEOC and OPM will lead to a barrage of lawsuits and unfounded complaints against men. The other two views, which are clearly related, seem to share the belief that sexual harassment is a form of sex discrimination and an abuse of power.

WHO ARE THE VICTIMS?

The MSPB survey found that age, marital status, and sexual composition of an employee's work group have a strong relationship to the degree of sexual harassment. In addition, factors such as educational level, race or ethnic background, job classification, sex of the immediate supervisor, and whether the employee works in a traditional or nontraditional job were shown to have some relationship to incidence of sexual harassment.

Those individuals most likely to be harassed sexually, male or female, were found to be (Merit Systems, 1981, 41-55)

1. Young (under 34).
2. Single or divorced.
3. Members of a minority group (males only).
4. Very dependent on their jobs.
5. Working for less than $11,000 annually if female and less than $15,000 annually if male.
6. Working as trainees or in nontraditional jobs.
7. Working in a work group made up predominantly of members of the opposite sex, reporting to a supervisor of the opposite sex.

The work environment was also found to have an effect on the incidence of reported harassment. Victims tended to have no particular workspace to call their own or occupied a workspace that was only "semiprivate." Victims reported being in organizations where employees did not perceive open communication or positive relationships with supervisors and shared the perception that management was not doing anything to stop the perpetrators of sexual harassment.

WHO ARE THE PERPETRATORS?

Most women surveyed by MSPB report that their harassers are male, and most males indicate that their harassers are female, although men are more likely than women to report being harassed by someone of the same sex.

Harassers of both men and women are reported to act alone rather than with another person. The harassers of women are identified as being older than the victim; the harassers of men are usually younger. Victims report that their harassers are usually married, of the same race or ethnic background (although minority women are more often harassed by someone of another race or ethnicity). Many victims also reported that their harasser had bothered others at work, negating the view that sexual harassment is a matter of isolated personal attraction.

A surprising result of the MSPB survey indicated that victims—both men and women—reported being harassed by fellow employees more often than by supervisors. Prior to the survey, most perpetrators were thought to be supervisors. Regardless of this finding, most victims held the supervisor responsible for the harassment, since part of the supervisor's responsibility is to assure that subordinates work in an environment free from harassment.

WHAT ARE THE EFFECTS
OF SEXUAL HARASSMENT?

Victims of sexual harassment report a range of feelings from embarrassment and humiliation to depression, anxiety, and actual physical illness. The Working Women's Institute, in a 1979 study of women who had been sexually harassed, concluded that sexual harassment diminished the victims' ability to work effectively and destroyed their ambition. Almost all the women questioned reported some type of emotional stress such as nervousness, fear, anger, and sleeplessness, and a majority (63 percent) reported headaches, nausea, and weight gain or loss. Sexual harassment, says the Institute, has become a "hidden occupational hazard" (Crull, 1979).

The effects of sexual harassment are not without cost to the employer. The MSPB study reports that a "conservative" estimate of the cost to the federal government over the two-year period studied was $189 million (Merit Systems, 1981: 77).

The greatest costs were associated with the loss of individual and work group productivity, as reported by the victims. According to the study, this estimate is conservative because (1) victims were far less likely to report a decline in their productivity than a decline in their physical or emotional well-being and (2) the study assumed that, when reported, individual productivity declined by only 10 percent and group productivity by only 1 percent.

Also included in the figure is the cost of job turnover resulting from those employees who left jobs as a result of sexual harassment. A total of $26.8 million is reported for replacing and training new employees in positions vacated by the victims of harassment.

WHAT DOES THE LAW SAY?

At best, the law surrounding sexual harassment is unclear and evolving. At its worst, it is "inconsistent, ambiguous and nascent" (Goldberg, 1978).

Unclear definitions of exactly what constitutes illegal behavior, conflicting views of who is responsible for illegal acts, and uncertainty about which laws or guidelines apply have resulted in a great deal of confusion. Unfortunately, many lawyers argue that the EEOC guidelines will not ameliorate the confusion, particularly since the EEOC "in determining whether alleged conduct constitutes sexual harassment . . . will look at the record as a whole and at the totality of the circumstances, such as the nature of the sexual advances and the context in which the alleged incidents occurred" and will determine the legalities of a particular action "from the facts, on a case by case basis" (EEOC, 1980).

Despite this ambiguity, victims or alleged victims of sexual harassment have in the past and will in the future turn to the courts to seek redress. These victims have two major alternatives in pursuing legal claims: civil and criminal actions. Despite the fact that criminal court cases offer some advantages—the statute of limitations is longer (usually two years, as opposed to six months under Title VII of the 1964 Civil Rights Act), and victims are able to obtain punitive as well as compensatory damages—the disadvantages of this type of action are also serious: charges of assault or battery must be proven beyond a reasonable doubt; court calendars are crowded; legal expenses may be burdensome; and only the perpetrator (who may well be "judgmentproof" or unable to pay damages), and not the employer, may be brought to trial.

As a result, most legal actions resulting from sexual harassment are filed under Title VII or under similar state statutes. Despite the EEOC's determination to view each allegation on a case by case basis, general criteria are emerging that differentiate sexual harassment from other supportable causes of action.

Several court cases bear testimony to the contradictory state of the art. One of the earliest sexual harassment cases is the 1974 case of *Barnes* v. *Train* (1974) in which a woman hired as an administrative assistant to the male director of the Environmental Protection Agency's Equal Opportunities Division filed a suit in district court alleging that her job was abolished because she refused to engage in sexual relations with the director. The district court dismissed the case, arguing that, although Barnes was discriminated against, the discrimination was not because she was a woman but because she refused to engage in sexual behavior with her supervisor. Thus, the district court decided that sexual harassment was not treatment "based on sex within its legal meaning."

Barnes appealed the ruling, and in *Barnes* v. *Costle* (1977) the appellate court reversed the decision, stating "We think that the discrimination as portrayed was plainly based on the appellant's gender. Retention of her job was conditioned upon submission to sexual relations—an exaction which the superior would not have sought from any male." The appellate court thus argued that sexual harassment did constitute sex discrimination. The Environmental Protection Agency was held accountable and Barnes received $18,000 in back pay as damages for lost promotions.

In *Corne* v. *Bausch and Lomb* (1975), two women sued for a violation of their civil rights under Title VII, stating that their male supervisor had taken unsolicited and unwelcome sexual liberties with both. The district court in Arizona dismissed the case on several counts: first, that Title VII outlawed sex discrimination where such discrimination grew out of a company policy, whereas the supervisor in this case was merely satisfying a "personal urge"; second, that Title VII did not prohibit "verbal and physical advances where the behavior was a nonemployment-related encounter"; and, third, that Title VII was inapplicable because the conduct could be directed equally toward men. The court also said "An outgrowth of holding such activities to be actionable under Title VII would be a potential federal lawsuit every time an employee made amorous or sexually oriented advances toward another. The only sure way an employer could avoid such charges would be to have employees who were asexual." The case was appealed and the decision of the Arizona district court was reversed by the Ninth Circuit Court of Appeals.

In *Miller* v. *Bank of America* (1976), this influential U.S. Court of Appeals for the Ninth Circuit ruled in bold language that an employer is liable for the sexually harassing conduct of its supervisors, even if the company has a policy against such conduct. Miller, a black employee of the Bank of America, filed suit in federal district court in 1976 claiming that her supervisor, a white male, promised her a better job if she would be sexually "cooperative." She claimed further that, when she refused to meet his demands, he caused her dismissal.

The bank policy of discouraging sexual advances and of disciplining employees found guilty of such conduct was undisputed, as was the fact that the bank had an established policy for investigating such complaints. Miller, however, chose not to pursue internal grievance procedures and filed a written complaint with the EEOC that was investigated and resulted in her "right to sue" letter for federal district court.

That court refused to hold the bank liable for the supervisor's conduct because Miller had failed to bring the matter to the bank's attention and because the court found that Miller could not prove that the bank had knowledge of the conduct.

In making its determination, the district court stated: "The attraction of males to females is a natural sex phenomenon and it is probable that this attraction plays at least a subtle part in most personnel decisions. Such being the case, it would seem wise for the court to refrain from delving into these matters short of specific factual allegations describing an employer policy which in its application poses or permits a consistent, as distinguished from isolated, sex-biased discrimination on a definable employee group."

The court of appeals, however, did not agree with the district court or with the bank's position. Instead, it applied the "usual rule" that an employer is liable for the wrongs committed by an employee acting in the course of employment, and, further, the appellate court stated unequivocally "We decline to read an exhaustion of company remedies requirement into Title VII."

In *Tompkins* v. *Public Service Electric and Gas Company* (1977), Tompkins, an office worker, complained to the company that her supervisor made physical sexual advances, had told her that a sexual relationship was essential to an effective working relationship, had threatened her with work-related reprisals when she refused, and had restrained her physically. Fifteen months after her complaint was filed, she was fired. The New Jersey State Court dismissed her case stating that Title VII "was not intended to provide a federal tort remedy for what amounts to a physical attack motivated by sexual desire on the part of a supervisor, and which happened to occur in a corporate corridor rather than in a back alley." The court stated further that sexual harassment is "neither employment-related nor sex-based, but a personal injury properly pursued in state court as a tort."

Tompkins appealed this finding, arguing that the employer corporation had knowledge of the harassment incident and that, instead of investigating or correcting the situation, it condoned further harassment by other employees. The Third Circuit agreed with Tompkins, who received $20,000 and attorney's fees, and ordered the employer to notify all employees that sexual harassment is against the law.

The decision of the appellate court in *Tompkins* is important in that it noted that employers are responsible for providing a work environment "free from the psychological harm flowing from an atmosphere of discrimination" and because it presented a three-part test in establishing illegal sexual harassment. First, the harassment by a supervisor must be linked to the victim's job status and coupled with a threat of demotion or with actual punitive conduct related to the individual's position in the organization. Second, the employer must be shown to either have had knowledge of the supervisor's acts or to be in a position where a reasonable employer in a similar position should have been aware of the harassment. Third, an employer in such a position is permitted a defense of "prompt remedial action."

The action taken by the employer in the case of *Heelan* v. *Johns Manville Corporation* (1978) was not deemed sufficient. Heelan claimed that, because she refused to have sexual relations with her supervisor, she was fired. She made a formal complaint but felt the company's response to be insufficient. The court held that "an employer is liable under Title VII when refusal of a supervisor's unsolicited sexual advances is the basis of termination." Heelan won a rumored $100,000 in an out-of-court settlement.

Recent cases have resulted in an evolved state of the art. In *Wright* v. *Methodist Youth Services* (1981), a supervisor's unwelcome homosexual advances were found to be a violation of Title VII by the Illinois Federal District Court, which noted that homosexual harassment "presents the obverse of the coin" of heterosexual harassment, which is prohibited by Title VII. Since heterosexual harassment cases, the court noted, are predicated on the notion that making a demand of a female employee that would not be made of a male employee involves sex discrimination, an "alleged demand of a male employee that would not be directed at a female" should also constitute a violation of Title VII.

A female engineer who was harassed and discriminated against by both co-workers and supervisors was entitled to collect punitive damages from her harassers in unusual awards made by a federal trial court in New Jersey. In *Kyriazi* v. *Western Electric Co.* (1981), Kyriazi, who was found to have been underpaid, denied promotions, harassed, and ultimately terminated for filing a discrimination charge, was also awarded reinstatement with retroactive benefits and back pay. The punitive damages were awarded under a state law prohibiting interference with contracts of employment. Her co-workers were held liable because they made Kyriazi's work environment intolerable, thus preventing her from practicing her profession, by shooting rubber bands at her, speculating loudly about her virginity, and circulating an insulting cartoon depiction of her, while the supervisors were found liable for having ignored this conduct, despite Kyriazi's complaints.

The cases mentioned here share a common denominator not found in *Bundy*

v. *Jackson* (1981): they involved adverse employment consequences either as a result of the victim's refusal of sexual advances or in retaliation for the filing of a complaint. In *Bundy,* however, the Court of Appeals for the District of Columbia Circuit held that an employer violates Title VII merely by subjecting an employee to sexual harassment, even if resistance to the advances does not cause loss of any tangible job benefits. Bundy complained to management that she had been harassed by three supervisors but that her complaints were not taken seriously. The district court found that the making of improper sexual advances to female employees was "standard operating procedure" at Bundy's place of employment and concluded that sexual harassment does not by itself represent discrimination with respect to the "terms, conditions or privileges of employment" within the meaning of Title VII.

The court of appeals reversed that decision. Drawing from race discrimination precedents, it held that Title VII is violated whenever an employer creates or condones a substantially discriminatory work environment, whether the complaining employee has lost any tangible job benefit as a result of the discrimination or not.

The court reasoned that, unless it extended Title VII protection to cases where the discrimination was limited to the creation of a work environment charged with sexual harassment, "an employee could sexually harass a female employee with impunity by carefully stopping short of firing the employee or taking any other tangible actions against her in response to her resistance." The victim of the harassment would face what the court described as a cruel trilemma: "She can endure the harassment. She can attempt to oppose it, with little hope of success, either legal or practical, but with every prospect of making the job even less tolerable for her. Or she can leave her job, with little hope of legal relief and the likely prospect of another job where she will face harassment anew." Concluding that it would not subject Bundy to these choices, the court ruled that Title VII was violated when her employer permitted the existence of a discriminatory work environment and ordered the district court to fashion appropriate injunctive relief. As a result of *Bundy,* an employer can now be held accountable for allowing the psychological and emotional work environment to become tainted by sexual innuendo and stereotyping.

In an effort to provide guidance to the district court in preparation of its injunctive decree, the court of appeals gave employers some suggestions as to how to avoid *Bundy*-type liability. Drawing upon the EEOC guidelines on sexual harassment, the court reminded employers that an employer may negate liability by taking immediate and appropriate corrective action when it learns of any illegal harassment but that the employer should fashion internal rules to ensure that such corrective action never becomes necessary.

It is not only the alleged victims of sexual harassment who have recourse under Title VII, but according to the guidelines, coworkers, as well. Section G notes that "Where employment opportunities or benefits are granted because of an individual's submission to the employer's sexual advances or requests for sexual favors, the employer may be held liable for unlawful sex discrimination against other persons who were qualified for but denied that employment opportunity or benefit."

HOW SHOULD THE ORGANIZATION
RESPOND?

Until recently, management's response to complaints of sexual harassment has generally been to do nothing. For a variety of reasons, organizations have failed to take the problem seriously or see it as a problem at all—despite evidence to the contrary—and have lacked adequate guidelines on how to develop preventive programs. As a result of the efforts of the House Committee on Post Office and Civil Service, the federal government and many of its major departments have taken a lead in developing appropriate organizational responses.

The legal cases cited, as well as the results of many surveys, indicate clearly that the key is preventive programs. As publicity spreads, organizations can expect an increase in formal complaints of sexual harassment, and the mere presence or absence of a preventive program may prove to be a major determinant in a court decision.

Such programs may not only minimize the employer's liability in sexual harassment cases, but they will also be welcomed by the potential victims of harassment—the employees. The MSPB study found, as did many others, that victims strongly agree that there is much that management can do to alleviate or eliminate the problem and that, while there is a remarkable amount of ignorance among employees about available remedies and courses of action, even those who were aware of their legal rights would prefer an effective "informal" solution to the problem.

While the EEOC guidelines and court decisions require positive, remedial action to avoid liability, and while data indicate that effective preventive programs are likely to result in cost savings to the employer (directly and indirectly, as a result of improved productivity and morale and reduced use of sick leave by victims), the question remaining is what, exactly, constitutes "positive preventive action"?

Many organizations have avoided issuing policy statements or developing preventive programs because they felt that to do so would be to admit that sexual harassment existed in their workplace. Now that the "pandemic" problem is known, the first step in developing any effective program is to convince management of the serious nature of the problem and the consequences of ignoring or dealing inappropriately with it. Once that is accomplished, the following steps are suggested. Organizations should

1. Issue a policy statement defining and condemning sexual harassment as a prohibited personnel practice. This policy must have the strong endorsement of management and be publicized widely: posted on bulletins, reprinted in newsletters, and placed in employee and manager handbooks.

2. Conduct an employee survey about the types and extent of sexual harassment, assuring employee anonymity and confidentiality. The survey should be worded carefully to cover the whole range of behavior and consequences. The results should be posted and reprinted and used to develop educational and training programs.

3. Provide special training for managers. The training, which will use infor-

mation gained through the employee survey as well as other material, should explain fully the agency stance on sexual harassment and emphasize the outcomes such behavior could have on the perpetrators, the victims and other employees. This training should also expose managers to the legal liabilities involved.

4. Conduct discussions of sexual harassment at employee meetings and during orientation sessions for new employees. Advise employees not only of the company policy on sexual harassment and the grievance channels available to them, but advise them what constitutes sexual harassment and the ramifications that may occur from both appropriate and inappropriate allegations. An example of this is the recent $23.7 million lawsuit filed by a Clark University professor against two faculty members and three other women who accused him of sexual harassment. Contending that the charges were "false and malicious" and ruined his reputation, he is suing each woman for millions of dollars.

5. Establish an investigative procedure, either as part of an existing program or as a special process. The first step in such an investigation is to assure the victim that his or her job is not in jeopardy and that all efforts will be made to protect the victim's identity and position in the agency. Advise the victim to document all incidents relating to the alleged harassment and search for other victims, particularly if the alleged harasser has a history of high turnover among subordinates of the opposite sex. In some cases, it may be advisable to consider the use of an outside consultant or investigator to enhance credibility and provide needed expertise.

6. Offer both the victim and the harasser the use of agency counseling programs, if available.

7. Set out a progressive disciplinary agenda and, if the allegations are found to be true, punish the perpetrator. Punishment could range from verbal reprimand to warning letters, transfer, denial of a bonus or promotion, poor performance appraisals, suspension or probation, or, ultimately, dismissal. Take care to ensure the perpetrator due process.

8. If no evidence of harassment is found, be sure that the allegation is not publicized and that there is no retaliation against the complainant.

9. Treat all complaints consistently and fairly. The key to a successful preventive program lies in a prompt, documented response—and in the credibility of the responsible individual or department handling the complaint. While many of the techniques and procedures developed for race and sex discrimination cases apply, the emotional and hierarchical nature of sexual harassment make it a unique situation in the workplace, with serious and potentially devastating implications for management.

REFERENCES

Barnes v. *Costle.* 1977.   501 F.2d 983.
Barnes v. *Train.* 1974.   13 FEP 123.
Bundy v. *Jackson.* 1981.   24 EDP 31439.

COLLINS, E. G. and T. B. BLODGETT. 1981. "Sexual Harassment . . Some See It . . Some Won't." *Harvard Business Review* 59 (March-April): 76–95.

Corne v. *Baush and Lomb.* 1975. 390 F. Supp. 161; 562 R.2d 55.

CRULL, P. 1979. "The Implications of Sexual Harassment on the Job: A Profile of the Experience of 92 Women." *Research Series Report No. 3.* New York: Working Women's Institute.

EQUAL EMPLOYMENT OPPORTUNITY COMMISSION. 1980. "Final Guidelines on Sexual Harassment in the Workplace." Washington, D.C.: G.P.O.

Federal Regulations 1980. 45: 74676.

GOLDBERG, A. 1978. "Sexual Harassment and Title VII." *Michigan Law Review* 76 (May): 1007–1035.

Heelan v. *Johns Manville Corporation.* 1978. 451 F. Supp. 1382.

Kyriazi v. *Western Electric Co.* 1981. 20 EDP 30273.

MERIT SYSTEMS PROTECTION BOARD. 1981 "Sexual Harassment in the Federal Workplace: Is it a Problem?" 344 46 3. Washington, D.C.: G.P.O.

Miller v. *Bank of America.* 1976. 418 F. Supp. 233.

OFFICE OF PERSONNEL MANAGEMENT. 1979. "Memorandum to Heads of Departments and Independent Agencies, Subject: Policy Statement and Definition of Sexual Harassment." Washington, D.C.: OPM, (December).

QUINN, R. E. 1980. "Coping with Cupid: The Formation, Impact, and Management of Romantic Relationships in Organizations." in D. A. Neugarten and J. M. Shafritz eds. *Sexuality in Organizations.* Oak Park, Ill.: Moore, 38–52.

SAFRAN, C. 1976. "What Men Do to Women on the Job: A Shocking Look at Sexual Harassment." *Redbook* (November): 149, 217–224.

Tompkins v. *Public Service Electric and Gas Company.* 1977. 422 F. Supp. 533.

UNITED NATIONS AD HOC GROUP ON EQUAL RIGHTS FOR WOMEN. 1977. "In House Memorandum on the Rights of Women." New York: United Nations.

U.S. HOUSE OF REPRESENTATIVES. SUBCOMMITTEE ON INVESTIGATIONS OF THE COMMITTEE ON POST OFFICE AND CIVIL SERVICE. 1980. "Sexual Harassment in the Federal Government." 96th Cong., 1st sess., serial number 96–57. Washington, D.C.: G.P.O.

Wright v. *Methodist Youth Services.* 1981.

Jeremy F. Plant
George Mason University

CHAPTER EIGHTEEN
ETHICS AND PUBLIC PERSONNEL ADMINISTRATION

Public personnel administration has in recent years begun to come to grips with the ethical problems of the public service.[1] The merit system that forms the core of the American system of personnel administration was created in part for its ethical underpinnings; indeed, "merit" implies not only the possession of skills useful in public service jobs, but integrity and freedom from political corruption. Woodrow Wilson, reformer and political scientist, considered civil service reform in 1887 "a moral preparation for what is to follow," the reconstruction of public administration on a scientific and nonpartisan basis. Issues with ethical aspects have become important in our public life since the time of Wilson because the relationship of personnel management and ethics is not so simple that it was solved with the end of the spoils system (if it has in fact ended!). We can identify a long list of issues and problems of government that are played out in the domain of personnel administration. In this list we can include programs for affirmative action; the right of public employees to strike; the problems of fraud, waste, and abuse; financial disclosure of private wealth; personal liability of public employees for damages to others incurred in the performance of the job; "revolving-door" patterns of individuals who use public employment as a way to enter and reenter lucrative positions in the private sector; and many more.

The justification for saying that public personnel administration is entering a new period in regard to ethics is twofold. First, ethics is being defined better in public administration, so that the *management* of ethics is beginning to emerge as a new role for personnel managers. The Civil Service Reform Act of 1978 is indicative of the trend to lodge actual responsibilities for ethics in personnel offices (Plant and Gortner, 1981: 5-9). Second, the perception of ethical problems in the public service is increasing in the mind of the public. Although few public officials are guilty of ethical transgressions, and studies have shown that most have a keen appreciation of the ethical dilemmas involved in public service jobs (Bowman, 1977), the confidence that the public once had in the honesty of its public service employees has been sorely tested by governmental scandals involving elected officials, and the occasional scandal involving the careerist.[2]

Can the public personnel system find ways to manage the needed programs of ethics? Will personnel administration be the focal point in government for the building of ethical awareness in the public service? Answering these questions in the affirmative requires that (1) we understand the various ways in which the ethical questions intrude upon the work of the public service and (2) select from among the different approaches by which public personnel administrators can help to build ethical understanding. This chapter examines the situations in which ethical questions become important for public administrators and suggests some ways in which the field of personnel management can adjust itself to be more useful in developing an awareness in government of the ethical dimension of public service.

Defining ethics is our first task. For our discussion, ethics will be defined as "right conduct," action that can be justified with individual and social standards of right and wrong. Since all public administration is concerned with the complex world of governance, it is necessary to add to our definition the concept of appropriateness: ethics is by nature situational insofar as right conduct means right conduct in particular situations of administration. Ethics may be based upon moral belief, but the test of ethical conduct is being able to *act* and be decisive in difficult contexts of action.

ETHICS IN PUBLIC ADMINISTRATION: A BRIEF HISTORICAL OVERVIEW

Among the early scholars who studied public administration, the discussion of ethics as part of the discipline[3] was considered either inappropriate or unnecessary: inappropriate because public administration was separate from politics and values, unnecessary because politics would settle the major normative issues of public life. Students of public administration were told the job of the public service was simply to carry out the decisions made by accountable elected officials. According to an eminent public official of the 1920s, carrying out value-free instrumental processes is the life of those who "are down in the stokehole of the ship of state, and [who] are concerned simply with the economical handling of fuel" (Dawes, 1923: 177).

A second factor that emphasized further the separation of politics and administration was the merit-based public personnel system. An admission that the public bureaucracy was involved in making ethical choices could be used to refute the merit principles used to separate the worlds of politics and personnel administration. Since public administrators were involved in, and had to maintain a stance of, nonpartisan and apolitical service to the public, they could not offer solutions to ethical problems. Instead it was the job of public administrators to carry out, efficiently and effectively, the choices made by politicians.

Not only was the consideration of public administration ethics inappropriate, it was unnecessary because the institutions of constitutional government and the structure of bureaucracy guaranteed accountability. Accountability became the key concept of early public administration thought as it considered problems of ethics in administration. So long as the actions of career administration were open to inspection by elected officials, ethics would be guaranteed by the constant surveillance of elected officials using formal controls outside the bureaucracy. Formal controls were lodged in all three branches of government, but the most important was the control of elected executives over the institutions of the executive branch.

With powerful political parties and interest groups involved in the accountability question, the guarantee of external controls over administrative action was made even stronger, and behind all the formal and informal structures of politics and government stood the law. Law was the underpinning and foundation of the rules by which the public policy process was played. Law placed carefully prescribed limits on the actions of public managers; therefore, it seemed unnecessary to debate the ethical aspects of public administration.

Beyond external controls there was the internal control of the hierarchy that also addressed the ethical standards of administration. Hierarchy, as Appleby (1949) has noted, serves as an ethical anchor for administration, and must be considered as a moral force as well as an instrumental, managerial force in administration. Hierarchy requires that each individual within the bureaucracy be accountable to a superior and that the superior assume responsibility for the actions of subordinates. Hierarchy, when functioning as it should, guarantees that someone is always on tap to see that subordinates act ethically and to answer any questions regarding the actions of bureaucracy. At the pinnacle of the hierarchy are political appointees who are held accountable by elected officials and the citizenry. The double-edged sword of accountability—external and internal control mechanisms—produced a thorough system of control over administrators. It was considered unnecessary for personnel administration to spend much time worrying over the ethical standards of public employees. People in positions of authority produced ethical behavior, not specialists within personnel offices.

While some students of public administration used these arguments to assume that ethics was not a problem of consequence for the public service, they failed as well to consider the issue of personal or individual ethics as it pertained to the public servant. Why was this so? First, when one discusses responsibility as personalized ethical conduct, it is ultimately necessary to deal with the problem of personal interpretation of events, decisions, situations. Once it is admitted that ethical questions are open to personal interpretation, it becomes obvious that the door is opened to individual perspectives that may lead to misinterpretation and aberrant behavior. There is no scientific way in which to study and define what is "correct" personal interpretation: no argument can be totally conclusive in the world of personal values. A second important factor in explaining the disinterest of public administration in concrete schemes of personal ethics is the reformers' belief that holding power in a democracy would reinforce the public servant's appreciation of the nebulous "public interest" and make him or her more conscious of the need to act in ethical ways. Both elected and career officials would be ethical if the political and administrative processes were cleansed of the evils of corruption, ineptness, and venality. Combining the scientific approach to management with the politics-administration separation of the reform movement became the basis of early public administration orthodoxy (Gulick and Urwick, 1937).

Public administration thinkers of the post–World War II period did not accept the orthodox view of public administration left from the merger of reform politics and scientific management techniques. They questioned the descriptive truth of the dichotomy between politics and administration, the simple notions of accountability by either internal or external control devices, and the idea that personal beliefs of individual bureaucrats would not be a major determining force in public decision-making.

Two forces bear notice in showing how public administration has adopted different guides for ethical awareness that it used in its early period. First is the development of research-oriented social science, which has led to a recognition that values and techniques important in administration can be kept separate only in the trivial, programmed tasks of administration. Important decisions require an awareness of the "seamless web" combining ethics and factual judgments (Simon, 1947). Research into human behavior and motivation (Maslow, 1943) has increased our understanding of the dilemmas created for individuals by large organizations. Leading an ethical existence in large bureaucracies is not an easy task, and the ethical underpinnings of life outside the organization may not be a satisfactory guide to making ethical choices within its confines (Argyris, 1957).

A second problem for public administration has been the awareness of students and practitioners in the field that leadership does not always work as the reformers told us it would. Administrative leadership, we were told, would solve the problem of linking the values of instrumental efficiency held by the bureaucracy and the values of democratic accountability and responsibility that form the core of our political community. The resolution of the conflict between democratic accountability and efficiency-effectiveness principles was to be found in an administrative leadership committed to social goals and political philosophy, yet was also skillful in utilizing the processes of scientific management. Leadership was the linchpin of the ethics of bureaucracy and the ethics of democracy.

Formal authority is acceptable as the basis of ethical leadership only if leaders can be trusted to (1) know what is "right" and appropriate in public sector management decisions and (2) have the will to carry out right conduct under conditions of adversity. During the last two decades, our faith in leadership to perform its role as "ethical anchor" has been sorely tested. The Watergate episode put to rest the notion that our democracy elevated the best to office or made true leaders out of political hacks. The failure of ethical leaders such as Presidents Ford and Carter to "lead through an idea" (Gulick and Urwick, 1937: 37-38) has also damaged the belief that leadership is the ethical foundation of public administration. Leaders must provide a sense of direction for government and make the career public officials see that there is a goal attached to their efforts so that a sense of accomplishment may be experienced. The scapegoating of "nameless, faceless bureaucrats" that leaders indulge in only harms their legitimacy as the ethical focal point of public administration.

Since it is impossible to separate technical problems and ethical concerns, and since it is not feasible to depend on either the structure or leadership of public organizations to provide definitive ethical guidelines and checks, scholars who have studied public administration have looked for other methods whereby bureaucrats can be induced or forced to maintain an ethical posture toward their work.[4] Personnel administration has had a strong interest in the continuing efforts of public administration to understand the meaning of ethics in the public service. This is a logical, (perhaps inescapable) interest since personnel administration deals with the human resources of the organizations of government. Public administration has moved away from formalism toward a greater interest in the human side of ethical behavior. The greater the concentration on human resources as a determinant of ethical behavior, the more important it is for personnel managers to adjust the traditional thinking and processes of their field to meet the demands for greater ethical awareness in public administration. The next section of the chapter looks at the role of personnelists in helping to produce a workable understanding of ethics in public service employment.

PERSONNEL ADMINISTRATION AND ETHICS: A CONCEPTUAL APPROACH

Personnel administration has absorbed many of the intellectual currents that have complicated the definitional problem of governmental ethics since the time of Woodrow Wilson. Perhaps the major recent change in emphasis, and one that is attributable largely to the infusion of ideas from the social sciences, is our belief in *positive ethical training.* According to believers in positive training, the role of the personnel department is to create, or to help mold, ethical individuals, that is, to create through training, education, and experiential learning devices individuals who do not need to be told what to do, what is right and what is wrong in public administration situations, who can feel their way through difficult decisions involving values.

Caiden (1971: 35) considers it personnel management's "basic aim to preserve personality from anonymity . . . the personnel staff should be the most worried about complaints of impersonality, bureaupathology, insensitivity, low valuation of life, and disrespect for human dignity. Their job is to humanize the system to make others aware that the end of all systems is the fulfillment of human needs." Such an approach to ethics based on humaneness is referred to by Choi (1979) as the "ethics of equity."

This positive approach to ethics has been overlayed on a personnel system designed to ensure other values as well as personal development, most notably the value of efficiency in operations. It was appropriate at one time for efficiency to be the primary value in the working of the public personnel system for the simple reason that the system didn't work well: efficiency and morality were seen as nonconflicting values in the reform period. Only after the system of government began to perform with acceptable levels of efficiency could it turn its attention to the less obvious and more complicated issue of personal development.

A conceptual approach to ethical awareness in public personnel administration is portrayed in Table 1. Two primary sets of variables exist. First is the approach taken to defining the problem of ethics. One way is the legalistic-formal approach emphasizing formal restrictions on behavior through codes of ethics, professional caveats, prohibition of political activities, and restriction of personal financial dealings. Arrayed counter to this approach is the dynamic-behavioral approach, which looks to develop in the individual public servant an awareness of client needs and desires, understanding of the meaning of right conduct in situations, personal self-development, awareness of stress on the job, the democratization of life in organizations.

TABLE 1 Variables in Public Administration Ethics

| | FOCUS OF CONCERN | |
APPROACH TO DEFINITION	INDIVIDUAL (MICRO)	SOCIETY OR SYSTEM (MACRO)
Dynamic/Behavioral	I Human Development and Improvement	II Social Equity/ Responsiveness
Legalistic/Formalistic	III Codes of Ethics	IV Utilitarianism

A second factor is the focus of concern: the microethical focus stresses the individual as an end in himself or herself and tries to assess what is right conduct for the individual in a particular administrative circumstance. The macroethical approach subordinates feelings and desires of individuals to the broader concerns of the system and society.

Typically, the two major sets of variables are intermingled in discussion, and three of the four cells described in Table 1 appear as models frequently cited in the literature on government ethics. Cell I is frequently found described in the literature based on human development (Rizzo, 1977). Cell II is advanced by advocates of the New Public Administration school (Fredericksen, 1971) and by disciplines of Rawls (1971). Its focus is social equity.

Cell III contains the formalistic approach to individual ethics that Rohr (1978) calls the "low road." While Rohr faults codes of conduct for their triviality and fear-based, nonlearning approach, others, notably, Kernaghan (1974), find the law and formal codes to be useful if tailored to the specific operating conditions of a program or agency.

Cell IV is the most elusive of the four to describe or find in real-world situations. Legal definitions of societal ethics are perhaps contained in formal constitutions. In undemocratic societies it quickly becomes heavy-handed authoritarianism. It is labeled as an approach for our purposes as utilitarianism and, in the democratic environment, finds its clearest operating milieu in emergencies and war, situations in which individual standards of right and wrong must be suspended to enforce societal values. The common element that cell IV demands is the requirement that individuals perform acts they deem personally immoral or reprehensible for the good of the community. Personnel administration may find it difficult to inculcate an understanding of utilitarian demands within the tradition of positive ethical training (Plant and Gortner, 1981: 4-5).

Moving from theories and concepts to practice is an essential skill for public administrators. It is especially difficult in the area of ethics, which many managers consider far removed from the real world of administrative practice. Yet the demands on personnel administration in the future will increasingly lie in the area of helping public administrators to translate ethical training into operational guides in a multitude of decision-making situations. For personnelists to have a lasting and significant impact on the ethical dimension of public administration, it is essential that they grapple with the political and managerial realities of modern administration. Perhaps the most important single institution affecting the public service is the modern chief executive. Earlier in the chapter we mentioned the critical role that leadership plays in ethical determinations. The prevalence of the executive leadership doctrine of public administration (Kaufman, 1956) makes it imperative for personnel administration to be cognizant of the ties between it and the modern executive (epitomized by the strong presidency). The executive sets goals, provides a plan for allocating resources, appoints senior-level officials, and influences the action of every agency of government. Furthermore, the doctrine has influenced the ethics of public administration by contrasting demands for loyalty against demands for universalized rules of ethical conduct. The next section examines the ethical role of the chief executives in modern-day administration, stressing the evolving links in the area of ethical leadership between the presidency and the personnel system.

ETHICAL DEMANDS
OF EXECUTIVE LEADERS

Managing ethics would be simplified for personnel administration if there were only one personnel system, with one set of rules and procedures governing all public employees. Such is obviously not the case. Mosher (1968) has noted the existence of several patterns of personnel management in the public service; the trends he saw as giving rise to diversity in the system—professionalism, unionism, changing patterns of education for public servants—have continued to be important forces in decentralizing the personnel system.

One important way in which public officials are different is in the appointment process: Do they owe their position to merit and competitive examination or to selection on the basis of political affiliation? The basis of selection will have important bearing on the ethical dilemmas likely to confront the individual. As Heclo (1977) has shown, it is not easy to differentiate the appointee from the high-level careerist at the top rungs of the bureaucracy. And, as Thayer (1981) has argued, the effect of the Civil Service Reform Act of 1978 may be to politicize the Senior Executive Service created by that legislation and push it closer to partisan politics.

A lesson of the American experiment of mixing political and career officials in the executive positions of government is this: any individual, regardless of how he or she is recruited and selected, who attains a position close to the top needs to understand the clash of ethics with demands for loyalty. The foremost dilemma of the top executive in government is the weighing of universal standards of conduct against demands for personalized loyalty to leader, team, ideology. Should the individual place loyalty to the person above loyalty to the organization, the community?

A public official must have the ability to understand the ethical quandary that excessive loyalty to any single reference point in the system, even the presidency, may produce. Personnel administration may find it necessary to provide more guidance to careerists and political appointees when it comes to understanding ethical problems caused by demands for loyal behavior.

Why is loyalty so important in understanding ethics? A direct outgrowth of executive leadership has been the view that loyalty—loyalty to person, to the incumbent, not loyalty to abstract notions of the public interest or public office—is an admirable, even necessary, virtue of high-level public service. Loyalty is no mean virtue, but it is often the natural result of attachment to primary reference points such as family, friends, neighborhood or community, church, and nation. Its weakness as a guide for ethical action in complex administrative situations is its simplicity, its irrationality. It ill-equips public officeholders to act in situations in which higher claims of morality or utilitarian motives of social efficiency must be weighed against expectations of unrelenting loyalty to a leader and his or her immediate circle of advisors.

Weisband and Franck, in their provocative account of executive loyalty, compare the claims of loyalty against the ethical autonomy they feel is required of all public officials (1975: 131):

> Loyalty to the Chief is not, of course, a quality to be deplored. Indeed, it is an appropriate, universally shared, and internalized ethic of key personnel in any functioning enterprise and, particularly, of governments. However, the extraordinary extent to which, among top federal executives, loyalty to the President has become the overriding ethic, taking precedence over all other considerations, is reported by many recent officials. And this has rightly become a matter of deep concern to the American public.

As the doctrine of executive leadership has come to dominate the thinking of public administration, the ascendency of loyalty as a primary attribute of the high-level public servant has become more and more evident. One reason for the supremacy of claims of loyalty is the expansion of offices of government in which staffing is chief executive dominated and therefore at least in part loyalty-based. Since 1970, in the federal government alone, there has been a significant expansion in the demands for loyalty in areas previously at arm's length from direct control of the executive. These offices include middle-management positions in OMB, certain positions in federal regional and area offices, and, with the 1978 reform of the upper levels of the career service, in a large body of civil servants who will be loosely assigned to management roles within the Senior Executive Service. SES participants will presumably find compelling career-based reasons for adding an operational definition of "loyalty to the chief" to the bureaucratic ethic of impartiality and political prudence they developed through years of socialization in the bureaucracy. The price of ascension to policy-sensitive positions for many will be a tug of war matching objectivity and ethical autonomy against loyalty to chief executive and his "team."

It is possible, of course, to argue that loyalty is demanded of, or comes naturally, to all public officials. The question is, loyalty to whom or what, and at what cost? The loyalty of bureaucrats is often loyalty to program, to agency or department, to region, to clientele, to allies in Congress, to cause or goals. It is difficult to function in the bureaucracy without visible loyalty to some important reference, and impossible to be accepted if considered *disloyal*. Is loyalty to the chief executive a higher loyalty than loyalty to one's organization? Does not the chief executive serve as direct representative of and emissary to the broader public that must be the measure of government activities and policies? Or is personalized loyalty, however understandable and practical, not in keeping with the demands for more universal standards of conduct?

In the world of administrative action, as Bailey (1964: 237) has observed, "there is no public decision whose moral effect can be gauged in terms of what game theorists refer to as a 'zero sum' result: a total victory for the right and a total defeat for the wrong." In situations dominated by the ethics of personal loyalty, however, there is a danger that just such black and white situations may be perceived. Loyalty is a simple virtue that makes out of complex situations simple stakes of right and wrong. Loyalty demands also discriminate against professionals working in administration in favor of personal staff members. The failure of executives to "lead by an idea" noted earlier in the chapter makes it necessary to analyze the leader's views on an issue-by-issue basis. Insiders are the only winners in this case. They are sensitive to the leader's opinion on the subject, or, if the leader is only involved superficially, it is the insiders who determine the position that the loyal follower should take. The career civil servant, loyal to profession, program, agency, and some notion of the public interest, will never seem loyal enough to the insiders, since the ethic of the careerist is to be "consistent enough to deserve ethical respect from revered colleagues and from oneself; to be pliable enough to survive within an organization and to suceed in effectuating moral purposes" (Bailey, 1964: 238).

Demands of executive leaders for loyalty create myriad problems for the career bureaucrat. Should one resign a position because it involves the implementation of policies that one finds morally repugnant? The sociability requirement of success within organizations may make it difficult to accept resignation as the only means of protest. Witness Weisband and Franck's analysis of one public servant's decision to resign quitely from a top position during the Vietnam war (1975: 181):

> If we were to be asked by an official like George Ball whether, in 1966, after resigning, he should have led a public campaign against the Johnson Administration's Vietnam policies, our answer would be something like this: "Yes, for the sake of the republic, for the good of the democratic political system, as well as for the cause of Vietnam disengagement. It would have been very useful to have had you take a lead in the antiwar movement. It would have restored the faith of the young in the system, would have given credibility and weight to the war's opponents, would have created the basis for an informed, civilized public debate of the Vietnam issues. But it would also, in all probability, have ended your political career and led to your being ostracized by the professional and social circles in which you work and relax. It would have

brought you to a severe crisis of self-esteem. You have spent your life as a team player, a loyal peer-grouper. You would suddenly have found yourself being categorized as a non-team-player by that small elite on whose amiability your professional and private life is built. The costs to you would have been enormous."

Up to this point, we have not shown how the president's personnel powers may be used to enforce loyalty in the public service. One way is through the White House personnel office and the educative role it assumes for political appointees. The classic document which tried to use the direct personnel role of the president vis-à-vis his appointees is the so-called "Malek Manual" of the Nixon administration. Thompson (1979: 113) described it in this way: "in some respects the Malek Manual is to personnel administration what Machiavelli's *The Prince* is to the broader field of political science."

Loyalty ideas are central to the logic of the manual. It tells appointees that bureaucrats are more loyal to Congress or to a vague sense of "the government" than to an elected president (Thompson, 1979: 160):

> The record is quite replete with instances of the failures of program, policy and management goals because of sabotage by employees of the executive branch who engage in the frustration of those efforts because of their political persuasion and their loyalty to the majority party of Congress rather than the executive that supervises them. And yet, in their own eyes, they are sincere and loyal to their government.

The manual is a guide to the use of questionable personnel procedures to ensure loyalty in the executive branch. It is most renowned for the section entitled "techniques for removal through organizational or management procedures." The manual begins to sound more and more like Machiavelli as it enumerates the various removal techniques to ensure executive control. These are listed in several sections. *Individual* techniques put the individual in a position whereby he or she is forced to leave a job or accept unpleasant, often distant work duties. *Layering* is a second approach; as the manual describes it, "the layering technique, as its full name [sic] implies, is an organizational technique to 'layer' over insubordinate subordinates, managers who are loyal and faithful. Other tactics are *shifting responsibilities* to isolate individuals or change job descriptions so that "those bureaucrats who have not quit in disgust are put into meaningless technical positions out of the mainstream of the department's operations." A final technique is called the *new activity* technique. It creates an office or task that is apparently meaningful but is in fact meaningless, a trap into which disloyal employees are directed.

Public personnel administration has to consider seriously the ethical problems created by the power of chief executives in the American system of government. Power is thought by many to corrupt, and some see in the power of the presidency a force that has tended to corrupt many individuals. The reorganization of the Civil Service Commission into two separate organizations, the Merit Systems Protection Board and the Office of Personnel Management, in the Carter administration makes the situation even more important for ethics in the public service. The Office of Personnel Management (OPM) will be much closer to the White House than was the bipartisan Civil Service Commission; its director is appointed by the president and serves as the president's chief advisor on personnel matters. Will this individual be a person who can communicate to the president the need to respect the ethical autonomy of public officials? Will career civil servants be subjected to a great deal of pressure from the president and his team of appointees? If so, what good is a system of merit that supposedly insulates careerists from politics? These questions can not be answered as yet; the system is still being developed and faces an uncertain future under the Reagan administration. But it is important for personnelists to ponder the relationship of politics—and its ethical dilemmas for public servants— with the ethical problems posed by a merit system that protects individuals from politics.

PROFESSIONALISM: A COMPETING ETHICAL FRAMEWORK

It is a mistake for personnel administration to assume that public officials are ethical vacuums before assuming positions in the public service. Personnelists need to assess the ethical training that individuals have received prior to joining the public service and see how to combine it with the necessity for public service ethical awareness. This is especially true for those public servants with professional backgrounds. The problem here for personnel administration will be the competition between the professional's specialized ethical guidelines and the need for a general ethics of the public interest.

Mosher (1968) addresses the issue of professionalism in government in a systematic and comprehensive manner. He sees a direct link between an educational system and the personnel system of a regime. American government is characterized by the employment of professionals trained in universities who "translate knowledge into action." Professions have an ethical basis that is linked with the educational processes that provide the skills expected of their adherents. These ethical rules are based on the assumption that the professional will administer general knowledge in a variety of individual circumstances. How to respond quickly and efficiently yet still in line with the general ethical framework of the profession is a needed skill. The meaning of life to the physician, the meaning of acceptable risk to the engineer, the rules of confidentiality for the journalist or attorney are examples of ethical guidelines that serve goals of efficiency as well as moral imperatives.

A second reason advanced by Mosher for the importance of ethical rules for professions is their tendency to be self-administering societies or guilds. Professions do not want to be told what is right and wrong in their arena of action. They feel better qualified than government or society to make this ethical determination.

The attention given to ethics by professionals in government is in many ways a solid basis for ethical conduct by government-employed professionals. Two problems often arise, however, if this is the *sole* ethical underpinning of the professionalized public employee. First, there is often a problem in interpreting the meaning of general professional ethics to the special circumstances of government employment. An attorney representing the public is in a very different ethical position than is one representing a private client. The education of professionals does not always equip them to handle the specialized problems of government activity. Second, the ethical framework provided by the individual's professional training may provide blinders in seeing the general ethical questions of public administration: the need for public accountability, the occasional political justification for action that professionally seems irrational and misguided.

A good example of the inadequacy of professional ethics as an all-encompassing substitute for a conception of the public interest is in the area of representative bureaucracy. Professionals see the entry of individuals to the closed society of the profession as a matter to be determined solely by merit, including the acceptance of ethical foundations of the profession. Public personnel systems often see the need to balance representativeness in government with professional competence. Representativeness usually requires the imposition of special standards for entry of underrepresented groups and in so doing threatens the rights of the professionals to govern their own professional affairs. The personnel office may, if unwary, be cast in the role of the enemy trying to bring unqualified individuals into the organization.

The conflict between professionals in government and personnel administration is often very acute in those professions that are found only in government: diplomacy, military service, police and public safety, and public health officers. These professions often exercise a great deal of control over promotions, entry qualifications, and other conditions of employment. Should personnel administration try to limit the independence of professions and push for a greater control over the total ethical dimension of public employment? Or should it recognize the tightly knit character of these professions as a valuable guide to ethical behavior and moral resilience under the stressful situations often found in public administration? The answer, of course, lies somewhere between the extremes. The ethics of the professional in government has always been a powerful guide to right conduct. It needs to be expanded and generalized in public conditions, not discarded in toto. Strong ethical foundations built upon realistic appreciation of ethical problems are needed to develop the public ethics of fairness, social equity, and justice in administration and to ensure the compatibility of administration and democracy.

Perhaps we may leave the subject of professional ethics in government with the reminder that professional decisions in the future will be more difficult to ground in simple formulas of correct action. The growth of government is usually in terms of greater complexity, not the expansion of the existing divisions. Program administration, an area of administration in which professionals dominate, now requires the balancing of demands from a variety of actors who approach a problem (say, the environment) from different perspectives. We need to have ethical guidelines that can help managers to reconcile the trade-offs of protecting the air, saving the economy of the Northeast, utilizing energy more efficiently, and developing a workable system of distributing money in the federal system—all at the same time. Easy solutions to ethical problems will not be possible, and personnel administration must ensure flexibility in responding to demands for more ethical public employees. Personnel offices, serving as aides to program managers, must be able to function as trainers of professionals and advisors to managers operating in conditions of ethical stress. No single professional specialty will be able to comprehend the ethical dilemmas in programs and policies that demand interorganizational cooperation and complicated balancing of competing demands.

ETHICS MANAGEMENT: WHAT SHOULD THE PERSONNEL OFFICE BE DOING?

Up to this point, we have looked at the ethics of personnel management as a problem of issues that encroach on the everyday work of the public service. These issues have included the role of politics in administration, especially the politics of a system that now puts so much power in the hands of chief executives and their appointees; professionalism, with its competing demands for ethical imperatives that may differ from general public service ethics; and the issue of representativeness, the quest for a representative government whose composition mirrors that of society and whose claims may create a conflict between the ethics of individuals and the moral basis of the community. The role of personnel administration in the world of ethical issues is (1) to understand the sides taken, the stakes involved, the salience of issues for contestants and (2) to adjust traditional management duties and personnel processes to take account of the ethical dimension of public administration. This section looks at the traditional duties of the personnel office and asks the question, "Can ethical understanding be added to the ongoing activities of the personnel office to achieve the goals of ethical *and* efficient administration?"

One way in which to answer the question is to assume that the holistic view of the ethical individual is a trainable goal of personnel administration that can be achieved through the training and educational processes of personnel development. Training is a key to evaluating ethical understanding, but personnel administrators must decide upon the method to be used and the focus of training. In regard to method, we can foresee a variety of choices. Case studies highlighting decisions with a known ethical component may be chosen. Guest speakers who have themselves been placed in ethically sensitive decision-making roles can be asked to share their experiences with public officials who may face similar dilemmas. Or the personnel office may try to ground ethical training in more abstract bases: the Kantian approach of Bok, Rohr's constitutionalism, or Rawls's concept of justice. And there is always what Rohr (1978) calls the "low road"—training to stay out of trouble—that concentrates only on specifics and does not ask deeper questions of right and wrong, corruption and legitimacy.

Regardless of the method to be employed in training and ethical development, a thorny problem remains: What should the focus of training be? Should it be the individual as an end in himself or herself, the organization, the work unit, government, the political system, humankind. There is a pedagogical problem in preaching about abstract views of ethics or altruistic schemes that do not relate to job situations. Yet there is perhaps a greater danger in focusing on the individual at work as an atomistic end with no higher or greater referent. It seems most reasonable to design training so that the individual is chosen at first as the referent, and each individual undergoing training is able to climb a ladder of generality, seeing the ethical issues that begin in the work on his or her desk leading up to implications for organization, government, and society.

There is also an ethic of ethical training that personnel administration must recognize explicitly and accept. Training in ethics is a sensitive matter. It requires that individual public servants, coming from different backgrounds and different job situations, be treated with dignity and integrity. Ethical training may require the individual to bear his or her soul on organizational matters, or interpersonal relationships—this information must be treated in confidence and not used for organizational control purposes. And the secular, heterogeneous nature of the public service requires the trainer to be conscious of the religious bases of particular ethical beliefs and to maintain a strict policy of noninterference in the philosophical and religious beliefs of individuals in training programs. Looking at the problem from the other side of the ledger, there is also the danger that ethics may become too loose a term, and ethical training sessions an opportunity for everyone to advance gripes about slow advancement, nasty bosses, and so on. A few general rules may be advanced to help the trainer understand his or her role:

1. Understand the nature of the work performed by individuals and the situations in that work that bring ethical problems to the surface.
2. Understand the prior education and training of the individual. This will give some clues as to probable levels of ethical awareness and the foundations of the individual's ethical understanding.
3. Remember that the more homogeneous the group of individuals being trained, the more difficult it will be for situations or issues to be chosen that have meaning for all members of the group.
4. Keep in mind the ethics of the trainer: fairness, willingness to listen to justifications for action, and the requirement that each member of a training group be treated fully as an individual.

Training of ethics is a different role for personnel administration, because it must define explicitly ethics and the means of improving ethical awareness in government. It highlights the *public* nature of public personnel administration and a public approach to ethical understanding. Yet it is not the only way ideas of ethical conduct enter the world of personnel administration. The caveats advanced for trainers have counterparts for all the other roles played by personnelists. Dealing as personnel does with human beings, it is necessary for all personnel specialists to recognize the ethical problems of public employment and humanize personnel matters while retaining the macroethical goals of accountability, representativeness, fairness. In most areas of personnel administration, it will require at the minimum the fair and impartial handling of procedures for implementing personnel laws and rules. A greater problem is recognizing the intersection of microindividual ethical schemes with societal issues in implementing the work of personnel administration.

PUBLIC PERSONNEL
AND ETHICS: PROBLEMS
AND PROSPECTS

Ethical awareness and understanding in the complicated and ambiguous world of the public service is not attained easily. Ethics will no doubt continue to be the subject of much concern for personnel administration in the years to come. The growing recognition that personnel administrators deal with the human resources of the public service, and should have a significant role in developing the human raw material of government, makes ethical training a significant aspect of personal development. The managerial movement in public administration, stressing the usefulness of staff roles such as personnel in helping the efficient management of public programs, is once again a basis of public administration thought. Ethics, it can be argued, is important in improving efficiency as well as personal development. Ethical dilemmas sap the energy of public servants, lead to declining levels of morale and enthusiasm, and create conflict that may prove detrimental to effective implementation of programs.

A second reason for the growth of interest in ethics in the public service is the now commonly held belief that ethics can be taught, can be treated effectively by training and education. Derek Bok, president of Harvard University, puts a great deal of faith in realistic, situational training by cases in which critical decisions must be made (Bok, 1976). And new and important groups of public officials are constantly being brought into the public services through the appointment processes of new administrations and the expansion of the merit-based civil service in new or differing programmatic areas. Both appointees and civil servants need counseling on ethics, and the personnel system must provide insights and opportunities for each.

Experience seems to indicate that personnel specialists can assist managers and workers in government in becoming more ethically aware (one hopes more ethical, but the responsibility of the personnel office is only to provide the opportunity for self-development) only if they are able to interpret general ethical guidelines in typical situations that confront public officials. In this respect, they need assistance from all sorts of program managers in government to make training or codes of conduct more truly guides to action. The goals of personnel administration in the field of ethics should be to provide the best possible service to individuals who cannot escape the dilemmas of exercising power in a democratic system, in the goldfish bowl of public action under scrutiny from all sorts of control agents—politicians, media, professional colleagues outside government, the universities, the citizenry.

The prospect is for greater attention to ethics in the public service. The major problem remains the lack of agreement on (1) the meaning of ethics in public administration and (2) the proper method of implementing programs of positive ethical training. As more and more work is done in the field, both by theorists examining the ethical foundations of governmental action and by practitioners training and developing individuals for the public service, we should arrive at a greater understanding of public service ethics. Ethics may not be as great a problem as most people outside government think it is, in the sense of wrongdoing and corruption. Ethical training, however, is not just designed to address this sort of problem. It is a form of education, and so is proactive and preventative. Its goal is the avoidance of transgressions by public servants, but through methods that do not center on coercion, force, or the destruction of professional pride and independence. Personnelists do not have to change into police officers or apologists for political power to serve as ethical facilitators.

Goals can be set, and should be set, for programs of ethics in personnel administration. They should be set in such a way that the breakdown of alternatives illustrated in Table 1 does not become a set of "either/or" choices but a guide to the full range of issues that ethical training should address. The goals for a program of ethics should include

1. Ensuring that major deviance from codes of ethics be brought to light and used as learning experiences in the training of public officials.
2. Preventing minor or subtle rules and regulations that create ethical problems for administrators and/or inhibit ethical awareness or conduct.
3. Assuming that rules, codes, and training make sense for individuals or groups covered—that, for instance, reasonable rules are made for such separate groups as the SES, top-level political appointees, and GS-9s.
4. Maximizing the investment in human capital by making public employment be recognized as a worthy and ethical calling by ensuring that individuals in sensitive situations know how to deal with ethical dilemmas.
5. Publicizing the investment made in personnel management's role in ethical training, so that the public will know the difference between the ethical grounding of the public service and that of elected politicians and will understand the ethical problems unique to nonelected, professional, career public servants.

A final goal of personnel administration is more outcome oriented, something that may be measured by the climate of public administration and the humaneness, in some total way, of its processes and activities. This is the goal of *civility*. Civility is basic to civilization, which of course shares its etymological roots, because it produces attitudes that lower conflict, raise trust, and make unlike individuals recognize the common bond of shared values and traditions. Civility at its best is a recognition of shared and common existence, at one point in time, in one society. It provides the slack needed for pluralism to function, for different roles to be played in the complex society in which we live. Producing an administrative state that is characterized by civility is a two-sided task: personnel administration can help public administration to act more ethically and intelligently, but it is important for politicians and the public to treat public administrators with respect, to feel the shared bonds of our society. Public administrators play a major role in our civilization and have played it with a remarkable degree of honesty and hard work. Yet they are often not treated with civility. The new role accorded the director of OPM as personnel advisor to the president and through him to the nation should be a "bully pulpit" to highlight the work done in advancing public sector ethics and to prevent the easy scapegoating of public officials for sins that more properly rest with politicians and the individual citizen.

NOTES

    1. An indication of this development is the recent symposium on ethics in *Public Personnel Management*, Vol. 10, no. 1 (1981), edited by James S. Bowman. The symposium provides an excellent overview of the thinking on ethics and the literature on the subject.

    2. The most spectacular disclosure of wrongdoing by careerists in recent years has no doubt been the scandal in the procurement activities of the General Services Administration uncovered in 1979 and 1980. For a review of the episode, the best source is probably the *Washington Post*.

    3. This section of the chapter is influenced heavily by the thoughts of my colleague and co-author Harold F. Gortner, director of the Public Administration Program of George Mason University. It is excerpted from a work in progress entitled *The Ethical Dimension of Public Administration* co-authored by Jeremy F. Plant and Harold F. Gortner.

    4. Perhaps the best bibliographical survey of the literature on ethics in the public service is "Ethics and the Public Service: An Annotated Bibliography and Overview Essay" by Elizabeth M. Gunn (Norma, Okla.: Bureau of Government Research, April 1980).

REFERENCES

APPLEBY, PAUL H. 1949. *Policy and Administration*. University, Ala.: University of Alabama Press.

ARGYRIS, CHRIS. 1957. *Personality and Organization*. New York: Harper and Row.

BAILEY, STEPHEN K. 1964. "Ethics and the Public Service." *Public Administration Review* 24 (December): 234–243.

BOK, DEREK. 1976. "Can Ethics Be Taught?" *Change* (October): 26–27.

BOWMAN, JAMES S. 1977. "Ethics in the Federal Service: A Post-Watergate View." *Midwest Review of Public Administration* 11 (March): 3–20.

CAIDEN, GERALD E. 1971. "Public Personnel Administration in the Doldrums?" *Public Personnel Review* 32 (January): 30–35.

CHOI, YEARN H. 1979. "Economy and Equity in Public Personnel Management: A Liberalism/Conservatism Synthesis." *Public Personnel Management* 8 (July–August): 222–228.

DAWES, CHARLES G. 1923. *The First Year of the Budget of the United States*. New York: Harper and Row.

FREDERICKSON, H. GEORGE. 1971. "Toward a New Public Administration." In Frank Marini, ed., *Toward a New Public Administration: The Minnowbrook Perspective*. San Francisco: Chandler, 309–331.

GULICK, LUTHER and L. URWICK. 1937. *Papers on the Science of Administration*. New York: Institute of Public Administration.

HECLO, HUGH. 1977. *A Government of Strangers*. Washington, D.C.: Brookings Institution.

KAUFMAN, HERBERT. 1956. "Emerging Conflicts in the Doctrines of Public Administration." *American Political Science Review* 50 (December): 1069-1071.

KERNAGHAN, KENNETH. 1974. "Codes of Ethics and Administrative Responsibility." *Canadian Public Administration* 17 (Winter): 527-541.

MASLOW, ABRAHAM H. 1943. "A Theory of Human Motivation." *Psychological Review* 50 (July): 370-396.

MOSHER, FREDERICK C. 1968. *Democracy and the Public Service*. New York: Oxford University Press.

PLANT, JEREMY F. and HAROLD F. GORTNER. 1981. "Ethics, Personnel Management, and Civil Service Reform." *Public Personnel Management* 10, Special Issue: 3-10.

RAWLS, JOHN. 1971. *A Theory of Justice*. Cambridge, Mass.: Belknap.

RIZZO, ANN-MARIE. 1977. "Changing Administrative Ethics: Approaches and Problems." Paper presented at the American Society for Public Administration annual conference, Peachtree Plaza Hotel, Atlanta, March 31.

ROHR, JOHN A. 1978. *Ethics for Bureaucrats: An Essay on Law and Values*. New York: Marcel Dekker.

SIMON, HERBERT A. 1947. *Administrative Behavior*. New York: Macmillan.

THAYER, FRED C. 1981. "Civil Service Reform and Performance Appraisal: A Policy Disaster." *Public Personnel Management* 10, Special Issue: 20-28.

THOMPSON, FRANK J., ed., 1979. *Classics of Public Personnel Policy*. Oak Park, Ill.: Moore.

WEISBAND, EDWARD and THOMAS M. FRANCK. 1975. *Resignation in Protest*. New York: Penguin.

WILSON, T. WOODROW. 1887. "The Study of Administration." *Political Science Quarterly* 2 (June): 197-222.

PART FOUR
MERIT SYSTEM REFORM AND THE FUTURE

Since the first tentative roots of public personnel administration as an identifiable and separate area of study and practice began to grow within the fertile fields of public administration, no other single theme has approached the preeminence of reform. Beginning in the late 1800s, early reform efforts were directed at spoils systems in all levels of government. As the merit ideology garnered support throughout the United States, legislative victories soon followed with the creation of civil service and merit systems in federal, state, and local governments.

But it shortly became apparent that the reforms and the institutions they established had unintended side effects. Politics remained firmly entrenched within the merit system structures and, as Wallace Sayre pointed out, techniques had begun to triumph over original merit purposes. By the 1960s, mainstream organizations such as the National Civil Service League challenged the conventional wisdom of reform and offered a new agenda, including such heretofore heretical suggestions as abolition of the traditional role of the civil service commission. In the first chapter of Part IV, Couturier and Schick set out the new reformist thinking vis-à-vis state and local merit systems.

That such reform proposals are not likely to come about any easier than those attempted in the past is illustrated by Ealy's case study of Georgia, which effectively demonstrates the validity of the criticisms offered by Sayre and others. Clearly, Couturier's and Schick's admonition regarding the need for reform to be considered and implemented within broader political and organizational contexts should be heeded. Personnel policymakers must travel beyond the narrow territory of techniques and expand their awareness of the intraorganizational, interorganizational, and interpersonal political issues given birth through reform efforts.

It is becoming increasingly evident that the goals of federal civil service reform as embodied in the 1978 Civil Service Reform Act have similarly been displaced, not so much by personnelists as by an insensitive Congress and executive branch. Lynn describes the major provisions of the act and considers the widening gap between the original intents of the reform and successful implementation. The outcomes of the act, both intended and unintended, are likely to spill over into merit system reform efforts at subnational levels, as state and local government policymakers observe the federal developments.

Merit system and personnel management reform should be viewed as a continuing struggle; there never will be "one best way" to design or reform personnel systems—conditions vary too greatly across time and jurisdictions. The future always holds the promise of new reform efforts, as personnelists constantly adjust to the changing environment of public personnel administration.

Jean J. Couturier
American University
and
Richard P. Schick
Consultant

CHAPTER NINETEEN
THE SECOND CENTURY OF CIVIL SERVICE REFORM: AN AGENDA FOR THE 1980s

A CENTURY OF CIVIL SERVICE
AND SOCIAL POLICY: 1881-1981

In 1881, the National Civil Service League (NCSL) was organized as a nonpartisan citizens' "good government" group. Its mission was to promote and monitor civil service systems in federal, state, and local governments. For one hundred years the NCSL pursued these goals, sometimes successfully, sometimes not. Three great periods of both reform and problems were (1) the patrician reforms of government, from 1881 to the turn of the century; (2) the depression years of the 1930s; and (3) the period of civil rights activism of the 1960s and 1970s. All three were periods of broad social change in which the civic issues transcended civil service problems.[1]

Problems relating to the structure, organization, and operation of state and local civil service systems have persisted since the passage of the first U.S. civil service law, the NCSL-authored 1883 federal Pendleton Act. These problems and the tensions they have generated spring, essentially, from two compromises—one political, one philosophical—made in the enactment of early federal, state, and local civil service systems. They have been perpetuated by subsequent legislation and regulation.

The political compromise was the attempt to permit the chief executive (president, governor, mayor) both to direct the conduct of public employees while, at the same time, philosophically to hold him or her responsible for serving "the public interest" in government employment.[2] This elaborate attempt to separate governing authority from political responsibility was bound to create conflict. An employee selection system based on practical, job-related selection standards, employee assignments, and incentives as well as on testing for theoretical concepts and abstract knowledge was bound to create even more conflict.

Ultimately, the elitists won. They managed to insulate the public employment system from the chief executive and to make it almost obsessively technocratic by applying the dubious concepts of the "scientific management" movement of the 1920s and 1930s to the selection process, thereby forcing public employers to rely on pencil-and-paper tests. It was not unusual for civil service examiners, in ranking applicants to determine "the best qualified" to carry out their test scores to the third decimal place, as though the test instruments had been proved capable of making such reliable, valid distinctions among prospective clerks, manual laborers, or trained professionals. As a consequence, our civil services have been too far removed from the people that they are supposed to serve. Many became procedurally rigid, regulatory in their approach to both the general public as well as to public employees, with socially regressive consequences (Couturier, 1971).

Because no system could be expected to serve such diverse constituencies adequately, civil service commissions became insular, isolated, and ultimately captives of the technicians employed to administer them. Thus, insiders came to "own" the civil services and to direct them for the benefit of those within, who had developed a new "patronage of the insider," able to manipulate the system in their own self-interests.

Civil service systems that were based on the nineteenth-century organizational structures and administered under arcane procedures embodied in the rules and regulations of half a century or more ago ultimately clashed with the needs of citizen and government managers who wanted to reorganize and restructure governmental services to meet the problems of the 1960s and 1970s.

Moreover, government employment underwent radical changes during the two decades. Few civil service systems adjusted gracefully to the realities of the growth of public employment, including increased federal intervention in state and local employment policies and practices; changing relationships among public employers, employees, and citizens interested in service delivery; and societal changes that greatly affected the way in which governments managed their public employment systems. These changes were of such overriding public importance that they often required a comprehensive restructuring of entire public employment systems. This restructuring required changes in the organizational relationships of civil service, the employee selection process, the civil rights of public employees, and the labor relations setting for public employment.

The growth of public employment is a clear response to the national change from a production society to a service society. A generation ago, 32 percent of the American work force was engaged in services and 68 percent was engaged in production. Today, these proportions are reversed. About a third of our population works for pay. This means that about 10 percent of all the people produce the hard goods: growing and harvesting corn, making cars, assembling the electronic gadgets that all of us consume. The rest of our workers spend their time serving the food, going to meetings, computing data, and delivering and managing health care, welfare systems, highway patrols, employment services, and myriad other social services.

Clearly, a large part of these various service functions are governmental. Thus, government has been creating two out of five new jobs in our society. Public employment at the federal, state, and local levels accounts for 20 percent of the work force. Governments today expend about 35 percent of the gross national product for governmentally provided and purchased goods and services. This growth in public employment to meet the needs of a service-oriented society has brought with it a responsibility for political managers to organize and direct a work force that meets those needs.

One dimension of the service society is expressed in the degree to which the federal government has become involved in state responsibility for managing the growth of public service employment. In 1939, the federal government began funding state employment, and afterward, county health and welfare services. Minimal "standards" were set for employing the staffs to run these programs with federal funds. Over the years, more programs were added until, in 1970, there were thirty-five federally financed programs mandating specific standards for state and local public employees.

As late as 1965, the federal government spent about $365 million for all national employment and training programs. Less than half of this was in the public sector. But, with the passage of the Comprehensive Employment and Training Act in 1973, the figure had risen to over $5 billion, with about 60 percent of that money going to pay for public service employment. In 1981, before radical budget slashes that eliminated the public employment program altogether, the federal government alone was spending $12 billion, nearly all of it for state and local public service jobs. Put another way, almost one-fifth of state and local revenues were paid by the federal government in 1974 ($41 billion). By 1977, this figure had risen to one-fourth of their revenues, or $60 billion.

Accompanying this growth in federal aid came a growing control of local civil services—a control that helped to stimulate state and local support for "de-regulation rebellion" of 1981 that saw CETA killed. By the mid 1970s, there were over 1,400 such grant-in-aid programs. One study that surveyed a mere 221 of these found 172 requirements for specific methods of managing state and local government personnel systems (ACIR, 1973: 79–88; U.S. Cong., 1974).

Added to these regulations was the extensive intervention of the courts in public service employment. Just over a decade ago, Federal District Judge Frank Johnson put the State of Alabama and ten of its departments under what was, in effect, a federal "trusteeship" for violating the civil rights of its employees (*Good Government*, 1970). He later found constitutional reasons to require massive expansion of the staffs of state-operated institutions. In subsequent court decisions, mental hospitals were required to provide larger staffs to offer adequate treatment. Prisons have been required to enlarge their staffs and reorganize their work patterns. Literally dozens of federal courts throughout the land have issued rulings on equal employment opportunity in state and local governments (Larsen, 1976).

The growth of public service employment and the constraints that this growth has placed on the freedom of states, counties, municipalities, and even school boards to manage their affairs suggests a new way of looking at local government management. State sovereignty has been eroded. There are those who believe fervently that de Tocqueville's view of competing governments is being replaced with a master-servant relationship. Ideological positions aside, it is virtually impossible to argue against the proposition that—through its grant-in-aid programs, its enlarging involvement in managing the environment and natural resources, its establishment of national employment rights laws, and its response to the demands of citizens and governments for financial aid and jobs creation in the form of public service employment programs—the federal government is now deeply and permanently a major partner in the management of the nation's public personnel systems.

The late 1960s and the 1970s can be characterized as an era of rising expectations of participation in decision making by those affected by government. Citizen interest in ecology, public service delivery, consumerism, energy, and governmental integrity was expressed, in part, by demands for greater citizen participation in the governmental decision-making processes affecting those issues.

Beyond citizen interests, public employee unions are vigorously pressing their own demands for participation in these decision-making processes. All these groups want more from the government. Fiscal crises more than occasionally result. Public officials call for greater public employee output for each input of effort. To some, this translates into demands for increased productivity; to others, it means decreased services; to still others, it means work speed-ups. In every case, the fundamental demand is for more services and a broadening of access to governmental decisions by those affected by government.

We have become a litigious society, quick to "drag the rascals to court." Employees increasingly demand legal "due process" in job selection and discipline. They join the general citizenry in concern for occupational health and safety, for secure pensions, for job enrichment, and for worker participation in management. Effective public personnel management systems are required now to reflect these new dimensions of our society.

These and other changes in both our society and governmental systems have produced a call for changes in most of our public employment systems—systems that were designed for bygone times—when the myths of scientific management went unchallenged in the public sector, along with an almost religious faith in credentials, especially educational ones.

Chief executives now demand the authority as well as the responsibility for achieving the program goals mandated by citizens. They recognize that organizational revitalization of the public employment system is basic to meeting those demands.

CURRENT CIVIL SERVICE
REFORM EFFORTS

When the National Civil Service League wrote the first civil service acts—the U.S. Pendleton Act and the New York State civil service law of 1883—the league also intended itself to be a watchdog and "improver" of the systems it advocated.

Over the years, it developed six "model" civil service laws. These became the foundation for almost every civil service system in the nation. By 1969, the then current model law—developed in 1953—was archaic. So the league, in 1969, conducted a broad national study of civil service systems. One part of this study was a "state-of-the-art" survey that asked about eighty questions of the six hundred largest units of state and local government, which together employed 75 percent of all employees outside the federal government, school districts, and special districts (Rutstein, 1971).

During this period, several hundred leaders in government, public administration, law, employee organizations, and academia were asked to critique the 1953 model law. A review committee of experts drew on these suggestions to develop a new model law. Their draft was reviewed by a task force of civic leaders and government organization representatives. After modification, the league's board of directors adopted a 1970 "Model Public Personnel Administration Law." (NCSL, 1970).

The model law had an extraordinarily wide exposure during this period. It went through three printings (60,000 copies), was covered by several major public executive associations, and was the subject of nearly two hundred conferences and national conventions of organizations representing public officials. What was the impact of this exposure?

In 1974, the NCSL did a follow-up survey of the 560 largest units of government having 500 or more employees and representing about 75 percent of all public employees outside of the federal government, school districts, and special districts. Sixty percent (338) of the large governments canvassed responded. The responding jurisdictions employ fully 55 percent of all state, county, and municipal employees. (The remaining 45 percent are employed in about 39,000 additional jurisdictions.) This survey group was basically the same as that surveyed in 1969. Thus, these consecutive surveys represented the most thorough studies undertaken in U.S. public personnel management to that time. The 1974–1975 survey sought to discover what specific changes had been made in public personnel systems since the model law was issued. Nineteen questions were asked. They fall into seven categories of changes advocated by the model law.

Two questions in the first of these categories dealt with the role of the chief executive. One asked if, during the preceding four years, the jurisdiction had acted to make the personnel director "appointive by and responsible to the jurisdiction's chief executive" and put "the director in charge of a centralized personnel department." A whopping 55 percent (180) of the respondents said "yes." This represented 49 percent of the 39 states responding, 59 percent (65) of the 110 answering counties, and 55 percent (50) of the 91 large cities that answered.

On the second question, 10 percent of the states, counties, and municipalities had, during the past four years, replaced the traditional independent civil service commission by a citizens' "oversight" group without rule-making authority. The earlier 1970 NCSL survey showed that 40 percent of these large jurisdictions operated without a civil service commission. Thus, it would seem that half of the large governments in the United States had abandoned the commission form for executive personnel management.

Several questions dealt with the second category of the employee selection process. The basic question asked whether these large governments had abandoned the traditional "rule of three" in favor of broader criteria for the certification of eligibles for employment. Fully 42 percent of the respondents said "yes" (62 percent of the states, 39 percent of the counties, and 39 percent of the cities). Within that group, 39 percent had moved to "pass-fail" certification, 25 percent went to the "rule of five," and 6 percent to the "rule of three groups" (highly qualified, qualified, and not qualified). Several jurisdictions noted that they already had, prior to 1971, adopted such provisions.

Data were requested on the third category of cooperative intergovernmental programs. Answers came in twelve subareas. Only 6 percent of the states, counties, and cities said that they had initiated such programs. Recruitment, training, and testing led the list of cooperative ventures. These were followed by interchanges of personnel among governments and joint establishment of eligible lists.

Regarding the fourth category of civil rights of employees, most jurisdictions (90 percent of states, counties, and cities) said that they had begun "aggressive outreach recruitment," and 82 percent had adopted "special programs aimed at hiring and training minorities, veterans, women, handicapped persons, and others who are disadvantaged." This was the case for 90 percent of the responding states and 81 percent, each, of the counties and cities. Significantly, the same question on the 1970 survey was answered affirmatively by only 51 percent of the states, 29 percent of the cities, and 18 percent of the counties.

The other three general areas of questions concerned changes in individual employee rights. Generally, civil services became much more liberalized in ways advocated by the model law, between 1971 and 1974-1975.

The model law called for the establishment of independent hearing officers (the fifth category of questions) to handle adverse actions. Thirty-seven percent of the states, 21 percent of the counties, and 29 percent of the cities in 1974-1975 had done so.

On political participation (category 6), 47 percent of the governments answered "yes" to the question "During the past four years, have you and/or your jurisdiction adopted provisions for lessening of restrictions on employee participation in the political process?" This question (asked before Congress passed liberalizing legislation for federal employees) received a 44 percent "yes" from the states, 57 percent from the counties, and 41 percent from the cities.

Collective bargaining for public employees (category 7) is now pervasive. When the NCSL advocated the right to bargaining in 1970 (and prior to that as early as 1919), there was not much formal union recognition (Couturier, 1972). However, the 1974-1975 survey showed that, between 1971 and 1974, an overwhelming 71 percent of the responding governments had, as the NCSL advocated, approved "the right of employees to organize, join and participate, or refuse to organize, join and participate in any employee organization to collectively bargain through representatives of their own choosing as to terms and conditions of employment." These rights were granted by 51 percent of the states, 77 percent of the counties, and 74 percent of the cities responding.

It is clear, then, that the hypotheses regarding areas of needed public personnel management reform of the November 1970 Model Public Personnel Administration Law were correct. Some of the issues were influenced heavily by general societal changes—some of which the league helped to achieve, some of which it anticipated, and some of which were underway but had not yet reached those who legislate change.

There are ways to assess the overall impact of the model law as a change agent. One way is to analyze the acknowledged awareness and impact of the model. Another is to summarize the acceptance of its major recommendations.

The 560 large units of government that employ the majority of state, county, and municipal employees were asked questions about the impact of the model law on their decisions. All told, 72 percent were familiar with specific key provisions. Of these, 88 percent said that they were "influenced by its recommendations in formulating personnel policy and regulations."

Another way is to look at the breadth of adoption among governments of the seven key provisions discussed earlier. A tabulation of the 338 jurisdictions responding to the 1974-1975 questionnaire shows that 28 percent of the states, 20 percent of the metropolitan counties, and 51 percent of the large cities adopted all or all but one of the recommendations of the Model Public Personnel Administration Law in the first four years after it was promulgated.

There is ample additional evidence of the impact of the National Civil Service League's 1970 model law. The federal Civil Service Reform Act of 1978 embodied the central provisions of the 1970 model law. The bifurcation of the old Civil Service Commission into an Office of Personnel Management (OPM) and separate Merit Systems Protection Board (MSPB) realized the most fundamental structural change advocated by the model law in separating civil service administration by OPM from oversight by the MSPB.

The Civil Service Reform Act (CSRA) left most of the merit principles and practices of the federal government untouched. Through policy changes, the OPM had already adopted many of the model law's recommendations regarding job-related and validated examinations, broad-band certification procedures, and affirmative action and special employment and training programs.

The CSRA also mandated streamlined employee grievance procedures for those employees not covered by collective bargaining agreements. The independent hearing officer concept of the model law, patterned after the federal hearing officer (now administrative law judge) process in the federal government was strengthened by the separation of the OPM and MSPB, prescribed originally by the model law.

A notable exception to NCSL policy recommendations was the refusal by Congress to modify the basic provisions of veterans' preference. This gives an edge in initial selection to all federal positions (competitive and noncompetitive) to qualified veterans and gives all veterans absolute preference in retention in the competitive service in the event of a reduction in force (RIF). The CSRA went beyond the model law in adopting the controversial Senior Executive Service (SES) for GS-16 through GS-18 managers, with its broad requirements for meritorious incentive pay and in-grade step increases for senior level employees in grades GS-13 through GS-15.

Much has been achieved in the last decade. The reforms noted here have not been adopted universally. But the pattern and the tone have been set and movement continues. It is time, then, to look to the future.

CIVIL SERVICE REFORM
ISSUES FOR THE 1980s

With so much of the 1970 model law now a reality at the federal, state, and local levels, a review of current issues in state and local public personnel administration, nevertheless, indicates a wide range of new issues. The following is a catalog of developing public employment issues that will become increasingly pressing for state and local governments.

Nine developing issues offer an agenda for the 1980s:

1. Budgeting and work force planning.

2. Contracting-out.
3. Pay.
4. Selection.
5. Performance appraisal.
6. Employee rights (privacy).
7. Collective bargaining.
8. Pensions.
9. Personnel program measurements and evaluation.

Budgeting and Work Force Planning

Few governments at any level do much systematic work force planning. This stems largely from attitudes caused by a surfeit of applicants for every job opening. It causes managers to lose sight of the need to control their work force through rational planning for the number and types of employees that will be needed under various contingencies. In the federal government, arbitrary personnel "ceilings" imposed by Congress and the Office of Management and Budget on the numbers of full-time federal employees at the end of the fiscal year contribute greatly to the lack of incentives for work force planning. Information on future employment levels, based on functional needs, is not required by officials and legislators who simply mandate across-the-board cuts as a way to control spending (GAO, 1977).

Similar budgetary constraints on personnel occur at the state and local levels. They are compounded by the problems of budget timing. Personnel managers are seldom part of the management team of budgetary and cabinet-level officials who determine the level and distribution of expenditures. More often, personnel staffs are treated as clerks, not as managers.

In jurisdictions where collective bargaining occurs, the bargaining process often drags on beyond the constitutionally or legislatively mandated budget approval date, thereby laying a floor under bargainable personnel expenditures, rather than a ceiling.

A constitutional amendment or law requiring the executive to develop and present work-load-related justifications for personnel staffing levels prior to each budget session, based at a minimum on consultation with personnel officials, could bring staffing resources more into line with management requirements. It is argued that this would force public managers to attempt real work force planning, planning that was based on a systematic survey of staffing needs, task analysis, and labor market availability of persons with needed knowledge, skills, and abilities. The annual budget may then become an outgrowth of actual staffing needs, rather than an arbitrarily imposed constraint.

Contracting Out

Unions often object to the practice of many governments to contract work out to private employers. Part of the impetus for contracting out is found in the budget ceilings for personnel, a practice, as indicated earlier, that is not limited to the federal government. Legislation has been proposed in many jurisdictions and in the Congress to prohibit or restrict management's power to contract out government work. Some believe that, in addition to being good for employee morale, this would force management to attend to internal staff development instead of relying on outside employers. Clearly, it would keep staff costs visible; for example, the number of government employees could not appear to be low because work was contracted out.

Pay

Two themes pervade recent state and local government pay legislation: one is a reiteration of the comparability principle of public and private sector wages; the other is incentive pay, based on employee performance.

Critics charge that comparability of private-public sector pay sometimes omits fringe benefits. Practitioners caution that compensation comparisons between employers cannot be made simply based on dollars spent for benefits. Other less tangible factors intervene. California's "total equivalent compensation" compensates for differences in standard workweeks due to holidays, hours, and leave. It includes

1. Salaries or wages for a normal work period.
2. Benefits paid through salaries (sick leave or equivalent, vacations, and holidays).
3. Benefits involving nonsalary costs for employers and, as applicable, employee contributions; these primarily include
   a. Service retirement.
   b. Social security.
   c. Death benefits (including life insurance).
   d. Disability benefits (long or short term).
   e. Health and medical benefits.
   f. Unemployment insurance.
   g. Workmen's compensation.
   h. Savings and profit-sharing plans.

Incentive pay plans are now being developed largely in response to collective bargaining. Increased costs of benefits, cash awards, and reduced hours of work are supposed to be offset by increased "productivity" of employees. This productivity is to be measured through increased worker outputs and/or improved quality of work. It is just a short step beyond the collective bargaining arena from this view of productivity to the broader application of the concept of incentive pay.

In 1980, OPM reported that the following jurisdictions had adopted or were considering adopting an incentive pay plan for a wide range of their employees, not just those at the executive level (for which another whole host of pay incentives will be described).

North Carolina returns to its employees one-fourth of all money saved through improved efficiency. The Kansas Department of Human Resources established on an experimental basis "incentive groups" of local offices to compete for semiannual cash awards for the three most productive offices. Productivity was defined operationally according to eight measures, including client satisfaction. Lakewood, Colorado also implemented incentive pay in 1979-1980, as did Ramsey County, Minnesota; Charlottesville, Virginia; New York City; Dayton, Ohio; and the states of Alaska, Arizona, California, Connecticut, Hawaii, Maine, Montana, Oregon, Utah, Washington, and Wisconsin.

At the federal level, the Civil Service Reform Act provided that "the head of each agency may provide for increases within the range of basic pay for any employee covered by the merit pay system." These determinations (1978 92 Stat. 1181, sec. 5402)

    (A) May take into account individual performance and organizational accomplishments, and

    (B) Shall be based on factors such as—
        (i) any improvement in efficiency, productivity, and quality of work or service, . . .
        (ii) cost efficiency;
        (iii) timeliness of performance; and
        (iv) other indications of effectiveness, productivity, and quality of performance . . .

Ideally, pay incentives are reputed to encourage better performance and, thereby, productivity. By providing sanctions (refusal to grant a pay increase) and rewards, they can contribute to managerial control of the work force. Unfortunately, incentive pay plans are only as reliable and credible to employees as the performance evaluation system that is used to allocate the incentives in the first place.

Selection

In explaining how the first (1883) civil service law would require selecting employees for their ability to perform on the job, the National Civil Service League pointed out that "The essential point is not to find coal heavers who can scan Virgil correctly, but coal heavers who, being properly qualified for heaving coal, are their own masters." Ninety years later, the U.S. Supreme Court said the same thing in its landmark, *Griggs* v. *Duke Power Co.* decision: "What Congress has commanded is that any test used [to select employees] must measure the person for the job and not the person in the abstract."

When the League conducted its survey of the state of the art of civil service in 1970, it found that few governments had ever validated any selection process by establishing a statistical correlation between performance on the job or ability to perform a job and relative scores on civil service entrance or promotion examinations. Instead, there was an obsessive reliance on ranking candidates according to examination scores ranging from 0 to 100. Selection was required from the "top three" (or one) names on the list of scorers, despite the lack of any scientific validation of the job relatedness of the test scores or one shred of evidence that the state of the art of civil service testing had been developed to the point where this kind of finite ranking and minute distinctions actually measured ability to perform on the job. In 1972, the chairman of the Equal Employment Opportunity Commission reported that 88 percent of state and local governments were still using written tests (Brown, 1972). The league's own survey found that 35 percent were using written examinations for *un*skilled laboring jobs (precisely those jobs for which the Supreme Court in the *Griggs* case had found written intelligence tests to be discriminatory).

In 1972, the Civil Rights Act of 1964 (under which the *Griggs* case was decided) was extended by the Congress to cover state and local (but not the federal) governments. Since then, hundreds of governments have been found guilty of discrimination by the courts. Quotas on minority hiring have been imposed to compensate for past discrimination and relieve disproportionate hiring patterns, based on the availability of minorities (and women) in local labor markets.

Enforcement of these decisions has resulted in the withholding of massive amounts of federal funds. Court supervision of daily personnel administration has been imposed and individual officials have been held personally liable. A special federal government Equal Employment Opportunity coordinating mechanism was established to reconcile differing federal positions and achieve uniform guidelines for all employers, private and public. In 1976, this group adopted selection guidelines for validated, job-related employee selection processes for state and local governments, stating (*Fed. Reg.*, 1976: 51376)

> These guidelines apply to selection procedures which are used as the basis for any employment decision. Employment decisions include, but are not limited to hire, transfer, promotion, demotion, job or work assignments, membership (for example in a labor organization), training, referral, retention, licensing, and certification.

In sum, these guidelines cover the entire personnel management system. This represents a mandate for good personnel management in which all aspects of employee selection, assignment, and retention must be job related. To accomplish this, validation must include not only employee intake but also periods of probationary training and evaluation, periodic review of employee performance, criteria for layoffs, and promotions.

Although the need to validate job-related selection criteria has been made commonplace by federal civil rights legislation, court decisions, the Uniform Guidelines on Employee Selection, and OPM merit system guidelines, there are some signs that current legal and technical developments could throw the whole concept of "merit" selection based on validated job-related criteria into question. On the other hand, psychometricians are giving credence to the notion of "validity generalization," that validity studies do not have to be situation specific, and that (Dunnette and Borman, 1979)

True validities for tests and particular job performance measures should be estimated from past studies by using a Bayesian approach [a statistical method]. Within such a framework, they argue that if evidence for past validity is strong [i.e., many studies with high validities], a validity study will usually not be necessary. If a study is necessary, the Bayesian approach allows the researcher to use both past validity information and the validity obtained in the study to estimate the true validity of the test for use in similar circumstances.

On the other hand, a study by the General Accounting Office showed that 99 percent of all blacks failed PACE (Professional and Administrative Career Examination), the federal civil service professional entrance examination, compared with 84 percent of all whites and that OPM's validation of the PACE did not conform to the Uniform Guidelines on Employee Selection Procedures mentioned (GAO, 1979b).

Opponents of PACE argued that any disparate impact whatsoever between black and white test-takers is intolerable. Proponents argued that the Supreme Court's 1970 landmark decision in *Griggs* requiring validation of employee selection devices specifically allowed disparate test results between blacks and whites if (and only if) the examination has a "business necessity" (i.e., if it is validated as job related). In 1980, the outgoing Carter administration agreed to drop the PACE examination entirely and substitute a quota plan for hiring minorities. However, the methods and costs of civil service test validations are still major state and local civil service problems.

The outcome of challenges to validity methods could result in the completely *random* selection of all applicants or in selective certification of a court-ordered quota of minority applicants in every case where the validation methodology is thought by the judge to be deficient. Random selection may become a viable alternative to the quagmire of employee selection device (test) validation. By definition, it gives an equal opportunity to all applicants. It moves the burden of demonstrating competence to the job situation itself by making the probationary period the sole test of performance and competence.

Performance Appraisal

Of all the administrative areas of civil service, performance appraisal seems to be getting the most attention. The Civil Service Reform Act gave this old personnel practice a new lease on life. Doubtless, the severe budgetary pinch experienced by state and local governments since the late 1970s has also stimulated performance appraisal as a way to get more work for less money. This fiscal crunch has accelerated the drive toward "economy and efficiency" through increased employee and managerial accountability. It has created a movement to use employee appraisals both for the traditional purposes of weeding out poor performers and for the added purpose of justifying pay increases. Moreover, the advent of collective bargaining has made management think twice about awarding employees more money or benefits without extracting a quid pro quo.

The biggest hindrance to employee performance appraisal, as with selection and productivity, has been a general inability to develop objective measures. Moreover, the need to validate performance criteria that have a bearing on the treatment of employees for pay, mobility, training, and counseling opportunities imposes additional burdens.

Employee Rights: Privacy

Based on the findings of the 1977 Privacy Protection Commission, a number of state and local governments have legislated specific prohibitions against the use of pretest interviews, polygraphs, psychological tests, and electronic surveillance in both the selection process and for employee retention and promotion, except in some police and related security functions. The states include Maine, Michigan, and Delaware and the District of Columbia. These laws also restrict the disclosure of personnel records to third parties.

The statutes on employee privacy rights also include provisions for access to personal records in personnel files to permit employees to see and correct performance, personal references, credit, disciplinary proceedings, medical, and other records. States with such laws are Tennessee, Pennsylvania, Connecticut, Ohio, and Maine.

The Privacy Protection Commission recommended the following "fair employment practices" principles (1977):

That an employer articulate, communicate, and implement fair information practice policies for employment records which should include:

(a) limiting the collection of information on individual employees, former employees, and applicants to that which is relevant to specific decisions;

(b) informing employees, applicants, and former employees who maintain a continuing relationship with the employer of the uses made of such information;

(c) informing employees as to the types of records that are being maintained on them;

(d) adopting reasonable procedures to assess the accuracy, timeliness and completeness of information collected, maintained, used or disclosed about individual employees, former employees, and applicants;

(e) permitting individual employees, former employees, and applicants to see, copy, correct or amend the records maintained about them;

(f) limiting the internal use of records maintained on individual employees, former employees, and applicants;

(g) limiting external disclosure of information in records kept on individual employees, former employees, and applicants, including disclosures made without the employee's authorization in respect to specific inquiries or requests to verify information about him; and

(h) providing for regular review of compliance with articulated fair information practice policies.

Collective Bargaining

A growing number of jurisdictions now permit public employee collective bargaining. The employee's right to join a union has been upheld by the courts as a fundamental First Amendment right of free association, but they have regarded collective bargaining as an aspect of contract law that requires the consent of both parties. Hence, governmental units may agree to participate in, or to avoid, collective bargaining with their employees, as they choose. Many municipalities and other local governments either have their own enabling legislation for collective bargaining, in lieu of state enabling legislation, or they bargain de facto, without specific enabling legislation.

Associations have been common in public employment for almost three quarters of a century. Traditionally, they have been mangement dominated. Nevertheless, they have played a vital role in seeking pay and benefit legislation, rule changes, and job reallocations and classifications and in establishing a unique system of employee participation in the crucial aspects of their employment relationship with government. Thus, they have lobbied for laws, litigated against their employers, and petitioned legislative bodies.

Current public employee collective bargaining issues have gone beyond rudimentary organizational rights and collective bargaining authorization to encompass the basic conditions of employment to be bargained over and the mechanisms by which the so-called "public interest" can be protected in the face of public employee demands. These include the "merit principle" and the ways by which public employees get and keep their jobs and gain mobility opportunities, the structure of "management" in the bargaining situation, and public access to what have traditionally been secret negotiations.

Ironically, collective bargaining is about the only major policy decision-making process where public access to information is espoused openly by many practitioners as detrimental rather than beneficial to public policy. Such secrecy makes it all the more difficult to hold public officials accountable for labor relations policies. By contrast, no one would think of adopting the annual budget without benefit of public hearings and discussion.

Several jurisdictions have provided either for totally open public employee negotiations, at which the interested public actually may observe what transpires at the bargaining table itself, or at least for access to information about the bargaining process, through which interested persons may discover the parties' initial bargaining positions.

States that have mandated some form of access are Minnesota (for all negotiations), Florida (all negotiations, including all public bodies in the State), Kansas (teachers), Idaho (teachers), Oregon (student access to teacher negotiations), Tennessee (teachers), Texas (police), and California (teachers).

According to the Labor-Management Relations Service of the National League of Cities, by 1980 an additional nine cities had permitted citizen observers into school negotiations (New York; Chicago; Philadelphia; Detroit; Baltimore; Toledo; Newark; Madison; and Plymouth, Massachusetts). Dayton, Ohio also opened up all public employee negotiations. However, these were unilateral decisions, made by the management party, not legislatively mandated provisions for public access.

In the first comprehensive study of the issue of the "public interest in government labor relations," the authors recommended at a minimum giving a citizens' advisory board access to information concerning negotiations. The board would be empowered to hire staff to analyze the parties' bargaining positions and budget and civil service impacts and to make public statements of its conclusions (Schick and Couturier, 1977).

It is argued by proponents of disclosure that it can alleviate unnecessarily extreme positions, thereby bringing the parties closer together before bargaining even starts. Public knowledge of the issues and parties' positions can help them to hold public officials accountable for their bargaining decisions and solidify public opinion in impasse situations.

Pensions

For many state and local governments, public employee pension obligations are a time bomb. Negotiated or granted during a period of massive growth in the number of public employees, many of these liabilities remain unfunded or underfunded.

"Purposeful underfunding" occurred on a massive scale in the 1960s and 1970s, when many of these benefits were won at the bargaining table. Since obligations would not come due for many years (such as the 1980s), elected officials were happy to pay only current benefits expenditures (which were relatively low, since most employees for whom benefits were earmarked were not yet near retirement age) rather than lay out money to cover future, real costs. Moreover, many pension plans have cost-of-living escalator clauses that exacerbate the obligations during periods of high inflation, such as during the decade from the mid-1970s onward.

As time passes and a larger proportion of the public work force that is covered by generous pensions begins to retire, the need for massive out-of-pocket expenditures (to make up for nonexistent or grossly underfunded trust funds) is likely to threaten the fiscal health of government as well as the economic well-being of retirees (GAO, 1979a; U.S. Cong., 1978).

Besides the issue of underfunding, state and local government pension plans are plagued by such expensive features as what is referred to as "the comparability basis." This means that many legislators and judges (the federal government being a conspicuous example) have been granted much more generous pensions than ordinary career civil servants. Moreover, many public employees can retire after only twenty years of service, thereby becoming eligible for "double dipping" or working at another job while on a public pension. Others, especially elected officials and judges, again, can receive benefits after only a short period on the job.

According to a 1976 Twentieth Century Fund study, conflicts of interest abound in the control and management of public employee pension funds. These range from politically motivated investments in banks or other enterprises controlled by powerful political interests, through incompetent fund management, to outright illegal use of funds. Subsidization of their own governmental jurisdiction through coerced purchases of questionably solvent securities, as in New York City's fiscal crisis of the late 1970s, is yet another problem (Kohlmeier, 1976).

Personnel Management Evaluation
and Reporting

Personnel program research, reporting, and evaluation entail relatively minor expenditures; yet few, if any, public employers have an adequate grasp of the implications of their own activities for work force planning, management, and assessing the labor market impacts of their policies and practices. Just as important as the customary in-house research on personnel methodology (such as test development and validation) is the managerial application of adequate employment data. If personnel staffs are going to become part of total governmental management, as prescribed by the first civil service reform discussed in this chapter, then they are going to have to develop, analyze, and contribute information that is useful to the other branches of public management in deciding goals and missions, work loads, and budgets.

Unless mandated by law, it is unlikely that the necessary resources will be devoted to such activities as labor market and employee mobility studies, development of data collection instruments and reporting formats, and other procedures useful to work force planning and management. Ironically, the Civil Service Reform Act's title on research and development is not a good model, since its emphasis appears to be on technological research and development (better examining procedures, appraisal systems, etc.) rather than on the managerial implications of work force data.

At present, it is hard to find a single jurisdiction in which the personnel director is responsible to the rest of the executive for research and annual reports on the status of the work force along a broad range of variables useful to the legislature, budgetmakers (who tend to ignore personnel entirely), and other executive functions, as well as to line management. This would include data on accessions of all kinds under relevant labor market conditions; employee mobility tracked throughout their careers; economic, social, and experience characteristics of applicants and employees; costs of various personnel activities; and budget and other policy effects of personnel policies and practices.

Such a "reform" would help to upgrade "personnel" from a clerical to a managerial function where it belongs—in theory if not in practice. This would require new staffing and training of personnel staffs and some additional expenditures (minor compared with the funds that are wasted as a result of bad personnel data) to develop the necessary reporting and data processing systems.

CONCLUSIONS

Where, then, do we go from here?

First, there is the unfinished agenda from the 1970s. Second, we have suggested a beginning agenda for the 1980s. Doubtless, neither will ever by realized fully, although progress will be made. The forces of changing societal needs will surely require modifications of the reform goals.

The National Civil Service League, in 1969, found its fifth model law (of 1953) out of date in barely fifteen years. It is reasonable to project that by 1985—the fifteenth anniversary of the 1970 Model Public Personnel Administration Law—we will see two developments: (1) a more nearly complete adoption of the league's principles and (2) a pressing need to reform the reforms of the 1970s.

NOTES

1. The authors of this article were staff members of the National Civil Service League during the 1960s and 1970s. Jean Couturier was executive director from 1963 to 1973, and Richard Schick was a senior researcher and project director from 1969 to 1979. It was during this period that most of the civil service reforms discussed in this article were developed and promoted by the league nationwide.

2. Two excellent histories of the early reform movement are William D. Foulke, *Fighting the Spoilsmen* (New York: Putnam, 1919), and Frank M. Stewart, *The National Civil Service Reform League* (Austin: University of Texas, 1929).

REFERENCES

ADVISORY COUNCIL ON INTERGOVERNMENTAL RELATIONS. 1973. *More Effective Public Service: The First Report to the President and Congress.* Washington, D.C.: G.P.O.
BROWN, WILLIAM H. 1972. "Moving Against Job Bias in State and Local Governments." *Good Government* 89 (Winter): 1–18.
"Court bars merit violations in grant-in-aid cases." 1970. Excerpts from a U.S. district court opinion of July 28, 1970, quoted in *Good Government* (Winter): 1–7.
COUTURIER, JEAN J. 1971. "Court Attacks on Testing: Death Knell or Salvation for Civil Service Systems?" *Good Government* 88 (Winter): 10–12.
——. 1972. "Chaos or Creativity in Labor-Management Relations." In Chester A. Newland, ed., *Managing Government Labor Relations.* Washington, D.C.: Manpower Press, 3–10.
——. 1976. "The Quiet Revolution in Public Personnel Laws." *Public Personnel Management* 5 (May–June): 150–159.
DUNNETTE, MARVIN D. and WALTER C. BORMAN. 1979. "Personnel Selection and Classification Systems." *Annual Review of Psychology* 30. 477–525.
FEDERAL REGISTER. 1976. 41 (November 23): 51376.
GENERAL ACCOUNTING OFFICE. 1977. "Personnel Ceilings—A Barrier to Effective Manpower Management." FPCD-76-88. Washington, D.C.: G.P.O., June 2.
——. 1979a. "Funding of State and Local Pension Plans: A National Problem." HRD: 79066. Washington, D.C.: G.P.O., August 30.
——. 1979b. "Federal Employment Examinations: Do They Achieve Equal Opportunity and Merit Principle Goals?" FPCD-79-46. Washington, D.C: G.P.O., May 15.
KOHLMEIER, LEWIS M. 1976. *Conflicts of Interest: State and Local Pension Fund Asset Management.* New York: Twentieth Century Fund.
LARSEN, RICHARD E. 1976. "A Memorandum on Test Validation." *Proceedings of the American Bar Association- National Civil Service League Confer-

ence on *Equal Employment Constitutional Law*. Washington, D.C.: American Bar Association.

NATIONAL CIVIL SERVICE LEAGUE. 1970. *A Model Public Personnel Administration Law*. Washington, D.C.: NCSL.

OFFICE OF PERSONNEL MANAGEMENT. 1979. "Conference Report on Recapturing Confidence in Government–Public Personnel Management Reform." Washington, D.C.: G.P.O., February 28.

PEIRCE, NEAL R. 1975a. "Attack on Merit Systems." *The National Journal* 7 (November 29): 1643–1648.

———. 1975b. "Civil Service Debate." *The National Journal* 7 (December 6): 1673–1678.

PRIVACY PROTECTION COMMISSION. 1977. *Final Report*. Washington, D.C.: G.P.O.

RUTSTEIN, JACOB J. 1971. "Survey of Current Personnel Systems in State and Local Governments." *Good Government* 88 (Spring): 1–28.

SCHICK, RICHARD P. and JEAN J. COUTURIER. 1977. *The Public Interest in Government Labor Relations*. Cambridge, Mass.: Ballinger.

U.S. CONGRESS. 1974. Senate, Committee on Government Operations, Subcommittee on Intergovernmental Relations. 93rd Cong., 2d sess. Washington, D.C.: G.P.O.

———. 1978. House, Committee on Education and Labor. "Pension Task Force on Public Employee Retirement Systems." 96th Cong. 12th sess. Washington, D.C.: G.P.O., March 15.

Steven D. Ealy

Armstrong State College

CHAPTER TWENTY
REFORM
OF THE GEORGIA
STATE MERIT SYSTEM

This chapter examines the politics and impact of the reform of the state of Georgia's classification and salary system. It shows that the modification of the personnel system had unanticipated consequences in the overall operations of state government, consequences far removed from those that we might expect to find when dealing with a limited and technical area of personnel administration.

These consequences were unanticipated because the state agency involved in this project, the Georgia State Merit System of Personnel Administration, did not view the reform of the personnel system in light of a broad political understanding of the role of the personnel system in the operations of state government. Rather, the Merit System, as is true for most personnel agencies, viewed its work in very narrow, technical terms and refused to acknowledge or admit that there was "spillover" from its project onto the daily operations of state government.

The charge that personnel agencies fail to consider the broad impact and the political context of their activity is not new. As long ago as 1948, Sayre described personnel administration as "the triumph of techniques over purpose" (1979: 30-35). By this he meant that personnel administration concerned itself mostly with rules and procedures that had been developed to ensure efficient administration, failing to consider the actual impact of those procedures on the operations of government. This study shows that, in some ways at least, not much has changed in public personnel administration in the thirty-three years since Sayre first made his complaint.

This limited view of the personnel function—concern only with technical matters—is an example of what some have called the "scientization of politics." Habermas has developed three models of politics to explain this concept. His political models present three different sets of relationships between political actors and technical or scientific experts (1970: 62-67).

A brief overview of Habermas's models will provide the context for this chapter, as well as an introduction to a discussion of the operations of Georgia's Merit System agency. In the *decisionistic model*, all policy questions are decided by the political actors, whereas the experts simply determine the most efficient way in which to achieve those policy goals. In the second, the *technocratic model*, the power relationship between political and technical actors is reversed, the policies are set by the experts on the basis of technical considerations. In this model, "rational administration," characterized by efficiency and stability, becomes the goal of government. The *pragmatistic model*, unlike either of the first two, involves mutual discussion and influence from political and technical actors. In this model, policy is based on a consideration of both political and technical questions.

THE GEORGIA MERIT SYSTEM
AND THE RECLASSIFICATION
SURVEY

In examining the theme of the scientization of politics through a study of Georgia's Merit System, this chapter deals with two aspects of the agency's operations. First, the Merit System as guided by a set of technical considerations in performing its duties is investigated. Then, the relationships that exist between the Merit System and various political actors in the state are discussed.

During the period of July 1975 to July 1979, the Georgia State Merit System of Personnel Administration was engaged in a reclassification survey designed to accomplish two goals.[1] First, the survey was to lead to a complete revision of the classification and compensation plan that covered all 45,000 merit employees within the state government. Second, every merit-covered position in the state was to be reviewed and placed into the new classification structure. Although this effort affected either directly or indirectly every aspect of Merit System activity, the survey was the primary responsibility of the Classification and Compensation Division (see Figure 1). Because of its comprehensive nature, this four-year project involved every department within Georgia state government. In addition, this survey was monitored with a great deal of concern by the Georgia General Assembly. Since the project provides a unique opportunity for analyzing the power and policy relations between the various actors, this study centers on the Merit System's conduct of the statewide reclassification survey.

The study of the classification survey is not intended to be comprehensive in its treatment of the problems created by this attempt to "rationalize" the state's classification system. As Shafritz has argued, "no accounting of the dysfunctional aspects of position classification can even pretend to be exhaustive. That would require a cataloguing of the grievances of all government employees abused by the system" (1973: 23). The purpose of this study, rather, is to show that the funda-

FIGURE 1

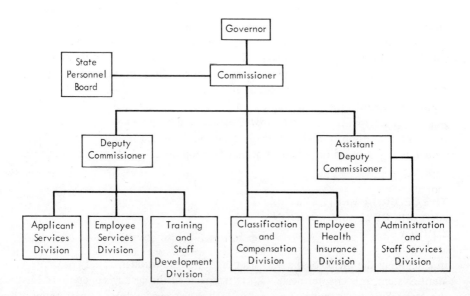

mental practical-political problems developing out of this survey can be traced to the technical orientation of the Merit System.

The following historical information is provided to set the classification survey in its proper context. The legislative basis for the reclassification survey was the Georgia Appropriations Act for fiscal year 1976, in which the General Assembly authorized expenditure of $140,000 "for a classification and compensation study to determine the proper salary relationships between the various class titles and not to determine what salary increases might be necessary to make the salaries paid under the Merit System Pay Schedule more competitive with private business and industry" (State Merit System, 1977: 1A).

The initial suggestion for such a survey came from the acting commissioner of the Merit System, who believed that a comprehensive reevaluation of the classification and compensation plan was needed for the following reasons. The last comprehensive review of the state's personnel classification system had occurred ten years earlier, in 1966. At that time 24,000 people were covered by the Merit System, and 1,250 job classes existed. Since that time the number of merit employees had nearly doubled, the number of classes had increased to 1,800, and a complex reorganization of the executive departments had taken place under the administration of Governor Jimmy Carter[2] (State Merit System, 1975). Despite these changes in state government, there existed little or no departmental support for the proposed survey.

Immediately following passage of the Appropriations Act, the Classification and Compensation Division of the Merit System began planning for the survey. Among the early actions of the merit system were decisions to use an outside consultant as technical advisor and supervisor for the survey and to establish a steering committee to oversee the survey. This committee was composed of members of the Merit System itself, representatives from both houses of the General Assembly, a representative of the Governor's staff from the Office of Planning and Budget, and the president of the Personnel Officers Council. The committee was to advise on the choice of consultant and thereafter to meet and provide guidance on a regular basis (Saylor, 1975).

The Merit System, without guidance from the steering committee, selected Hay Associates of Chicago as technical advisor. The Merit System's primary criterion for a consultant was the ability to develop an objective classification system (State Merit System, 1975). Hay Associates was selected because of its use of a point system as the basis for its quantitative evaluation of job content. The Hay proposal for the survey included a timetable for survey activity. Initially the survey was to be completed in an eighteen-month time frame, but it actually took forty-eight months to complete.[3]

Rather than deal with this project chronologically, we focus on a number of issues raised by the operations of the Merit System during the four years of this survey. First, we deal directly with the technical orientation that guided Merit System activity, as seen in its attempt to eliminate all nontechnical questions concerning reclassification activity. Next, we consider the political relationships between the major actors involved in the survey.

OBJECTIFICATION
AND THE ELIMINATION
OF NONTECHNICAL QUESTIONS

The Classification Division concerned itself exclusively with a few specific questions relating to position classification during the survey. The problems with which the Merit System concerned itself were the development of a technically sound and workable classification structure, the assignment of pay grades to each of the classes in the new plan, and the allocation of existing positions to the appropriate classes in the new plan. The Merit System focused on these technical questions, to the exclusion of all other concerns.

Technical interest, according to Habermas (1973: 264), is concerned with the understanding and manipulation of objective (physical) reality. To achieve these goals, the technical orientation eliminates from consideration the concerns raised from both political and moral standpoints. This means that practical problems are either translated into technical problems, which are susceptible to scientific solution, or they are identified as nonrational and therefore insoluble. In either case, the practical problems of daily life, which find expression in moral and political questions, are suppressed by the interest in technical action (1973: 275-276).

In the survey, the Merit System attempted to "objectify" the personnel system of the state to facilitate its technical control. This required the elimination of all questions which were not readily solvable through the application of the Merit System's quantitative classification technique. The approach taken by the Merit System abstracted the classification system from the actual work environment of state government. The Merit System treated the classification system as if it were totally separate from other operations of state government to reduce all problems encountered to technical questions. This approach had two major consequences. First, the abstraction from the life-world of government led to a failure to deal with the practical consequences that the demands of the survey were placing on state government. Second, the narrowing of the area of discussion to technical questions led to the exclusion of moral, management, and operational questions. This narrowing of concern reinforced the tendency to ignore practical questions.

Abstraction from the Life-World
of Government

While the Merit System's attempt to treat the classification survey as if it were isolated from the life-world of state government can be seen clearly in a number of areas, two examples are used to illustrate this tendency.

Stabilization of the classification plan. Acting Commissioner Ralph Moor, in his first memorandum to department heads concerning the survey, told them that it was "imperative that the departments drastically curtail routine requests" for position actions during the course of the survey, so that "the classification system may be held more or less static" (Moor, 1975). Technical and practical problems confront each other directly in this request. The technical problems of evaluation would be simplified with a static personnel system. The practical demands of department programs required the continuous reallocation of old positions, the creation of new positions, and the establishment of new classes.

The Merit System "solution" to this conflict was to take away the departments' authority to allocate and reallocate positions within their organizations and to require Merit System approval for all such actions. This centralization did not stop the demand for position actions, but it did allow the Classification Division to control the level and rate of change within departments. This move to gain total control of the classification system resulted in ever-increasing amounts of work for the Classification Division, however, and placed greater demands on the time of division technicians. As a result, the requests for position actions were processed slowly, thus creating problems for the departments and taking time away from the division's survey efforts, thereby creating more pressure and problems within the division. The division's leadership, however, preferred the tighter control, despite the resulting disruptions caused by the decreasing efficiency and quality of work.

Impact on employees. A second example of the attempt to separate the survey from the life-world of state government involves the impact of the Merit System's recommendations on the employees of the state. From the standpoint of state employees, the only importance of the survey was the "bottom line," the direct effect of the survey on their positions. The survey dealt with two aspects of every position in state government: the pay grade and the class title of the position. Both items were of great concern to employees. The pay grade was important, of course, because that directly affects the standard of living of the employee. But the title of the position is also very important, for the title helps to provide the identity of the position incumbent.[4]

One decision made early in the survey by the Merit System was to develop a completely new set of classification titles for the plan developed in the survey. This decision was based on the desire to simplify operations for the Merit System. The change in titles would lessen the chance of confusing existing position classifications while the Classification Division was working with both the current and the new survey classification structures.

The impact of this decision was felt throughout state government, but it was greater within departments that employed professional and educational personnel. The decision to change titles was, in effect, a direct blow to the self-image of many employees and led to a loss of morale. Within the Department of Education, personnel whose titles were changed to general classes from education-specific classes (for example, from "education program specialist" to "research specialist") were especially angered. These people feared that the title changes would actually affect their relationships with other department employees. To some extent these fears were justified, for the Department of Education is extremely status oriented, and status revolves around degrees, credentials, and titles.

In addition to revamping the titles, the survey also changed the salary schedule and the specific salary grades attached to positions. The adjustment in the assignment of grades to classes meant the adjustment of positions in relation to each other, and the attendant new relations caused concern among some of the affected employees.

The major concern with new salaries was related to the impact of these changes on individual positions. The Merit System had recognized that disaster would result if salaries were actually cut for employees whose positions were downgraded.[5] The solution was to downgrade the position but to continue to pay the incumbent the same salary as that received previously. What the agency did not consider was the impact on individuals of being told that they had been overpaid and would continue to be overpaid. Again, the self-image of the employee rather than his or her level of earnings was the real heart of the matter.[6]

During the course of the survey, some positions had their classification changed as many as five times. These changes, of course, also affected the proposed pay grades for these positions. This show of apparent indecision by the Merit System had a tremendous, negative impact throughout the state. The Department of Human Resources, after consultation with the Merit System, notified all its 22,000 employees of the Merit System's "final recommendation" on their new classifications early in 1978. The Merit System, however, continued to review positions and to make changes in its recommendations up until the day of implementation.

The morale of state employees seemed to ebb lower as the survey progressed. The loss of confidence and growth of fear was not restricted to the employees affected directly. The changes that took place appeared at times to be random, and even the people who had not been affected feared that they would be before implementation.

Exclusion of nontechnical questions The problems that were generated by the survey—morale problems among state employees, difficulties in maintaining high program standards (both because of morale problems and because of work disruptions due to the survey), loss of personnel, and work disruptions—were ignored by the Merit System in its planning and execution of the survey These problems were ignored because of the systematic elimination of all but technical questions from Merit System consideration. Thus, moral questions, management problems, and operational difficulties were all excluded from consideration by the Merit System.

1. *Operational difficulties.* The Classification Division's concern with a technically sound classification system extended only to the abstract soundness of the plan, not to the operational soundness of the plan. For example, the development of new training and experience requirements for each of the classes was done by the Classification Division itself. This part of the class specification, however, was of little concern to the Classification Division in its routine activity. The training and experience requirements determine who is or is not eligible for appointment to a particular class, and the responsibility for dealing with that question belongs to the Applicant Services Division of the Merit System. Applicant Services is charged with

designing instruments to use in assigning merit scores to applicants, and it uses the standards contained in the class specification as the basis for developing its tests and other rating devices.

The standard Hay training and experience requirements (T&Es) had but tangential relation to the responsibilities of actual positions within a class, however, and often were not related directly to the description of a class contained in the rest of the specification. These T&E requirements tended toward artificial rather than real work standards. For example, it was common to develop an entire set of T&Es for a classification series with a number of levels merely by stacking additional years of experience and/or education onto the standard selected for the lowest level. In such an instance the lowest level might require a B.A. degree with no experience. Each higher level then would require the degree plus an additional year of experience.

The first operational problem that ensued from this was the inability of the Applicant Services Division to develop measurement instruments appropriate to the specifications' requirements. An additional difficulty was that, in stacking, the requirements at the upper levels of the series would come into conflict with the pay levels assigned to these classes—the stacking placed higher educational and experience requirements than were appropriate for the assigned pay levels. A final difficulty was the impact of these specifications on equal employment programs. Under the concept of equal employment, minimum rather than ideal or desirable standards are to be set, which allows for the widest range of people possible to be considered for a position. The stacking of T&Es, however, tended to set the training and experience levels higher than those actually needed to perform a job effectively.

Within the Merit System these problems were the immediate concern of Applicant Services, and the director of that division called them to the attention of the Survey Steering Committee. The Applicant Services' division director was told by the commissioner to remain silent on these difficulties. This silence extended beyond public discussion and into the private meetings of the Merit System. The Classification Division refused to discuss the possibility that these problems could arise. The Hay consultant maintained that these types of problems had·not occurred elsewhere, and the Classification Division Director argued that the plan developed was more objective than any the Merit System had ever used previously (this, of course, sidestepped the whole question of the existence of these problems). Thus, the operational difficulties the survey would create even for other sections of the Merit System itself were not addressed by the Classification Division.

2. *Management problems.* In the field, the major difficulties created by the survey also affected the operational effectiveness of state government, but from a different angle. Employee morale fell during the survey, and this drop in morale had an unavoidable impact on the quality of work performed. When this change in morale, and its attendant difficulties, was brought to the attention of the Classification Division, the division simply ignored the role of the survey in creating these problems. These problems, the division maintained, had nothing to do with the survey, for these were "management problems." If employees were not performing

adequately, then it was the manager's responsibility to take appropriate action as outlined in state personnel regulations. As indicated earlier, the negative impact of the survey on the rest of state government was simply excluded by the Merit System from discussion.

3. *Moral questions.*   Finally, the Merit System systematically excluded from discussion all questions concerning the legitimacy of what it was doing. The legislation authorizing the survey was not specific in terms of operational procedures, and it was the fairness of the survey procedures and policies that was questioned most often by those outside the Merit System. The major question in this area concerned the "final recommendation" on both individual positions and on the pay grades for specific classes. At what point was the Merit System to stop changing these recommentations? As noted, even when the Classification Division had informed a department that recommendations had been finalized, further changes would be made. The division's position was that every effort to make the new plan correct technically would be made, and if this required reviewing position allocations, then that would be done. This process did not stop even on the date of implementation, however, for many changes in which recommendations were lowered were made after July 1, 1978. The Merit System response to inquiries about this activity was that the affected positions had been misclassified originally.

This points to another type of activity that occurred during the survey. During the period of analysis, departments would, at times, negotiate with Classification Division technicians concerning problems of particular interest to the department. When agreement was reached, the department would act on the agreement, only to find that the division leadership had modified the agreement unilaterally, without even informing the department of the change. When challenged, the division's response was that the technician had made an error and that that error had merely been corrected. Good faith agreements thus became less important than technical correctness. In fact, technical questions were given so much weight that they completely overshadowed the ethical questions involved.[7]

One final example of this elimination of ethical questions during the survey is offered. When the General Assembly refused to appropriate funds sufficient to implement the survey totally, the Classification Division was forced to modify its recommendations to keep costs within allocations. In making these revisions in the classification structure, the division decided simply to cut back the recommended increases for a number of large classes at the bottom of the pay scale. Unfortunately, these were the very classes that needed salary upgrading the most. The reason for their selection, according to the Merit System, was that, by cutting them, maximum dollar amounts would be saved with minimum recommendation changes. Thus, the efficiency of the operation, rather than the equity of the outcome, was the motivating factor in this decision. Even this view of efficiency is somewhat deceptive, however, for, while fewer class recommendations had to be changed, many more individual positions were affected by this decision. One of the claims for the survey had been that it would increase the internal equity of the class and pay structure. But by letting the goal of efficiency, rather than the question of fairness, guide key decisions, the survey increased internal inequity.

TECHNICAL-POLITICAL
RELATIONS DURING
THE SURVEY

The Merit System, and in particular the Classification Division of the Merit System, is the State of Georgia's "technical expert" in the area of personnel classification policy. Both the Classification Division and the Hay consultants shared a common motive: the rationalization of state personnel practices. Both the consultant and the Merit System approached the survey in terms of the technical problems presented in revising the state's classification plan. From this perspective, Hay Associates and the Classification Division combined to form a technical base of expertise for the survey.

In this framework, the political actors of Georgia government were the General Assembly and the departments falling under Merit System regulation. The General Assembly represented political power in terms of authority to make the final decision concerning the implementation of the survey. The departments and agencies of the state represented political concerns in terms of the impact of the survey on their personnel and programs. The departments thus saw the survey in terms of practical, rather than technical, problems.

As shown, in dealing with both these political actors, the Merit System sought to eliminate practical questions and to focus attention on technical questions. In general the Merit System was successful in this endeavor, but because of the different legal relationships between these actors and the Merit System, different models of political-technical relations apply to Merit System-General Assembly relations and to Merit System-departmental relations.

The relationship between the Merit System and the General Assembly may be characterized by the decisionistic model of political practice. Once the General Assembly passed legislation initiating the survey, it lost control of the activity of the Merit System. This was the case for a number of reasons. The General Assembly's interest in the classification survey was motivated by two factors: concern with budget restrictions and pressure from unhappy constituents who were employed by the state.[8] While it was possible for both factors to influence the views of individual representatives or senators, in general these two issues were considered separately. This fragmentation was, in fact, institutionalized by the division of responsibility within both houses of the General Assembly. On the one hand, the substantive committees charged with oversight of the Merit System were oriented toward personnel policy and toward increasing expenditures for the salaries of state employees. On the other hand, the appropriations committees in each house were made up of some of the most fiscally conservative members of the legislature. The concern of the appropriations committees was simply to keep the state budget as low as possible. For example, leading members of the House Appropriations Committee expected the Merit System to balance proposed pay increases at the lower end of the salary scale with proposed pay reductions at the upper end of the scale, so that no additional state funds would be necessary to implement the classification survey. The infighting that took place between the substantive and the fiscal committees weakened the legislature's ability to control the operations of the Merit System, for these committees refused to work in unison toward a common goal.

In addition to the internal divisions within the General Assembly, the second major reason for its lack of control over the Merit System was its lack of knowledge and expertise in the area of personnel policy. Because the House has no formal research office, and the Senate has a very small research staff, the General Assembly has very little professional assistance in evaluating and investigating programs. For this reason the legislature's concern with the survey tended to be reactive and to be motivated by constituent complaints of abuse or injustice. This type of concern, while it could and did force modification or review of specific individual cases, had no impact on the overall direction and conduct of the survey.

For these and other reasons (e.g., the General Assembly is limited constitutionally to a forty-day session per year), the legislature was involved in the survey only at the most general level and was denied effective input into the final plan. The General Assembly's sole function was to render the final decision for implementation in the form of allocating or rejecting funds in the budget. Because of the legislature's lack of understanding, its decision would be, in either case, somewhat arbitrary. The major argument in favor of implementation was that all the money and time spent would be wasted if the survey recommendations were simply dropped. Thus, the relationship between the Merit System and the General Assembly approximates Habermas's decisionistic model.

The relationship of the Merit System to the other departments, however, coincides more nearly with the technocratic model. The Merit System controlled the development of the new classification plan. The departments were presented with a plan reflective of Merit System desires rather than their own needs. While the Merit System placed great demands on the departments, the departments had no base from which to exercise any control over the Merit System. Merit System planning eliminated most of the questions of importance to the departments, and Merit System control of the survey communications networks effectively eliminated departmental feedback of survey difficulties and problems. Department personnel staffs were thus placed in the position of having to carry out instructions that actually created practical problems for their agencies without having the information necessary to explain or justify these actions and requirements to administrators or to affected employees.

Internal relations within the Merit System itself can be placed in this typology, for the Merit System was not monolithic in its approach to and support for the survey. Within the Merit System three specific actors may be identified: the Classification and Compensation Division, the Applicant Services Division, and the commissioner's office. Both the Classification Division and the Applicant Services Division had responsibility for specific technical areas of the state's personnel system. The commissioner had responsibility for the overall operations and direction of the Merit System. During the survey, however, the Merit System position was generally determined by the Classification Division, with the commissioner serving mainly as a buffer between that Division and the outside political forces discussed earlier. The commissioner, in general, surrendered his control over the survey to the Classification Division. His intervention was similar to that of members of the legislature: in some specific individual cases he overruled decisions made by the Classification Division. Normally, however, the commissioner did not involve himself in the planning or implementation of the survey, and when he did, it was done with a view to defending the actions of the Classification Division.

While the Classification Division was responsible for the survey, its actions affected directly the Applicant Services Division's ability to perform its functions. As shown, in cases of conflict between these two divisions, the Classification Division's position prevailed. The commissioner's role in these disputes was to instruct Applicant Services to abide by the department line, the line set by the Classification Division. Thus, within the Merit System itself, general personnel concerns were replaced by specific classification concerns as the guiding principles for the survey.

For the Merit System, then, the technocratic model seems most applicable, with the Classification Division's setting policy for the rest of the department. Many of the problems of the survey resulted directly from these internal relationships, for no one in the Merit System viewed the survey in terms of the state's total personnel program. Thus, the technical expert, the Classification Division, made decisions that were carried out and supported by the commissioner and the other divisions within the department.

THE POLITICS OF PERSONNEL
AND THE POLITICS OF POWER

To this point, it has been argued that the scientific interest in rationalization leads to bureaucratic imperialism and the drive for domination. As a case study of this thesis, it has been shown that the basis of the Georgia Merit System of Personnel Administration's operations during the classification survey was what Habermas calls "the technical interest in instrumental control" (1973: 309).

This drive for control by a personnel agency is not unique to the Georgia Merit System. According to Shafritz, position classification in the public sector has retained its influence in personnel policy formation because its "pseudo-scientific pretentiousness" gives it an apparently legitimate technical basis. Shafritz (1973: 61–62) also states that, although the argument for position classification is made in terms of equity and impartiality, the real source of its durability is the control mechanism that it provides.

Personnel agencies fill two roles simultaneously. These are the service function providing assistance to other departments and the police function ensuring that personnel policies are not violated. While Shafritz (1973: 47–62) argues that these two roles must be maintained in some type of equilibrium, the argument here is that the policing role will dominate any time that technical rationalization becomes the agency's basis for action. Emphasis of the policing role facilitates control.

The technical drive for control is not found in isolation but, rather, often coincides with the desire for power at a much more personal level. In reviewing the survey, it is often difficult to separate these two factors. The application of "objective techniques" in fact often served as a façade to cover actions based on personal bias or whim. The claim of objectivity—"we rate positions, not the people in them"— was undercut by the common approach to discussing the proper allocation of positions. During these discussions, positions were identified by the name of the incumbent, and attention often focused on that individual's performance and the classification technician's evaluation of the individual.

This desire for domination also extended into the dealings of the Classification Division with other departments, especially in cases of friction between a technician and department personnel offices. A technician could "get" a department by downgrading positions or by holding them at a lower level than that desired by the department. In addition to this type of petty domination, there was a tendency to expand classification concerns to cover all personnel matters in dealing with a department. Thus, during the course of the survey, the Classification Division would use its authority to approve or disapprove new positions or reallocations of old positions in an attempt to structure the organization of a department, rather than simply to verify that a new position or reallocated position would be performing duties appropriate to its class of assignment.

The drive for domination is seen clearly in the position of the director of the Classification and Compensation Division. According to the director, the major mistake made by the Merit System during the survey was its heavy reliance on department personnel officers. If the survey were to be done again, there would be even more control and even greater centralization of survey activity. This claim was coupled with the statement that the Merit System "never had any intention of letting the departments participate" in designing and implementing the survey.[9]

According to the analysis of the division director, most of the difficulties that arose during the survey were the fault of the departments. If the department personnel officers had only supported the survey effort completely, it would have been much more successful with many fewer problems. What this analysis fails to recognize is that there was really no reason why the departments should have supported the survey. It was not their project—they did not recommend it, plan it, execute it, or have the opportunity to evaluate it. They had no stake in the survey—it was creating problems for them where there were no problems before.

The reason that the other departments and state employees had no stake in the survey was that the Merit System had intentionally cut itself off from the concerns of these parties. By eliminating all the issues of interest to these actors, and by emphasizing only technical personnel questions, the Merit System effectively prevented the type of cooperative and critical interaction characteristic of Habermas's pragmatistic model.

Rather than critical interaction, the relations between the Merit System and these other actors are described better in terms of fear and distrust. Edelman (1964: 92) has accurately characterized the feeling that existed during the course of the survey:

The leader who makes no effort to identify himself with approved community symbols or roles, but whose tenure is secure, thereby greatly increases public anxiety and irrationality. Men expect that leaders' acts will be rationalized as dealing with problems of general concern, even if there is no discernible payoff. An official or oligarchy that refuses to justify its actions is bound to make people wonder whether the problems they do not know how to handle themselves are being dealt with at all or whether some other grand design, benign or malevolent, motivates the leaders' acts. Fear and irrationality are the response to inexplicable and seemingly arbitrary acts.

As has been argued at length, the perception that the Merit System was motivated by goals not shared with the rest of state government, that the aims of the Merit System were often incompatible with the aims of departments and employees, is basically correct.

This state of affairs in public personnel administration is certainly not new. As noted earlier, Sayre described personnel administration as "the triumph of techniques over purpose." This study shows that, at least in these general terms, Sayre's critique can be applied accurately to the operations of the Georgia State Merit System. A closer look at Sayre's (1979: 32) argument reinforces this basic conclusion, for he claims that personnel administration is "characterized more by procedure, rule, and technique than by purpose or results . . . . Quantitative devices have overshadowed qualitative. Standardization and uniformity have been enshrined as major virtues."

Procedures, rules, techniques, quantitative devices, uniformity, and standardization are all elements of a technical approach to personnel administration. Purpose and qualitative concerns, on the other hand, raise practical and political questions that cannot be decided on the basis of a narrowly defined rationality. If public personnel administration is ever to become more than the application of pseudo-scientific techniques, it must first overcome its self-imposed technical limitations. Personnel questions must be placed in their broader context; personnel policy should aim to facilitate the overall goals of the organization. Personnel questions must be answered in terms of their political as well as their technical implications. Open communications between all those involved, from the personnel specialists, to the individuals affected, to the program managers, must be instituted.

If such changes are to occur, it is obvious that organizational changes will be required that make control of the personnel program by personnel specialists impossible. Such institutional restructuring will certainly need to be accompanied by a deemphasis on the personnel agency's policing role and an increased emphasis on the service dimension of the agency's responsibility. Given the inherently dysfunctional nature of personnel (especially classification) operations, such changes are necessary. But the fact that they are necessary does not guarantee that they will occur, because personnel departments motivated by the technical interest in control will not willingly give up their perceived power. This then requires that the political actors within government reassert their right to set personnel policy. This includes political actors within personnel agencies themselves. Through such a reassertion, the politics of control can be modified into the politics of cooperation.

Despite the opposition and resistance that such an effort would encounter from personnel administrators and technicians, the accompanying changes in policy setting and implementation would be worth the effort. After all, personnel administration is too important to be left to the personnel specialists.

NOTES

1. For a complete review and evaluation of this project, see Steven D. Ealy, *Communication, Speech, and Politics: Habermas and Political Analysis* (Washington, D.C.: University Press of America, 1981), pp. 21–83, 171–205. Most of the information contained in this paper was obtained from unpublished documents in the files of the Georgia State Merit System of Personnel Administration and from a series of interviews with individuals involved with the survey.

2. For a discussion of Carter's reorganization, see George E. Berkley, *The Craft of Public Administration*, 2nd ed. (Boston: Allyn & Bacon, 1978, pp. 64–71).

3. See Hay Associates, "Proposal to Update Classification Plan" (Chicago: Hay Associates, 1975). A major dysfunctional feature of this survey was the enormous amount of time required to complete it.

4. Pay and title are, respectively, examples of what Frederick Herzberg calls "hygiene factors" and "motivators" (1973: 91-113). Also see Linda Burzotti Nilson and Murray Edelman (1979).

5. As indicated in a memorandum from Jerry W. Saylor to Charles E. Storm, May 11, 1977.

6. A related example of Merit System insensitivity to employee needs should be noted. The Merit System originally provided each employee of the state with a new class title only, without any salary information, and asked for an evaluation of the new classification system. In a very real sense, however, a classification plan is incomplete without an indication of the pay levels of the various classes, for it is in the comparison of these pay grades that the relative value of the various classes is determined. The Merit System's reason for withholding the salary information was its desire for an "objective" evaluation of the classification structure itself, undistorted by either approval or disapproval of the pay grades assigned to particular classes. In taking this approach, however, the Merit System had removed the sole basis for evaluation and comparison used by most state employees.

7. In this case, especially, the political desire for domination and the technical desire for control are difficult to separate. A power technique used frequently by Classification Division leadership was to change unilaterally or cancel agreements made with departments. This strategy was based on the notion that uncertainty and insecurity on the part of the departments would increase the control of the division over the departments.

8. These two dimensions were neatly brought together in a statement made by State Senator Roscoe Dean. Speaking at a meeting of the Senate Governmental Operations Committee, Dean "warned that state employees who thought they were getting big raises are now unhappy with smaller pay hikes . . . under the scaled down reclassification appropriation. Dean said employees will blame the legislators who enacted the budget, not the administrators who parcelled out the money. 'We've got to have this thing changed and we've got to have it changed before election time,' he said" ("State Salary 'Mess' Cited," *The Atlanta Constitution*, May 12, 1978, p. C-8).

9. Interview with Jerry W. Saylor.

REFERENCES

EDELMAN, MURRAY. 1964. *The Symbolic Uses of Politics*. Urbana: University of Illinois Press.
HABERMAS, JÜRGEN. 1970. "The Scientization of Politics and Public Opinion"

and "Technology and Science as 'Ideology'." In Jeremy Shapiro, trans., *Toward a Rational Society*. Boston: Beacon Press, 62–80.

——. 1973. "Dogmatism, Reason, and Decision: On Theory and Praxis in Our Scientific Civilization." In John Viertel, trans., *Theory and Practice*. Boston: Beacon Press, 253–282.

HERTZBERG, FREDERICK. 1973. *Work and the Nature of Man*. New York: New American Library.

MOOR, RALPH C. 1975. Memorandum to All Department Heads and Personnel Officers (July 3).

NILSON, LINDA BURZOTTI and MURRAY EDELMAN. 1979. "The Symbolic Evocation of Occupational Prestige." *Society* 16 (March–April): 57–64.

SAYLOR, JERRY W. 1975. Memorandum to Ralph C. Moor (May 19).

SAYRE, WALLACE. 1979. "The Triumph of Techniques Over Purpose." In Frank Thompson, ed., *Classics of Public Personnel Policy*. Oak Park, Ill.: Moore, 30–34.

SHAFRITZ, JAY. 1973. *Position Classification: A Behavioral Analysis for the Public Service*. New York: Praeger.

STATE MERIT SYSTEM OF PERSONNEL ADMINISTRATION. 1975. "Request for Proposal." Atlanta, Georgia, April 24.

——. 1977. *Report and Recommendations: Statewide Classification Survey*. Atlanta: State Personnel.

Naomi B. Lynn

Kansas State University

CHAPTER TWENTY-ONE
THE CIVIL SERVICE REFORM ACT OF 1978

Only rarely in the field of public personnel administration does a major innovation occur. Such a break with past practice was caused by the Civil Service Reform Act of 1978 (CSRA). The legislation was based on long planning and extended discussion by professional administrators, scholars, and elected representatives. Nonetheless, however, in its early years the act became the subject of controversy and even disillusionment. It may yet fulfill its promise, but to do so will require efforts and commitments that are not yet in existence.

INTRODUCTION

To get a perspective on the sort of problems that have arisen under the CSRA and to gain insights into the prospects for resolving these problems it will be helpful to do two things: (1) to review a model presented by Downs that can serve as a heuristic device and (2) to review the history of legislation and events that led to the enactment of the 1978 law.

The Downs Model

Downs (1967: 18-21) has presented a pattern of bureaucracies' life cycles. At first, the young organization starts with a mission and its members seek to carry it out. They gain skills as they acquire experience, and the bureau's productivity rises. After a time, systems that have worked well become the basis for a formal structure of rules and regulations. This makes it easy for new people to learn the system, but it makes it hard for them to respond creatively to new situations. The organization's members age and become more conservative, unless there is rapid institutional growth. The image of an aging rigid organization had characterized the federal bureaucracy under the Civil Service Commission.

Critics of bureaucracies often emphasize the problems of the later phases of the life cycle. As we consider the problems and prospects of CSRA, however, it is important to keep in mind that the structures that have come out of the act are still very young. The reform process has created two new agencies that could be viewed as organizations in Downs's first phase. Organizations that have not yet passed the "initial survival threshold" (Downs, 1967: 9) experience the inevitable problems of the early phases of the learning curve.

Background of the CSRA

The passage of the Civil Service Reform Act of 1978 was the culmination of years of recognition that the federal civil service system was in need of major overhaul. It should not be viewed as an initiative of the Carter administration, although that administration played a major role in securing its passage. Its roots can be traced to earlier commissions, such as the second Hoover Commission. The federal personnel system had grown rapidly with little systematic attention being given to developing a consistent management approach. By 1966 it became apparent that lack of coordination and unnecessary duplication were exerting a heavy toll on federal personnel practices. A civil service commissioner, John Macy, convened a task force consisting of the directors of all the Civil Service Commission bureaus to try to develop a system for handling executive personnel. The result of the task force's effort was to bring all the executive personnel functions into a central point in the Civil Service Commission—the Bureau of Executive Management, later called the Bureau of Executive Personnel. The newly established bureau was also assigned the task of studying and making recommendations for strengthening the personnel system. By 1970 these efforts had resulted in the preparation of proposed legislation aimed at reform. The recommendations were the result of careful study and analysis of public administration principles rather than a reflection of presidential priorities. Among the suggestions were three-year contracts for career executives and the establishment of a Federal Executive Service. The legislation was controversial and lacked the necessary enthusiastic support of President Richard M. Nixon. The final bill died with the end of the congressional session. The task force continued its work and had a legislative package prepared when President Jimmy Carter entered office. The proposals were evaluated and modified by the Carter administration and then presented to Congress.

The Act's Implementation: Structures and Purposes

The Civil Service Reform Act was signed into law on October 13, 1978. Its stated purpose is "to provide a competent, honest and productive work force reflective of the nation's diversity, and to improve the quality of public service" (Civil Service Reform Act, 1978: 92 Stat. 1111). The legislation abolished the Civil Service Commission and established in its place the Office of Personnel Management (OPM) and the Merit Systems Protection Board (MSPB) and its special counsel. It also replaced the Federal Labor Relations Counsel with the Federal Labor Relations Authority (FLRA).

The Office of Personnel Management is headed by a director appointed to a four-year term by the president. The Merit Systems Protection Board is composed of three members appointed by the president. Not more than two can belong to the same party; the term of each member is seven years. The special counsel of the MSPB is appointed by the president for a term of five years. Members of the MSPB and the special counsel may be removed by the president only for inefficiency, neglect of duty, or malfeasance in office.

Features of CSRA

Concerning the civil service system (GAO, 1980: 2, 3), CSRA

1. Stated the fundamental merit principles and defined prohibited personnel practices (Title I).

2. Set up a basis for changing performance appraisal systems to link performance of employees to all types of personnel actions (Title XI).
3. Revised the laws for taking action against employees for unacceptable performance and misconduct and for adjudicating appeals from such action (Title XI).
4. Made a number of changes in the process for filling jobs, in applying veterans preference in personnel management, in authorizing new programs to hire disabled veterans, and in setting up recruiting programs for minorities and women (Title III).
5. Established the Senior Executive Service (Title IV).
6. Provided for establishing a system of merit pay for supervisors and managers in grades GS-13 through GS-15 (Title V).
7. Authorized research and demonstration projects in the field of public management (Title VI).
8. Established the labor relations program of the federal service on a statutory basis (Title VII).
9. Provided for grade and pay retention for federal employees whose positions are downgraded through no fault of their own (Title VIII).

In summary, the CSRA resulted in a major restructuring of the civil service system. It sought greater flexibility, increased protection of individual employee rights, and increased protection from political abuse. It was the result of years of careful study, refinement, compromise, and political realities. Its prospects are good. Its problems are just beginning to surface.

All the topics listed cannot be covered in detail in this chapter. Two major features of the reform merit special attention. They are the Senior Executive Service and the Merit Systems Protection Board.

SENIOR EXECUTIVE SERVICE

The Senior Executive Service (SES) is a critical component of the CSRA. It was designed to provide a cadre of top-level government managers who were to be rewarded on the basis of merit. Since the system provides for "rank in person," these individuals would have increased mobility and give agencies greater flexibility in assigning executives. Transfers are envisioned among agencies and geographic areas. SES is to be administered in a manner that will provide conditions of employment and compensation likely to attract and retain high-caliber individuals. It also aims to make executives more accountable for the performance and productivity of subordinates. Those who perform at an exceptional level receive bonuses and cash awards. Appointments to SES become final only after a one-year probationary period. Those who are dismissed for failure to meet performance standards are entitled to a lower-level civil service position in any agency. Theoretically, they can return to their positions without having any stigma attached to the move. SES covers positions that are classified GS-16, 17, and 18 and executive levels IV and V (or their equivalents).

Politicization

The reform seeks to achieve a balance between two democratic but sometimes contradictory goals—assuring bureaucratic responsiveness to the political system and assuring a politically neutral civil service system. To strengthen responsiveness, political appointees were given greater control over subordinates. For example, prior to civil service reform there was no centralized system for hiring and compensating federal executives. Congressional interference in personnel decisions often resulted in careerists whose first loyalty was to their congressional sponsor. Political appointees had limited flexibility in assigning or shifting personnel to meet special needs (Marzotto, Ban, and Goldenberg, 1981). Under the SES there is a single set of personnel procedures. Political heads of agencies may reassign executives as needed.

In recognition of possible political abuse, steps were taken to strengthen the neutrality of the service. The CSRA specifies that the total number of noncareer appointees in all agencies may not exceed 10 percent of the total number of senior executive positions in all agencies. The total number of limited-emergency appointees and limited-term appointees may not exceed 5 percent of the number of SES positions. In addition, 45 percent of senior executive positions are career reserved; they cannot be filled by political appointees.

Despite these structural features, the principal apprehension expressed by executives about CSRA is fear of politicization. Many of them see the reforms as a return to the spoils system (Lynn and Vaden, 1979, 1980). They believe that it will be easier to move "politically inspired" appointees to the upper levels of SES by bringing them in at a lower rank and then moving them ahead rapidly, using the authority that political appointees have in the new flexible system. They see the increased managerial controls as a vehicle for more partisan control. They fear that bonuses will be used to reward favorites. Some do not believe that political appointees will have the experience or judgment to make objective and professional performance evaluations. Under CSRA, political appointees may reassign career executives 120 days after assuming office. As Bernard Rosen, the former executive director of the U.S. Civil Service Commission, has pointed out, a political appointee "can not only reduce the pay of career executives who report to him, but he can banish them programmatically and even geographically" (Rosen, 1981: 204).

Career bureaucrats watched with concerned interest the reassignments that took place as the Reagan administration finished its first 120-day period. At the time of this writing it appeared that wholesale shifts had not occurred; this may reflect the slowness of the administration in making subcabinet appointments. Or it may reflect the political appointees' recognition of their need for executive expertise and their desire to keep the goodwill of SES members, without which their agencies could not function. If career executive apprehensions about politicization are reinforced in the future, we can anticipate a rather quick drop in their support of CSRA. As will be shown, this support is already tenuous (Lynn and Vaden, 1979, 1980).

Performance Appraisals

Performance appraisals receive more emphasis in civil service reform legislation than does any other aspect of personnel management. CSRA requires each agency to set up new performance systems that contain specific standards that are to serve as the basis for merit pay, removal or demotion of unacceptable performers, and other personnel decisions. Previously, employees were appraised against a list of traits such as "maturity, judgment, initiative, ' and so forth. Appraisals were rarely tied directly to other personnel actions, such as rewarding or promoting employees. Most managers found it convenient to rate everyone 'satisfactory." Under CSRA, agencies are mandated by statute to develop appraisal systems aimed at improving performance and assessing individual strengths and weaknesses. The legislation mandates written performance standards, negotiation of performance standards before the performance period begins, and the identification of critical elements of a job so employees will know which part of their jobs it is essential to perform well. If the system works properly, employees should be able to see a clear relationship between actual performance and merit pay. This makes it critically important that employees understand what is expected of them and what performance standards will be used to evaluate them.

Even before the passage of CSRA, career executives expressed misgivings about the implementation of a performance appraisal system. Many were convinced that objective measures would be impossible to achieve. Representatives of the Federal Executive League, in testimony before the House Subcommittee on Civil Service, expressed the doubt that "a measure of agency productivity could be developed which could be used to evaluate the performance of anyone other than the Secretary and the subordinate agency heads. To do this would be to tie productivity improvement to performance objectives outside the control of individual supervisors and managers" (Seidman, 1979). They went on to point out that statutory, resource, and political limitations that restrict a manager's freedom of action would complicate this issue further.

SES members were asked to establish performance appraisal systems by July 1979. The General Accounting Office has expressed the concern that this close deadline may not have given the agencies enough time to test the systems adequately before they were implemented (GAO, 1980: 13). In similar testimony the National Academy of Public Administration, a nonprofit organization whose basic purpose is to improve the public service, stated that the increased work load related to establishing the system coupled with the lack of additional resources could limit the quality of these early efforts (Berlin, 1980: 75-82). They estimate that it will take at least five years to perfect standards and appeal systems. To complicate matters, the first director of OPM, Alan K. Campbell, did not give much guidance on such key matters as the criteria for bonuses.

A 1979 survey of 14,000 federal workers found that 56 percent did not believe that a promotion or better job would result from high performance ratings. Only 25 percent believed that performance evaluations were helpful in measuring effectiveness (OPM, 1980). Performance appraisals and their use and misuse are sources of serious concern among federal employees. Some of this concern is related to the previously discussed fear of politicization. The performance appraisal system puts additional power in the hands of political appointees since bonuses and pay increases will be determined on the basis of these appraisals, as will sanctions, such as transfers to undesirable locations, frozen salaries, and decreases in pay. The delegation of this additional power was motivated by the perceived need to make career executives more responsive to political superiors. However, as with all power, there is always the possibility of abuse. To safeguard against this, executives who believe that they are treated unfairly may present their case to their agency's Performance Review Board. If their contention involves prohibited personnel practices (such as race or sex discrimination), they may appeal to the Merit Systems Protection Board. Apparently, these safeguards are not sufficiently adequate to offset misgivings about possible abuse, and as Buchanan (1981: 353) has aptly observed, "the long term success of the SES depends heavily on positive, supportive attitudes within the ranks. The apparent absence of such support in the early going is a significant, though potentially reversible, threat to success."

A major intent of the legislation is to improve program effectiveness. One mechanism for achieving this goal was to be performance appraisal systems. Buchanan (1981), in his study of SES, found that there is not necessarily a correlation between measures of individual effectiveness and program effectiveness. He found that little attention was given to defining, measuring, and linking these objectives. Buchanan concludes that, if SES fails to make these linkages, the 'ability of the SES to bring about improved program effectiveness will be compromised" (1981: 349–358).

Bonuses

The Civil Service Reform Act permits supervisors to give performance awards to up to 50 percent of the career executives, in amounts up to 20 percent of the base salary. Annually, as many as 5 percent of the SES may receive the rank of "meritorious executive" with a monetary award of $10,000. One percent may receive the rank of "distinguished executive" with a special award of $20,000 (CSRA, 1978: Title IV). Bonuses were considered a critical part of the reform legislation, because its originators were convinced that additional incentives were needed to improve performance and to motivate top managers to assume the additional responsibilities and risks required by the changes.

Since the awarding of bonuses was an innovative change, the first agencies to distribute bonuses received considerable congressional attention. This focus and study of awardees drew attention to some recipients that members of Congress did not believe merited awards. They saw bonuses as a means of getting around the pay freeze and paying certain people more than they deserved. Some members of Congress had not fully understood the implications of the bonus system when they voted for the original legislation. Congress reacted by lowering bonuses from 50 to 25 percent ("Bonus v. Malice," 1980: A26). OPM, fearing that if the full 25 percent quota received bonuses the entire system would be in jeopardy, lowered it to 20 percent and quickly issued guidelines. This action undermines the motivating intent of the legislation. Large numbers of career executives are now all too aware that their chances of receiving bonuses are minimal. A career executive summarized general reaction to congressional and OPM action as follows: "The prostitution of the bonus system by the Congress . . . has made me and my associates quite cynical. Whatever motivational factors were there in theory are in fact disappearing" (Rosen, 1981: 206).

Executives have expressed the view that cronyism is a natural bureaucratic phenomenon. As the number of those eligible for bonuses was reduced, the suspicion of cronyism grew. With only a few bonuses to award, there seems to be a natural tendency for agency heads to give them to those they know. A similar sort of thing was suspected by some observers when strikingly high percentages of the bonuses in some agencies went to those who served on the performance review boards. In the Department of Housing and Urban Development, for example, 50 percent of bonuses went to this group of "insiders." No bonuses went to the Air Force and Department of Education (Lanouette, 1981: 1298).

Pay

The limitations on bonuses have added to the frustrations that career executives are experiencing as a result of the widening gap between federal and private sector salaries. In 1975, Congress passed the Executive Salary Cost-of-Living Adjustment Act, which links the salaries of Congress to federal executives, and after CSRA this included all members of SES. Executive salaries in several of the upper levels are all frozen at $50,112.50, because Congress has refused to grant raises to itself and consequently to federal executives. The result has been that those at many different levels of responsibility receive exactly the same pay, and many executives have had their pay frozen for years.

OPM sent a questionnaire to a random sample of career executives who had left government service in 1980. Sixty-six percent of those surveyed said they resigned to accept a higher-paying position outside government (Commission on Executive, Legislative, and Judicial Salaries, 1980: 20). Other studies have also found a direct relationship between the lack of increase in pay for career executives because of frozen executive pay levels and the dramatic rise in the retirement rates of these employees (Commission on Executive, Legislative, and Judicial Salaries, 1980: 21). *The Wall Street Journal* (1981: 22), in reporting that more than 45 percent of nearly 1,000 senior executives polled stated that they may leave the government within the next two years, concluded that the setting of limits on expected bonuses and the lack of pay raises are hurting morale and contributing to "an unprecedented wave of resignations and early retirements." The General

Accounting Office has recommended breaking the linkage between the executive schedule and congressional salaries. It has further concluded that executive pay compression is detrimental to the overall success of the SES (GAO, 1980: 41).

Civil service reform restructured the civil service system. Executives were asked to make sacrifices in terms of security, increased responsibility, and rapid accommodation to change. A selling point was the promise of increased financial rewards. These have not been forthcoming. The immediate price may be the necessity to hire and promote less knowledgable and less experienced managers as the best people are lost to the private sector. This could have a devastating effect on the efficiency and success of SES and on the quality of public service performance and delivery.

MERIT SYSTEMS
PROTECTION BOARD

The Merit Systems Protection Board (MSPB) and its special counsel serve as the main enforcement components of the CSRA. The early years of this board saw the structural flaws in the legislation complicated by a drastic cut in funding.

Protection of Merit Principles

Title I of the CSRA contains the statement of merit principles (CSRA, 1978: Title I). Recruitment is to be based on ability, skills, and knowledge; moreover, the federal service is to be a work force that contains all segments of society. Employees are to be treated fairly and equitably without regard to such matters as race, religion, sex, age, or handicapped condition. Adequacy of performance is the standard to be used in making retention decisions. Employees are to be protected against reprisals for disclosing information about violations of law or regulations or about mismanagement, gross waste of funds, or dangers to the public ("whistleblowing").

The MSPB is given broad authority to hear matters related to observance of merit system principles and to make rulings on them. The board also can conduct studies and review OPM rules and regulations. Decisions of the MSPB can be appealed to the U.S. Court of Appeals.

The functioning of the MSPB can be seen in the case of *Wells* v. *Harris*, (1980). One of OPM's first regulations issued on January 16, 1979, when it was less than a month old, gave agencies the right to shortcut some of the act's procedural protections. Essentially, employees could be discharged before specific merit-based performance appraisal systems were in place. The Social Security Administration, before establishing performance standards, disciplined employees who were said to be deficient in their performance of critical elements of their assigned tasks. This policy was challenged before the MSPB, and the board struck down both the OPM's policy and Social Security's action under it. The OPM did not appeal the decision, probably because of its specific and narrow implications.

The Special Counsel

The Office of Special Counsel serves an important function in the act. The special counsel receives and investigates allegations of prohibited practices. This is fairly similar to the board's charge to hear and adjudicate matters related to Title II of the act. Where the emphasis of the board may be on the issuing of rules, and the special counsel may specialize in investigation and actions regarding individual cases, the division of labor between the two relatively independent entities is not spelled out precisely enough to avoid confusion and misunderstanding.

Throughout the CSRA's first two years, only acting special counsels were in office. To compound the inherent problem that this posed, the office's funding was cut in half by Congress from $4 million to $2 million per year. As Swygert, one of the acting special counsels, said, "What does that tell you?" [about Congress' attitude toward and support for the function] ("Fund and Appointment Woes . . .," 1980: B-10). He considered it a major accomplishment merely to keep his office open.

Outlook for Effectiveness

The problems that have plagued the MSPB and the special counsel are the result of three circumstances that have impaired their effectiveness. First is the ambiguity in the law; this created a power vacuum that both agencies moved to fill. Second, the lack of a permanent special counsel led to confusion and delay in handling cases. Third, the cut in the budget encouraged the agencies to compete for the remaining funds. Efforts spent fighting over bones cannot be used to protect those who deserve it.

CONCLUSION

The CSRA is based on well-established management concepts that should provide a sound basis for public policy. Unfortunately the potential effectiveness of the reform law has been severely limited by congressional and administrative action.

To the extent that CSRA has been a disappointment to the nation and has caused considerable disillusionment among the managers it was designed to motivate, the blame can be shared by Congress, the president, and the bureaucracy's top managers. It is well established that, once reform measures are passed, presidents lose interest in them. In this case the situation was compounded by a change of administration very early in the life of the act. Congress chose to intervene before the legislation had a fair trial. The heads of OPM were politically very knowledgable and effective in selling the changes to Congress, but they had a *laissez-faire* management attitude that did not result in a good internal implementation approach.

To establish a bonus system with great fanfare and then to cut off its funding may be worse than never bringing up the subject in the first place, especially since the question of money as a motivator is far from settled. In 1978 the stated national policy was to seek an excellent executive corps; by the early 1980s the policy in practice appeared to be that saving money was to be given top priority. The demoralization of the SES and the drastic budget cut of the special counsel of the MSPB are striking examples of the harm caused by recent congressional action and presidential disinterest.

Contributing to the problem are ambiguities in the act and implementation approaches followed in the new law's crucial early phase. One example of ambiguity is that the MSPB and its special counsel were given very similar charges and almost full independence from each other. Alan K. Campbell, the director of OPM, led the way in getting passage of the act and rapidly established its basic structures but then developed an almost *laissez-faire* attitude. Campbell was very supportive of the concept of decentralization; perhaps a firm central direction was needed. An emphasis on follow-through and an attention to detail in implementation would have been helpful.

Performance standards that have been established are often unmanageably complex. A balance between this complication and an excessively simplistic approach has yet to be found.

"Whistleblowers" receive special protection in the new law, reflecting the general public approval for this courageous and often lonely activity. Because of low funding and the problems of getting started, however, the support of whistleblowers has been less extensive than many had hoped for.

It is easy to become discouraged by the record thus far, and some have expressed this discouragement (Lanouette, 1981: 1296-1299). Perhaps, however, it is good to recall Downs's insights into the life cycle of bureaus. This one is only a few years old, and it has had its infancy in periods of economic difficulty and political change. There is still ample reason to hope that it can meet the challenges it faces. Adequate financial support will be crucial. Also helpful will be a willingness to make any needed legislative amendments that appear warranted once adequate monetary support is in place. Some ground has been lost since 1979, but the long-run outlook for turning the federal public service back on the course plotted by CSRA is far from hopeless.

REFERENCES

BERLIN, S. S. 1980. Hearings before the Subcommittee on the Civil Service of the Committee on Post Office and Civil Service House of Representatives. 96th Cong., 2d sess., May 18.
"Bonus v. Malice". 1980. *The New York Times* (June 25): A26.
BUCHANAN, B. 1981. "The Senior Executive Service: How We Can Tell If It Works." *Public Administration Review* 41 (May–June): 349-358.
Civil Service Reform Act of 1978. 1978. 92 Stat. 1111.
COMMISSION ON EXECUTIVE, LEGISLATIVE, AND JUDICIAL SALARIES. 1980. *Report.* Washington, D.C.. G.P.O., December.
DOWNS, A. 1967. *Inside Bureaucracy.* Boston: Little, Brown.

"Fund and Appointment Woes Slow Agency to Protect 'Whistleblowers'." 1980. *The New York Times* (November 3): B:10.

GENERAL ACCOUNTING OFFICE. 1980. *Report to the Congress of the United States–Civil Service Reform Where It Stands Today.* Washington, D.C.: G.A.O.

LANOUETTE, W. J. 1981. "SES–From Civil Service Showpiece to Incipient Failure in Two Years." *National Journal* 13 (July 18): 1296–1299.

LYNN, N. B. and R. E. VADEN. 1979. "Bureaucratic Response to Civil Service Reform." *Public Administration Review* 39 (July-August): 333–343.

——. 1980. "Federal Executives: Initial Reactions to Change." *Administration Society* 12 (May): 101–120.

MARZOTTO, T., C. BAN, and E. N. GOLDENBERG. 1981. "Controlling the Bureaucracy: Will SES Make a Difference." Paper presented at Annual Meeting of the American Society for Public Administration, Detroit, Michigan, April 1981.

OFFICE OF PERSONNEL MANAGEMENT. 1980. "Federal Employee Attitudes Phase I: Baseline Survey 1979 Government-wide Report." Washington, D.C.: G.P.O.

ROSEN, B. 1981. "Uncertainty in the Senior Executive Service." *Public Administration Review* 41 (March–April): 203–207.

SEIDMAN, E. 1979. Hearings Before the Subcommittee on the Civil Service of the Committee on Post Office and Civil Service, House of Representatives. 95th Cong., 2d sess., July 12.

Wall Street Journal, The. 1981. "Federal Executives Dissatisfied with Reform" (June 18): 21.

WELLS v. *HARRIS.* 1980. MSPB Order No. RR-80-3.

ABOUT
THE AUTHORS

JEAN J. COUTURIER is director of Research and Sponsored Programs for the American University's College of Public and International Affairs. He was formerly professor and director of Northwestern University's public and nonprofit management graduate programs. From 1963 to 1974 Dr. Couturier served as executive director of the National Civil Service League. He is the author of over sixty published articles and books, including an award-winning book on public sector labor relations published by Princeton University.

CHARLES E. DAVIS is assistant professor of public management at Suffolk University. Current research interests are in public personnel management and environmental policy, and he has recently authored and co-authored articles appearing in the *Journal of Public and International Affairs*, *Public Productivity Review*, *Industrial and Labor Relations Review*, and other professional journals.

JOHN J. DEMARCO is an assistant professor of public administration at the University of Georgia. He recently completed a year with the Office of Personnel Management as a NASPAA fellow. His research interests are in the areas of public personnel, public management, and organizational decision making.

STEVEN D. EALY is assistant professor of political science and history at Armstrong State College. He is author of *Communication, Speech and Politics: Habermas and Political Analysis*. His research interests include personnel management and political theory.

STEVEN W. HAYS is associate professor and vice chairman, Department of Government and International Studies, University of South Carolina. He was formerly chairman of the Department of Public Administration, California State University, Dominguez Hills. Dr. Hays has published widely in the areas of personnel management, judicial administration, and organizational theory.

W. DONALD HEISEL is adjunct professor of political science and senior research associate, Institute of Governmental Research, University of Cincinnati. Prior to his University of Cincinnati affiliation, he was a practitioner in local government and served as personnel director for the City of Cincinnati for thirteen years. He is an honorary life member of the International Personnel Management Association.

ALBERT C. HYDE is a professor in the School of Business and Public Administration at the University of Houston at Clear Lake City. He was formerly the project director for the State Department's Human Resources Information Systems Task Force. He has authored and co-authored a number of books and articles in the general field of public personnel administration.

RICHARD C. KEARNEY is an associate professor in the Department of Government and International Studies at the University of South Carolina. He is the author of a number of articles on public employee unions and collective bargaining, personnel administration, and nuclear waste management. He is also author of a forthcoming book on public employee unions to be published by Marcel Dekker.

WILLIAM KELSO is associate professor and director of the public administration program at the University of Florida. He is the author of *American Democratic Theory: Pluralism and its Critics*. He has recently completed an article on benefit-cost analysis for a book on public decision making. He has also published articles in the *Midwest Review of Public Administration*, *Public Personnel Administration*, *International Journal of Public Administration*, and *The Bureaucrat*.

DONALD E. KLINGNER is an associate professor and director of the Department of Public Administration at Florida International University in Miami. He has written and consulted widely in the area of public personnel management.

MARY M. LEPPER is associate professor of public administration at the Maxwell School of Citizenship and Public Affairs, Syracuse University. She has taught in California and Colorado. From 1971 to 1973, she was associate director of the Executive Seminar Center, Civil Service Commission, Berkeley, California. From 1973 to 1978 she was associated with the Office for Civil Rights, Department of Health, Education and Welfare. She has published a number of articles on affirmative action and equal employment opportunity for higher education institutions and public sector employment.

CHARLES H. LEVINE is the Edwin O. Stene Distinguished Professor of Public Administration at the University of Kansas. A graduate of Indiana University, he was previously director of the Institute for Urban Studies and the Bureau of Governmental Research at the University of Maryland. He has published several studies and books on the topic of fiscal stress, including *Managing Fiscal Stress* (1980) and *Fiscal Stress and Public Policy* (with Irene Rubin, 1980).

NAOMI B. LYNN is a professor of political science at Kansas State University. She holds a master's degree from the University of Illinois and a doctorate from the University of Kansas. Her publications include *The Fulbright Premise: Senator J. William Fulbright and Presidential Power in Foreign Policy* and articles published in *Public Administration Review*, *American Journal of Political Science*, *Administration and Society*, *The Bureaucrat*, and *Public Personnel Management*. She is a member of the National Council of the American Society for Public Administration and the Executive Council of the American Political Science Association. She serves on the editorial boards of four scholarly journals.

MICHAEL S. MARCH is professor of public affairs at the University of Colorado at Denver. He holds a Ph.D. in political economy and government from Harvard University and served for thirty-three years in the federal service, largely in the

Bureau of the Budget and Office of Management and Budget. During his federal career he conducted extensive studies of many retirement and income maintenance programs, including civil service and military retirement, railroad retirement, veterans' pensions, and social security.

MONICA MILLER-SPELLMAN is a chief information specialist for the Colorado State Department of Personnel. She consults with both private and public employers and community organizations on equal employment opportunity issues. She drafted the Colorado Civil Rights Commission's Guidelines on Sexual Harrassment.

DAIL ANN NEUGARTEN is an associate professor and associate dean of the Graduate School of Public Affairs, University of Colorado at Denver. She has recently co-edited a book of readings entitled *Sexuality in Organizations: Romantic and Coercive Behavior at Work*. She is involved in research on the topic of productivity in the public sector.

STEVEN M. NEUSE is an associate professor of political science and M.P.A. director at the University of Arkansas at Fayetteville. He has published several articles in the field of personnel administration. Currently he is investigating the role of the TVA as an international technology transfer agent.

JEREMY F. PLANT is an associate professor in the Department of Public Affairs at George Mason University. He has researched and written widely in the area of public sector ethics.

T. ZANE REEVES is professor and director of the Division of Public Administration at the University of New Mexico. He was formerly director of the public administration programs at California State University, Dominguez Hills (1979-1981) and Pepperdine University (1975-1979). His research interests include public financial management and personnel administration and labor relations. He has published widely in these areas and has co-authored textbooks on collective bargaining and personnel management.

DAVID H. ROSENBLOOM is professor of public administration at the Maxwell School, Syracuse University. He is the author of numerous works on law and public personnel administration, including *Federal Service and the Constitution*. He has taught at the University of Kansas, the University of Tel Aviv, and the University of Vermont.

RICHARD P. SCHICK is a consultant to a large number of agencies, including the Department of Labor and the Department of Housing and Urban Development. He has an extensive background in labor relations, economics, and public employment research. Among his many publications is a book that arose from a Department of Labor study of local citizen groups' attempts to access their local governments' labor relations decision-making processes. This book was named as one of the "Outstanding Books in Industrial Relations and Labor Economics" of 1977.

JAY M. SHAFRITZ is a professor in the Graduate School of Public Affairs at the University of Colorado at Denver. He has taught at the State University of New York at Albany, Rensselaer Polytechnic Institute, Howard University, and the University of Houston at Clear Lake City. He is the author of several books and journal articles dealing with position classification, sexual harrassment, and other facets of personnel management.

RONALD D. SYLVIA is assistant professor of political science at the University of Oklahoma. He received his B.A. degree from California State University at San Bernardino and his M.P.A. and Ph.D. from Kent State University. He has published articles in the fields of personnel management, organization theory, and psychology as well as political science.

JOHN CLAYTON THOMAS is associate professor of public administration at the L. P. Cookingham Institute of Public Affairs, University of Missouri, Kansas City. His research interests include urban politics and administration, with a particular interest in public personnel administration in local governments. He has published articles in such journals as *Public Personnel Management, Public Administration Review,* and *Administration and Society.*

FRANK J. THOMPSON is an associate professor of political science and director of the Doctoral Program in Public Administration at the University of Georgia. He participated in the Oakland Project while at the University of California and subsequently served as a Public Administration fellow with the Health Resources Administration. His published works include *Personnel Policy in the City: The Politics of Jobs in Oakland* and, more recently, *Health Policy and the Bureaucracy: Politics and Implementation.*

CHARLIE B. TYER is an associate professor in the Department of Government and International Studies and director of the Bureau of Governmental Research and Service at the University of South Carolina. His research and writing have focused upon staff functions, particularly financial and personnel management and public planning. His articles have appeared in many professional journals, and he serves as managing editor of the *Review of Public Personnel Administration.*

JONATHAN P. WEST is director of the M.P.A. Program and associate professor of politics and public affairs at the University of Miami. His research interests are in public personnel management and public policy and he has recently authored or co-authored articles in *Public Personnel Management, Midwest Review of Public Administration, Social Science Quarterly,* and *International Journal of Public Administration.*

GEORGE G. WOLOHOJIAN is a management analyst at the National Oceanic and Atmospheric Administration of the U.S. Department of Commerce. A graduate of the Maxwell School of Syracuse University, he has served as a faculty research associate of the Bureau of Governmental Research at the University of Maryland and taught at Northeastern University. He has published several articles on fiscal stress, retrenchment, and cutback management.

INDEX

Merit Systems Protection Board:
description, 8, 143, 299, 318, 354–56
performance appraisal, 12
sexual harassment, 277–78, 286
Special Counsel, 355
Miller v. *Bank of America*, 283
Minimum wage, 45
Model Public Personnel Administration
Law, 315, 317–18, 328
Morton v. *Mancari*, 37
Mosher, Frederick, 4
Motivation:
performance appraisal, 120
promotional policy, 95
rewards, 18, 73–74
See also Merit pay
Mount Healy City School District Board of Education v. *Doyle*, 39

NAACP, 85–86
National Academy of Public Administration, 351
National Association of Letter Carriers v. *Civil Service Commission*, 31–32
National Association of Schools of Public Affairs and Administration, 140–41
National Association of Social Workers, 199
National Center for Productivity and Quality of Working Life, 183
National Civil Service League, 312, 315–16, 321, 328
National Education Association, 198–99
National Income Security Commission, 169
National League of Cities, 325
National League of Cities et al v. *Usury*, 45
National Railroad Passenger Corporation, 9
National Treasury Employees Union, 199
New Federalism, 44, 48
New public administration, 295
Nixon, Richard M., 7–8, 299, 348
Nondiscrimination, 218–19, 223, 230.

See also Affirmative action; Discrimination; Equal employment opportunity

Occupational Safety and Health Act of 1970, 44
Occupational Safety and Health Administration, 24
Office of Management and Budget, 212
Office of Personnel Management:
ethics enforcement, 299–300, 306
Intergovernmental Personnel Act, 46
job centers, 206
merit standards, 49–50
performance appraisal, 12
purpose, 318, 348
relation to MSPB, 354
sexual harassment, 277, 279
training, 138–39, 142
Omnibus Crime Control and Safe Streets Act, 47
On-the-job training (OJT), 149. *See also* Training
Operations research, 148
Organizational Development, 143–44, 146–47
Orientation programs, 145
Overtime pay, 45. *See also* Compensation
Owen v. *City of Independence*, 39, 55

Paired comparisons, 124. *See also* Performance appraisal
Patronage, 5. *See also* Spoils
dismissals, 32–33, 40
selection, 95–96
Pay. *See* Compensation
Peltier v. *City of Fargo*, 236
Pendleton Act, 4, 312, 315
Pensions, 154–70
benefits, 156–57, 162–64
contributions to, 160–61
costs of, 164–66
history, 154